Xamarin Mobile Development for Android Cookbook

Over 80 hands-on recipes to unleash the full potential of Xamarin in the development and monetization of feature-packed, real-world Android apps

Matthew Leibowitz

D1664331

PUBLISHING

BIRMINGHAM - MUMBAI

Xamarin Mobile Development for Android Cookbook

First published: November 2015

Production reference: 1191115

Published by Packt Publishing Ltd.
Livery Place
35 Livery Street
Birmingham B3 2PB, UK.

ISBN 978-1-78439-857-6

www.packtpub.com

Credits

Author
Matthew Leibowitz

Reviewers
Ole Falkerslev Kristensen
Frédéric Mauroy
Luca Zulian

Commissioning Editor
Amarabha Banerjee

Acquisition Editor
Reshma Raman

Content Development Editor
Dharmesh Parmar

Technical Editor
Abhishek R. Kotian

Copy Editor
Pranjali Chury

Project Coordinator
Paushali Desai

Proofreader
Safis Editing

Indexer
Monica Ajmera Mehta

Graphics
Disha Haria

Production Coordinator
Arvindkumar Gupta

Cover Work
Arvindkumar Gupta

About the Author

Matthew Leibowitz is a professional software engineer living in South Africa, and is currently working in a Xamarin development team. He has many years of professional experience as a programmer in developing systems ranging from servers, to desktops, to mobile devices.

He has a passion for programming and has recently been awarded Xamarin Certified Mobile Developer certification for his work. He has written various articles on his blog and has participated in several forums.

With his experience and great passion for development, Matthew spends his days continually looking for new ways to create a better experience for users and other developers. Some of his work is seen on GitHub under the username mattleibow. In addition to his public code, Matthew is active on Twitter with the same username.

I would like to thank my family for enduring my late nights and putting up with my strange behavior for the time it me took to put all this together. They have been very encouraging and have inspired me to share my knowledge with the world.

About the Reviewers

Ole Falkerslev Kristensen was a software developer at Nokia Mobile phone for more than 10 years, working with C, C++ and C#. He is now a professional Xamarin.Android developer in a startup company with 4-5 employees for the last 3 years.

He has also developed Android Apps for A.M.O Professional Loyalty programs and events apps. Also, he has also developed in Xamarin iOS.

Frédéric Mauroy discovered computers in the mid-80s and got his joy of programming with Basic. This new-found passion naturally led him to pursue an education in IT, where he learned C and C++. His first job allowed him to hone his skills in C, and he later sled towards C# with the amazing .Net framework. Having mainly worked in ASP.Net, he also developed Windows applications, and more recently, mobile applications for Android and iOS using PhoneGap and Xamarin.

He has made mobile applications for Viashopia and Alert112. You can get more details at the following links:

http://mauroy.eu

http://viashopia.com

http://alert112.com

Luca Zulian lives in Milan, Italy, and he is a skilled Microsoft .NET Framework developer, specializing in patterns and practices. In his many years as developer, he worked with numerous languages and technologies, and started with mobile development from a native approach to land on the Xamarin world. Now, he is experienced in large-scale enterprise applications along with a continuous phase of learning new languages and tools.

www.PacktPub.com

Support files, eBooks, discount offers, and more

For support files and downloads related to your book, please visit www.PacktPub.com.

Did you know that Packt offers eBook versions of every book published, with PDF and ePub files available? You can upgrade to the eBook version at www.PacktPub.com and as a print book customer, you are entitled to a discount on the eBook copy. Get in touch with us at service@packtpub.com for more details.

At www.PacktPub.com, you can also read a collection of free technical articles, sign up for a range of free newsletters and receive exclusive discounts and offers on Packt books and eBooks.

https://www2.packtpub.com/books/subscription/packtlib

Do you need instant solutions to your IT questions? PacktLib is Packt's online digital book library. Here, you can search, access, and read Packt's entire library of books.

Why subscribe?

- ► Fully searchable across every book published by Packt
- ► Copy and paste, print, and bookmark content
- ► On demand and accessible via a web browser

Free access for Packt account holders

If you have an account with Packt at www.PacktPub.com, you can use this to access PacktLib today and view 9 entirely free books. Simply use your login credentials for immediate access.

Table of Contents

Preface

With a rapid increase in the use of mobile devices everywhere, developing for Android takes advantage of this trend to reach the widest market available to any mobile platform. Along with creating awesome Android apps, Xamarin allows the use of the mature .NET Framework. .NET is a massive framework that is supported on almost all platforms, including iOS, Windows, Mac OS X, and Linux.

Developing apps with Xamarin.Android allows you to use and reuse your code and skills on different platforms, making you more productive in any sort of development. Although not a write-once-run-anywhere framework, Xamarin provides native platform integration and optimizations. There is no middleware; Xamarin.Android talks directly to the system, taking your C# and F# code directly to the low levels.

What this book covers

Chapter 1, Working with Xamarin.Android, allows us to create native Android apps with the strengths of C# and .NET. Using C#, we can develop native Android apps and at the same time have the ability to share code with other platforms.

Chapter 2, Showing Views and Handling Fragments, explores one of the most important parts of Android apps—the user interface, as it is the most visible part of an app. When creating apps for Android, there are numerous different ways available to create these interfaces.

Chapter 3, Managing App Data, consists of the program that almost all apps make use of to process data. Android provides many ways to manage data, each being different and useful for different purposes. Data can be stored in a file, a dictionary, or in a SQLite database.

Chapter 4, Presenting App Data, is only useful to a user if the user is able to view it. Android has several means to present data, the most common being some form of list or collection.

Chapter 5, Communicating with the Outside World, explains communication, which is possibly the most important part of interaction, both between humans and technology. Most Android devices are built with Cellular, Wi-Fi, Bluetooth, or NFC communication technologies.

Chapter 6, Using Background Tasks, is where the users expect mobile apps to be fluid, dynamic, and most of all, responsive. Long-running tasks, even those running for a few milliseconds, must be run in the background to keep an app responsive.

Chapter 7, Notifying Users, explains notifications, which draw the user's attention to let him/her know something has happened. Android apps can present notifications in several ways, ranging from a quick popup to a persistent message from a remote server.

Chapter 8, Interacting with Other Apps, explains that users have many apps installed on their Android devices. By developing apps to be aware of other apps, our apps can communicate and request data from these other apps.

Chapter 9, Presenting Multimedia, consists of an explanation of audio, video and photos, the most vivid means to convey information to the user. By making use of Android's many features, an app can present a user with dynamic images and sounds. This can be used to provide a function or enhance other functionality.

Chapter 10, Responding to the User, explicates that a user can interact with Android apps in many ways. The user can manipulate virtual objects using the device's touch screen, or trigger the sensors by moving the device in the physical world.

Chapter 11, Connecting to Wearables, is one of the newest things with regard to technology; it is the increase in wearable devices. Android Wear is a special version of Android that allows device manufacturers to create wearables and permit typical Android apps to run on them.

Chapter 12, Adding In-App Billing, elucidates Android app developers can capitalize on the fact that users are willing to pay for new or additional features in the app. This is especially the case with mobile games that support purchasing virtual products or subscriptions.

Chapter 13, Publishing Apps, posits that once an Android app has been created, the next step is to release it into the world. Google has created the Google Play store, which can be used to distribute mobile and wearable apps. Before distribution, mobile apps can be compressed and protected against malicious users.

What you need for this book

This book will provide you with the necessary knowledge and skills to be part of the mobile development era using C#. Covering a wide range of recipes such as creating a simple application and using device features effectively, it will be your companion during the complete application development cycle.

Starting from installing the necessary tools, you will be guided step-by-step on everything you need to develop an application, ready to be deployed. You will learn best practices for interacting with the device's hardware, such as the GPS, NFC, and Bluetooth. Furthermore, you will be able to manage multimedia resources, such as photos and videos captured with the device's camera, and much more!

Who this book is for

If you are a C#/.NET developer with no previous experience in Android development, or you are a Java developer who wants to create complete Android applications in C# and deploy them to the Play Store, then this book is ideal for you. Having no experience with Xamarin will not hamper your interests.

Conventions

In this book, you will find a number of text styles that distinguish between different kinds of information. Here are some examples of these styles and an explanation of their meaning.

Code words in text, database table names, folder names, filenames, file extensions, pathnames, dummy URLs, user input, and Twitter handles are shown as follows: "We can include other contexts through the use of the `include` directive."

A block of code is set as follows:

```
[Activity(
  Label = "My App",
  MainLauncher = true,
  Icon = "@drawable/icon")]
public class MainActivity : Activity
{
}
```

When we wish to draw your attention to a particular part of a code block, the relevant lines or items are set in bold:

```
<?xml version="1.0" encoding="utf-8"?>
<resources>
  <string name="buttonText">Hello World!</string>
</resources>
```

Any command-line input or output is written as follows:

```
adb shell bmgr backup <android-package-name>
adb shell bmgr run
adb shell bmgr restore <android-package-name>
```

New terms and **important words** are shown in bold. Words that you see on the screen, for example, in menus or dialog boxes, appear in the text like this: "Click on the **Download Xamarin for Windows** or **Download Xamarin for OS X** links, depending on the operating system you are using."

 Warnings or important notes appear in a box like this.

[💡 Tips and tricks appear like this.]

Reader feedback

Feedback from our readers is always welcome. Let us know what you think about this book—what you liked or disliked. Reader feedback is important for us as it helps us develop titles that you will really get the most out of.

To send us general feedback, simply e-mail `feedback@packtpub.com`, and mention the book's title in the subject of your message.

If there is a topic that you have expertise in and you are interested in either writing or contributing to a book, see our author guide at `www.packtpub.com/authors`.

Customer support

Now that you are the proud owner of a Packt book, we have a number of things to help you to get the most from your purchase.

Downloading the example code

You can download the example code files from your account at `http://www.packtpub.com` for all the Packt Publishing books you have purchased. If you purchased this book elsewhere, you can visit `http://www.packtpub.com/support` and register to have the files e-mailed directly to you.

Errata

Although we have taken every care to ensure the accuracy of our content, mistakes do happen. If you find a mistake in one of our books—maybe a mistake in the text or the code—we would be grateful if you could report this to us. By doing so, you can save other readers from frustration and help us improve subsequent versions of this book. If you find any errata, please report them by visiting `http://www.packtpub.com/submit-errata`, selecting your book, clicking on the **Errata Submission Form** link, and entering the details of your errata. Once your errata are verified, your submission will be accepted and the errata will be uploaded to our website or added to any list of existing errata under the Errata section of that title.

To view the previously submitted errata, go to `https://www.packtpub.com/books/content/support` and enter the name of the book in the search field. The required information will appear under the **Errata** section.

Piracy

Piracy of copyrighted material on the Internet is an ongoing problem across all media. At Packt, we take the protection of our copyright and licenses very seriously. If you come across any illegal copies of our works in any form on the Internet, please provide us with the location address or website name immediately so that we can pursue a remedy.

Please contact us at `copyright@packtpub.com` with a link to the suspected pirated material.

We appreciate your help in protecting our authors and our ability to bring you valuable content.

Questions

If you have a problem with any aspect of this book, you can contact us at `questions@packtpub.com`, and we will do our best to address the problem.

1
Working with Xamarin.Android

In this chapter, we will cover the following recipes:

- ▶ Creating Xamarin.Android projects
- ▶ Creating user interface layouts
- ▶ Creating an option menu
- ▶ Supporting previous Android versions
- ▶ Adding an action bar
- ▶ Navigating with the action bar
- ▶ Adding action bar action items
- ▶ Creating contextual action mode menu
- ▶ Sharing code with other platforms

Introduction

Xamarin.Android allows us to create native Android applications using the same UI controls we would use in Java, with the flexibility of C#, the power of the .NET **Base Class Library**, and two first-class IDEs.

Android development with Xamarin can be done on either Mac OS X or Windows, using either Visual Studio or Xamarin Studio. This variety provides us with our choice of how we want to work to create awesome apps.

This book will enable us, as developers, to create amazing, professional apps for the Android ecosystem. This knowledge can be used on so many platforms, from TVs and smartphones to watches, wearables, and many other Android-powered devices.

This chapter covers some of the most common tasks and steps to getting our app ready for development. We will learn how to create a new app, add support for the old versions of Android, and get started with the user interface used in all Android apps. We will also look at just how powerful the Xamarin.Android platform is by looking how we can share code with many other platforms, including Windows Phone, iOS, Windows, and Mac.

Creating Xamarin.Android projects

Before any apps can be created, the development environment has to be set up and the software downloaded and installed.

Getting ready

Before we start creating any Android apps, we need to get our tools in place using the installer from Xamarin.

1. Go to `http://xamarin.com/download`:

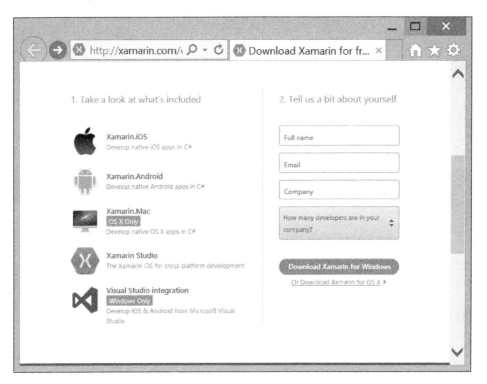

2. Enter your details for registration.

3. Click on the **Download Xamarin for Windows** or **Download Xamarin for OS X** links, depending on the operating system you are using.

4. Once the download has completed, launch the installer, following the on-screen instructions. Setup will continue to download and install all the required components:

5. Once the installer has finished, you should have a working installation of Xamarin Studio, the IDE designed for cross-platform development.

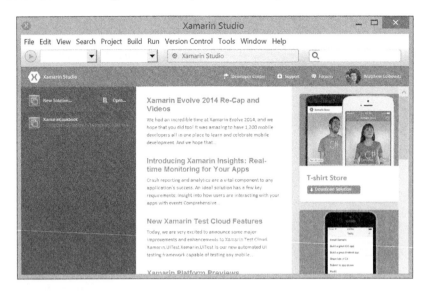

How to do it...

Creating Xamarin.Android projects is very simple!

1. Open Xamarin Studio.

2. Select **File**, then **New**, and then **Solution...**:

3. Select **C#**, then **Android**, and then **Android Application**:

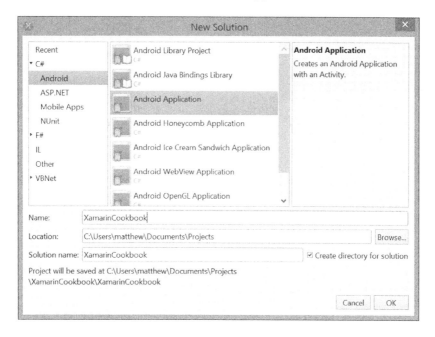

4. Enter a name for your app, for example XamarinCookbook.

5. Click on **OK**.

6. We now have a fully functional Xamarin.Android app, which can be deployed to a device or an emulator.

7. In the target device dropdown, select either an emulator or your device (if you have attached an Android device).

8. Finally, click on **Run** and the app will install and launch.

How it works...

Xamarin.Android allows us to write native Android apps using .NET and C# or F#. Xamarin. Android does not abstract or emulate any Android features. Rather, it is an alternate programming language available for the development of Android apps.

 Whatever can be done in Java, and much more, can be done in C#.

Some of the benefits of using Xamarin.Android are found in the small things. For example, if we are using Android Studio or Eclipse, we will have to make changes in AndroidManifest.xml. If we are using Xamarin.Android, we can do much of this work by using the familiar attributes.

 Various attributes can be used to provide the same functionality that modifying the AndroidManifest.xml file would bring.

To add the <activity> element into the manifest with Xamarin.Android, we add the [Activity] attribute on an activity as follows:

```
[Activity(
   Label = "My App",
   MainLauncher = true,
   Icon = "@drawable/icon")]
public class MainActivity : Activity
{
}
```

This will create a section in ApplicationManifest.xml at compile time, as highlighted in the following code:

```
<activity android:label="My App"
   android:icon="@drawable/icon"
   android:name="mynamespace.MainActivity">
   <intent-filter>
     <action android:name="android.intent.action.MAIN" />
     <category android:name="android.intent.category.LAUNCHER" />
   </intent-filter>
</activity>
```

If we want to add permissions to our app, all we need to do is add this:

```
[assembly: UsesPermission(Manifest.Permission.Camera)]
```

There are many other attributes that help us build the manifest file, such as the [Service] and [IntentFilter] attributes.

Creating user interface layouts

All apps require some form of user interface for the user to input data or view the output of information.

How to do it...

Creating an interface for our apps is very easy. There are two ways to create user interfaces, with code or with XML:

▸ If we are using code to create a button on the screen, we would do something similar to this:

```
protected override void OnCreate(Bundle bundle)
{
  base.OnCreate(bundle);

  LinearLayout layout = new LinearLayout(this);
  layout.Orientation = Orientation.Vertical;

  Button button = new Button(this);
  button.Text = "Hello World!";
  layout.AddView(
    button,
    ViewGroup.LayoutParams.MatchParent,
    ViewGroup.LayoutParams.WrapContent);

  SetContentView(layout);
}
```

Both XML and code can be used to create equivalent UIs, but using XML, we have additional capabilities:

▸ The equivalent interface in XML would be created and stored in the `layout` sub-folder of the `Resources` folder and reads as follows:

```
<?xml version="1.0" encoding="utf-8"?>
<LinearLayout
 xmlns:android="http://schemas.android.com/apk/res/android"
  android:id="@+id/layout"
  android:layout_width="match_parent"
  android:layout_height="match_parent"
  android:orientation="vertical">
  <Button
    android:id="@+id/button"
```

```
      android:layout_width="match_parent"
      android:layout_height="wrap_content"
      android:text="Hello World!" />
</LinearLayout>
```

Once we have created the interface in XML, we have to indicate to the activity which layout file is to be used. This is done by invoking the `SetContentView()` method in the `OnCreate()` method of the activity. For example, say we named our layout file `Main.axml`:

```
protected override void OnCreate(Bundle bundle)
{
    base.OnCreate(bundle);

    // note the name "Main"
    SetContentView(Resource.Layout.Main);
}
```

Regardless of whether the layout was created in code or through XML files, we are able to access the various controls similarly:

> ▸ In order to access the control at runtime, we make use of the `FindViewById` method on the activity or a view (use the `View` property of a fragment):
>
> ```
> Button btn = FindViewById<Button>(Resource.Id.buttonId);
> ```

How it works...

Separating the UI from the code allows us to easily make changes for updates as well as to support different screen configurations. The benefit of this is that it allows us to modify the UI without updating the code. And part of this is the fact that the Android system can switch the entire layout at runtime. Different layouts for different screen configurations can be selected simply by changing the suffix of the `layout` folder name.

 Fragments can be used in addition to layouts to create advanced interfaces consisting of self-contained, reusable regions.

For example, if we want our `Main` layout to have the `LinearLayout` method to be vertical in portrait orientation and horizontal in landscape orientation, all we have to do is create two layout files with the same name in different folders as follows:

```
<project-root>/Resources/layout/<layout-file-name>.axml
<project-root>/Resources/layout-land/<layout-file-name>.axml
```

There are many uses for the suffixes, and there are many different suffixes. Each of the resource subfolders can have suffixes, including `values`, `layout`, `menu`, and `drawable`. Each of the folders can have combinations of the suffixes for language or culture, screen orientation, screen density, screen size, and platform version. More information can be found online at `https://developer.android.com/guide/topics/resources/providing-resources.html#AlternativeResources`.

The Android layout structure usually follows the structure of the type, with the element name matching the type name and property names matching the attribute names. For example, the `Button` type has a `Text` property; thus, the XML will have a `<Button android:text="..." />` element.

Although we can nest one or more layouts within another layout, we should strive to keep our layout hierarchy as shallow as possible. The layout will be drawn faster if it has fewer nested layouts.

 A wide view hierarchy is better than a deep view hierarchy.

One of the most important attributes in layouts is the `id` attribute. This attribute is used to uniquely identify a view within a tree. An ID need not be unique throughout the entire tree, but it should be unique within the part of the tree that is being searched.

 The ID need not be unique, but it's best to be completely unique when possible so that the specific view can be found in the hierarchy.

There's more...

Layout files are an easy way to create the UI separate from the code, and in the same way, resource files can be used to separate the localizable text from the layout. This is achieved by placing the strings into a resource file and then, referencing each the string from the layout. Say we have a button that has some text:

```
<Button android:text="Hello World!" />
```

This value can be extracted and placed into a file under the `values` folder of the project resources (`<project-root>/Resources/values/<file-name>.xml`):

```
<?xml version="1.0" encoding="utf-8"?>
<resources>
  <string name="buttonText">Hello World!</string>
</resources>
```

The layout file can then be updated to reference the value:

```
<Button android:text="@string/buttonText" />
```

Using this pattern, we are able to not only extract strings but any value for any attribute, including layout information. An example would be to extract an element's padding and use a larger padding for larger screens. These types of resources are placed in the `values` folder with a suffix, such as `-large` for large screens.

See also

▸ *Chapter 2, Showing Views and Handling Fragments, Creating and using fragments*

▸ Providing Resources | Android Developers, `https://developer.android.com/guide/topics/resources/providing-resources.html#AlternativeResources`

Creating an options menu

Android provides the user with the ability to display a special type of menu that contains a set of items that pertains to the entire app, instead of the current activity.

How to do it...

Adding an options menu to our app is very simple, and only two things are required: a menu structure and code to connect the menu with the activity. In order to use a menu layout file, a resource file needs to be added:

1. First, we create a new XML file with the name of the menu, for example `Options.xml`, in the `menu` folder under the `Resources` folder.

2. Then, we create the menu structure in this file, for example, create three menu items: `refresh`, `settings`, and `about`.

```xml
<?xml version="1.0" encoding="utf-8" ?>
<menu xmlns:android=
"http://schemas.android.com/apk/res/android">
  <item
    android:id="@+id/action_refresh"
    android:icon="@drawable/ic_action_refresh"
    android:title="@string/action_refresh" />
  <item
    android:id="@+id/action_settings"
    android:title="@string/action_settings" />
  <item
    android:id="@+id/action_about"
    android:title="@string/action_about"/>
</menu>
```

3. Once we have the structure, we override the `OnCreateOptionsMenu()` method and inflate the resource:

    ```
    public override bool OnCreateOptionsMenu(IMenu menu)
    {
      MenuInflater.Inflate(Resource.Menu.Options, menu);
      return true;
    }
    ```

4. If we want to respond to items being selected in that menu, all we need to do is override the `OnOptionsItemSelected()` method:

    ```
    public override bool OnOptionsItemSelected(IMenuItem item)
    {
      if (item.ItemId == Resource.Id.action_refresh) {
        // do something here...
        return true; // we handled the event
      }
      return base.OnOptionsItemSelected(item);
    }
    ```

How it works...

Menus, especially the options menu, are both simple and important to Android apps. The Options menu contains items that are relevant to the current activity. They are important, but they are often not commonly used and so don't have a dedicated space in the layout.

An Android screen with an options menu at the bottom

As with traditional layout files, using resource files for menus allows greater flexibility for the many screen configurations as well as for simplifying customizations to menus.

Each menu item contains a unique ID, which allows the system to recognize the item when the user selects it, and a title, which is used to present the item to the user. There are also additional properties, the most commonly used of these being the icon. When using action bars, this icon is used to display an image alongside, or in place of, the title.

Although not required, it is recommended that most menu items include an icon.

The `MenuInflater` instance creates the menu structure from the resource file and inflates it into the `IMenu` instance. All the menu items in the resource will be added as children to the menu.

 The `OnCreateOptionsMenu()` method should return `true` if the menu is to be displayed. Returning `false` will result in the menu not being displayed.

When we handle the menu item selections, the menu item that was selected is passed into the `OnOptionsItemSelected()` method. If the event was handled, `true` should be returned; otherwise, the system will keep on processing the event.

We can use any of the properties on the menu item, but one of the more commonly used ones is `ItemId`, which contains the ID that was used in the resource file. This ID can be used to determine which item was selected.

Supporting previous Android versions

As the Android operating system evolves, many new features are added and older devices are often left behind.

How to do it...

In order to add the new features of the later versions of Android to the older versions of Android, all we need to do is add a small package:

1. An Android app has three platform versions to be set. The first is the API features that are available to code against. We set this to always be the latest in the **Target Framework** dropdown of the project options.

2. The next version to set (via **Minimum Android version**) is the lowest version of the OS that the app can be installed on. When using the support libraries, we can usually target versions down to version 2.3.

3. Lastly, the **Target Android version** dropdown specifies how the app should behave when installed on a later version of the OS. Typically, this should always be the latest version so the app will always function as the user expects.

If we want to add support for the new UI paradigm that uses fragments and action bars, we need to install two of the Android support packages:

- ▸ Create or open a project in Xamarin Studio.
    1. Right-click on the project folder in the **Solution Explorer** list.
    2. Select **Add** and then **Add Packages...**.
    3. In the **Add Packages** dialog that is displayed, search for **Xamarin.Android. Support**.
    4. Select both **Xamarin Support Library v4** and **Xamarin Support Library v7 AppCompat**.
    5. Click on **Add Package**.

There are several support library packages, each adding other types of forward compatibility, but these two are the most commonly used.

1. Once the packages are installed, our activities can now inherit from the `AppCompatActivity` type instead of the usual `Activity` type:

   ```
   public class MyActivity : AppCompatActivity
   {
   }
   ```

2. Finally, we specify that the activity theme be one of the `AppCompat` derivatives using the `Theme` property in the `[Activity]` attribute:

   ```
   [Activity(..., Theme = "@style/Theme.AppCompat", ...)]
   ```

How it works...

As Android is developed, new features are being added and designs change. We want to always provide the latest features to our users, but some users either haven't or can't upgrade to the latest version of Android. By including the Android Support Libraries in our app, we can make use of the new features, but still support the old versions.

 Types from the Android Support Library are available to almost all versions of Android currently in use.

Xamarin.Android provides three version numbers to specify what and how types can be used. The target framework version specifies what types are available for consumption as well as what toolset to use during compilation. This should be the latest as we always want to use the latest tools.

However, this will make some types and members available to apps even if they aren't actually available on the Android version that the user is using. For example, it will make the ActionBar type available to apps running on Android version 2.3. If the user were to run the app, it would probably crash.

In these instances, we can set the minimum Android version to be a version that supports these types and members. But, this will then reduce the number of devices that we can install our app on. This is why we use the support libraries; they allow the types to be used on most versions of Android.

 Setting the minimum Android version for an app will prevent the app from being installed on devices with earlier versions of the OS.

The Android support libraries provide us with a type that we know we can use everywhere, and then that base type manages the features to make sure they function as expected. For example, we can use the ActionBar type on most versions of Android because the support library made it available through the AppCompatActivity type.

Because the AppCompatActivity type is an adaptive extension for the traditional Activity type, we have to use a different theme. This theme adjusts so that the new look and feel of the UI gets carried all the way back to the old Android versions.

 When using the AppCompatActivity type, the activity theme must be one of the AppCompat theme variations.

There are a few differences when using the support library. With native support for the action bar, the AppCompatActivity type has a property named ActionBar; however, in the support library, the property is named SupportActionBar. This is just a property name change, but the functionality is the same.

Sometimes, features have to be added to the existing types that are not in the support libraries. In these cases, static methods are provided. The native support for custom views in menu items includes a method named SetActionView:

```
menuItem.SetActionView(someView);
```

This method does not exist on the IMenuItem type for the older versions of Android, so we make use of the static method on the MenuItemCompat type:

```
MenuItemCompat.SetActionView(menuItem, someView);
```

There's more...

Besides using the Android Support Libraries to handle different versions, there is another way to handle different versions at runtime. Android provides us with the version number of the current operating system through the `Build.VERSION` type.

This type has a property, `SdkInt`, which we can use to detect the current version. It represents the current API level of the version. Each version of Android has received a series of updates and new features. For example, Android 4 has received numerous updates since its initial release, new features being added each time.

Sometimes the support library cannot cover all the cases, and we will have to write specific code for particular versions:

```
int apiLevel = (int)Build.VERSION.SdkInt;
if (Build.VERSION.SdkInt >= BuildVersionCodes.IceCreamSandwich) {
  // Android version 4.0 and above
} else {
  // Android versions below version 4.0
}
```

Although this can be done, it introduces spaghetti code and should be avoided. In addition to different code, the app may behave differently on different versions, even if the support library could have handled it. We will now have to manage these differences ourselves each time a new version of Android is released.

Adding an action bar

Almost all apps require some form of commanding, usually being frequently used. As a result, these commands should be presented in an easily consumed region of the screen, regardless of differences in screen configuration.

How to do it...

Adding an action bar is very simple and does not need many changes to our app, even if they are to run on the old versions of Android:

1. By default, on Android 4.0, apps will have an action bar. To access this, we can use the `ActionBar` property on the `Activity` type:

    ```
    ActionBar.Title = "Xamarin Cookbook";
    ```

To provide an action bar to previous versions of Android, we use the Android Support Libraries:

1. First, we need to install the **Xamarin Support Library v7 AppCompat Component** or **NuGet**.

2. Then, we need to ensure our activities inherit from the `AppCompatActivity` type instead of the usual `Activity` type:

```
public class MyActivity : AppCompatActivity
{
}
```

3. Next, we add the `Theme` property to the `[Activity]` attribute:

```
[Activity(..., Theme = "@style/Theme.AppCompat")]
```

4. Finally, if we need to access the `ActionBar` instance, it is available via the `SupportActionBar` property on the activity:

```
SupportActionBar.Title = "Xamarin Cookbook";
```

How it works...

Certain commands are used very frequently in an app. These commands are often the main set of actions available to the current app screen. Because these commands are so important, they have a dedicated area in the app, often at the top of the screen. In a to-do list app, this might be the action to add a new task. In a shopping app, this might be the option to search for a product.

An Android screen with an action bar at the top

While adding an action bar on older Android versions, it is important to inherit it from the `AppCompatActivity` type. This type includes all the logic required for including an action bar in the app. It also provides many different methods and properties for accessing and configuring the action bar. In newer versions of Android, all the features are included in the `Activity` type.

Although the functionality is the same, we do have to access the various pieces using the support members when using the support libraries. An example would be to use the `SupportActionBar` property instead of the `ActionBar` property. If we use the `ActionBar` property, the app will crash on devices that don't natively support the `ActionBar` property.

In order to render the action bar, the activity needs to use a theme that contains a style for the action bar or one that inherits from such a theme. For the older versions of Android, we can use the `AppCompat` themes, such as `Theme.AppCompat`.

There's more...

With the release of Android version 5.0, Google introduced a new style of action bar. The new `Toolbar` type performs the same function as the action bar but can be placed anywhere on the screen. The action bar is always placed at the top of the screen, but toolbar is not restricted to that location and can even be placed inside other layouts.

To make use of the `Toolbar` type, we can either use the native type, or we can use the type found in the support libraries. Like any Android View, we can add the `ToolBar` type to the layout:

```
<android.support.v7.widget.Toolbar
  android:id="@+id/my_toolbar"
  android:layout_width="match_parent"
  android:layout_height="?attr/actionBarSize"
  android:background="?attr/colorPrimary"
  android:elevation="4dp"
  android:theme="@style/ThemeOverlay.AppCompat.ActionBar"
  app:popupTheme="@style/ThemeOverlay.AppCompat.Light"/>
```

The difference is in how the activity is set up. First, as we are not going to be using the default `ActionBar` property, we can use the `Theme.AppCompat.NoActionBar` theme. Then, we have to let the activity know which view is the `Toolbar` type:

```
var toolbar = FindViewById<Toolbar>(Resource.Id.toolbar);
SetSupportActionBar(toolbar);
```

See also

- ▶ The *Supporting previous Android versions* recipe
- ▶ The *Adding action bar action items* recipe

Navigating with the action bar

The action bar is used to allow the user to navigate to a parent activity, as well as show the user where they are in the app.

How to do it...

Navigation with the action bar is an upward navigation, rather than a backward navigation. This navigation is very simple to add and involves only two steps. If we support versions of Android versions below 4.1, we will make use of the support library.

1. First, we need to ensure that our source activity is accessible using a known name by adding a `[Register]` attribute:

   ```
   [Register("com.xamarincookbook.MainActivity")]
   public class MainActivity : AppCompatActivity
   {
   }
   ```

2. Next, we let the system know which activity we want to navigate up to using a `[MetaData]` attribute:

   ```
   [MetaData(
      "android.support.PARENT_ACTIVITY",
      Value = "com.xamarincookbook.MainActivity")]
   public class RecipeDetailsActivity : AppCompatActivity {
   }
   ```

3. Then in the child activity, we let the action bar know that we want to allow upward navigation:

   ```
   SupportActionBar.SetDisplayHomeAsUpEnabled(true);
   ```

If the Android version is 4.1 and above, we use the native types and members:

1. First, we set the `ParentActivity` property on the `[Activity]` attribute:

   ```
   [Activity (ParentActivity = typeof(MainActivity))]
   public class RecipeDetailsActivity : Activity
   {
   }
   ```

2. Then, we let the child activity's action bar know that we want to allow upward navigation:

   ```
   ActionBar.SetDisplayHomeAsUpEnabled(true);
   ```

How it works...

The action bar can facilitate direct navigation in two ways: navigating up to the parent activity and navigating down to a child activity. Navigating down is often done by adding action items to the action bar.

Action bar automatically navigates up to the parent activity when the user taps the icon, which is different from the traditional back navigation. The up navigation within an app is based on the hierarchical relationships between activities, that is, navigation to the parent activity. The back navigation is navigation back through the history of activities, in reverse chronological order.

 If an activity is the topmost one in an app and it does not have a parent activity, it should not present an up button.

Sometimes the back navigation is the same as the up navigation. This happens when the previously viewed screen is also the hierarchical parent of the current screen. However the up navigation will keep the user in the app, but back navigation may return the user to the home screen or another app.

When adding the `[MetaData]` attribute to the activity, we need to reference the final compiled name of the parent activity. Xamarin.Android mangles the final name of the types to avoid possible conflicts, so we have to let the compiler know exactly what name to use. We do this using a `[Register]` attribute on the parent activity, and we then use the same value for the value component of the metadata.

The action bar lets the user know where they are in the app by using the action bar's title, which is usually the current activity's label. This can be customized by assigning a new `string` value to the `Title` property on the `ActionBar` instance.

There's more...

Sometimes the up navigation will take the user to different parent activities, depending on how the user arrived at the current activity. In these cases, we override several members in our activity. If our app is not going to have the activity instantiated on any other apps, we only need to override the `SupportParentActivityIntent` or `ParentActivityIntent` properties:

```
public override Intent SupportParentActivityIntent {
   get {return new Intent(this, typeof(MainActivity));}
}
```

If our activity is going to be used by other apps, we also need to override the `OnCreateNavigateUpTaskStack()` or `OnCreateSupportNavigateUpTaskStack()` method.

See also

▶ The *Adding an action bar* recipe

Adding action bar action items

The fundamental purpose of an action bar, besides navigation, is to present the user with a set of actions that can be performed.

How to do it...

By simply using the action bar, all the action items are added to the overflow:

1. The XML for ActionBar items is exactly the same as the options menu:

```
<menu ... >
  <item
    android:id="@+id/action_refresh"
    android:icon="@drawable/ic_action_refresh"
    android:title="@string/action_refresh"/>
</menu>
```

However, we can customize what items are displayed, and how they are displayed:

1. To add action items with images to the actual `ActionBar` property, as well as more complex items, all that is needed is an attribute in the XML, showAsAction:

```
<menu ... xmlns:app="http://schemas.android.com/apk/res-auto">
  <item ... app:showAsAction="ifRoom"/>
</menu>
```

2. If we wish to add custom views, such as a search box, to the action bar, we make use of the `actionViewClass` attribute:

```
<menu ... xmlns:app="http://schemas.android.com/apk/res-auto">
  <item ...
  app:actionViewClass="android.support.v7.widget.SearchView"/>
</menu>
```

3. If the view is in a layout resource file, we use the `actionLayout` attribute:

```
<menu ... xmlns:app="http://schemas.android.com/apk/res-auto">
  <item ... app:actionLayout="@layout/action_rating"/>
</menu>
```

4. Sometimes, we may wish to only display the icon initially and then, when the user taps the icon, expand the item to display the action view:

```
<menu ... xmlns:app="http://schemas.android.com/apk/res-auto">
   <item ... app:showAsAction="ifRoom|collapseActionView"/>
</menu>
```

How it works...

Action item buttons are just traditional options menu items but are optionally always visible on the action bar.

The underlying logic to handle item selections is the same as that for the traditional options menu. No change is required to existing code inside the `OnOptionsItemSelected()` method.

The value of the `showAsAction` attribute can be `ifRoom`, `never`, or `always`. This value can optionally be combined, using a pipe, with `withText` and/or `collapseActionView`.

Creating contextual action mode menu

Some controls or regions in the user interface allow for additional actions to be performed. However, due to limited screen space, these actions need to be hidden until the user requests them.

How to do it...

1. The first thing that needs to be done is to let the activity or fragment know that we want to display a popup menu when the user long-taps on a view:

```
this.RegisterForContextMenu(someView);
```

2. Then, following the pattern of the options menu, we create or inflate the menu items in the `OnCreateContextMenu()` method:

```
public override void OnCreateContextMenu(
    IContextMenu menu,
    View view,
    IContextMenuContextMenuInfo menuInfo) {
    base.OnCreateContextMenu(menu, view, menuInfo);
    MenuInflater.Inflate(Resource.Menu.Main_Options, menu);
}
```

3. Lastly, we can respond to item selections, as we did with the options menu, in the `OnContextItemSelected()` method:

```
public override bool OnContextItemSelected(IMenuItem item) {
    if (item.ItemId == Resource.Id.action_refresh) {
```

```
        // do something here...
        return true;
    }
    return base.OnContextItemSelected(item);
}
```

How it works...

We can provide a context menu for any view, but they are most often used for items in a list, grid, or other view collection. One way to show a contextual menu is to use a floating or pop-up menu, and it is the recommended way for apps supporting versions of Android below version 3.0.

 If the views or list view is not registered with its activity or fragment, the context menu will not be displayed, even if the methods are implemented.

When the user long-taps on a view that has been registered for a context menu, the activity or fragment attempts to display a menu that is created or inflated in the `OnCreateContextMenu()` method.

After the user selects an item from the contextual menu, the `OnContextItemSelected()` method on the activity or fragment is invoked. In this method, we initiate the desired operation that was selected. We can identify the selected item using the `ItemId` property.

There's more...

Using the `IContextMenu` instance that is passed into the `OnCreateContextMenu()` method, we can change or remove the header of the popup menu. The header could be a combination of an icon and/or text or a separate custom view:

```
menu.SetHeaderTitle("My Context Menu Heading");
```

See also

- ▸ The *Creating an options menu* recipe
- ▸ The *Creating contextual action mode menu* recipe

Creating contextual action mode menus

The action bar provides the user with a set of actions; however, these actions are usually just the most commonly used. Sometimes, the context of the app changes, so the presented actions need to adjust to what is commonly used in the new context.

How to do it...

There are a few steps to implementing a contextual action bar:

1. The first step is to implement the `ActionMode.ICallback` interface. This interface can either be implemented in a new, separate class or on the actual activity or fragment:

```
public class MainActivity :
  AppCompatActivity, ActionMode.ICallback {
  public bool OnCreateActionMode(
    ActionMode mode, IMenu menu) {
  }
  public bool OnPrepareActionMode(
    ActionMode mode, IMenu menu) {
  }
  public bool OnActionItemClicked(
    ActionMode mode, IMenuItem item) {
  }
  public void OnDestroyActionMode(ActionMode mode) {
  }
}
```

2. In the `OnCreateActionMode()` method, we create the menu as we would any options menu:

```
public bool OnCreateActionMode(ActionMode mode, IMenu menu)
{
  mode.MenuInflater.Inflate(Resource.Menu.options, menu);
  return true;
}
```

3. Because we are not going to be updating the action mode once displayed, we can return `false` in the `OnPrepareActionMode()` method:

```
public bool OnPrepareActionMode(
  ActionMode mode, IMenu menu) {
  return false;
}
```

4. We handle any item selections in the `OnActionItemClicked()` method:

```
public bool OnActionItemClicked(
  ActionMode mode, IMenuItem item) {
  if (item.ItemId == Resource.Id.action_refresh) {
    // do something here...
    return true;
  }
  return false;
}
```

5. We don't need to do anything when we leave action mode, so we leave the `OnDestroyActionMode()` method empty:

```
public void OnDestroyActionMode(ActionMode mode) {
}
```

6. An instance of `ActionMode.ICallback` is passed to the `StartSupportActionMode()` or `StartActionMode()` methods:

```
someView.LongClick += (sender, e) => {
   if (actionMode == null) {
      // start the action mode
      actionMode = StartSupportActionMode(this);
      someView.Selected = true;
   }
};
```

How it works...

The contextual action mode menu is actually a separate action bar-like UI element that overlays but does not replace the actual action bar.

 Contextual menu items do not need to have the `showAsAction` attribute set in order to be displayed (it is ignored); by default, everything is visible.

This menu provides a set of commands that can be displayed based on some context, usually after a selection of an item on the screen. Selections are usually done after a long-tap, similar to traditional context menus; however, instead of a popup, the action bar is transformed. This provides a consistent interface without disrupting the flow of the task.

In order to enter action mode, we invoke the `StartSupportActionMode()` method. If we are not using the support libraries, we invoke the `StartActionMode()` method. This will return an `ActionMode` instance, which can then be used to customize the appearance of the action mode overlay.

When entering action mode, the `OnCreateActionMode()` method is invoked. Here we create the various action items that will be presented on the actions bar.

The `OnPrepareActionMode()` method is invoked whenever the action mode changes or is invalidated. This method allows us to optionally modify the UI. We must return `true` if any changes were made and `false` if nothing was modified.

When the user selects an action item, the `OnActionItemClicked()` method will be invoked. The current action mode and the selected item are provided so that we can perform the task.

There's more...

If we are using lists and supporting Android 3.0 and above, there is an extra feature that we can make use of: multiple selections. There is currently no native support for a similar functionality on older versions of Android; however, there is no reason why we can't use this feature on newer Android versions.

Implementing this requires a few extra steps but is actually an extension of the normal contextual action mode. Instead of implementing the `ActionMode.ICallback` interface, implement the `AbsListView.IMultiChoiceModeListener` interface (which actually derives from `ActionMode.ICallback`). This adds one extra method:

```
public void OnItemCheckedStateChanged(
  ActionMode mode, int position, long id, bool isChecked) {
  // handle item selections and deselections
}
```

And finally, we let the list view know about the multiselect availability by passing the instance. This is done instead of registering the context menu for floating menus:

```
listView.ChoiceMode = ChoiceMode.MultipleModal;
listView.SetMultiChoiceModeListener(this);
```

See also

▸ The *Adding action bar action items* recipe
▸ The *Creating a contextual menu* recipe

Sharing code with other platforms

One of the major reasons for using Xamarin.Android is the use of C# as the programming language. But this is not the only benefit as that same C# code can be shared with other platforms, such as iOS, Windows, or Mac OS.

How to do it...

First, we are going to create the project structure that we are going to use to create our cross-platform app. In this example, we will only target Xamarin.Android and the Console, but extra platforms can be added.

1. Open Xamarin Studio or Visual Studio and create an empty solution. For example, we are going to call this one `XamarinCodeSharing`.

2. In this solution, create three projects:

   ❏ An Android project named `XamarinCodeSharing.Droid`

   ❏ A console application named `XamarinCodeSharing.Desktop`

   ❏ A portable class library named `XamarinCodeSharing.Core`

3. Open the project settings for `XamarinCodeSharing.Core`. If you are using Xamarin Studio, navigate to **Build | General**. Or if you are using Visual Studio, navigate to **Library** and then click on **Change** under the **Targeting** section.

4. Note the various platform options available, including iOS, Android, Windows, and several others, some with version options. Ensure that the **.NET4.5** and the **Xamarin. Android** boxes are selected as these are the platforms we are going to need.

5. To make things easier, we are going to use a `NuGet` package, `Microsoft.Net. Http`, which simplifies the process of using HTTP and REST services. Install this package into each of the three projects.

6. Add a project reference from `XamarinCodeSharing.Droid` to `XamarinCodeSharing.Core` and a project reference from `XamarinCodeSharing.Desktop` to `XamarinCodeSharing.Core`.

7. Now that we have our project structure in place, we are going to write some code that will access the web service, and then see how that code is reused without modification or even recompilation. What we are going to do next all takes place in the `XamarinCodeSharing.Core` project.

8. To make things easy, we can just delete the file that the IDE created. Xamarin Studio created a file named `MyClass.cs`, and Visual Studio created a file named `Class1.cs`.

9. We can now create a new class named `BlogItem`, which will represent the actual blog entries. This bit is very simple and is just a set of properties:

```
using System;

namespace XamarinCodeSharing.Core
{
  public class BlogItem
  {
    public string Title { get; set; }
    public string Link { get; set; }
    public DateTime PublishDate { get; set; }
    public string Description { get; set; }
  }
}
```

10. In the same project, create another new class named `XamarinBlog`, which both represents the blog as well as provides a means to download the blog:

```
using System;
using System.Collections.Generic;
using System.IO;
using System.Linq;
using System.Net.Http;
using System.Threading.Tasks;
using System.Xml.Linq;
using System.Net;

namespace XamarinCodeSharing.Core {
  public class XamarinBlog {
    private const string BlogUrl =
    "http://blog.xamarin.com/feed";

    // blog metadata properties
    public string Title { get; set; }
    public string Link { get; set; }
    public List<BlogItem> Items { get; private set; }

    // Download the feed, parse it and return a blog object
    public static async Task<XamarinBlog> Download() {
      HttpClient client = new HttpClient();
      HttpResponseMessage response = await
      client.GetAsync(BlogUrl);

      // if all went well, read the feed, otherwise fail
      if(response.IsSuccessStatusCode) {
        return await ParseResponse(response.Content);
      }
      else {
        throw new Exception("There was a problem.");
      }
    }

    // Read the response out of the content and
    // create objects
    private static async Task<XamarinBlog>ParseResponse(
    HttpContent content) {
      XamarinBlog blog = new XamarinBlog();

      using(Stream stream = await
      content.ReadAsStreamAsync()) {
```

```
XDocument doc = XDocument.Load(stream);
XElement channel = doc.Root.Element("channel");

// load the blog metadata out of the xml
blog.Title = WebUtility.HtmlDecode(
channel.Element("title").Value);
blog.Link = WebUtility.HtmlDecode(
channel.Element("link").Value);

// load the blog items out of the xml
var items = from item in channel.Elements("item")
select new BlogItem {
  Title = WebUtility.HtmlDecode(
  item.Element("title").Value),
  Link = WebUtility.HtmlDecode(
  item.Element("link").Value),
  PublishDate = DateTime.Parse(
  WebUtility.HtmlDecode(
  item.Element("pubDate").Value)),
  Description = WebUtility.HtmlDecode(
  item.Element("description").Value),
};
blog.Items = items.ToList();
}

return blog;
}
}
}
```

There are several important points to note here. We are using the `async` and `await` keywords to make asynchronous code easier to read, something which is not available in Java. Another feature is LINQ to XML to make working with XML easier to parse, another feature not available to Java. And finally, `WebUtility.HtmlDecode` is used as all the data is HTML encoded inside the XML.

Now that we have created the main logic of the app, we can look at those native implementations. First, we will create the Console app that will run on almost any desktop operating system, such as Windows, Mac OS, and most of the flavors of Linux:

1. To do this, we can just replace the code in the `Program.cs` file with the following:

```
using System;
using XamarinCodeSharing.Core;
using System.Threading.Tasks;

namespace XamarinCodeSharing.Desktop {
  class MainClass {
    public static void Main(string[] args) {
      GetBlogItems().Wait();

      Console.WriteLine("Press any key to quit.");
      Console.ReadKey();
    }

    private static async Task GetBlogItems() {
      Console.WriteLine("Downloading blog...");
      XamarinBlog blog = await XamarinBlog.Download();
      Console.WriteLine("Download finished.");
      Console.WriteLine();

      Console.WriteLine("{0} ({1} items)",
      blog.Title, blog.Items.Count);

      foreach (var item in blog.Items) {
        Console.WriteLine(item.Title);
        Console.WriteLine(
          item.PublishDate.ToString("d MMMM yyyy"));
        Console.WriteLine(item.Description);
        Console.WriteLine();
      }
    }
  }
}
```

If we run the desktop project now, the console will start up, download the blog feed, and then display each entry along with a short summary. Last but not least, we want to get that mobile version going. And what better platform to support first than Android?

1. Switching to the Xamarin.Android project, we can replace the code in the `MainActivity.cs` file with the following:

```
using System.Collections.Generic;
using System.Linq;
using Android.App;
using Android.OS;
using Android.Runtime;
using Android.Widget;
using XamarinCodeSharing.Core;

namespace XamarinCodeSharing.Droid {
  [Activity(
    Label = "XamarinCodeSharing.Droid",
    MainLauncher = true,
    Icon = "@drawable/icon")]
  public class MainActivity : ListActivity {
    private const string TitleKey = "title";
    private const string SubtitleKey = "subtitle";

    protected async override void OnCreate(Bundle bundle) {
      base.OnCreate(bundle);

      var progress = new ProgressDialog(this);
      progress.SetTitle("Downloading blog...");
      progress.SetMessage(
        "Please wait while we download the Xamarin
        blog...");
      progress.Show();

      XamarinBlog blog = await XamarinBlog.Download();
      var items = from item in blog.Items
      select new JavaDictionary<string, object> {
        { TitleKey, item.Title },
        { SubtitleKey, item.Description }
      };

      ListAdapter = new SimpleAdapter(
        this,
        items.Cast<IDictionary<string, object>>().ToList(),
        Android.Resource.Layout.SimpleListItem2,
```

```
            new []{ TitleKey, SubtitleKey },
            new []{ Android.Resource.Id.Text1,
            Android.Resource.Id.Text2 });

        progress.Dismiss();
        progress.Dispose();
      }
    }
  }
```

If we run this Android app now, we shall get that app that downloads the latest Xamarin blog posts and displays them in a neat list.

How it works...

Portable class libraries is one of the most important aspects of code reuse. Although there are many different ways to reuse code, such as file linking or shared projects, none can match the reliability and ease of simply reusing the compiled assembly. This assembly can be tested and verified and then used and reused without fear of problems arising on different platforms.

Why? It is because each platform in each portable class library profile promises to support all the features, for all platforms, in that profile, and all those features function exactly the same.

Using Xamarin.Android, we now have all the features of the .NET runtime available, the same runtime that runs on almost all devices. Along with that same runtime, we can now build libraries that run on that runtime, and those libraries will run on all platforms that have the same runtime. Those platforms include iOS, Android, Windows Phone, Mac OS, Windows, Linux, and even more, such as PlayStation!

Although we can never achieve 100 percent code reuse, as each platform has differences (especially in the user interface), much of the code lives below the surface and can be reused. And using the commonality of the runtime and languages, we can create abstractions that can work around the platform differences, resulting in even more code reuse.

Although we only covered two platforms in this example, we can already see that it takes more code to work with the data than it does to display it. Adding extra platforms, such as Windows Phone and iOS, will result in this ultra-simple example app being able to support the major mobile operating systems, with the only difference being the UI.

2
Showing Views and Handling Fragments

In this chapter, we will cover the following recipes:

- ▶ Using custom views with layouts
- ▶ Creating and using fragments
- ▶ Preserving view and fragment state
- ▶ Navigating between fragments
- ▶ Fragments and the action bar
- ▶ Animating fragment navigation
- ▶ Animating view and object properties
- ▶ Animating views on the UI
- ▶ Adding a navigation drawer with fragments
- ▶ Applying local styles and global themes

Introduction

All apps have one thing in common: they all have some sort of user interface. Whether it is a rich set of controls or just a simple notification that something happened, all apps present the user with a means to consume information or provide data.

Users desire an interface that is easy to use and beautiful to look at. Often, the simplest way to improve the interface is to add a transition between states. This provides a way to move the user from one state to another, but without a sharp and sudden change.

In order to move the user between states or allow the user to initiate such a movement, the app needs to provide a set of actions or navigation points. As navigation through the app is often not the primary function of the app, these controls should be placed within easy reach but should not obstruct the real functionality.

Animations and transitions do not change the functionality of an app, but they do make the user experience more enjoyable. Navigation is often the most jarring change, and transitions provide a smoother experience.

Not only do transitions improve navigation, but designing the user interface for navigation also makes the experience better. Taking advantage of new and popular navigation concepts, the app can become a pleasure to use.

Using custom views with layouts

One of the most important parts is the user interface, as it is the most visible part of an app. When we create apps for Android devices, sometimes we may need to create custom views.

How to do it...

Creating a new UI control involves creating a new type, inheriting either directly or indirectly from one of the `View` types. Here's how it's done:

1. If we want to create more advanced button control, we must create a new type inheriting from the `Button` type. We also need to ensure that the namespace is user friendly as it will be used in the layout files:

   ```
   namespace XamarinCookbook.Views {
     public class TimedButton : Button {
     }
   }
   ```

2. Now we can implement the functionality that this button provides:

   ```
   public int Interval { get; set; }

   private async void OnClicked(object sender, EventArgs e) {
     // disable the button for several seconds
     if (Interval > 0) {
       Enabled = false;
       await Task.Delay(Interval * 1000);
       Enabled = true;
     }
   }
   ```

3. As this control can be created in code, we must implement the constructor that accepts a `Context` instance:

```
public TimedButton(Context context)
: base(context) {
  Interval = 5; // default
  Click += OnClicked;
}
```

4. Additionally, this control will be inflated from layout resource files, so we implement the constructor that accepts an `IAttributeSet` instance:

```
public TimedButton(Context context, IAttributeSet attrs)
: base(context, attrs) {
  Interval = 5; // default
  Click += OnClicked;
}
```

To make use of the view in our UI layouts, we can either instantiate the control in code or we can add them to our layout resource files.

1. Like any other control, we can instantiate the custom control:

```
var button = new TimedButton(this);
```

2. Similarly, we can add our custom control to layout resource files as well:

```
<xamarincookbook.views.TimedButton
   android:id="@+id/myButton"
   android:layout_width="match_parent"
   android:layout_height="wrap_content"
   android:text="@string/hello"/>
```

Although we can add properties to custom controls, we cannot set them in the layout resource files. To do this, we must create an attributes file:

1. To set attributes in the XML files, we need to declare them by adding a `value` resource (`Resources/values/TimedButtonAttr.xml`):

```
<?xml version="1.0" encoding="UTF-8" ?>
<resources>
  <declare-styleable name="TimedButton">
    <attr name="interval" format="integer" />
  </declare-styleable>
</resources>
```

2. Once we have this resource file, we need our custom button to actually use the values specified in the XML attributes, and this just requires an update to the constructor with the `IAttributeSet` parameter:

```
public TimedButton(Context context, IAttributeSet attrs)
: base(context, attrs) {
    // get our custom style
    TypedArray styled = context.Theme.ObtainStyledAttributes(
        attrs, Resource.Styleable.TimedButton, 0, 0);

    try {
        // set the property from the attribute
        Interval = styled.GetInt(
            Resource.Styleable.TimedButton_interval, 5);
    } finally {
        // clean up
        styled.Recycle();
        styled.Dispose();
    }

    Click += OnClicked;
}
```

3. Finally, we can add the custom attributes to the `view` instance in our layout resource file:

```
<xamarincookbook.views.TimedButton
    ...
    xmlns:app="http://schemas.android.com/apk/res-auto"
    app:interval="3"/>
```

How it works...

Creating a custom view is no different from subclassing an existing type and adding functionality. However, to use this new type, we have to add support for it so that it can be used in layouts that will be inflated. This is just an extra, optional constructor, but it is recommended to add an attributes resource file.

Using this view in a layout resource is no different from adding the standard Android views to the layout. But we can see that we have to specify the full namespace of the button, and this is lowercase. This is exactly the same as adding views from the Android support libraries.

 Android requires that views provide the full namespace, in lowercase, in the layout resource files. The type name should keep original casing.

All Android views require at least a constructor that accepts an instance of `Context`. This allows the view to properly handle the various lifecycle events.

The additional constructor takes the usual `Context` property, but additionally, it also takes the `IAttributeSet` parameter. This is used by the layout inflator to pass the attributes from the XML to our custom view, which in turn we can use to initialize any members.

The attributes are declared in a resource, `<declare-styleable>`, so that they can be used in code to retrieve the attribute values. This element will contain all the `<attr>` elements that represent each available XML attribute that can be used in the layout.

Custom attributes are not prefixed with `android:` but with a local, app-specific namespace from `http://schemas.android.com/apk/res-auto`.

When the view is inflated from an XML layout, all the attributes from that element are passed to the constructor via `IAttributeSet`. Although it's possible to read values from `IAttributeSet` directly, doing so does not allow resource values to be resolved, such as when using string resources.

We can obtain the resolved and styled attributes from the result of the `ObtainStyledAttributes()` method on the `Context` themes. This method returns a `TypedArray` object, from which we can easily retrieve the values that we can use to initialize members.

 The `TypedArray` objects are a shared resource and must be recycled after use.

There's more...

Sometimes we wish to create a new view that is actually just a collection of other views, with some relationship between them. This is very easily done by simply subclassing a layout type, such as `LinearLayout`, instead of a button. This allows us to add subviews that will make up our new compound view.

See also

▶ *Preserving view and fragment state*

Creating and using fragments

Sometimes normal layouts aren't dynamic enough or we may have to reuse sections of the UI and its related code.

Getting ready

To add fragments to our app we need to be targeting Android version 3.0 and above; for versions below that, we need to have installed the **Xamarin.Android.Support.v4** package.

How to do it...

In order to make use of fragments in our apps, we need to create a new fragment type. Then, either in the layout or in the code, we can insert the fragments into their appropriate places in the UI. Let's take a look at the following steps:

1. To make a master-detail app, we need a menu or list of items to select. For the menu fragment we are going to inherit from `ListFragment`, which is very similar to `ListActivity`, and set the `ListAdapter` property:

```
public class MenuFragment : ListFragment {
  public override void OnStart() {
    base.OnStart();

    ListAdapter = new ArrayAdapter(
      Activity,
      Android.Resource.Layout.SimpleListItem1,
      new [] {"First", "Second", "Third", "Fourth"});
  }
}
```

2. The other part of a master-detail app is the details. This fragment is going to be a normal fragment, and we will use a separate layout resource to define the UI structure:

    1. The UI for this fragment can be any view hierarchy. Here it is defined in a layout resource file named `ContentFragment.axml`:

    ```
    <?xml version="1.0" encoding="utf-8"?>
    <LinearLayout
    xmlns:android="http://schemas.android.com/apk/res/android"
      android:orientation="vertical"
      android:layout_width="match_parent"
      android:layout_height="match_parent">
      <TextView
        android:id="@+id/textView"
        android:text="Select an item to the left..."
    ```

```
        android:gravity="center"
        android:layout_width="match_parent"
        android:layout_height="match_parent"
        style="@android:style/TextAppearance.Large" />
</LinearLayout>
```

2. The code for the content fragment inflates the resource in the `OnCreateView()` method:

```
public class ContentFragment : Fragment {
  public override View OnCreateView(
    LayoutInflater inflater,
    ViewGroup container,
    Bundle savedInstanceState) {
      return inflater.Inflate(
        Resource.Layout.ContentFragment, container, false);
    }
}
```

3. If we are going to update the UI from outside the fragment, we need to make sure that the fragment provides a means to do so:

```
public void Update(string text) {
  var textView = Activity.FindViewById<TextView> (
    Resource.Id.textView);
  textView.Text = string.Format(
    "You have selected '{0}'...", text);
}
```

3. Now that our fragments are complete, we can start creating the app that will be using these fragments:

1. We are going to create a layout for the main activity in a file named `Main.axml`. The layout will display both fragments side by side, by setting the `orientation` attribute to `horizontal`:

```
<?xml version="1.0" encoding="utf-8"?>
<LinearLayout
xmlns:android="http://schemas.android.com/apk/res/android"
  android:orientation="horizontal"
  android:layout_width="match_parent"
  android:layout_height="match_parent">
  <fragment
    android:name="xamarincookbook.MenuFragment"
    android:id="@+id/menu"
    android:layout_weight="2"
    android:layout_width="match_parent"
    android:layout_height="match_parent" />
```

```
<fragment
  android:name="xamarincookbook.ContentFragment"
  android:id="@+id/content"
  android:layout_weight="1"
  android:layout_width="match_parent"
  android:layout_height="match_parent" />
</LinearLayout>
```

2. We now have to set up the activity to load the layout using the
    SetContentView() method:

```
protected override void OnCreate(Bundle bundle) {
  base.OnCreate(bundle);
  SetContentView(Resource.Layout.Main);
}
```

4. Once we have the basic structure set up for both the fragments and the activity, we
    add the ability for the menu fragment to communicate with the parent activity, and in
    turn, the content fragment. Let's take a look at the following steps:

    1. The menu fragment only does one thing—it lets the activity know that the
        user has selected an item—so we create an interface that represents a
        contract between the fragment and the activity:

```
public interface IMenuSelected {
  void OnMenuSelected(string text);
}
```

    2. Next, we ensure that the activity implements the IMenuSelected interface
        and its OnMenuSelected() method. This method then retrieves the content
        fragment and updates it. Let's take a look at the following code snippet:

```
public void OnMenuSelected(string text) {
  var contentFragment =
    SupportFragmentManager.FindFragmentById(
      Resource.Id.content) as ContentFragment;
  contentFragment.Update(text);
}
```

    3. In the menu fragment, we need to get hold of the activity that we will be
        communicating with. This can be done by overriding the OnAttach()
        method of the menu fragment and keeping a reference to the parent activity:

```
private IMenuSelected menuSelected;

public override void OnAttach(Activity activity) {
  base.OnAttach(activity);
  menuSelected = activity as IMenuSelected;
}
```

4. Then, to let the activity know when the user selects a menu item, we subscribe to the list's select event and invoke the `OnMenuSelected()` method of the activity:

```
public override void OnStart() {
  // ...
  ListView.ItemClick += (sender, e) => {
    if (menuSelected != null) {
      menuSelected.OnMenuSelected(items[e.Position]);
    }
  };
}
```

How it works...

A `Fragment` element represents a behaviour or section of the user interface in an activity that can be reused across multiple activities and combined with other fragments. Fragments can be viewed as a subactivity that is semi-self-contained and has its own lifecycle.

Fragments allow us to create more dynamic and more flexible interfaces. They can be swapped and moved at runtime, without having to manage complex view hierarchies. They should be designed as a modular component, without directly manipulating the activity or other fragments. This makes them easier to reuse and maintain.

 The activity containing the fragments needs to inherit from `AppCompatActivity` when supporting Android versions below version 3.0.

As a fragment is usually used as part of the user interface with a layout, the interface can be inflated or created in the `OnCreateView()` method of the fragment. This method should return the view that is the root of the fragment's view hierarchy.

 A subclass of `ListFragment` does not need to implement the `OnCreateView()` method as it automatically has a `ListView` instance.

The `OnCreateView()` method has arguments that provide access to the view that is going to be used as a parent as well as the `Bundle` type that contains saved data from the previous instance of this fragment.

 Fragments may be destroyed and re-created during the lifetime of a single activity.

Fragments can be added to the activity either with code using fragment transactions or by using the XML layout. In this recipe, we will look at the XML. Later, we will see how to use code for dynamic layouts. This is very similar to adding traditional views, except we use the `<fragment>` element and specify the type name in the `name` XML attribute, instead of using the type name as the element name.

 We can access fragments in the view hierarchy by making use of the `FragmentManager` instance and its `FindFragmentById()` method.
If a fragment is added to an activity layout by defining the fragment in the layout XML file, the fragment cannot be removed at runtime.

If a fragment wishes to communicate with the activity, an interface is used. This interface is provided by the fragment and implemented by the activity. The fragment can then capture a reference to the activity in the `OnAttach()` method—which will have the implemented interface—and use that for communication. The fragment can then verify that the activity implements the interface and make a decision on what to do with it. Communication is performed by calling methods on the interface from the fragment.

 Communication between fragments is done via the activity and should not be done directly.

See also

▸ *Preserving view and fragment state*

▸ *Navigation between fragments*

Preserving view and fragment state

It is important to save the state of a view, fragment, or activity. Each has a limited lifetime and may be stopped at any point, such as when the user closes the activity, navigates away from, or even rotates the device.

How to do it...

In order to preserve the state across certain actions, such as when the user switches between apps, we should save the state to the instance state parcel. Let's take a look at the following steps:

1. Saving state for a view is done by inheriting from a type that implements the `IParcelable` interface, such as `BaseSavedState`:

   ```
   private class InstanceState : BaseSavedState {
   ```

```
  public InstanceState(IParcelable superState)
  : base(superState) {
  }

  public InstanceState(Parcel parcel)
  : base(parcel) {
    Interval = parcel.ReadInt();
  }

  public int Interval { get; set; }

  public override void WriteToParcel(
    Parcel dest, ParcelableWriteFlags flags) {
      base.WriteToParcel(dest, flags);
      dest.WriteInt(Interval);
    }
  }
```

2. Now, Android needs a way to construct the instance state. This is achieved by providing an implementation of the `IParcelableCreator` instance:

```
private class InstanceStateCreator:
  Java.Lang.Object, IParcelableCreator {
    public Java.Lang.Object CreateFromParcel(
      Parcel source) {
        return new InstanceState(source);
      }
    public Java.Lang.Object[] NewArray(int size) {
      return new InstanceState[size];
    }
  }
```

3. Finally, we need to connect `IParcelableCreator` with `IParcelable` by creating a special method in the `IParcelable` implementation:

```
[ExportField("CREATOR")]
private static InstanceStateCreator InitializeCreator() {
  return new InstanceStateCreator();
}
```

4. Next, to actually save the data, we need to provide the data in the `OnSaveInstanceState()` method of the view:

```
public override IParcelable OnSaveInstanceState() {
  IParcelable state = base.OnSaveInstanceState();
  InstanceState instance = new InstanceState(state) {
    Interval = Interval
```

```
    };
    return instance;
}
```

5. To start the restore process, we override the `OnRestoreInstanceState()` method and read the data out:

```
public override void OnRestoreInstanceState(
    IParcelable state) {
    InstanceState instance = state as InstanceState;
    if (instance == null) {
        base.OnRestoreInstanceState(state);
    }
    else {
        base.OnRestoreInstanceState(instance.SuperState);
        Interval = instance.Interval;
    }
}
```

Preserving state for a fragment or an activity is much easier and can be done simply by saving and restoring the values to the `Bundle` object that is passed around. Let's take a look at the following steps:

1. Saving state happens in the `OnSaveInstanceState()` method:

```
public override void OnSaveInstanceState(Bundle outState) {
    base.OnSaveInstanceState(outState);
    outState.PutString("KEY", "VALUE");
}
```

2. To restore state, we can make use of the `OnCreate()` method, and additionally (for fragments only), the `OnCreateView()` method:

```
public override void OnCreate(Bundle savedInstanceState) {
    base.OnCreate(savedInstanceState);
    if (savedInstanceState != null) {
        string value = savedInstanceState.GetString("KEY");
    }
}
```

> The `Bundle` type may be `null` inside the `OnCreate()` and `OnCreateView()` methods, so it needs to be checked first.

3. For activities only, there is also the `OnRestoreInstanceState()` method:

```
protected override void OnRestoreInstanceState(
    Bundle savedInstanceState) {
    base.OnRestoreInstanceState(savedInstanceState);
    string value = savedInstanceState.GetString("KEY");
}
```

> The `OnRestoreInstanceState()` method of the activity is only called when there is a `bundle` object to restore, so a null check isn't necessary.

How it works...

Views are frequently created and destroyed in Android, and often we have to save the current state of the view between these operations. One of the classic examples is the instance of the device rotation; the entire activity is destroyed along with the fragments and views. Android usually takes care of this for us, but sometimes, especially in the case of custom views, we need to do this ourselves.

Views store their state in a `Parcel` object, and we can let Android know what to store in that `Parcel` object by giving it an object that contains instructions on what to store and what to retrieve. This object is an instance of `IParcelable`.

Instead of implementing all the bits from the `IParcelable` interface, we'd rather inherit from `BaseSavedSate`, which has most features already implemented, allowing us to only have to implement two members:

- The `WriteToParcel()` method, which allows us to write values (using a simple interface) to the `Parcel` object that will be persisted
- The constructor which receives an instance of a `Parcel` object, which we can use to read the previously saved values.

When a view is reconstructed from the values in the `Parcel` object, Android uses an instance of an `IParcelableCreator`. This type contains members that allow Android to construct our `IParcelable` instance, with which we can read the values that we had previously saved. There are two methods that we need to implement:

- The `CreateFromParcel()` method, which allows us to recreate our `IParcelable` instance from the `Parcel` object
- The `NewArray()` method, which allows Android to create a collection of our `IParcelable` instance

An instance of `IParcelableCreator` must inherit from `Java.Lang.Object` as the `IParcelableCreator` interface inherits from the `IJavaObject` interface.

We have to let Android know which creator to use, so we provide a field in the `IParcelable` instance. Android has a specific name for this field, `CREATOR`, and this is provided to Android by means of the Xamarin.Android exports helpers using the `[ExportField]` attribute.

Once we have our `IParcelable` instance, our `IParcelableCreator` instance, and the special field, `CREATOR`, we need to pass the state from our view into `IParcelable`. This is done by simply creating an instance of `IParcelable`. We then wrap the state from the base class, add any values we wish to save to our instance, and finally, pass it back to Android.

When Android tries to restore our view, it remembers which creator to use and constructs an instance of `IParcelable`. We then read off the values from the `Parcel` object into our view.

In order to read and write values, we create properties in `IParcelable` that hold the values from the view or from the `Parcel` object, depending on what direction the data is moving in.

Saving state for activities and fragments is much easier and only requires that we implement the `OnSaveInstanceState()` method, in which we write values to `Bundle`, a simple type of `IParcelable`.

To restore state in an activity or fragment, there are many areas we access the `Bundle` object, such as in the `OnCreate()`, `OnRestoreInstanceState()`, or `OnCreateView()` methods.

There's more...

We can use the `Bundle` type instead of creating the `IParcelable` and `IParcelalbleCreator` instances. In order to do so, we must be sure to save the state from the base into the bundle so that the base can restore its own state later on.

Although we don't have to create a custom type to store the view state, doing so makes it easier to manage and more flexible. In addition to possible future flexibility, we can abstract the state management a bit, keeping the view a bit cleaner.

See also

▸ *Using custom views with layouts*

▸ *Creating and using fragments*

Navigating between fragments

Fragments can be navigated through and back, like activities. Sometimes we have a layout that will be displayed when a user selects an option, and we want the back navigation to be as seamless as pressing the back button.

How to do it...

When it comes to navigation with fragments, we do not insert the fragments into the layout. Rather, we use an empty container layout. Then, at runtime, we insert the correct fragment:

1. First, we are going to add a new layout for portrait view. Landscape will be the original two-pane layout, and the new portrait view will have the single pane, but with swapping (Resources/**layout-port**/Main.axml):

```xml
<?xml version="1.0" encoding="utf-8"?>
<FrameLayout
xmlns:android="http://schemas.android.com/apk/res/android"
  android:id="@+id/fragmentContainer"
  android:layout_width="match_parent"
  android:layout_height="match_parent"/>
```

2. Next, we need to initialize FrameLayout by loading the first fragment, MenuFragment, at startup. If FrameLayout is obtainable, then we are in portrait mode, so we load the menu fragment:

```csharp
protected override void OnCreate(Bundle bundle) {
  //...
  FrameLayout container = FindViewById<FrameLayout>(
    Resource.Id.fragmentContainer);
  if (container != null) {
    Fragment menu =
      SupportFragmentManager.FindFragmentById(
        Resource.Id.menu);
    if (bundle == null || menu == null) {
      menu = new MenuFragment();
      SupportFragmentManager
        .BeginTransaction()
        .Add(Resource.Id.fragmentContainer, menu)
        .Commit();
    }
  }
}
```

3. Now we need to handle the menu selections and swap the menu out with the content. If we are in portrait mode, we use a transaction to show the content fragment with arguments. Otherwise, we just find the content fragment and update it:

```
public void OnMenuSelected(string text) {
  FrameLayout container = FindViewById<FrameLayout>(
    Resource.Id.fragmentContainer);

  if (container != null) {
    Bundle args = new Bundle();
    args.PutString(ContentFragment.ArgumentsKey, text);
    ContentFragment content = new ContentFragment();
    content.Arguments = args;

    SupportFragmentManager
      .BeginTransaction()
      .Replace(Resource.Id.fragmentContainer, content)
      .AddToBackStack(null)
      .Commit();
  }
  else {
    ContentFragment content =
      SupportFragmentManager.FindFragmentById(
        Resource.Id.content) as ContentFragment;
    content.Update(text);
  }
}
```

4. In order for the fragment to receive the updates from the activity, we need to read the arguments that were passed in from the main activity. This we do in the `OnStart()` method of the content fragment as the view will already be constructed, allowing us to update it. Let's take a look at the following code snippet:

```
if (Arguments != null) {
  currentText = Arguments.GetString(ArgumentsKey);
}
```

How it works...

When creating dynamic layouts, we can sometimes just design several layout files, each with variations based on the target screen configuration or device. However, greater flexibility can be achieved if we use fragments and switch them around at runtime. Fragments can be used to create dynamic and flexible interfaces and allow reuse of the layouts as well as the logic behind it.

Because we are going to load, unload, and replace fragments at runtime, we make use of `FragmentManager`. This type provides access to the `FragmentTransaction` API, which encapsulates changes to fragments—such as add, remove, and replace—into a single, reversible operation.

 In order to remove a fragment at runtime, it has to be created at runtime. If it was inserted in the XML layout, it can't be removed.

Using this API, we can perform actions such as add or replace as well as assign transitions with `SetTransition` and then apply the transaction with `Commit`. These changes can be added to the back stack, using `AddToBackStack`, so that we can "roll back" to the previous fragment when the user taps the **Back** button.

Fragment operations require a view that acts as a container for the fragments. Each `Add`, `Replace`, and `Remove` operation in a transaction is passed the ID of the container as a parameter along with the fragment.

When initializing the fragments in the `OnCreate()` method of an activity, we need to check to see if the fragments don't already exist. Android will restore the state automatically, including the fragments and fragment back stack, so we only have to set up the fragments initially.

If a fragment is removed without it's being added to the back stack, it is destroyed and is not available when going back. If `AddToBackStack` is called, the current fragment is stopped but then resumed when navigating back.

 Fragment transactions have to be added to the back stack in order to be able to pop back to it from a transaction.

In order to pass values using fragment navigation, we use the `Arguments` property, which is a `Bundle` type. This allows us to pass values in key-value pairs to the fragment. Inside the fragment, we can then query the `Arguments` property to read the values.

See also

▸ *Creating and using fragments*

Fragments and the action bar

We can access the action bar from a fragment and make customizations to aid the user on a per-fragment basis. Items can be added, and you can also customize the up navigation, keeping a consistent structure with the rest of the app.

How to do it...

When a fragment is added to the activity, we can allow that fragment to add items to the action bar. This is similar to providing items from the activity. Let's take a look at the following steps:

1. First, we want to add items to the action bar from the fragment, so we let the activity know we have a menu:

```
public override void OnCreate(Bundle savedInstanceState) {
    base.OnCreate(savedInstanceState);
    SetHasOptionsMenu(true);
}
```

 If the target Android version is below version 3.0, the `HasOptionsMenu` property is used instead of the `SetHasOptionsMenu()` method.

2. We then create the menu structure in the `menu` resource folder:

```
<menu
xmlns:android="http://schemas.android.com/apk/res/android"
    xmlns:yourapp="http://schemas.android.com/apk/res-auto">
    <item android:id="@+id/action_share"
        android:icon="@android:drawable/ic_menu_share"
        yourapp:showAsAction="ifRoom"
        android:title="@string/action_share" />
</menu>
```

3. And finally inflate it in the `OnCreateOptionsMenu()` method of the fragment:

```
public override void OnCreateOptionsMenu(
    IMenu menu, MenuInflater inflater) {
        inflater.Inflate(Resource.Menu.ActionBarItems, menu);
    }
```

Another thing we may want to do is to make the home button in the action bar and change to an up button when we navigate down to a fragment:

1. To do this, we add logic to show the up arrow when there are items on the fragment back stack:

```
private void OnBackStackChanged() {
  bool hasBack =
    SupportFragmentManager.BackStackEntryCount > 0;
  SupportActionBar.SetDisplayHomeAsUpEnabled(hasBack);
}
```

2. And then, we call that method to update the home button when the back stack changes, also making sure to call it when the activity starts:

```
protected override void OnCreate(Bundle bundle) {
  . . .
  SupportFragmentManager.BackStackChanged += delegate {
    OnBackStackChanged();
  };
  OnBackStackChanged();
}
```

3. Finally, we override the home button press so that we can pop the fragments:

```
public override bool OnSupportNavigateUp() {
  SupportFragmentManager.PopBackStack();
  return true;
}
```

How it works...

If a fragment wants to place items on the action bar, we have to let the activity know. The way we do this is by setting the `HasOptionsMenu` property to `true`, or on Android versions 3.0 and above, by passing `true` to the `SetHasOptionsMenu()` method.

We can then go ahead and create and inflate the menu structure in the same manner as if we were adding an options menu to an activity. There is an `OnCreateOptionsMenu()` method in the fragment that performs the same function as the method on the activity.

Another useful thing for us to do is to make the home button into an up button after we navigate to a child fragment. This is simple to add by subscribing to the `BackStackChanged` event on the fragment manager. In this event, we can check to see if there is anything on the back stack and update the home button.

The home button should be refreshed in the OnCreate() method as the activity may have just been restored from a saved state, such as after a device orientation change.

After adding the up arrow to the home button, we can override the OnSupportNavigateUp() method or the OnNavigateUp() method to pop the back stack of the fragment manager.

See also

▸ *Navigating between fragments*

Animating fragment navigation

Navigating between fragments is easy to do, but it appears very sharp and does not provide a smooth user experience. We can improve this by adding transitions to the navigation.

How to do it...

When navigating between fragments, we can add an animation, or rather a transition to make the overall change seem less sharp and more appealing:

1. One of the simplest ways to add animations to transitions is to simply make use of the built-in animations, such as fade or open. This is set by calling the SetTransition() method:

```
SupportFragmentManager
    .BeginTransaction()
    .SetTransition(FragmentTransaction.TransitFragmentOpen)
    .Replace(Resource.Id.fragmentContainer, content)
    .AddToBackStack(null)
    .Commit();
```

In order to create more fragment transitions, we have to create animations. This is a relatively straightforward process, but it does differ depending on the Android version we are supporting. Typically, we would create either two or four separate animations, for each stage of the transition:

1. For Android versions below 3.0, we can make use of animation resource files, saved in the anim resource folder. Here is an example of one of the required animations, card_slide_in_bottom.xml:

```
<?xml version="1.0" encoding="utf-8"?>
<translate
xmlns:android="http://schemas.android.com/apk/res/android"
```

```
android:interpolator="@android:anim/decelerate_interpolator"
  android:fromYDelta="50%p"
  android:toYDelta="0"
  android:duration="@android:integer/config_mediumAnimTime"/>
```

2. In order to use these custom animations in the actual navigation, specify the four animation resources to use in the `SetCustomAnimations()` method:

```
SupportFragmentManager
  .BeginTransaction()
  .SetCustomAnimations(
    Resource.Animation.card_slide_in_bottom,
    Resource.Animation.card_slide_out_top,
    Resource.Animation.card_slide_in_top,
    Resource.Animation.card_slide_out_bottom)
  .Replace(Resource.Id.fragmentContainer, content)
  .AddToBackStack(null)
  .Commit();
```

Similar to using animations, on Android versions 3.0 and above, we have to make use of the new `ObjectAnimator` and `ValueAnimator` types. Let's take a look at the following steps:

1. Here is an example of one resource, `card_flip_left_in.xml`, saved in the `animator` resource folder:

```
<?xml version="1.0" encoding="utf-8"?>
<set
xmlns:android="http://schemas.android.com/apk/res/android"
>
  <objectAnimator
    android:valueFrom="1.0"
    android:valueTo="0.0"
    android:propertyName="alpha"
    android:duration="0"/>
  <objectAnimator
    android:valueFrom="-180"
    android:valueTo="0"
    android:propertyName="rotationY"
    android:interpolator=
    "@android:anim/accelerate_decelerate_interpolator"
    android:duration="@integer/card_flip_time_full"/>
  <objectAnimator
    android:valueFrom="0.0"
    android:valueTo="1.0"
    android:propertyName="alpha"
```

```
        android:startOffset="@integer/card_flip_time_half"
        android:duration="1" />
    </set>
```

2. To add custom animations on Android versions 3.0 and above, we use these animators:

```
FragmentManager
  .BeginTransaction()
  .SetCustomAnimations(
    Resource.Animator.card_flip_right_in,
    Resource.Animator.card_flip_right_out,
    Resource.Animator.card_flip_left_out,
    Resource.Animator.card_flip_left_in)
  .Replace(Resource.Id.fragmentContainer, content)
  .AddToBackStack(null)
  .Commit();
```

How it works...

Setting animations between fragment navigations just requires that we invoke a single method, with values of the various animation resources.

The simplest way to add an animation is to use one of the predefined transitions. These simple animations are specified using the `SetTransition()` method and passing a value from the `FragmentTransaction` type. The available animations are: `TransitFragmentOpen`, `TransitFragmentClose`, and `TransitFragmentFade`. The first two are usually used by the Android system; however, the last one can also be used by our app.

A more flexible means for specifying an animation is to use the `SetCustomAnimations()` method. This method takes four parameters, `push enter`, `push exit`, `pop enter`, and `pop exit`. Depending on the target Android version, we will either specify `Animation` resources (Android versions below 3.0) or `Animator` resources (Android version 3.0 and above). The first two animations apply to the transitions taking place when a new transaction is being placed on the stack, and the last two are for when the transaction is popped off the stack.

A view animation, which is available from the versions of Android below 3.0, can perform a series of simple transformations (position, size, rotation, and transparency) on the contents of a `View` object. These animation resources are placed in the `anim` folder, and each resource can contain combinations of the various transformations.

Property animators, introduced in Android version 3.0, provide a framework that allows us to animate any object's properties over time, even if that object is not a view. These animation resources are placed in the `animator` resource folder and are not available for the older Android versions.

The view animation system is relatively limited in that it only provides the ability to animate `View` objects and only a few aspects of them. The view animation system also only modifies where the view was drawn and not the actual view.

See also

▸ *Animating view and object properties*

▸ *Animating views on the UI*

Animating view and object properties

The property animation system provides a way for us to animate properties of any object, such as its position or opacity. It is also able to animate properties of custom types.

How to do it...

The `ValueAnimator` type lets us animate values of some type for the duration of an animation by specifying set values to animate through. Let's take a look at the following steps:

1. We obtain a `ValueAnimator` type by calling one of its factory methods, such as `OfInt`, `OfFloat`, or `OfObject`. The instance is then used to tween a value from one value to another:

    ```
    ValueAnimator animator = ValueAnimator.OfInt(1, 1000);
    animator.SetDuration(5000);
    animator.SetInterpolator(new BounceInterpolator());
    animator.Start();
    ```

2. We can also use the `ObjectAnimator` property to tween a property value from one value to another, in this case the `Alpha` property:

    ```
    ObjectAnimator animator = ObjectAnimator.OfFloat(
       myButton, "alpha", 1.0f, 0.0f, 1.0f);
    animator.SetDuration(5000);
    animator.SetInterpolator(new BounceInterpolator());
    animator.Start();
    ```

3. If we want to create a custom object to animate, we have to add the `[Export]` attributes and inherit from `Java.Lang.Object`:

    ```
    public class MyType : Java.Lang.Object {
      int myValue;
      public int MyValue {
    ```

```
      [Export("getMyValue")]
      get {
        return myValue;
      }
      [Export("setMyValue")]
      set {
        myValue = value;
      }
    }
  }
}
```

4. To animate custom properties, we use the camel case name of the property:

```
ObjectAnimator animator = ObjectAnimator.OfInt(
  myObject, "myValue", 0, 100);
```

We can extend the value animator with a custom type converter so that we can tween types that are unknown to Android. Let's take a look at the following steps:

1. We implement the `ITypeEvaluator` interface, which has a single `Evaluate()` method:

```
public class StringEvaluator :
  Java.Lang.Object, ITypeEvaluator {
    public Java.Lang.Object Evaluate(
      float fraction,
      Java.Lang.Object startValue,
      Java.Lang.Object endValue) {
        int level = (int)(fraction * 10);
        return string.Format ("Level {0}", level);
      }
  }
```

2. And then we pass an instance of the type converter to the `ValueAnimator` instance:

```
ValueAnimator animator = ValueAnimator.OfObject(
  new StringEvaluator(), 1, 1000);
animator.SetDuration(5000);
animator.SetInterpolator(new LinearInterpolator());
animator.Start();
```

There is also the ability to create animation sequences in XML and use those instead of creating it in code. Let's take a look at the following steps:

1. The animator resource XML is stored in the `values` resource folder:

    ```xml
    <?xml version="1.0" encoding="UTF-8"?>
    <set
    xmlns:android="http://schemas.android.com/apk/res/android"
      android:ordering="sequentially">
      <objectAnimator
        android:propertyName="alpha"
        android:duration="2500"
        android:valueTo="0.0" />
      <objectAnimator
        android:propertyName="alpha"
        android:duration="2500"
        android:valueTo="1.0" />
    </set>
    ```

2. Like views and menus, we inflate the animator by its resource ID:

    ```
    Animator animator = AnimatorInflater.LoadAnimator(
      this, Resource.Animator.property);
    animator.SetTarget(myButton);
    animator.Start();
    ```

There are several events that we can subscribe to in order to be notified about important events during the animation. Let's take a look at the following steps:

1. Some events are general, such as start and stop:

    ```
    animator.AnimationStart += delegate {
    };
    animator.AnimationEnd += delegate {
    };
    ```

2. And there is the event that fires for every frame for the `ValueAnimator` type:

    ```
    valueAnimator.Update += (sender, e) => {
      Java.Lang.Object value = e.Animation.AnimatedValue;
      float fraction = e.Animation.AnimatedFraction;
    };
    ```

How it works...

The property animation system is a robust framework that allows us to animate almost anything. We can define an animation to change any object property over time, regardless of whether it draws to the screen or not. A property animation changes a property's value over a specified length of time.

The `ValueAnimator` class lets us animate values of some type for the duration of an animation by specifying set values to animate through. We obtain a `ValueAnimator` class by calling one of its factory methods, such as `OfInt`, `OfFloat`, or `OfObject`.

`ObjectAnimator` is a subclass of the `ValueAnimator` class, with the ability to animate a named property of a target object. In order for an object to be animated, the object must inherit from the `Java.Lang.Object` type.

This object must have `getter()` and `setter()` functions in the underlying Java. This is usually not a problem for Android objects as they will have these methods. For our new C# objects, we have to make sure that we tell the runtime what methods to generate. We can create a property and annotate `getter` and `setter` with the `[Export]` attribute, passing the name that it should generate in the Java.

`TypeEvaluator` is an object with a single method, `Evaluate()`, that allows us to return an appropriate value based on the current point of the animation. This method receives a `fraction` parameter, which is the current, interpolated fraction from the interpolator. This fraction is then used to calculate the actual value of the animation from the start and end values.

Animations have various events that we can subscribe to, such as the general animation lifecycle events, and the actual frame update events. The general events, such as `AnimationStart`, `AnimationEnd`, and `AnimationRepeat`, can be used to perform actions when the state of the animation changes. The `Update` event is very powerful and is used especially by the `ValueAnimator` class as it fires each time there is a change in the animation frame. We can use this event to obtain the current animation position.

The property animation system also lets us declare property animations with XML instead of doing it programmatically. By defining our animations in XML, we can easily reuse our animations in multiple activities and more easily edit the animation sequence.

There's more...

Just like with type evaluators, we can also create custom interpolators. We do this by implementing `IInterpolator` and the `GetInterpolation()` method. As this is an object that will be passed to the Java API. It also needs to inherit from `Java.Lang.Object`.

See also

 ▸ *Animating fragment navigation*

 ▸ *Animating views on the UI*

Animating views on the UI

View Animation is the older system and can only be used with views. It is relatively easy to set up and offers enough capabilities to meet many application's needs.

How to do it...

We can add basic animations to simple view operations, such as hide and show. Let's take a look at the following step:

1. This is done by adding the `animateLayoutChanges` attribute to the XML layout:

```
<LinearLayout
xmlns:android="http://schemas.android.com/apk/res/android"
  android:orientation="vertical"
  android:layout_width="match_parent"
  android:layout_height="match_parent"
  android:animateLayoutChanges="true">
</LinearLayout>
```

We can also create animations for views by using XML, which can then be used to animate views. Let's take a look at the following steps:

1. This is similar to creating animators, but it works on all versions of Android and resides in the `anim` resource folder:

```
<?xml version="1.0" encoding="utf-8"?>
<set xmlns:android=
"http://schemas.android.com/apk/res/android"
android:interpolator=
"@android:anim/accelerate_decelerate_interpolator">
  <scale
    android:fromXScale="1.0"
    android:toXScale="0.0"
    android:fromYScale="1.0"
    android:toYScale="0.0"
    android:pivotX="50%"
    android:pivotY="50%"
    android:duration="500"
    android:fillBefore="false"/>
  <rotate
```

```
            android:fromDegrees="0"
            android:toDegrees="-45"
            android:toYScale="0.0"
            android:pivotX="50%"
            android:pivotY="50%"
            android:duration="500"/>
    </set>
```

2. To use this animation, we just have to inflate it and start it:

```
Animation animation = AnimationUtils.LoadAnimation(
    this, Resource.Animation.hyperspace);
hyperButton.StartAnimation(animation);
animation.AnimationEnd += delegate {
    hyperButton.Visibility = ViewStates.Gone;
};
```

Animations can be created using code or resource files, but another way is to make use of the fluent API:

▶ To use the fluent API for animations on newer versions of Android, we can just invoke the `Animate()` method:

```
apiButton.Animate()
    .ScaleX(0.0f)
    .ScaleY(0.0f)
    .SetDuration(500)
    .Rotation(-45f)
    .SetInterpolator(new DecelerateInterpolator());
```

▶ As the `Animate()` method is only available to the later versions, we can make use of the support library to prevent the app from crashing on older devices. Instead, we use the `ViewCompat` type and invoke the static `Animate()` method:

```
ViewCompat.Animate(apiButton)
    .ScaleX(0.0f)
    .SetDuration(500)
    .Rotation(-45f);
```

How it works...

A layout animation is an animation that the system runs automatically each time there is a layout configuration change. This easily sets the `animateLayoutChanges` attribute in the XML layout. This will animate various layout changes, such as adding or removing views.

For more advanced view animations, such as changing position, size, rotation, or transparency, an animation sequence can be defined in a resource file. These files are placed in the `anim` resource folder. Using animation resource files makes it easier to read and maintain.

The same animations that are performed using the resources can be performed using the fluent API. The method chaining is started by calling the `Animate()` method on a view. We can then start chaining transformations as well as duration and interpolators. This API is only available on versions of Android above 3.1.

 View animations are not applied to the view; the appearance changes, but not any other properties or behaviors.

When using the fluent API to apply animations, we need to make sure that we use the `ViewCompat` type on Android versions prior to 3.1. When running on older Android versions, no animation will occur, but the app will be prevented from crashing.

It is important to apply the changes of view animations after the animation has completed. Animations are not applied after an animation occurs, and although the view appears to be removed or in a new position, the actual view is still in its original position. This view, although not visible, can still be interacted with and will respond to events as if it were never animated.

There's more...

As an alternative to the `StartAnimation()` method, we can define a starting time for the animation with the `Animation.SetStartTime()` method and then assign the animation to the view with the `View.Animation` property.

Adding a navigation drawer with fragments

The navigation drawer is a panel that transitions in from the left edge of the screen and displays the app's main navigation options.

How to do it...

We can add a navigation drawer to our app by setting the `DrawerLayout` type as the root layout container, with the contents of the drawer and the main content as subviews:

1. The `DrawerLayout` type should be the root of our layout file, with two subviews: the first is the main content and the second is the drawer. Let's take a look at the following code snippet:

```xml
<?xml version="1.0" encoding="utf-8"?>
<android.support.v4.widget.DrawerLayout
xmlns:android="http://schemas.android.com/apk/res/android"
```

```
android:id="@+id/drawerLayout"
android:layout_width="match_parent"
android:layout_height="match_parent">
<FrameLayout
  android:id="@+id/drawerContent"
  android:layout_width="match_parent"
  android:layout_height="match_parent" />
<ListView
  android:id="@+id/drawerList"
  android:layout_width="240dp"
  android:layout_height="match_parent"
  android:layout_gravity="start"
  android:choiceMode="singleChoice"
  android:divider="@android:color/transparent"
  android:dividerHeight="0dp"
  android:background="#111" />
</android.support.v4.widget.DrawerLayout>
```

2. Now we add an adapter to the list view that we are using and the event to handle item clicks:

```
protected override void OnCreate(Bundle bundle) {
  base.OnCreate(bundle);
  SetContentView(Resource.Layout.Main);

  DrawerLayout drawerLayout =
    FindViewById<DrawerLayout>(Resource.Id.drawerLayout);
  FrameLayout drawerContent =
    FindViewById<FrameLayout>(Resource.Id.drawerContent);
  ListView drawerList =
    FindViewById<ListView>(Resource.Id.drawerList);

  drawerList.Adapter = new ArrayAdapter(
    this,
    Android.Resource.Layout.SimpleListItem1,
    new []{"First", "Second", "Third", "Fourth"});

  drawerList.ItemClick += (sender, e) => {
    ContentFragment content = new ContentFragment();
    Bundle args = new Bundle();
    args.PutInt(ContentFragment.ArgumentsKey, e.Position);
    content.Arguments = args;

    SupportFragmentManager
```

```
        .BeginTransaction()
        .Replace(Resource.Id.drawerContent, content)
        .Commit();

    drawerList.SetItemChecked(e.Position, true);
  };
}
```

3. In order to know when the user opens or closes the drawer, we need a drawer toggle:

```
private class DrawerToggle : ActionBarDrawerToggle {
  public DrawerToggle(
    Activity activity, DrawerLayout drawerLayout)
  : base(
    activity, drawerLayout,
    Resource.String.drawer_open,
    Resource.String.drawer_close) {
    }

  public override void OnDrawerClosed(View drawerView) {
    base.OnDrawerClosed(drawerView);
    var handler = DrawerClosed;
    if (handler != null) {
      handler(this, EventArgs.Empty);
    }
  }

  public override void OnDrawerOpened(View drawerView) {
    base.OnDrawerOpened(drawerView);
    var handler = DrawerOpened;
    if (handler != null) {
      handler(this, EventArgs.Empty);
    }
  }

  public event EventHandler DrawerClosed;
  public event EventHandler DrawerOpened;
}
```

4. We then attach the drawer toggle to the drawer. When the drawer opens, we change the title of the screen to be the app title, and when it closes, we set the title to be the current page title:

```
private DrawerToggle drawerToggle;

protected override void OnCreate(Bundle bundle) {
   ...
   drawerList.ItemClick += (sender, e) => {
      ...
      drawerLayout.CloseDrawer(drawerList);
   };

   drawerToggle = new DrawerToggle(this, drawerLayout);
   drawerToggle.DrawerClosed += delegate {
      SupportActionBar.Title = "Xamarin Cookbook Item";
   };
   drawerToggle.DrawerOpened += delegate {
      SupportActionBar.Title = "Xamarin Cookbook";
   };
   drawerLayout.SetDrawerListener(drawerToggle);

   SupportActionBar.SetDisplayHomeAsUpEnabled(true);
   SupportActionBar.SetHomeButtonEnabled(true);
}
```

5. If we want to display the hamburger icon as the home button, we have to connect the activity event methods to the drawer toggle:

```
protected override void OnPostCreate(
   Bundle savedInstanceState) {
      base.OnPostCreate(savedInstanceState);
      drawerToggle.SyncState();
}

public override void OnConfigurationChanged(
   Configuration newConfig) {
      base.OnConfigurationChanged(newConfig);
      drawerToggle.OnConfigurationChanged(newConfig);
}
```

6. And if we want the drawer to open when the user taps the home button, we have to connect the home button to the drawer toggle:

```
public override bool OnOptionsItemSelected(IMenuItem item)
{
    if (drawerToggle.OnOptionsItemSelected(item)) {
        return true;
    }
    return base.OnOptionsItemSelected(item);
}
```

7. Finally, we should hide the options menu items when the drawer is open. To do this, we can invalidate the options menu when the drawer is opened or closed:

```
SupportInvalidateOptionsMenu();
```

8. To check if the drawer is open, we can use the `IsDrawerOpen()` method:

```
bool isOpen = drawerLayout.IsDrawerOpen(drawerList);
```

How it works...

The navigation drawer is a panel that displays the app's main navigation options on the left edge of the screen. It is hidden most of the time but is revealed when the user swipes a finger from the left edge of the screen or (while at the top level of the app) touches the app icon in the action bar.

The drawer layout subviews can be of any type; however, there is usually some container for the fragments and a list of options in the drawer. The order in which the views are added in is important. To keep the drawer above the main content, it must be added after the main content. It is also important for us to keep the drawer width a bit narrower than the screen to ensure that there is always a bit of main content for the user to see.

 In order to support RTL languages, the drawer's horizontal gravity should be set to `start` instead of `left`.

Users can open and close the navigation drawer with a swipe gesture from or towards the left edge of the screen, but if we're using the action bar, we should also allow users to open and close it by touching the app icon. The app icon should also indicate the presence of the navigation drawer with a special icon. We can implement all this by using the `ActionBarDrawerToggle`.

We have to link the drawer toggle to the activity events in order for the drawer to respond to various events. We let the action bar know that we want to show an icon in the home button by enabling the home button and overriding the `OnPostCreate()` and `OnConfigurationChanged()` methods.

By overriding the `OnOptionsItemSelected()` method, we can intercept taps to the home button and pass it on to the drawer toggle, which will then show or hide the drawer.

 The action bar should display the app title when the drawer opens and a title for the current context when it closes.

In order to remove conflicting information from the screen, we should remove the action bar items that do not apply to the drawer and any contextual action bar items when the drawer is opened. The following image is the Android navigation drawer:

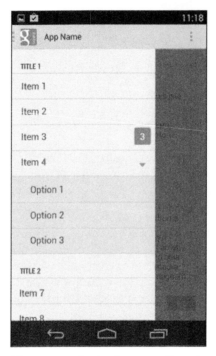

An app with an open navigation drawer over the main content.

See also

▶ *Creating and using fragments*

Applying local styles and global themes

Themes are Android's mechanism for applying a consistent style to an app or activity. A style specifies the visual properties of the elements that make up your user interface, such as color, height, padding, and font size.

How to do it...

1. We can create styles for views using the various attributes:

```
<TextView
    style="@android:style/TextAppearance.Medium"
    android:layout_width="match_parent"
    android:layout_height="wrap_content"
    android:textColor="#7F3300"
    android:typeface="monospace"
    android:gravity="center"
    android:text="Inline Styles" />
```

2. These styles can be extracted into a separate file so that they can be reused across views, as with string resources. In this case, we inherit from the Android style `TextAppearance.Medium`, but this is not always necessary. Let's take a look at the following code snippet:

```
<?xml version="1.0" encoding="UTF-8"?>
<resources>
    <style name="MyStyle"
        parent="@android:style/TextAppearance.Medium">
        <item name="android:layout_width">match_parent</item>
        <item name="android:layout_height">wrap_content</item>
        <item name="android:textColor">#7F3300</item>
        <item name="android:typeface">monospace</item>
        <item name="android:gravity">center</item>
    </style>
</resources>
```

3. Using styles in a layout resource is done by using the `style` attribute:

```
<TextView style="@style/MyStyle" android:text="Styled" />
```

4. This can also be done for the actual activities, but in this case, we inherit from an activity style, `Theme.Light`:

```
<?xml version="1.0" encoding="UTF-8"?>
<resources>
    <color name="mycolor">#007F0E</color>
    <style name="MyTheme" parent="android:Theme.Light">
        <item name="android:windowBackground">
            @color/mycolor </item>
        <item name="android:colorBackground">
            @color/mycolor</item>
    </style>
</resources>
```

How it works...

A style is a collection of properties that specify the look and format for a view or window. A theme is a style applied to an entire activity or application, rather than an individual view.

 Styles and themes are saved in the `values` resource folder with the `.xml` extension.

Styles can be inherited and extended, meaning we can take an existing style and add a few additional attributes and customizations. Inheritance is achieved by using the `parent` XML attribute on the `<style>` element.

There is also a shortcut for inheriting our own styles by using a special naming system. If we were to create a style named `MyStyle.Bigger`, this new style would inherit all the attributes from the `MyStyle` style. This only applies to local styles and not Android styles.

Due to inheritance and the ability to have same-name resources in different folders, we can create advanced styling that is based on various device configuration options, such as orientation, screen size, or Android version. For example, we could have a larger padding for larger screens and use new features on newer devices.

3
Managing App Data

In this chapter, we will cover the following recipes:

- ▶ Storing data with SharedPreferences
- ▶ Using files and the filesystem
- ▶ Reading bundled assets and resources
- ▶ Parsing, processing, and generating XML
- ▶ Accessing data with ADO.NET
- ▶ Accessing data with SQLite.NET
- ▶ Encrypting databases with SQLCipher
- ▶ Consuming content providers
- ▶ Creating content providers
- ▶ Backing up preferences and files to the cloud
- ▶ Backing up data to the cloud

Introduction

Data is possibly the single most valuable entity in the world, whether it is personal data about a user or person, or it is general data about the world. Companies spend billions collecting this data, and it is sought after by other companies.

What makes data so valuable? Data is correct and accurate, and it can be used to make decisions, which are both helpful as well as potentially lucrative. Data is valuable because of what can be done with it.

Companies spend billions collecting data and then spend billions more protecting it. Data can lose some of its value when it becomes public knowledge; not that the data becomes less valuable but rather the value from the decisions made. If the data becomes public, then other companies can use it to get a competitive advantage.

In addition to losing competitive advantage, personal data can be used to compromise personal security and privacy. The data can be used to impersonate a user, and possibly, do harm.

Regardless of where the data came from or what it is used for, data needs to be stored and processed. Data only attains its true value if it can be queried and then processed into information.

Data can be stored in key-value pairs, structured files, and relational databases. There are many other ways to store data, but the storage mechanism is chosen to best suit the querying or processing requirements.

Mobile apps are no different; over time, they can collect data about users and their preferences. This data is then stored locally or on the cloud. This data is backed up and encrypted for security purposes.

Storing data with SharedPreferences

Sometimes, an app needs to store data after it closes so that it can be retrieved later. This data is often very simple, so a database may be unnecessary.

How to do it...

There are two parts to using the `ISharedPreferences` instance: read and write. Both are similar but write has a few extra steps. Let's take a look at the following extra steps included:

1. In order to either read from or write to the preferences, we have to first obtain the preferences by name:

   ```
   ISharedPreferences prefs = GetSharedPreferences(
       "MyPreferences", FileCreationMode.Private);
   ```

2. Once we have the preferences, we can simply query a value using a key along with a default value:

   ```
   if (prefs.Contains("MyKey")) {
      int myIntValue = prefs.GetInt("MyKey", 0);
   }
   ```

3. To write values to the preferences, we request the ability to edit it using the `Edit()` method of the instance:

```
ISharedPreferences prefs = GetSharedPreferences(
    PreferencesName, FileCreationMode.Private);
ISharedPreferencesEditor editor = prefs.Edit();
```

4. Once we have the editor, we can write or update the values in the preferences instance using one of the various `"put"` methods:

```
editor.PutInt("MyKey", myIntValue);
```

5. The last thing there is to do is to save the changes made with the editor:

```
editor.Commit();
```

How it works...

The `ISharedPreferences` type provides a general framework that allows us to save and retrieve persistent key-value pairs of primitive data types. We can save any primitive data types, such as `bool`, `float`, `int`, `long`, and `string`. This data will persist across user sessions, even if our app is killed.

There are two basic ways to obtain an `ISharedPreferences` instance:

- Using the `GetSharedPreferences()` method on a `Context`, which provides a named preferences
- Using the `GetPreferences()` method on an `Activity`, which provides an activity-based preferences

When obtaining a preferences instance, there is an additional argument passed, `FileCreationMode`. This argument determines where the preferences can be accessed from. Usually only `FileCreationMode.Private` is needed.

When we want to write values to the preferences, all we have to do is obtain an `ISharedPreferencesEditor` instance. We then use that editor to put our values, by key, into the preferences, ensuring that we commit our changes.

We don't always have to write our changes every time something needs to be updated. We can improve performance if we read out the values when the activity is created and only write them back when the activity is stopped.

 Performance can be improved by saving and retrieving values from the preferences only when necessary.

There's more...

Shared preferences are not strictly used for saving "user preferences," such as what ringtone a user has chosen. If we need to include user preferences for our app, we can make use of the `PreferenceFragment` or `PreferenceFragmentCompat` instances. This provides a framework through which we can create user preferences, which will be automatically persisted (using shared preferences).

When creating a preference activity, we first create the XML representation of the screen hierarchy. In this case, it is just a single screen with a single preference, `preferences.xml`, saved in the XML resource folder:

```
<PreferenceScreen xmlns:android=
"http://schemas.android.com/apk/res/android">
  <EditTextPreference
    android:defaultValue="anonymous"
    android:dialogTitle="User Name"
    android:key="UsernameKey"
    android:summary="Your user name."
    android:title="User Name"/>
</PreferenceScreen>
```

To support the older version of Android, we can use the **Xamarin Support Library Preference v7** Component or NuGet. We then create a fragment, which inherits from the `PreferenceFragmentCompat` type, which will inflate the XML into a UI layout:

```
class SettingsFragment : PreferenceFragmentCompat {
  public override void OnCreatePreferences(Bundle b, string root)
  {
    AddPreferencesFromResource(Resource.Xml.preferences);
  }
}
```

We can now display that fragment in any activity, but typically we would create a settings activity. One thing that we do need to do when using the support libraries is to ensure that we specify the `preferenceTheme` value for the activity theme:

```
<resources>
  <style name="PrefsTheme" parent="@style/Theme.AppCompat">
    <item name="preferenceTheme">
    @style/PreferenceThemeOverlay</item>
  </style>
</resources>
```

To make use of the preferences, we use the `PreferenceManager` type. This is similar to getting an activity's shared preferences:

```
var prefs = PreferenceManager.GetDefaultSharedPreferences(this);
var username = prefs.GetString("UsernameKey", "anonymous");
```

A preference fragment is just an extension of the base `Fragment` type and can be used like any other fragment. No UI is specified as the UI is created from the preference XML resource. The activity that holds the fragment can be displayed as any other activity.

Using files and the filesystem

Many apps require access to the filesystem for accessing databases, reading content, and many other reasons.

How to do it...

There are two main areas for storing files: internal storage and external storage. Making use of the internal storage or app sandbox is very easy:

1. Writing files to the filesystem is very simple, and all that is required is the path to the sandbox for our app:

   ```
   string sandbox = FilesDir.AbsolutePath;
   ```

2. Once we have this path, we can use the types from the .NET BCL to manipulate the files:

   ```
   string file = Path.Combine(sandbox, "myFile.txt");
   bool exists = File.Exists(file);
   File.WriteAllText(file, "this is my value");
   string value = File.ReadAllText(file);
   ```

3. Sometimes, we only need to store files temporarily. In such cases, we can make use of the cache location:

   ```
   string cache = CacheDir.AbsolutePath;
   ```

Using the external storage only has a few extra requirements. Typically, the way external storage is used is the same as the way internal storage is used, except that we have a different root folder:

1. If we wish to write to the external storage, we need to ask for permission to do so:

   ```
   [assembly: UsesPermission(
     Manifest.Permission.WriteExternalStorage)]
   [assembly: UsesPermission(
     Manifest.Permission.ReadExternalStorage)]
   ```

2. Once we have the permission to access the filesystem, we will verify that the external media is attached and writeable:

```
bool writeable =
    Android.OS.Environment.ExternalStorageState ==
    Android.OS.Environment.MediaMounted;

bool readable = writeable ||
    Android.OS.Environment.ExternalStorageState ==
    Android.OS.Environment.MediaMountedReadOnly;
```

3. We can obtain the path to the external location and then work as we would with the internal storage filesystem:

```
string external = GetExternalFilesDir(null).AbsolutePath;
string externalCache = ExternalCacheDir.AbsolutePath;
```

4. There are also a few extra external locations, such as the public directories. This is where Android places and reads files from things such as music, movies, and downloads:

```
string downloadsDir =
    Android.OS.Environment.GetExternalStoragePublicDirectory(
        Android.OS.Environment.DirectoryDownloads)
    .AbsolutePath;
```

5. We can also see how much space or free space is available by querying the file location:

```
long freeSpace = FilesDir.FreeSpace;
long totalSpace = GetExternalFilesDir(null).TotalSpace;
```

How it works...

Working with the Android filesystem is similar to using the file systems on any .NET-supported platform. We can make use of all the features in .NET, as well as many of the Java features. However, Android does not allow access to all file locations on the device, especially the system locations or other app sandboxes.

Usually an app will access its own internal sandbox location obtained from `FilesDir` and possibly the app cache location obtained from `CacheDir`. Files saved to the internal storage are private to our app and neither other apps nor the user can access them.

When the user uninstalls our app, the internal files are removed automatically. In addition, the user may remove them through the device settings screens. As a result, we must first check whether a file exists before trying to read it.

 Files saved to the files and cache directories are deleted, and not preserved in any way, when the app is uninstalled.

Access to the external storage is no different but requires app permissions. Starting from Android 4.4, these permissions are not required if the only external access is through the `GetExternalFilesDir()` method and the `ExternalCacheDir` property. External files are visible to the user, especially if the files connect it to a computer as a USB mass storage device.

Files saved to the cache, whether internal via `CacheDir` or external via `ExternalCacheDir`, are meant to be temporary. Android may delete these files when the device starts to run out of free space or if the app is uninstalled. However, we should not rely on the system to clean up these files and maintain the cache ourselves.

It is very important to remember that external storage may become unavailable if the user mounts the external storage on a computer or removes the media. As a result, it is essential to check the availability of the external storage before use. In the `Android.OS` namespace, the `Environment` type contains the properties, methods, and other types used to determine the state of the external storage. The `ExternalStorageState` property may be `MediaMounted`, which is writeable, or `MediaMountedReadOnly`, which is read only.

 External storage mediums are not always available and access should be verified before being used.

There are special public locations that are used by Android to hold the user's downloads—photos, music, and other files. These locations are obtained by passing the desired directory constant to the `GetExternalStoragePublicDirectory()` method on `Environment`.

We can see how much free space is available by using the `FreeSpace` or `TotalSpace` properties on the Java `File` objects, such as the result from the `FilesDir` property. The values returned aren't the exact space available, but a representation of how much free space can be available. If there is a few extra MB over the size to be saved, then it is probably OK to continue.

There's more...

The external storage may not actually be the SD card but rather a section of the device's internal memory marked as external.

The actual SD card can be accessed using the result of `GetExternalFilesDirs()` or `ContextCompat.GetExternalFilesDir()`, which is an array of the external storage mediums available, one of which will be the actual SD card. Similarly for the cache, the locations are found in the result of `GetExternalCacheDir()` or `ContextCompat.GetExternalCacheDir()`.

Reading bundled assets and resources

Almost all apps include some sort of content with the app package; it can be a database, image, or just plain text.

How to do it...

We can only get read-only access to bundled assets and resources but that is often all that is needed, as most app data comes from other sources such as the Internet or device sensors. We will create and add three basic types or resources by performing the following steps:

1. Starting with assets, create a folder named `Assets` at the root of the project.

2. Create a new file in the new `Assets` folder and save some text into that file, for example, a file named `MyAsset.txt` with the following contents:

   ```
   Hello Asset World!
   ```

3. Now, mark the file as an asset by selecting the file. In the **Properties** pane, select **AndroidAsset** from the **Build action** dropdown.

4. Next, for raw resources, create a folder named `raw` in the `Resources` folder.

5. In the new `raw` folder, again create and save any text file, for example, a file named `MyRaw.txt` with the following contents:

   ```
   Hello Raw World!
   ```

6. Similar to marking a file as an asset, we select **AndroidResource** from the **Build action** dropdown in the **Properties** pane.

7. Finally, for special resources, ensure that there is a folder named `values` under the `Resources` folder.

8. In the `values` folder, create a new XML file with the Android-style resources, for example, a file named `MyResources.xml` with the following content:

   ```xml
   <?xml version="1.0" encoding="UTF-8" ?>
   <resources>
     <string name="myString">Hello Resource World!</string>
   </resources>
   ```

9. Again, we mark this file as **AndroidResource** in the **Properties** pane.

Once we have the resources created, we can now start writing code to access them:

1. Starting with resources, we can access string resources using the `Resources` property:

```
string stringValue =
    Resources.GetString(Resource.String.myString);
```

2. Accessing raw files is a little more complicated as we use the `Stream` element:

```
using (Stream raw =
    Resources.OpenRawResource(Resource.Raw.MyRaw))
using (StreamReader reader = new StreamReader(raw)) {
    string rawValue = reader.ReadToEnd();
}
```

3. And the same with assets, we use a `Stream` instance:

```
using (Stream asset = Resources.Assets.Open("MyAsset.txt"))
using (StreamReader reader = new StreamReader(asset)) {
    string assetValue = reader.ReadToEnd();
}
```

How it works...

There are three main types of app content: assets, raw resources, and special resources.

Special resources, or resources, are the most common and easiest to use. These resources can be accessed in layout files and in code. There are two main groups of special resources; there are Android-specific resources, such as animations, layouts, and menus, and there are value resources, such as strings, Booleans, and integers.

These value resources are accessed via various getter methods on the `Resources` property, and they return the value of the resource directly. They are stored in the `values` resource folder and are structured as basic XML elements with a name attribute.

Each resource folder can have a suffix that is used to determine the resource file that is to be loaded. There are many different suffixes that can be used, and a full list can be found on the Android developer website at `http://developer.android.com/guide/topics/resources/providing-resources.html`.

If there are two folders with the same name and different suffixes, such as `values` and `values-land`, Android will correctly select the appropriate file when the `Resources` property is used. This feature is especially useful for creating alternative resources, such as layouts, menus, and values based on the device characteristics, such as orientation and screen size, as well as device settings, such as language or culture.

Android resources can be used to provide alternative resources based on both device configurations and user configurations, and they do not require any special or additional logic in the code.

Another benefit of using resources is the fact that the compiler generates a type that contains all the various resources. For example, if we create a string resource with the name `myString`, the compiler will generate a field named `myString` in the `String` type nested inside the `Resource` type. This provides compile time checking and resource validation allowing us to write `Resource.String.myString` when accessing the string resource, instead of having to use string keys.

All resource types, from animations to values, have the benefit of allowing the Android runtime to select a variation of a resource, making resources very useful. The same is true for raw resources, which are just a type of resource. One main difference is that raw resources allow us to specify any resource type as a resource, such as the database files, binary data files, and ZIP files. Although these types aren't used by Android, we can use them in our code.

We access raw resource files through the `OpenRawResource()` method on the `Resources` property, passing in the ID of the raw resource. This method returns a stream with which we can work as we would work on any other stream.

Assets, on the other hand, are quite different. They are simply are files that bundled in the app package and stored in the `Assets` folder. Using assets allows us to dynamically load and list the files at runtime, but we have to do the work ourselves. Assets can also be organized into a folder hierarchy, which is not supported by resources.

 Android assets can be used to hold any file type in a hierarchical structure and can be accessed dynamically.

Also, some features are only available to assets; these features include using a custom typeface or loading cascading style sheets. The reason for this is that assets actually have a URI for accessing any particular file: `file:///android_asset/<some-file-name>` (note the three slashes). We can load pages into the web browser component using this URI, and the browser can resolve the resource paths automatically.

 The `assets` folder hierarchy can be multiple levels deep, something that cannot be done when using Android resources.

Accessing assets is done through the `AssetManager` instance, accessed either through the `Assets` property or the `Resources.Assets` property. We use the `Open()` method and pass in a path relative to the `assets` folder. Just as we did with raw resources, we obtain a stream that we use to read the contents of a particular asset.

See also

> ▸ The *Using files and the filesystem* recipe

Parsing, processing, and generating XML

Some apps, especially apps used with existing systems, need to be able to parse and generate XML.

Getting ready

For this recipe, we need to have an existing XML file stored in the `Assets` folder. The structure of the XML file that we will use in this recipe is as follows:

```xml
<?xml version="1.0" encoding="UTF-8"?>
<bookshelf>
  <book title="book title">
    <authors>
      <author firstname="name" lastname="surname"/>
      <author ... />
    </authors>
  </book>
  <book>...</book>
</bookshelf>
```

How to do it...

There are many ways to handle XML, but in this recipe, we will use **Language-Integrated Query** (**LINQ**) to XML. One of the most common things to do with XML is to read it, usually from a remote source. Let's take a look at the following steps:

1. Ensure that the project includes the `System.Xml.Linq.dll` reference.

2. In this instance, we will just read an asset and load it into an `XDocument` instance, keeping a reference to the root `XElement`:

```csharp
XElement root;
using (var asset = Resources.Assets.Open("bookshelf.xml"))
{
  XDocument doc = XDocument.Load(asset);
  root = doc.Root;
}
```

3. If we wish to access the child elements with the name `book`, all we have to do is execute the following code:

```
var books = root.Elements("book");
```

4. If we wish to select all the authors in all books (in this case, the elements three levels deep), we chain the `Elements()` methods:

```
var authors = root
  .Elements("book")
  .Elements("authors")
  .Elements("author");
```

5. We can also do SQL-like queries, for example, list all the values from the title attributes from all the books:

```
var titles = from book in root.Elements("book")
                from title in book.Attributes("title")
                select title.Value;
```

6. Even more advanced queries can be created using filtering, ordering, and even grouping:

```
var longTitles =
   from title in root.Elements("book").Attributes("title")
   where title.Value.Length > 10
   orderby title.Value
   select title.Value;
```

In addition to parsing XML files, we can also easily create entire XML document structures with LINQ to XML using the `XDocument`, `XElement`, and `XAttribute` types:

1. By chaining and nesting the various constructors, we can construct an XML document:

```
var doc = new XDocument(
  new XElement("bookshelf",
    new XElement("book",
      new XAttribute("title", "C# 5.0 in a Nutshell"),
      new XElement("authors",
        new XElement("author", "Joseph Albahari"),
        new XElement("author", "Ben Albahari")))));
```

2. We can also build entire documents by chaining constructors and nesting subqueries:

```
var generatedDoc = new XDocument(
  new XElement("bookshelf",
    from book in root.Elements("book")
    select new XElement ("book",
      new XAttribute("title",
        book.Attribute("title").Value),
      from author in
```

```
          book.Elements("authors").Elements("author")
      select
        new XElement("author",
          author.Attribute("lastname").Value))));
```

How it works...

Working with XML on Android with Java is very similar to using the `XmlReader` or `XmlDocument` type in the .NET world. It is relatively complex and does not always produce neat and maintainable code. Using .NET, we can make use of LINQ and LINQ to XML. This makes working with XML much easier when compared to what is needed when developing with Java.

LINQ extends the .NET languages by adding query expressions, which are similar to SQL statements and can be used to conveniently extract and process data from almost any type of data collection.

As XML is basically a collection of elements and attributes, we can use LINQ when working with XML. LINQ to XML enables us to query and modify XML documents from within any .NET language. It provides a new way to work with XML, which is more lightweight and easier to work with than the original XML readers and DOM models.

The most important advantage of LINQ to XML is that it enables us to write SQL-like queries on the in-memory XML document. This ability allows us to retrieve collections of elements and attributes, similar to what an `XPath` would allow us to do.

 LINQ to XML allows the creation and parsing of entire XML documents in memory in an easy-to-understand manner.

When working with LINQ to XML, an `XDocument` represents the entire document along with the metadata. An `XElement` object is an element in the XML document that has a `Value` object and has a collection of `XAttribute` and child `XElement` instances. We can access these types using the corresponding methods. If we want to access the collection of child elements, we use the `Elements()` method, which returns an `IEnumerable` instance of `XElement`.

Using `IEnumerable` means that LINQ to XML can make use of deferred execution and lazy evaluation. Deferred execution means that the evaluation of an expression or chain of methods is delayed until the value is actually required, such as when iterating through the collection. Deferred execution can greatly improve performance when we have to manipulate large data collections, especially when there is a series of chained queries or manipulations.

LINQ to XML makes use of deferred loading where possible, thus improving performance on large documents and with complex queries.

Another advantage of LINQ to XML is the ability to use query results as parameters to `XElement` and `XAttribute` constructors, enabling us to construct entire document trees from queries and constructors. This approach of creating documents enables us to quickly and easily transform one XML tree structure into a totally new structure.

There's more...

If the XML document uses a default namespace, we need to ensure that all our queries include the namespace. For example, in a document without namespaces, we access elements by calling the `Elements()` method with the name of the element:

```
var elements = root.Elements("book");
```

If the document uses a namespace for those book elements, we also use a namespace:

```
XNamespace ns = "http://www.cookbook.com/samples/v1";
var elements = root.Elements(ns + "book");
```

When creating elements, we can also specify the namespace:

```
XNamespace ns = "http://www.cookbook.com/samples/v1";
var element = new XElement(ns + "book");
```

Namespaces can be used with any XML node, such as elements or attributes.

See also

▶   More information on LINQ can be found on the MSDN website:
    http://msdn.microsoft.com/en-us/library/bb397926.aspx

▶   More information on LINQ to XML can be found on the MSDN website:
    http://msdn.microsoft.com/en-us/library/bb387098.aspx

Accessing data with ADO.NET

Many apps need to use databases, irrespective of whether the app is database-centric or even just to store pieces of data in a structured form. Android provides SQLite as a database engine and .NET provides ADO.NET as an interface.

Getting ready...

This recipe demonstrates how we can make use of ADO.NET to interact with a SQLite database using SQL. It is assumed that you have some SQL knowledge to construct queries.

How to do it...

Using ADO.NET with SQLite is easy and not much different from working with any ADO.NET provider. It is fairly straightforward to create and interact with a SQLite database:

1. To start with, we need to add a reference to `System.Data` and `Mono.Data.SQLite`.

2. We can now start selecting what database file we will use. If a database file does not exist, one will be created for us. To do this, we use a connection string:

```
var databasePath =
  Path.Combine(FilesDir.AbsolutePath, "database.sqlite");
var connectionString =
  string.Format("Data Source={0}", databasePath);
```

3. We can now create the connection to the database from the connection string. When we open the connection, we initiate the process that allows us to communicate with the database:

```
using (var conn = new SqliteConnection(connectionString)) {
  conn.Open();
  // use the database here
}
```

4. Using the open connection, we can start creating the database structure. To create a simple table, we execute normal SQL commands:

```
string createTable = @"
  CREATE TABLE IF NOT EXISTS [MyTable] (
    id INTEGER PRIMARY KEY AUTOINCREMENT,
    firstName TEXT,
    lastName TEXT
  );";

using (var cmd = new SqliteCommand(createTable, conn)) {
  cmd.ExecuteNonQuery();
}
```

5. Once we have a table, we can insert values into the table by using commands and parameters:

```
string insertQuery = @"
   INSERT INTO [MyTable] (firstName, lastName)
   VALUES (@firstName, @lastName);";

using (var cmd = new SqliteCommand(insertQuery, conn)) {
  cmd.Parameters.AddWithValue("@firstname", "Bill");
  cmd.Parameters.AddWithValue("@lastName", "Gates");
  cmd.ExecuteNonQuery();
}
```

6. In order to read the data in the database, we use commands and data readers:

```
string selectQuery = "SELECT * FROM [MyTable]";

List<string> names = new List<string>();
using (var cmd = new SqliteCommand(selectQuery, conn))
using (var reader = cmd.ExecuteReader()) {
  while (reader.Read()) {
    names.Add(reader ["lastname"].ToString ());
  }
}
```

7. If we have multiple operations that we need to perform on the database, we can use transactions:

```
using (var trans = conn.BeginTransaction()) {
  // a series of operations
  trans.Commit();
}
```

How it works...

ADO.NET provides an interface for working with many different types of data sources, ranging from databases to XML files. Using a means of abstraction, ADO.NET can handle almost any type of database, from servers such as a SQL Server to embedded ones, such as SQLite.

More information about using ADO.NET can be found on the MSDN website: https://msdn.microsoft.com/en-us/library/e80y5yhx.aspx.

When accessing a database, there are a few steps which open a connection, executing commands, and iterating results with readers.

 Making use of the using statements ensures that the connection, command, or reader is correctly closed and disposed of in order to free up objects and file locks.

When connecting to a database, we need to make use of a connection. A connection contains all the information required to identify, locate, authenticate, and communicate with the database. In the case of SQLite, we make use of a SqliteConnection type, passing in a connection string that contains a path to the data source or database file.

Once we have a connection, we need to ensure that we open it. This initiates the connection and prepares the connection for communication with the actual database.

 Connections can be and should be closed as soon as they are no longer in use so that they can be returned to the connection pool, allowing ADO.NET to optimally manage and reuse the connections.

Once we have an open connection, we can start executing commands. A command, or a SqliteCommand command in the case of SQLite, contains information about a particular action that we wish to perform. The information includes a SQL query and, optionally, parameters and values, which will be substituted during the execution.

Commands have three basic types of execution: readers, scalars, and nonqueries. For example, when creating a table, no rows or values are returned, so we execute using the ExecuteNonQuery() method as this is an instruction to the database to do something. If we only expect a single value result, we can use the ExecuteScalar() method, which returns a single primitive type. Often, we will request multiple rows from the database, for which we use the ExecuteReader() method that gives us a result in the form of a data reader.

A data reader in the case of SQLite is an instance of the SqliteDataReader type. This provides a means to iterate through the rows returned and handle them as we wish. The reader has several methods that we use to access the data returned. A reader is a forward-only, read-only stream of data that allows us to access data one row at a time. We can check whether any rows are returned using the HasRows property, and we can also check the number of rows returned using the RowsAffected property. As we step through the data reader using the Read() method, we can access individual columns using the indexer or the various getter methods.

 When a command is going to be executed multiple times with different values, parameters can be used. This allows the values to be swapped without having to recreate the command, thus improving the performance.

We can use transactions to group a series of commands into a single, reversible operation. We use transactions to roll back any and all operations in a series, if any operation in that set fails. Using transactions ensures that our database remains consistent even if there is a failure in either the system or the app.

See also

▶   The *Accessing data with SQLite.NET* recipe

▶   The *Encrypting SQLite databases with SQLCipher* recipe

Accessing data with SQLite.NET

Many apps need to use databases, whether the app is database-centric or even just to store pieces of data in a structured form. A lightweight ORM can be used to make data access easier.

How to do it...

Accessing the database is very easy when using **SQLite.NET**, especially since we don't have to write a single line of SQL. Let's take a look at the following steps:

1. Before we can make use of SQLite.NET, we need to add the component. Right-click on the **Components** folder in the project and click on **Get More Components....** In the dialog that appears, we search for and add the `SQLite.NET` component.

2. Once the component is downloaded, we can start creating the C# types that will represent the tables:

    ```
    public class MyTable {
      [AutoIncrement, PrimaryKey]
      public int Id { get; set; }
      public string FirstName { get; set; }
      public string LastName { get; set; }
    }
    ```

3. Now that we have our tables, we can choose where we want the database to be created to or accessed from:

    ```
    var databasePath = Path.Combine(
      FilesDir.AbsolutePath, "database.sqlite");
    ```

4. The next thing to do is to create and open a connection to the database using the path:

    ```
    using (var conn = new SQLiteConnection(databasePath)) {
      // connection is now open for use
    }
    ```

5. With our open connection, we can create the table without having to write a SQL query:

```
conn.CreateTable<MyTable>();
```

6. Now that we have a table, we can populate it, again without any SQL:

```
var row = new MyTable {
   FirstName = "Bill",
   LastName = "Gates"
};
conn.Insert(row);
```

7. Reading values from the table is just as easy, and still does not require any SQL:

```
List<MyTable> allRows = conn
    .Table<MyTable>()
    .ToList();
```

8. If we want to do filtering or ordering, we can use the normal `IEnumerable` extension methods:

```
List<MyTable> filtered = conn
    .Table<MyTable>()
    .Where(r => r.LastName == lastName)
    .OrderBy(r => r.FirstName)
    .ToList();
```

9. When we need to use transactions, there are two ways to do this. We can use the `BeginTransaction()`, `Commit()`, and `Rollback()` methods:

```
try {
   conn.BeginTransaction();
   // do something
   conn.Commit();
}
catch {
   conn.Rollback();
}
```

10. Alternatively, we can use the `RunInTransaction()` method:

```
conn.RunInTransaction(delegate {
   // do something
});
```

How it works...

SQLite.NET is a lightweight ORM for SQLite, providing a means to map tables and rows to objects. As this mapping takes place automatically, we have to write very few, if any, SQL statements. SQLite.NET is not a fully featured ORM, but it is often sufficient to be used in most mobile applications.

One of the main advantages of using an ORM is that there is greater type-safety as we don't have to use string-based column names for each query. And, we don't have to use string queries at all as this is generated automatically, making the code far neater and much more maintainable.

Instead of creating SQL to generate a table in the database, we create a C# type that is annotated with attributes to describe how the table is to be constructed in the database. Column types and names are pulled from the object's properties automatically.

There are also several attributes that are used to describe how keys and indexes will be created. Some of these attributes, such as [PrimaryKey], [Unique], and [AutoIncrement], provide additional information on the column type. There are also the [Table] and [Column] attributes that provide a means to override default names.

There are a few features of SQLite.NET that we can use to manage the database, such as creating and dropping tables and indexes. These methods, such as CreateTable, are found on the SQLiteConnection type. These methods allow us to manage the database without having to write SQL.

Inserting rows into a table in the database is as simple as creating a new instance of an object and passing it to the Insert() method. SQLite.NET will automatically discover the correct table and add the values from the properties into a new row in that table. We can also update and delete records in a table by passing the appropriate object to the Update() or Delete() methods.

Reading values from the table is also easy and we can make use of LINQ. The query is started by requesting a table from the connection using the Table() method and then we use LINQ to build up our query from that object. The executions of these queries are deferred until we actually start reading the values. We can make use of most of the typical LINQ commands, such as Where, OrderBy, Skip, and Take, although joins aren't supported at this time.

We can also use transactions in two ways. We have the usual begin and commit actions when using the BeginTransaction(), Commit(), and Rollback() methods. Also, we have a helper method, RunInTransaction(), which takes a delegate or an action. This method wraps the action in a transaction and automatically rolls it back in case of an exception.

There's more...

SQLite.NET also has an asynchronous API. We access this using `SQLiteAsyncConnection` instead of the `SQLiteConnection` type. The advantage of using the asynchronous API is that the tasks can run on a different thread to the UI, making our apps more responsive. This asynchronous API is very similar to the synchronous API, except that the names of the methods end in `Async`.

For example, `CreateTable` becomes `CreateTableAsync`. Let's take a look at the following commands:

```
using (var conn = new SQLiteAsyncConnection(databasePath)) {
  await conn.CreateTableAsync<MyTable>();
}
```

See also

▸ The *Accessing data with ADO.NET* recipe

▸ The *Encrypting SQLite databases with SQLCipher* recipe

Encrypting databases with SQLCipher

Encryption adds another level of security to our apps and data. If we have an app that contains sensitive information, such as passwords or confidential data, then encryption can help protect this data.

How to do it...

Adding encryption to our apps is as simple as adding a reference and creating a password or encryption key. Let's take a look at the following steps:

1. Remove the **Mono.Data.Sqlite** reference if you are using ADO.NET, the **SQLite.NET** component, or the NuGet package if we are using SQLite.NET.

2. Add the **SQLCipher Android** component to the project from the Xamarin Component Store. This can be done by right-clicking on the **Components** folder under the project. In the dialog that appears, we can search for **SQLCipher** and install the Android package.

3. Once the component is installed, we modify our code that opens the database connection to include a password. If we use ADO.NET to access databases, we can first set the password before opening the connection:

```
using (var conn = new SqliteConnection(connectionString)) {
  conn.SetPassword("StrongPasswordHere123");
  conn.Open ();

  // normal database access
}
```

4. If we use SQLite.NET to access the database, we modify the connection constructor to include the password:

```
using (var conn = new SQLiteConnection(
  databasePath, "StrongPasswordHere123")) {

  // normal database access
}
```

How it works...

SQLCipher provides transparent and secure 256-bit AES encryption of SQLite database files; all that we have to do is to specify a password. Passwords can be either a string or a byte array passed to the connection.

If we use the ADO.NET API, we call the `SetPassword()` method; if we use the SQLite.NET API; we pass the password in with the constructor. Other than this, there is no extra work for us to do.

 Avoid hardcoding the key, especially in plain text, within the app, but rather encrypt or obfuscate the key. If the app is compromised, the key will not be easily available.

SQLCipher works with the SQLite engine to transparently encrypt the pages before being written to disk and decrypt them when read back into memory. Due to its small footprint and great performance, it can be used to protect SQLite databases in embedded and mobile environments, such as on Android devices.

SQLCipher includes its own build of SQLite as the native SQLite does not support all the features required to handle transparent database encryption. However, there is very little modification to the actual SQLite implementation and most changes are extensions to support the encryption process.

See also

▶ More information on SQLCipher can be found on the Zetetic LLC website: `https://www.zetetic.net/sqlcipher`

▶ The *Data access with ADO.NET* recipe

▶ The *Data access with SQLite.NET* recipe

Consuming content providers

The most common way for apps to share structured data is to use content providers. These providers present data in a table-like form for easy consumption.

Getting ready...

If we are targeting an Android version earlier than 3.0, we will need to add the **Xamarin Android Support v4** NuGet package.

How to do it...

Content providers give us a way to access data from other apps and services on the device. Here, we will view the contacts through an Android content provider. Let's take a look at the following steps:

1. As we are going to access the contacts, we have to request permission to do so:

   ```
   [assembly: UsesPermission(
     Manifest.Permission.ReadContacts)]
   ```

2. Now that we have the permission, we will need a URI that directs us to the contact content provider:

   ```
   string uri = ContactsContract.Contacts.ContentUri;
   ```

3. Next, we will request the contact ID and the display name using the column constants. There are several columns that can be selected, and we can request any combination of them:

   ```
   string[] projection = {
     ContactsContract.Contacts.InterfaceConsts.Id,
     ContactsContract.Contacts.InterfaceConsts.DisplayName
   };
   ```

4. If we want to add a filter, we can do so. Here, we select all the contacts with the letter e in their name:

```
string filter = string.Format("{0} like ?",
    ContactsContract.Contacts.InterfaceConsts.DisplayName);
string[] filterArgs = { "%e%" };
```

5. We can also apply a sort, or ordering, to our selection:

```
string sort = ContactsContract.Contacts.
InterfaceConsts.DisplayName;
```

6. Now that we have the target and the request data, we can use a `CursorLoader` type to start the connection:

```
var loader = new CursorLoader(
    this, uri, projection, filter, filterArgs, sort);
```

7. Once we have the connection, we can connect and get a cursor to the data:

```
var cursor = (ICursor)loader.LoadInBackground();
```

8. We can move through the results provided by the cursor, similar to what we did with a data reader in ADO.NET:

```
if (cursor.MoveToFirst()) {
    int idIdx = cursor.GetColumnIndex(projection[0]);
    int nameIdx = cursor.GetColumnIndex(projection[1]);
    do {
        long id = cursor.GetLong(idIdx);
        string name = cursor.GetString(nameIdx);
    }
    while (cursor.MoveToNext());
}
```

9. When we are finished with the cursor, we need to ensure that we close it:

```
cursor.Close();
```

How it works...

Using a `ContentProvider` type allows us to access data from both a central repository as well as access data from other apps or services installed on the device. Content providers offer a consistent and uniform interface for accessing data from any provider. They make accessing any data type or structure similar to accessing tables from a database.

An app can access data from a content provider through a `CursorLoader` or `ContentResolver` type. Both allow data queries, but a content resolver has additional operations for inserting, updating, and deleting, and the loader supports background threads.

Cursors should be released as soon as they are no longer in use in order to free up any resources that are in use by the cursor.

The resolver's `Query()` method, or the loader's constructor, accepts several parameters that provide the means to obtain data. The first parameter is the URI that determines which and what content provider to access. The URI identifies the provider, or the authority, to be accessed and the particular data in the provider or the path.

The next parameter is the projection, or the columns, to be returned in the resulting query. This consists of a collection of the column names.

The next two relate to the `where` clause or the filter aspect. This consists of two parts, the first being the actual textual statement and the second being the collection of parameter values. The `where` clause should use a parameter—the ? character—which will be substituted with the appropriate value from the array when the query is executed.

The final parameter is the column used to sort the resulting data and the name of the column we wish to sort by.

In order to obtain the values from the result, we can make use of the several getter methods, such as `GetString()` or `GetLong()`. There is also the `GetColumnIndex()` method, which allows us to find columns by name instead of position.

There's more...

Using a `CursorLoader` allows us to make requests on a separate thread to the UI (however, in this example we don't do that). We can also use the `ContentResolver` property on the `Context` type. This gives us access to more actions, such as insert, update, and delete; however, these operations occur on the UI thread.

In order to delete data, we construct a `where` clause and pass in an array of values to the `Delete()` method, as we would when filtering the query. The items returned in the filter will be removed.

In order to insert data, we pass a set of key-value pairs via a `ContentValues` object. Items are added via the `Put()` method with the key being the column name.

Updating data is simply a combination of the delete and insert aspects. We pass a query and arguments along with the collection of values to the `Update()` method. The items returned by the filter are updated with the values provided.

See also

▸ The *Creating content providers* recipe

Creating content providers

If an app wants to allow its data to be available to other apps on the devices, it needs a way to control access. Content providers can be used as a public endpoint to the data, but they allow the app to maintain control over the data.

How to do it...

Creating content providers allows us to share data with other apps in a uniform manner. It is, for the most part, straightforward. Let's take a look at the following steps:

1. First, we inherit from the `ContentProvider` base type:

```
public class NumberStringsContentProvider : ContentProvider
{
  public override bool OnCreate () {
  }
  public override string GetType (Uri uri) {
  }
  public override ICursor Query (
    Uri uri, string[] projection,
    string selection, string[] selectionArgs,
    string sortOrder) {
  }
  public override int Delete (
    Uri uri, string selection, string[] selectionArgs) {
  }
  public override Uri Insert (
    Uri uri, ContentValues values) {
  }
  public override int Update (
    Uri uri, ContentValues values,
    string selection, string[] selectionArgs) {
  }
}
```

2. Then, we set up the content URI and authority that is used to access our provider:

```
public const string Authority =
  "com.xamarincookbook.provider";
private const string BasePath = "numberstrings";
public static readonly Uri ContentUri =
  Uri.Parse("content://" + Authority + "/" + BasePath);
```

3. Using that authority, we add an attribute to this type:

```
[ContentProvider(
    new [] { NumberStringsContentProvider.Authority })]
```

4. Given the authority, we can create the various URI patterns or data paths:

```
private enum Code {
    All,
    ByNumber,
    ByText
};
private static UriMatcher uriMatcher;
static NumberStringsContentProvider() {
    uriMatcher = new UriMatcher(UriMatcher.NoMatch);
    uriMatcher.AddURI(Authority, BasePath, (int)Code.All);
    uriMatcher.AddURI(Authority,
        string.Format("{0}/#", BasePath), (int)Code.ByNumber);
    uriMatcher.AddURI(Authority,
        string.Format("{0}/*", BasePath), (int)Code.ByText);
}
```

5. For each of the URI patterns, we define a MIME type:

```
public static class MimeTypesConsts {
    public static readonly string NumberStrings =
    string.Format("{0}/vnd.{1}.NumberStrings",
        ContentResolver.CursorDirBaseType, Authority);
    public static readonly string String =
    string.Format("{0}/vnd.{1}.NumberString",
        ContentResolver.CursorItemBaseType, Authority);
    public static readonly string Number =
    string.Format("{0}/vnd.{1}.NumberNumber",
        ContentResolver.CursorItemBaseType, Authority);
}
```

6. Now that we have our definitions in place, we can start the implementation. The first thing to do is to return the correct MIME type for a particular URI pattern. This is done by implementing the `GetType()` method:

```
public override string GetType(Uri uri) {
    switch ((Code)uriMatcher.Match(uri)) {
        case Code.All:
            return MimeTypesConsts.NumberStrings;
        case Code.ByNumber:
            return MimeTypesConsts.Number;
        case Code.ByText:
            return MimeTypesConsts.String;
```

```
          default:
            throw new Java.Lang.IllegalArgumentException();
    }
}
```

7. As this provider is not going to do much, we can create an empty implementation for the `OnCreate()` method:

```
public override bool OnCreate() {
    return true;
}
```

8. In this example, we will make a simple two-column table with one column for an integer and another column for the string representation of that number:

```
private Tuple<int, string>[] data = {
    new Tuple<int, string>(0, "Zero"),
    new Tuple<int, string>(1, "One"),
    new Tuple<int, string>(2, "Two"),
    ...
};
```

9. We also need to create a set of columns for this provider to be used in projections:

```
public static class InterfaceConsts {
    public const string Number = "number";
    public const string Text = "text";

    public static string[] AllColumns = {
        InterfaceConsts.Number,
        InterfaceConsts.Text
    };
}
```

10. Using this, we can implement the `Query` type to return data based on the parameters (in this example, we just assume the projection is `AllColumns`):

```
public override ICursor Query(
    Uri uri, string[] projection,
    string selection, string[] selectionArgs,
    string sortOrder) {
    Code code = (Code)uriMatcher.Match(uri);
    if (code == Code.All) {
        MatrixCursor cursor = new MatrixCursor(projection);
        foreach (var item in data) {
            var builder = cursor.NewRow();
            // create the row based on the projection
            builder.Add(item.Item1).Add(item.Item2);
```

```
        }
        return cursor;
    }
    // handle the rest of the parameters
}
```

11. Similarly, an implementation can be created for the `Delete()`, `Insert()`, and `Update()` methods. We can implement them according to how we want the provider to work with the requests. We read the parameters and decide on what should be done.

How it works...

A content provider makes data available to other apps, which is why we create a content provider if our app needs to share data with other apps. However, we can make content providers even if we only wish to make the data available within our app. But, this does reduce the amount of code that can be shared across other platforms. In order to increase code sharing, our provider can just be a wrapper to the shared data.

Data is shared using a structure similar to a database table with the queries and commands similar to that of SQL. Although requests aren't entirely text-based, the `where` clause is partially string-based. This allows for a semi type-safe interface. The data requested is returned as a cursor to the first row in the result and moved sequentially through the result set.

Content providers are accessed through a URI, which contains two main parts, the authority which identifies the provider, and the path, which points to a specific resource in the provider. The authority is usually similar to that of the app package name, being a unique, reverse Internet domain name. The path is usually the table name or resource.

For example, if we have an app that has the app package name of `com.cookbook.fungame`, and we have a provider that accesses some form of scoreboard, we can use the `com.cookbook.fungame.provider` authority and the `scores` path. We can also include an ID to a particular user, `22`. In this case, our content URI will be `content://com.cookbook.fungame.provider/scores/22`.

When responding to requests, we use a `UriMatcher()` method to distinguish the content URI that was passed to the provider. We construct the matcher from a URI set consisting of the authority, path, and, optionally for some entries, wildcards. Wildcards can be the asterisk, `*`, for any string or the hash, `#`, for any series of digits.

The data that is shared can exist in any type or form. This is one of the reasons for using a content provider: creating a uniform interface for any data type. Data can be from a database, XML, or even from a remote, network-based data store.

If we will be providing data in a tabular form, we should have a primary key or ID column to identify a particular row or item. This column can have any name; however, the best choice is to use the value of `BaseColumns.ID`. Using this name is required when linking a result set to a list view, as one column is required to have the name `_id`. For these operations, we implement the `Query()`, `Insert()`, `Update()`, and `Delete()` methods.

If we will be providing data in the form of files, we implement this by overriding the `OpenFile()` method for arbitrary files or `OpenAssetFile` for assets. In these methods, we open the file and return it to the consumer.

When creating our content provider, we inherit from the `ContentProvider` type and register it with the Android system by applying the `[ContentProvider]` attribute, using the authority URI as a parameter.

The provider is not automatically launched when the app is launched. When the provider is first accessed by a consumer, only then is the `OnCreate()` method called.

 Code executed in the `OnCreate()` method should do as little as possible, and tasks should be deferred until they are actually needed.

The `Query()`, `Insert()`, `Update()`, and `Delete()` methods are each a varying combination of parameters, including a projection, filter clause, value collections, and a sort parameter. We use these parameters to build up and execute queries, which return the data or some other result to the consumer. These methods need to be thread-safe as we can call them multiple times on different threads.

The `Query()` method should always return an `ICursor` type. If an error occurs, throw an exception, and if no data is available, return an empty cursor. The `Insert()` method should add a new item to the data source and return the URI to that item. The `Delete()` and `Update()` methods should return the number of items removed or updated, if any.

The `GetType()` method returns a string representing the MIME type of the data returned, using Android's vendor-specific MIME format. There are two parts, the Android-specific part and the provider-specific part, separated by a slash.

There are two options available for the Android-specific part. For multiple rows, we use the `vnd.android.cursor.dir` or `ContentResolver.CursorDirBaseType` fields, and the `vnd.android.cursor.item` or `ContentResolver.CursorItemBaseType` fields for single row results. The next part is a combination of the provider authority and the specific type. Continuing with the preceding example, we will use `vnd.android.cursor.dir/vnd.com.cookbook.fungame.provider.scores` for multiple rows and `vnd.android.cursor.item/vnd.com.cookbook.fungame.provider.scores` for a single row.

  ▸ The *Consuming content providers* recipe

Backing up preferences and files to the cloud

Most apps will need some sort of backup for the various customizations that the app permits, especially if the app does not have a dedicated server to store those settings. The Android Backup Service provides a simple means of preserving data.

How to do it...

Adding backup support for shared preferences and files is very easy and very simple. Let's take a look at the following steps:

1. Before we start, we have to register our app with the Android Backup Service:
    `http://developer.android.com/google/backup/signup.html`

    On the form, enter the application package name and click on **Register**.

2. Make a note of the key that is provided and create a `[MetaData]` attribute in our app with the value being the key:

    ```
    [assembly: MetaData(
      "com.google.android.backup.api_key",
      Value = "AndroidBackupServiceKey")]
    ```

3. To create our backup agent, we need to inherit from `BackupAgentHelper`:

    ```
    public class BackupHelper : BackupAgentHelper {
      public override void OnCreate() {
      }
    }
    ```

4. Then, we need to register our agent with the Android application:

    ```
    [assembly: Application(
      BackupAgent = typeof(XamarinCookbook.BackupHelper))]
    ```

5. The last thing that our agent needs is to know what to backup. In the `OnCreate()` method, we add helpers:

```
AddHelper(
   "PrefsHelper",
   new SharedPreferencesBackupHelper(this, "GamePrefs"));
AddHelper(
   "FileHelpers",
   new FileBackupHelper(this, "scores.xml"));
```

6. All we have to do now is tell Android that a backup is needed whenever the preferences or files change:

```
using (BackupManager bm = new BackupManager(this)) {
   bm.DataChanged();
}
```

How it works...

Most apps and games have some sort of data that should be preserved across devices or app installs. It can be scores, progress, or app configurations. There are two types of backup agents that we can create: a helper-based agent and a more comprehensive agent. This recipe looks at the former and the next recipe looks at the latter.

There are two simple data types that can be backed up using helpers, almost without any code: shared preferences and files. This backup API is only designed for small pieces of data, less than one megabyte, and should not be used to store large data.

Each app requires a special Android Backup Service Key, which can be obtained from the `http://developer.android.com/google/backup/signup.html` service. This key is then added to the Android manifest by adding an assembly `[MetaData]` attribute.

We also have to register the backup agent with the app by passing the type of the agent to the `BackupAgent` property of the `[Application]` attribute.

Creating an agent is as simple as inheriting from the `BackupAgentHelper` type and implementing the `OnCreate()` method. In this method, we can add all the helpers that we require.

Each helper is constructed with a list of files or a list of shared preferences that we need to backup. After construction, we add each helper to the agent along with a unique key.

Once we have created and registered our backup agent, we need to let Android know every time the data changes, so it can back it up. To do this, we instantiate a `BackupManager` and call `DataChanged`. This does not run the backup immediately, but instead queues it up for the most opportune time determined by the Android OS.

There is no way to programmatically start a backup or restore on demand. Only requests to back up or restore can be queued with Android. Not all devices support backup and restore, and there are no guarantees about data security.

It is also very simple to test the backup process while developing our app. We can request a backup to happen immediately by executing the following commands:

```
adb shell bmgr backup <android-package-name>
adb shell bmgr run
```

Once we have run the backup, we can either clear all data associated with the app or uninstall and reinstall the app. Both actions can be done from the **Settings** app on the device. Once we have done either of these, we can start the restore task:

```
adb shell bmgr restore <android-package-name>
```

We can then launch the app and check whether the app has the data that was backed up. We can also override the `OnBackup()` and `OnRestore()` methods of the agent and insert breakpoints. When we run the command lines, they will be hit accordingly.

Sometimes, Android does not think it should run the backup or restore process. This can be for any number of reasons, but we can force the backup to occur by disabling and then re-enabling it:

```
adb shell bmgr enable false
adb shell bmgr enable true
```

Once the agent has started, we can then request a backup as normal. The reason this works is that when the backup agent is disabled, it wipes all the data from the service. As there is no data anymore, it will always perform the backup.

There's more...

Although not usually necessary, we can request a restore. This, like requesting a backup, is done through the `BackupManager` type and not performed immediately. To request a backup, we call the `RequestRestore()` method.

See also

- The *Storing data with SharedPreferences* recipe
- The *Using files and the filesystem* recipe
- The *Backing up data to the cloud* recipe

Backing up data to the cloud

Often, an app will need to backup it's data, especially if the data took time, effort or money to collect. The Android Backup Service provides a means of preserving data that is more complex than simple shared preferences or files.

Getting ready...

In order to work with the backup API, we have to have registered our app package name with the Android Backup Service.

We do this on `http://developer.android.com/google/backup/signup.html`.

How to do it...

In this recipe, we will save a value to a file and read from a file. This can be a far more comprehensive set of actions on a larger dataset, but not necessary, for example:

1. Our app is not going to do much with the data, so we can save our single value to the filesystem as a basic write operation:

   ```
   File.WriteAllText(dataPath, clickCount.ToString());
   ```

2. Additionally, to read the data on the app start, we will do a basic read:

   ```
   if (File.Exists(dataPath)) {
     clickCount = int.Parse(File.ReadAllText(dataPath));
   }
   ```

Now that we have the data moving in our app, we need to hook up the backup. Although this example uses a simple file stored locally, we can back up data in a database using an algorithm to determine whether a backup needs to be done. Let's take a look at the following steps:

1. Just as we did when we used backup helpers (refer to the previous recipe), we need to register the agent with the application using the backup key:

   ```
   [assembly: MetaData(
     "com.google.android.backup.api_key",
     Value = "AndroidBackupServiceKey")]
   ```

2. In the case of our agent, we inherit it from the base `BackupAgent` instance:

   ```
   public class BackupHelper : BackupAgent {
     public override void OnBackup(
       ParcelFileDescriptor oldState,
       BackupDataOutput data,
   ```

```
    ParcelFileDescriptor newState) {
      // backup logic
    }
  public override void OnRestore(
    BackupDataInput data,
    int appVersionCode,
    ParcelFileDescriptor newState) {
      // restore logic
    }
}
```

3. We now need to create the logic that actually creates the backup logic. We do this in the `OnBackup()` method in four main steps. First, we read the state or metadata associated with the last backup, if any:

```
var stateDate = DateTime.MinValue;
if (oldState != null) {
  using (var descr = oldState.FileDescriptor)
  using (var file = new FileInputStream(descr))
  using (var invoker = new InputStreamInvoker(file))
  using (var stream = new DataInputStream(invoker)) {
    stateDate = DateTime.FromBinary(stream.ReadLong());
  }
}
```

4. Next, we get the state of the data that we need to backup, in our case, the file's last write date:

```
var fileDate = DateTime.MinValue;
if (File.Exists(dataPath)) {
  fileDate = File.GetLastWriteTimeUtc(dataPath);
}
else {
  stateDate = DateTime.MinValue;
}
```

5. Now, we can compare the states, and if they differ, we perform the backup. Here, we just back up the entire contents of the file, but we can back up any data or subset of data:

```
if (stateDate != fileDate) {
  var buffer = File.ReadAllBytes(dataPath);
  data.WriteEntityHeader("DataHeader", buffer.Length);
  data.WriteEntityData(buffer, buffer.Length);
}
```

6. Whether or not we do a backup, we now have to let the agent know what state we are in, and in our case, just the last time the file was modified:

```
using (var descr = newState.FileDescriptor)
using (var file = new FileOutputStream(descr))
using (var invoker = new OutputStreamInvoker(file))
using (var stream = new DataOutputStream(invoker)) {
  stream.WriteLong(fileDate.ToBinary());
}
```

7. Now we need to work on the restore logic in the `OnRestore()` method. We first have to go through all the bits of data that were backed up until we find the header we are looking for, that is, what we know our is app saved:

```
while (data.ReadNextHeader()) {
  if (data.Key == "DataHeader") {
    var buffer = new byte[data.DataSize];
    data.ReadEntityData(buffer, 0, data.DataSize);
    File.WriteAllBytes(dataPath, buffer);
    break;
  }
  else {
    data.SkipEntityData();
  }
}
```

8. Lastly, we have to let the agent know about the current state of the backup, and again in our case, just the time of the last modification of the file:

```
if (File.Exists(dataPath)) {
  using (var descr = newState.FileDescriptor)
  using (var file = new FileOutputStream(descr))
  using (var invoker = new OutputStreamInvoker(file))
  using (var stream = new DataOutputStream(invoker)) {
    var fileDate = File.GetLastWriteTimeUtc(dataPath);
    stream.WriteLong(fileDate.ToBinary());
  }
}
```

How it works...

We can easily back up shared preferences or entire files, but sometimes, we need to have more flexibility or control. To do this, we can create an instance of the base `BackupAgent` instance.

There are several advantages of using the base agent directly as opposed to the helpers. The most notable advantage is the ability to version data and appropriately upgrade or downgrade the data. There is also the powerful ability to back up and restore partial data, such as a section of a larger file. We can also back up specific tables in a database. This will allow us to better version the data as well as reduce the size by excluding static data.

There are two stages to any backup process: backup and restore. The backup stage consists of four main steps:

1. The first step is to read the state or metadata associated with the last backup from the `oldState` parameter. This state is used to identify the backed up data but is not the data itself; it can be anything, even a simple, last-modified timestamp of the data. If the state is `null`, then no backup or restore has been performed and we should take a backup.

2. We now need to be able to make a decision to backup, so we need to obtain the state of the data itself. If we are backing up data only if it has changed, we need to obtain the timestamp of the last change. If we are backing up a database, we may use the last login date.

3. Now that we have both the state of the backup and the state of the data, we can determine whether a backup is needed. To perform a backup, we populate the `BackupDataOutput` object with a set of key-value entities. We first write a header using the `WriteEntityHeader()` method, and then the actual data using the `WriteEntityData()` method. If we are backing up a database table, we can read the contents into an XML document and then write that.

4. Finally, we have to let Android know the state of the backup in the `newState` parameter. Even if nothing was backed up, we can still write a value representing the fact that nothing was done, that is, the original value. This state is passed in as the `oldState` parameter the next time a backup is run. If we are backing up a table, we can write the last login date.

Performing a restore is a bit easier as we only have to execute two steps:

1. We have to first go through the data in the `BackupDataInput` object and work with the keys we recognize. We can loop through the headers using the `ReadNextHeader()` method, and if we are working with different app versions, we may choose to ignore some using the `SkipEntityData()` method. If we want to read the data, we use the `ReadEntityData()` method.

2. After we have restored the data, we now update the state of the data by writing to the `newState` parameter. If we are restoring a section of a file, we can use the timestamp. This state is passed in as the `oldState` parameter when a backup is run.

The `OnBackup()` method is called when the backup manager decides that it is time to run a backup. We can request a backup using the backup manager, but cannot control when it is run. The `OnRestore()` method is called by the backup manager as well, but is also automatically called when the app is installed. Like backups, we can request a restore but cannot directly control when it happens.

There's more...

During a restore, we are provided an `appVersionCode` values that we can use to handle restore data versioning. When the data is backed up, this value represents the version code of the app that was used to create the backup.

See also

▶ The *Backing up preferences and files to the cloud* recipe

4

Presenting App Data

In this chapter, we will cover the following recipes:

- ▶ Implementing a `ListView`
- ▶ Using a `SimpleAdapter`
- ▶ Using custom `ListView` items
- ▶ Using a `BaseAdapter` with arbitrary data
- ▶ Using a `CursorAdapter`
- ▶ Optimizing the `ListView`
- ▶ Enabling fast scrolling
- ▶ Using section indexes
- ▶ Integrating app searchability

Introduction

Data is the most important feature of many apps, and the best way to use this data is often to present it first. Data comes in many shapes and forms, but in order to be managed or manipulated, it has to be presented.

Data can be in the form of images, text, or other forms, but often the most common way of presenting data is in a list. Lists provide a structured way in which data can be quickly viewed and compared.

There are many ways to present data in the form of a list. It can simply be presented as text blocks one below the other; however, this is often difficult to read. If each chunk of data is carefully arranged and presented, the data becomes more useful. Not only how the data is arranged but also how the data is rendered aids viewing.

Humans can easily pick out patterns and identify specific items if the data is arranged in a form that is both neat and clean. By spacing and ordering items, data becomes easier to consume.

Another important aspect of data presentation is the ability to quickly locate or navigate to a specific piece of data. This involves scrolling, but can be further enhanced by searching or the ability to jump to a specific section in the larger data.

Data is important and, when arranged with navigational support, it becomes useful and useful data is information.

Implementing a ListView

Almost all apps have some sort of collection of data that will be presented to the user, with the easiest and most common way being some sort of list.

How to do it...

If we want to present a collection of items to the user, we can use a `ListView` instance:

1. In order to show a list, we need to add a `ListView` element to our layout resource (we can do this in the code as well):

```
<ListView
    android:layout_width="match_parent"
    android:layout_height="match_parent"
    android:id="@+id/listView" />
```

2. We then get hold of the `ListView` instance in our code so that we can use it:

```
ListView listView = FindViewById<ListView>(
    Resource.Id.listView);
```

3. Now that we have the view, we need the data (which we will generate here):

```
IEnumerable<int> numbers = Enumerable.Range(1, 1000);
IEnumerable<string> strings = numbers.Select(
    i => string.Format("Item Number {0} Here!", i));
List<string> data = new List<string>(strings);
```

4. We then create an `IListAdapter` instance to connect the data to the view:

```
ArrayAdapter<string> adapter = new ArrayAdapter<string>(
    this, Android.Resource.Layout.SimpleListItem1, data);
```

5. We can then assign the adapter to the `listView` instance:

```
listView.Adapter = adapter;
```

6. Finally, if we want to handle item selections, we attach the following code to the `ItemClick` event:

```
listView.ItemClick += (sender, e) => {
  using (var dialog = new AlertDialog.Builder(this)) {
    int position = e.Position;
    string value = data[position];
    dialog.SetTitle("Item Selection");
    dialog.SetMessage(value);
    dialog.Show();
  }
};
```

How it works...

Presenting collections of data to a user is very common and is easily implemented using a `ListView` type. There are a few other types of views that we can use to display data, such as the `Spinner` and `GridView` type, but these are just variations of the list view.

The `ListView` type presents the data by applying a particular item template to each data item. The data is rendered onto the view or collection of views and then displayed in a scrollable list. The list view has many available customizations and can be styled to a great degree.

The list view makes use of adapter types that implement the `IListAdapter` interface, which maps the data to the `ListView` items. The adapter takes each item in the data collection and creates an item for the list view based on the provided template. In the case of our example, we use a simple adapter, the `ArrayAdapter<T>` type, which takes a string data item and renders it using the `SimpleListItem1` item template, which happens to be a single `TextView` element.

If we want to be able to handle item selections, we can subscribe to the `ItemClick` event. This event provides an `ItemClickEventArgs`, which gives us access to several details of the selected item, including the actual list item view and the position of the item in the adapter.

There's more...

Lists are so common in mobile apps that there is a special class to display lists of data—the `ListActivity` type. This class is simply an activity with a list view built in, so we don't have to worry about a layout. To access the list view, we use the `ListView` property; to access the adapter, we use the `ListAdapter` property.

When we want to handle item selections, there are two ways we can go about this. We can either subscribe to the `ItemClick` event on the list view or we can override the `OnItemClick()` method of the `ListActivity` type.

See also

▶ The *Using custom ListView items* recipe

▶ The *Using a BaseAdapter with arbitrary data* recipe

▶ The *Enabling fast scrolling* recipe

Using a SimpleAdapter

If we want more control over the parts of the data to be rendered and how the data is rendered for each item, we can use a different adapter and different item templates.

How to do it...

List views allow us to entirely customize each item view through item templates. Android has a few predefined templates that we can use:

1. We can make use of the simple, single-line text items using the `ArrayAdapter<T>` type and a simple string collection:

   ```
   var adapter = new ArrayAdapter<string>(
       this, Android.Resource.Layout.SimpleListItem1, data);
   ```

2. Android also provides a means to handle more complex data. To do this, we use a collection of the `JavaDictionary<string, object>` objects:

   ```
   var data = new JavaList<IDictionary<string, object>>();
   ```

3. We can add items to this list like any other collection using the `Add()` method:

   ```
   data.Add(new JavaDictionary<string, object> {
       { "name", "Bruce Banner" },
       { "status", "Bruce Banner feels like SMASHING!" }
   });
   ```

4. With more complex data, we need to use the `SimpleAdapter` type, which allows us to map a particular key in the dictionary to a view in the item:

   ```
   var adapter = new SimpleAdapter(
       this, data, Android.Resource.Layout.SimpleListItem1,
       new[] { "name" }, new[] { Android.Resource.Id.Text1 });
   ```

5. The `SimpleAdapter` type also allows us to map multiple keys to multiple views in each item; to do this, we use a different item resource:

```
SimpleAdapter adapter = new SimpleAdapter(
   this, data, Android.Resource.Layout.SimpleListItem2,
   new[] {
      "name",
      "status"
   }, new[] {
      Android.Resource.Id.Text1,
      Android.Resource.Id.Text2
   });
```

6. There are also items that support checkboxes, or some other means of showing that the item is selected:

```
var adapter = new SimpleAdapter(
   this, data, Android.Resource.Layout.SimpleListItemChecked,
   new[] { "name" }, new[] { Android.Resource.Id.Text1 });
```

7. In order to support selection, we have to ensure that the list view `ChoiceMode` is either `Multiple` or `Single`:

```
listView.ChoiceMode = ChoiceMode.Single;
```

How it works...

Passing collections between .NET and Java is slightly more complex than it appears. When we pass a collection to Java, only a *copy* of the collection is passed. This means that, if the collection is modified by some object on the Java side, the changes are not reflected on the .NET side. Xamarin.Android has a way of addressing this problem by providing various Java collections, such as `JavaList` and `JavaDictionary`. These collections are simple wrappers to the underlying Java collections.

 When collections are passed to Java objects, a copy of the collection is created in Java, and that copy is used instead of the .NET collection.

There are advantages of using both types of collections. If we use the .NET collections, the objects exist in .NET and a copy is passed to Java. This copy is not linked to the original, and is managed separately by both the .NET and Java garbage collectors. The downside is that the .NET collection is not updated when the Java collection is; however, this method is not used very often.

If we use the Java collections, the collection is created in Java and a wrapper is created in .NET. This allows a collection to be updated if the other one is. However, every time we wish to access the items or update the collection, the item is passed to the underlying Java collection and back again.

 The .NET collections are useful when the operation is performed in .NET. The Java collections are useful if the data will be updated from the native Java.

The `SimpleAdapter` type allows us to easily map a slightly more complex datatype to a structured view. When constructing the adapter, we provide the data along with two arrays that are used to map an item property to a view.

The data is a collection of dictionaries, with each dictionary representing an item from the list. The dictionary is used to *label* a value. Each of the dictionaries should contain the same set of keys, as these represent the attributes of the data.

The last two parameters in the constructor, two arrays, are used together to map a dictionary key to a view ID. The first array contains the collection of dictionary keys, and the second contains a collection of IDs. The size of the arrays should be the same as each item corresponds directly to the item in the same position in the other array.

The adapter iterates through the items in the arrays and, after obtaining the value from the dictionary using the key in the first array, it updates the corresponding view using the ID in the second array.

There's more...

As the `SimpleArray` type takes a resource ID for the item template as a parameter, we can create our own item layouts and use those IDs instead of the Android ones. If we need to have even more control over the adapter, we can create our own adapter by inheriting from the `BaseAdapter` type.

See also

- ▸ The *Using custom ListView items* recipe
- ▸ The *Using a BaseAdapter with arbitrary data* recipe

Using custom ListView items

Using a list view, we can entirely customize the way each item looks. We don't have to stick to a simple template, but rather provide a much more detailed view.

How to do it...

All we need to do in order to create a custom item template is to create a custom layout, either by code or in a layout resource:

1. First, we create the item template using normal layout files.

   For example, we can create a layout named `ListItemLayout.axml` with three content views—an image view and two text views:

   ```xml
   <?xml version="1.0" encoding="utf-8"?>
   <LinearLayout
     xmlns:android="http://schemas.android.com/apk/res/android"
     android:layout_width="fill_parent"
     android:layout_height="wrap_content">
     <ImageView
       android:id="@+id/icon"
       android:layout_width="wrap_content"
       android:layout_height="match_parent"
       android:layout_weight="0" />
     <LinearLayout
       android:orientation="vertical"
       android:layout_weight="1"
       android:layout_width="fill_parent"
       android:layout_height="fill_parent">
       <TextView
         android:layout_width="fill_parent"
         android:layout_height="wrap_content"
         android:layout_weight="1"
         android:id="@+id/firstRow" />
       <TextView
         android:layout_width="fill_parent"
         android:layout_height="wrap_content"
         android:layout_weight="1"
         android:id="@+id/secondRow" />
     </LinearLayout>
   </LinearLayout>
   ```

2. Assuming that we are going to use the `SimpleAdapter` type, we can construct our data in the following form:

   ```
   var data = new JavaList<IDictionary<string, object>>();
   data.Add(new JavaDictionary<string, object> {
       { "name", "Bruce Banner" },
       { "status", "Bruce Banner feels like SMASHING!" }
       { "icon", Resource.Drawable.hulk }
   });
   ```

3. Now that we have our data, we can create the adapter, which will do all the work to update the view with the data:

```
var adapter = new SimpleAdapter(
    this, data, Resource.Layout.ListItemLayout,
    new[] {
        "name",
        "status",
        "icon"
    }, new[] {
        Resource.Id.firstRow,
        Resource.Id.secondRow,
        Resource.Id.icon
    });
```

How it works...

Many apps will want to customize the list view in order to have more complex items as well as to continue using the same theme throughout the app. In order to achieve this, we create custom items for the list view and style the list view itself. For example, consider the inbox of the Gmail app or the results of the Google Now app; each is a list view, but each item has been greatly customized and has many data points.

Custom list view items are simply normal views, such as an inflated layout, that are repeated for each item. Each list view item can contain any view or any view structure, just like in an activity layout. Although this is the case, we need to keep in mind that the item view is in a scrollable list; thus, we shouldn't put another scrollable view inside a list view item.

Another thing we should remember is that the item view will be repeated many times, so we should not create an overly complex view. We should strive to keep our list items as shallow as possible to increase performance, especially as there will be many items and they will be moving on the screen when the user scrolls.

 The ListView items should be kept as shallow as possible to increase performance.

There's more...

If we want to specify an actual custom type, such as from a SQLite.NET data type, then we can create an instance of the BaseAdapter type. This provides a clean way to map any datatype to any view with full control over each item. The SimpleAdapter type tries to handle several view types, but is not designed for very complex items.

See also

▸ The *Using a BaseAdapter with arbitrary data* recipe

▸ The *Optimizing the ListView* recipe

Using a BaseAdapter with arbitrary data

Sometimes, we need to have the flexibility to completely customize the way a datatype is rendered for each item. To do this, we can make use of the `BaseAdapter` type and custom item layouts.

How to do it...

If we want to specify an actual custom type, then we can create an adapter, derived from the `BaseAdapter` type:

1. A list can bind to any data type collection, as long as we have an adapter that understands how to present each item. For example, we can bind to an arbitrary type:

```
public class Person {
  public int Id { get; set; }
  public string Name {get;set;}
  public string Status {get;set;}
  public bool IsMale { get; set; }
}
```

2. The adapter that we will create can inherit from the generic `BaseAdapter<T>` adapter:

```
public class PeopleAdapter : BaseAdapter<Person> {
  public override int Count { get; }
  public override Person this[int index] { get; }

  public override long GetItemId(int position) {
  }
  public override View GetView(
    int position, View convertView, ViewGroup parent) {
  }
}
```

3. Next, we add a constructor that provides us with access to a context and the data that we store in fields:

```
private readonly Context context;
private readonly List<Person> data;

public PeopleAdapter(Context context, List<Person> data)
{
    this.data = data;
    this.context = context;
}
```

4. We can now implement the simple property, `Count`, which simply returns the size of the collection, and the indexer, which returns the particular data item:

```
public override int Count {
    get { return data.Count; }
}
public override Person this[int index] {
    get { return data[index]; }
}
```

5. There is also the `GetItemId()` method, which we use to return an ID or just the item's position:

```
public override long GetItemId(int position) {
    return data[position].Id;
}
```

6. Finally, we will implement the `GetView()` method. First, we get hold of the data item for this list item:

```
Person person = data[position];
```

7. Now that we have the data, we start constructing the view. First, we check whether we can reuse any old view from the `convertView` parameter, and if we can't, we inflate or create a new view:

```
if (convertView == null) {
    var inflater = LayoutInflater.From(context);
    convertView = inflater.Inflate(
        Resource.Layout.ListItemLayout, parent, false);
}
```

8. Once we have the view, we can put the values from the data item into the various subviews in the item. We can access any subview of the item view just as we can for any other view:

```
var firstRow = convertView.FindViewById<TextView>(
  Resource.Id.firstRow);
var icon = convertView.FindViewById<ImageView>(
  Resource.Id.icon);
```

9. Once we have the various views, we can assign the data to them:

```
int image = person.IsMale
  ? Resource.Drawable.male
  : Resource.Drawable.female;
icon.SetImageResource(image);
firstRow.Text = person.Name;
```

10. Lastly, we return the view:

```
return convertView;
```

How it works...

We can put any data into a list view, but we do need to let the list view know how to handle as well as present the data. Our data can come from any source, such as a database, file, or a collection. To do this, we use a list adapter, which inherits from `IListAdapter`, or more specifically, the generic `BaseAdapter<T>` type.

This adapter has four members that we need to override, three of which are very simple and, usually, require only a single line of code.

The `Count` property is very simple and it just returns the number of items that are in the data. The indexer is also very simple and simply returns the data item for a particular position in the data collection.

In the case of the `GetItemId()` method, we should try and return the item's ID. If the item does not have an ID that we can use, we can just return the item's position, the method's parameter.

 A data item's position in the adapter can be used as the ID if it does not have a specific ID.

The `GetView()` method is where we can translate the data item into a view for a list item. Here, we can obtain the data item and display it in any form of our choice. Once we have the data item, which we obtain using the position parameter, we need a view to display it in.

Instead of creating a new view for each item, we should try to reuse views. An old view comes through to us via the `convertView` parameter. This view is actually one of the items that we created previously but has scrolled off the screen. This view may be `null`, for example, when the items are first rendered; so, we do have to construct the view before using it.

Reusing views reduces the amount of memory required to display the data as well as improving performance, especially when scrolling, as the list view does not have to reconstruct the view each time.

[🔆💡 Views should be reused whenever possible to improve performance and memory usage.]

Once we have the view, either reused or created, we can then update the various subviews as we wish using the data for that item. The process of updating a view is exactly the same as for a normal view in the activity.

There's more...

We can also override the nongeneric `BaseAdapter` type. This type does not have the indexer, but instead has a `GetItem()` method, which returns a `Java.Lang.Object` element. There are a few steps in converting, or actually wrapping, a .NET object into a Java object, which the `GetItem()` method on the generic adapter does for us. The generic adapter uses the value returned by the indexer and wraps it in a `Java.Lang.Object` element.

See also

- ► The *Using custom ListView items* recipe
- ► The *Optimizing the ListView* recipe
- ► The *Using section indexes* recipe

Using a CursorAdapter

Sometimes our data comes from a source that returns an `ICursor` element; thus, we can make use of the `SimpleCursorAdapter` type without having to create a collection of data objects.

How to do it...

Using the `SimpleCursorAdapter` type with an `ICursor` instance is almost the same as using the `SimpleAdapter` type with an object collection:

1. When using a `CursorAdapter` type, all we need is an `ICursor` instance from either the `ContentResolver` or `CursorLoader` types:

```
var uri = ContactsContract.Contacts.ContentUri;
string[] projection = {
  ContactsContract.Contacts.InterfaceConsts.Id,
  ContactsContract.Contacts.InterfaceConsts.DisplayName,
  ContactsContract.Contacts.InterfaceConsts
    .ContactStatusLabel,
};
ICursor cursor = ContentResolver.Query(
  uri, projection, null, null, null);
```

2. Once we have the cursor, we can hand it over to the `SimpleCursorAdapter` type, which is very similar to the `SimpleAdapter` type:

```
SimpleCursorAdapter adapter = new SimpleCursorAdapter(
  this, Android.Resource.Layout.SimpleListItem2, cursor,
  new[] {
    ContactsContract.Contacts.InterfaceConsts.DisplayName,
    ContactsContract.Contacts.InterfaceConsts
      .ContactStatusLabel
  }, new[] {
    Android.Resource.Id.Text1,
    Android.Resource.Id.Text2
  });
```

3. We can then assign this adapter to the list view as we would do for any other adapter:

```
listView.Adapter = adapter
```

How it works...

When our data comes from a content provider, we are presented with an `ICursor` instance. In order to handle this type of result, we make use of the `SimpleCursorAdapter` type, which is very similar to the `SimpleAdapter` type.

The main difference is that, instead of accepting a collection of items as data, the `SimpleCursorAdapter` type accepts an `ICursor` instance. And, instead of using dictionary keys to map data to a view resource ID, we use the column names from the projection.

This is very useful if we are trying to read data from an `ICursor` instance, but we don't need to create an object collection just in order to bind to a list view. As content providers are used to share content between apps, we may have to consume one at some time.

There's more...

If we want to have greater flexibility for more complex data, we can do something similar to what we do when using a `BaseAdapter<T>` type. In order to have more control, we inherit from the `CursorAdapter` type, which works with an `ICursor` instance instead of a collection of data items.

The `CursorAdapter` type is different in that we don't have to implement the various data members, such as `GetItem()`, `GetItemId()`, `Count`, and the indexer. The reason for this is that the implementation of these members is handled by the CursorAdapter automatically; comes from the cursor; all we have to do is work with the view.

Again, unlike the `BaseAdapter` type, we don't implement the `GetView()` method but rather it is split into two more specific methods, `NewView()` and `BindView()`. In the `GetView()` method, we will inflate or create the view and then assign the data to the view. With the `CursorAdapter` type, we will inflate or create the view in the `NewView()` method and then only assign the data to the view in the `BindView()` method. The actual implementation is very similar, but it is split into two methods.

See also

- ▸ The *Implementing a ListView* recipe
- ▸ The *Using a SimpleAdapter* recipe

Optimizing the ListView

In order to make scrolling through out lists as smooth as possible, we need to ensure that the construction and manipulation of the items run as fast and as efficiently as possible.

How to do it...

One way in which we can optimize the list items is to reuse the item view:

- ▸ This is very easy to do, and all we need is to check is whether we can use the `convertView` parameter before trying to create a new instance of the item:

```
if (convertView == null) {
    var inflater = LayoutInflater.From(context);
    convertView = inflater.Inflate(
```

```
        Resource.Layout.ListItemLayout, parent, false);
    }
    var firstRow = convertView.FindViewById<TextView>(
        Resource.Id.firstRow);
    firstRow.Text = person.Name;
```

Another way is to store references to the various subviews so that we don't have look for them each time, as follows:

1. Create a type that will hold a reference to those subviews:

```
private class ViewHolder : Java.Lang.Object {
    public ImageView Icon;
    public TextView FirstRow;
    public TextView SecondRow;
}
```

2. Then, when we inflate the view for the first time, we search for the various views and store them in the fields:

```
var viewHolder = new ViewHolder {
    Icon = convertView.FindViewById<ImageView>(
        Resource.Id.icon),
    FirstRow = convertView.FindViewById<TextView>(
        Resource.Id.firstRow),
    SecondRow = convertView.FindViewById<TextView>(
        Resource.Id.secondRow)
};
```

3. Once we have created the view holder object, we can assign it to the list item's view using the `Tag` property:

```
convertView.Tag = viewHolder;
```

4. Next time we have to populate the view, we don't have to search for the various subviews, but we can just get the references from the item:

```
var viewHolder = (ViewHolder)convertView.Tag;
```

5. When we want to update the item, all we have to do is use the `viewHolder` object:

```
viewHolder.FirstRow.Text = person.Name;
```

How it works...

As the user is able to scroll quite fast through a list, the list needs to be able to create and update the items as fast as possible. If there is any delay, the user will notice it immediately and this makes the experience less polished.

There are two very common, and incidentally, very expensive operations that we perform for every item. These operations are inflating the views and locating the particular subviews. Every item has to be created at some point, and in order to update, the text of one item will have to find the view that will contain that text. Also, as there may be thousands of items, this executes multiple times in a second.

> The construction or inflation of views as well as searching for views in a hierarchy are very expensive and some of the most common operations performed by any app.

There are a few ways in which we can improve list and app performance, one being in the construction of the view. Instead of reconstructing the view for each item, we need to try and reuse the already existing view. An item scrolling off the screen is placed in a recycle bin in order that the item may be reused at some point. This recycle bin allows Android to limit the number of items constructed, improving both memory consumption as well as the number of CPU operations.

Android provides an easy means to reuse a view in the `GetView()` method. One of the parameters passed into this method, the `convertView` parameter, is an available view from the recycle bin. We can then use this view and simply update the contents with the data from the new item. As this view is actually an existing item that scrolled off the screen, we need to ensure that we reset any values that we may have set. This pattern is called **Virtualization**.

> View construction performance can be improved by reusing old views.

Another way to improve performance is to reduce the number of times we search for a view within the item. Even though we may only have a few views to update in the item, we need to remember that there may be many items, and searching for a view requires that the entire item hierarchy be searched.

We can limit the number of times we search for a view by saving the references to each view item in the item itself. We can do this by creating an object that will hold the references to all the views that we will update and then assign that object to the item. We assign the object to the item by assigning the object to the `Tag` property of the item's view. We call this pattern the **View Holder pattern**.

> View finding performance can be improved by storing references to the various subviews when they are found.

There's more...

There are many other performance improvements that we can do for lists. We can cache various pieces of data, such as images. We can also move expensive operations to another thread. This can be further improved by ensuring that we don't run operations unnecessarily, such as when the list is scrolling at high speed. We can also improve performance by ensuring that some of the operations are done beforehand, and the results are cached.

See also

- ▸ The *Using custom ListView items* recipe
- ▸ The *Using a BaseAdapter with arbitrary data* recipe
- ▸ The *Enabling fast scrolling* recipe
- ▸ The *Using section indexes* recipe

Enabling fast scrolling

Locating a specific item in a large list is fairly difficult, so we should provide a means to help the user get there quickly.

How to do it...

In order to help the user navigate through large lists, Android provides a few means to skip large sections of data. One of these aids is Fast Scroll, or simply, using a scroll thumb.

- ▸ In order to enable the thumb, we set the `FastScrollEnabled` property:

  ```
  listView.FastScrollEnabled = true;
  ```

- ▸ Alternatively, if we are using the layout resources, we can set the `FastScrollEnabled` property as follows:

  ```
  android:fastScrollEnabled="true"
  ```

- ▸ If we are targeting Android versions 3.0 and later, and want the thumb to always be visible, we can use the `FastScrollAlwaysVisible` property:

  ```
  listView.FastScrollAlwaysVisible = true;
  ```

How it works...

Paging through large data collections does not provide a great user experience. Android provides a few means to make the process of skipping over large sections of data easier without the user having to fling the list repeatedly. The simplest way is to enable **Fast Scroll**, which provides a scroll thumb that can be dragged, thus making it possible to scroll through the list very rapidly.

 Paging through large data collections is not very user-friendly, and there should be a means for the user to jump closer to the desired position.

The thumb is initially disabled, but we can enable it by setting the `FastScrollEnabled` property to `true`. Once enabled, the thumb will appear if the list is large enough, usually if the total number of items is four times the number that can fit on the screen.

We can also enable fast scroll from the layout resources. To do this, we set the `android:fastScrollEnabled` attribute to `true`. This does exactly the same thing as the `FastScrollEnabled` property, but we can keep all our view code inside the layout resource.

If we enable fast scroll, the thumb will only appear if the user is actually scrolling through the list. In order to ensure that the thumb is always visible, even when not scrolling, we set the `FastScrollAlwaysVisible` property to `true`.

Even though the scroll thumb is very simple, it is a quick means of improving the user experience when we have large lists.

There's more...

When using the thumb, it is very difficult to see where in the list we are, so we can make use of **section indexes**. This is a small popup that appears as we scroll, displaying an index, such as the first letter of the items. The section index and the thumb make navigating through lists much easier, as the user can skip to a section by dragging the thumb to the desired section.

See also

- ▸ The *Optimizing the ListView* recipe
- ▸ The *Using section indexes* recipe

Using section indexes

Even if we have enabled fast scroll, it is still difficult to know where we are in the list. To get around this, we make use of section indexes.

How to do it...

Making a list show a section index popup while scrolling is quite easy, requiring only that the adapter implements the `ISectionIndexer` interface. Let's take a look at the following steps:

1. In order to enable the section index, we need to ensure that fast scroll is enabled on the list view:

    ```
    listView.FastScrollEnabled = true;
    ```

2. Then we ensure that the list adapter implements the `ISectionIndexer` interface:

    ```
    public class PeopleAdapter :
      BaseAdapter<Person>, ISectionIndexer {
      public int GetPositionForSection(int section) {
      }
      public int GetSectionForPosition(int position) {
      }
      public Java.Lang.Object[] GetSections() {
      }
    }
    ```

3. We can calculate all of these values on-the fly but, for performance reasons, we do some of it in the constructor. Here, we group the data by the first letter of the name:

    ```
    private readonly Context context;
    private readonly List<Person> data;
    private readonly Dictionary<string, List<Person>> sectionData;
    private readonly List<string> sections;

    public PeopleAdapter(Context context, List<Person> data) {
      this.data = data;
      this.context = context;

      sectionData = data
        .GroupBy(p => p.Name.Substring(0, 1).ToUpper()
        .ToDictionary(g => g.Key, g => g.ToList());
      sections = sectionData.Select(s => s.Key).ToList();
    }
    ```

4. Once we have the main groups, we can start by implementing the `GetSections()` method, which returns all the sections in the data:

```
public Java.Lang.Object[] GetSections() {
    return sections
        .Select(s => (Java.Lang.Object)s)
        .ToArray();
}
```

5. Next, we implement the method that returns the position of a section that contains a particular data item:

```
public int GetSectionForPosition(int position) {
    Person person = data[position];
    string key = sectionData
        .First(g => g.Value.Contains(person))
        .Key;
    return sections.IndexOf(key);
}
```

6. Lastly, we implement the method that returns the position of the first item in a particular section:

```
public int GetPositionForSection(int section) {
    string key = sections[section];
    Person person = sectionData[key].First();
    return data.IndexOf(person);
}
```

How it works...

Even if we have enabled fast scroll, it is still difficult to know where we are in the list as the items are moving very quickly. We might not be able to see which items they are, so we have to stop scrolling and check. We can add to the improvement of fast scroll by using a section index.

A section index is a simple popup that appears as we fast-scroll, displaying a value that we choose representing the section of the list that the visible items are in. The section index value can be anything as it is simply a grouping mechanism that we determine. For example, it can be the first letter of the items.

 The section index is a simple popup that appears in order to let the user know the section of the list that they are in.

After enabling fast scroll, the only additional thing we need to do is ensure that our adapter implements the `ISectionIndexer` interface. There are three methods to implement—two provide a means for the list to find particular positions and one provides the indexes.

The `GetSection()` method returns a simple array of all the indexes; this is only requested once and can be precalculated to improve performance. In this method, we return an array of the extracted indexes from the data. The order of the items is important as we will refer to a particular item by position.

The `GetSectionForPosition()` method returns the position of a section that contains the particular data item. This position refers to a position in the array returned by the `GetSection()` method. In order to get this position, we are provided with the position of the data item, which we can use to work backwards to obtain the section.

The `GetPositionForSection()` method returns the position of the first item in a particular section. This position refers to a position in the original data collection. We are provided with the position of a section and work forward to obtain the first item in that section.

There's more...

As the sections will only change if the data is changing, we can precalculate the entire set of sections and indexes, and then just return the values from the respective methods.

Depending on the type of adapter we use, adding items to it may automatically let the list view know that it needs to refresh the sections. If we are using a custom adapter, we will have to manually do this by invoking the `NotifyDataSetChanged()` method on the adapter. This will trigger the list view to obtain a new set of sections.

As the `GetSections()` method is only called once every time the data changes, we can place the logic that precalculates the sections and indexes here, reducing the load on the other methods to a simple lookup.

See also

▸   The *Using a BaseAdapter with arbitrary data* recipe
▸   The *Optimizing the ListView* recipe
▸   The *Enabling fast scrolling* recipe

Integrating app searchability

Many apps work with collections of data, and users search through that data in order to find what they are looking for. Android has several search mechanisms that are integrated with the OS.

How to do it...

Integrating search into our app is very easy, only requiring a search activity and a few attributes on the activities:

1. In order to handle searching, our app has to have an activity that will handle search intents:

```
public class SearchActivity : Activity {
  protected override void OnCreate(Bundle bundle) {
    ...
    HandleIntent(Intent);
  }
  protected override void OnNewIntent(Intent intent) {
    HandleIntent(intent);
  }
  private void HandleIntent(Intent intent) {
    if (intent.Action == Intent.ActionSearch) {
      string query =
      intent.GetStringExtra(SearchManager.Query);
    }
  }
}
```

2. Because Xamarin.Android will hash the type namespaces when it generates the Java code, we have to let it know what name we want for the search activity using the `[Register]` attribute:

```
[Register("com.xamarincookbook.SearchActivity")]
```

3. Once we have the search activity, we need to add attributes to it to let Android know that it can accept search intents:

```
[IntentFilter(new[] { Intent.ActionSearch })]
```

4. We now have to create an XML file, in the `xml` folder under `Resources`, that contains various properties for the search metadata.

    For example, the contents of the `searchable.xml` file can be as follows:

```
<?xml version="1.0" encoding="utf-8"?>
<searchable xmlns:android=
"http://schemas.android.com/apk/res/android"
  android:label="Xamarin Cookbook"
  android:hint="Search Xamarin Cookbook for code"
  android:voiceSearchMode=
    "showVoiceSearchButton|launchRecognizer">
</searchable>
```

5. The XML file is associated with the search activity using an attribute with the key `android.app.searchable`:

```
[MetaData(
  "android.app.searchable",
  Resource = "@xml/searchable")]
```

Our search activity is finished, so we can start building the activities that are searchable or expose some search functionality:

1. We need to let the other activities know where to send their search intents. This can be done in two ways, one of which is to add an attribute on each activity, as follows:

```
[MetaData(
  "android.app.default_searchable",
  Value = "com.xamarincookbook.SearchActivity")]
```

2. Or, add an assembly-level attribute for all activities:

```
[assembly: MetaData(
  "android.app.default_searchable",
  Value = "com.xamarincookbook.SearchActivity")]
```

3. Next, we add the search view to the menu resource, where we are using the support library to provide the widget:

```
<item
  xmlns:app="http://schemas.android.com/apk/res-auto"
  android:id="@+id/searchItem"
  android:title="Search"
  android:icon="@android:drawable/ic_menu_search"
 app:actionViewClass="android.support.v7.widget.SearchView"
  app:showAsAction="always" />
```

4. When we inflate the action bar, we need to let the search view know about our search properties, ensuring that we cast the `ActionView` to the support library search view:

```
public override bool OnCreateOptionsMenu(IMenu menu) {
  MenuInflater.Inflate(Resource.Menu.ActionBar, menu);

  var searchItem = menu.FindItem(Resource.Id.searchItem);
  var view = searchItem.ActionView.JavaCast<SearchView>();

  var manager = SearchManager.FromContext(this);
  var info = manager.GetSearchableInfo(ComponentName);

  view.SetSearchableInfo(info);

  return true;
}
```

How it works...

Most apps that provide collections of data need some way of searching through that data. This is not just adding a filter to a list, but rather searching for a piece of data across the entire app. For example, if we are making a social network app, we may want to search through the people, places, and events from a single location.

The first thing we need is an activity that will be responsible for responding to search requests. This activity is not special in any way, except that there should be some code that handles the search intent. Intents are used by Android to pass data between various apps and activities.

To do this, we check the `Action` property of the activity's `Intent` property. If we are searching from another activity, the `Intent` property can be read from the `OnCreate()` method. If we are searching from the search activity, the activity is not reconstructed, so we read the `Intent` property from the parameter in the `OnNewIntent()` method.

In order to obtain the search query from the `Intent` property, we use the `GetStringExtra()` method and pass in the `SearchManager.Query` value. This will return a string representing what the user requested.

 The search query is read out of the `Intent` property extras using the `SearchManager.Query` key.

Once we have the search activity set up, we need to add various attributes that describe how the activity will receive the search intent. We add an `[ActionFilter]` attribute, with a value of `ActionSearch` that lets Android know that we wish to receive the search intents. We also add a `[MetaData]` attribute that points to the configuration of the search activity. This configuration is a simple XML resource that describes various properties, such as the hint in the search box or whether voice search is enabled.

 The `[ActionFilter]` attributes are used to let the Android OS know which intents an app can receive and understand.

Xamarin.Android tries to avoid any possible naming conflicts when it merges all the types in the assemblies by hashing the generated namespaces. To avoid our search activity being lost with a random name, we use the `[Register]` attribute to give it a specific name.

Now that our search activity is complete, we need to let Android know which activities can make use of the search activity. This is done by adding a `[MetaData]` attribute to the various activities, passing in the full name of the search activity.

We can either attribute each activity to use the search activity or we can apply a global attribute for all activities. We can also use a combination of both, allowing us to override the global attribute for a specific activity.

If we want to start a search, we have several options depending on what version of Android we are targeting. We can make use of the search dialog or overlay for all versions of Android. This is simply requested by invoking the `OnSearchRequested()` method from any activity.

If we are targeting Android version 3.0 and later; we can make use of the `SearchView` option in the action bar. This also is available to the older versions of Android if we are using the support libraries.

 The new `SearchView` action bar item can be used in older Android versions through the support libraries.

When we inflate the action bar, we need to ensure that we attach the search configuration to the search view, as we did with the `[MetaData]` attribute on the search activity.

There's more...

If we are supporting Android versions 4.1 and later, we can integrate with Google Now. First, we add a new `[IntentFilter]` attribute to the search activity:

```
[IntentFilter(
   new[] { "com.google.android.gms.actions.SEARCH_ACTION" },
   Categories = new[] { Intent.CategoryDefault })]
```

Then, we need to extend our intent handling, such as in the `OnCreate()` method, to accept the new intent from Google Now:

```
if (intent.Action == Intent.ActionSearch ||
   intent.Action == "com.google.android.gms.actions.SEARCH_ACTION") {
      string query = intent.GetStringExtra(SearchManager.Query);
}
```

 Integrating with Google Now requires that the app support the additional intent.

In order to test if our integration with Google Now is working, we have to first publish our app to the Play Store. If we download our app and then search for something like: "Ok Google, search for <search query> in <app package name>".

However, if we wish to make sure that our app launches correctly, we can launch it from the command line using ADB:

```
adb shell am start -a com.google.android.gms.actions.SEARCH_ACTION -e query "<search query>" <app package name here>
```

5
Communicating with the Outside World

In this chapter, we will cover the following recipes:

- ▸ Consuming REST services with HttpClient
- ▸ Obtaining a network state
- ▸ Handling network state changes
- ▸ Using the `DownloadManager` element
- ▸ Accessing Bluetooth
- ▸ Transferring data via Bluetooth
- ▸ Receiving NFC events
- ▸ Writing NFC tags
- ▸ Transferring data via NFC
- ▸ Obtaining location coordinates and addresses

Introduction

Communication is one of the most important aspects of human existence. Everyone communicates with someone else at some point in their lives.

We as humans speak, write, draw, and move to send a message or convey some sort of message to someone else. Babies cry, children speak, and adults write to let someone else know what they are doing or what they want the other person to do.

Communication can be an instruction to do something, or it can be an expression of feelings. Communication can also be a means of sharing data or information.

Mobile apps are very similar to humans when it comes to communication, not because apps inherently want to share, but rather as a result of having a user. Users of the app want to share or communicate, and thus the app is designed to share or communicate.

Not only do users want to share data they have communicated with the rest of the world, such as through social media, they may also want to share data with a specific device. These devices may belong to another person or to the user themselves.

Information can be shared over the Internet using Wi-Fi or mobile data, and sharing is really only limited by the user's imagination. There are also various short range communication technologies in the world.

Bluetooth and **Near Field Communications** (**NFC**) are very common, whether to play sound over wireless speakers, or to identify an object. These forms of communication are often designed for one-on-one interactions, thus making them more personalized means of communication.

Consuming REST services with HttpClient

If we have an app that displays data, the chances are that it comes from somewhere outside the device, say somewhere like the Internet.

Getting ready

To work with JSON responses, we need to install the `Newtonsoft.Json` NuGet package or the `Json.NET` component. This is an advanced JSON parser; however, we can make use of the `DataContractJsonSerializer` type or any other serializer for JSON.

How to do it...

In order to obtain data from the Internet or a local network, we use HTTP requests. In this recipe, we access data from `http://jsonplaceholder.typicode.com/posts/1`:

1. Access JSON data from the HTTP location in the form:

```
{
  "userId": 1,
  "id": 1,
  "title": "sunt aut facere repellat provident occaecati",
  "body": "quia et suscipit\nsuscipit recusandae conse"
}
```

2. For any Internet communication, we need to request permission from Android:

```
[assembly: UsesPermission(Manifest.Permission.Internet)]
```

3. Then, to access the data from the remote source, we make use of `HttpClient` and the `GetStringAsync()` method:

```
using (var client = new HttpClient()) {
  var uri = "http://jsonplaceholder.typicode.com/posts/1";
  var result = await client.GetStringAsync(uri);
}
```

4. We can try and parse the result ourselves, or we could create a .NET type that will be used to deserialize it:

```
public class Post {
  public int Id { get; set; }
  public int UserId { get; set; }
  public string Title { get; set; }
  [JsonProperty("body")]
  public string Content { get; set; }
}
```

5. Now it is time to map the JSON string to the .NET type:

```
var post = JsonConvert.DeserializeObject<Post>(result);
```

If we want to send data to the server, we can do something similar, but instead of doing a GET, we do a POST to `http://jsonplaceholder.typicode.com/posts`:

1. First, we have to create our object that we want to send:

```
var newPost = new Post {
  UserId = 12,
  Title = "My First Post",
  Content = "This is some real deep stuff in here!"
};
```

2. Once we have our data, we must serialize it into JSON:

```
var jsonData = JsonConvert.SerializeObject(newPost);
```

3. After that, we need to create the HTTP content and header that we are going to send. Because we are sending JSON data, we specify the content type as `"application/json"`:

```
var content = new StringContent(
  jsonData, Encoding.UTF8, "application/json");
```

4. Finally, we send the serialized object:

```
var uri = "http://jsonplaceholder.typicode.com/posts";
var result = await client.PostAsync(uri, content);
```

Doing a POST will return a result from the server, which we use to determine whether everything went well:

1. We can use the `EnsureSuccessStatusCode()` method to throw an exception if there is a problem:

    ```
    result.EnsureSuccessStatusCode();
    ```

2. Or we can check the `IsSuccessStatusCode` property for a successful result:

    ```
    var success = result.IsSuccessStatusCode;
    ```

3. If there is data in the content of the response, we can read it out of the `Content` property:

    ```
    var resultString =
        await result.Content.ReadAsStringAsync();
    var post =
        JsonConvert.DeserializeObject<Post>(resultString);
    ```

How it works...

There are many ways for an app to communicate with the outside world. These include technologies used on the Internet, such as HTTP and FTP, as well as via more local technologies such as Bluetooth or NFC. However, one of the most common and most frequently used is HTTP.

HTTP is a way in which two devices can communicate, often through a network such as the Internet. Messages are sent out and received by a server. The server then responds with another message. Data can be transferred via HTTP and is used to provide data from a server to a local app, and vice versa.

 The `HttpClient` property provides a very simple and easy-to-use interface for sending and receiving data over HTTP or HTTPS.

If we want to send an HTTP message, we can make use of the `HttpClient` property provided by .NET. To request data from a server, all we have to do is request it via the `GetStringAsync()` method, passing the URI of the resource. There are other types that can be received easily, such as byte arrays via the `GetByteArrayAsync()` method or a `Stream` instance via the `GetStreamAsync()` method. If we want more control over how the request is sent and handled, we can use the `GetAsync()` method. We can then process the result of these methods using a serializer or parser.

If we want to send data to the server, we have several other methods such as the `PostAsync()` method or the `PutAsync()` method. These methods take both the URI and the content that needs to be sent. We typically use POST to send data to the server, but some servers handle PUT messages differently, which we may want. We may want the server to do something different when using PUT.

The content sent to the server is wrapped in an `HttpContent` type. This type contains the various headers as well as the actual body that we want to send to the server. Headers are used to describe the content as well as how to handle the request. A header can include the content type, content length, or any authorization requirements. The body is the data that we wish to send. The body could be anything, but in most cases, we would serialize the data and send it. We have to be sure that we send the data in a format that the server can understand, for example in XML or JSON.

 It is important that the HTTP content is in a format that is understood by the server, otherwise the response will be an error code.

Once the server has received our message, whether through GET or POST, it will respond with a code specifying whether there were errors or not. We can then use this code and respond to the user accordingly.

It is important to remember that sending data over the network is very slow compared to normal CPU operations. Thus, to avoid any app performance issues, we carry out network operations on a separate thread. This is very easy to do with the `async` and `await` keywords in C#. The compiler will automatically rewrite our code to start a new thread.

 Sending data over a network is slow and should be done on a separate thread.

As transferring data wirelessly requires battery, and possibly mobile data, it is important that we try and cache what we can. Caching will reduce the need for communication, thus reducing the load on the battery as well as the amount of data consumed.

Another battery-saving technique is prefetching. Prefetching requests data before it is actually needed to reduce the number of requests it has to make later. Each time the wireless controller is woken up, battery is consumed to restore the controller. If we bundle all our requests into a single request, the controller only has to be woken once instead of multiple times.

 Caching and prefetching can be used to reduce battery consumption and data usage as well as improve app performance.

See also

 ▸ The *Obtaining a network state* recipe
 ▸ The *Handling network state changes* recipe

Obtaining a network state

When we want to send or request data from a remote source, such as the Internet, we need to make sure that we can access the network.

How to do it...

In order to access the state of the network, we make use of the `ConnectivityManager` instance:

1. When we want to access the state of the network, we have to request permission from Android first:

    ```
    [assembly: UsesPermission(
      Manifest.Permission.AccessNetworkState)]
    ```

2. Now that we have permission, if we want the network state, we need to get hold of the `ConnectivityManager` instance through the static `FromContext()` method:

    ```
    var manager = ConnectivityManager.FromContext(this);
    ```

3. Once we have the manager, we can get hold of the current state:

    ```
    var networkInfo = manager.ActiveNetworkInfo;
    ```

4. If the info is `null`, then we have no connection at all, but if there is a connection, we can access various properties:

    ```
    if (networkInfo != null) {
      var isConnected = networkInfo.IsConnected;
      var type = networkInfo.Type;
      var subtype = networkInfo.Subtype;
    }
    ```

5. We can also request the state for a specific type connection, such as Wi-Fi:

    ```
    var wifiInfo =
    manager.GetNetworkInfo(ConnectivityType.Wifi);
    ```

6. Once we have the state, we can begin any network operations:

    ```
    if (networkInfo != null && networkInfo.IsConnected) {
      // begin download
    }
    ```

How it works...

Before we attempt to transfer data across a network, we should verify that the network is indeed available. This is especially so for mobile devices, as the user can disable the network at any time as well as go out of range of network points.

On Android, we use the `ConnectivityManager` instance to obtain network information such as the type of network and whether it is connected. Once we have the manager, we can obtain information about the current connection, if there is one, using the `ActiveNetworkInfo` property. This information allows us to make decisions on whether to actually try and communicate, or maybe wait until a more opportune time.

Obviously, we can only send data when the connection is available, trying to do so otherwise will result in an exception. If there is no connectivity, the client will attempt to send the data, but as it cannot locate the remote host, it will probably throw a `WebException` exception with a `Status` instance of `NameResolutionFailure`.

If we verify that the connection is available first, we can reduce the number of errors that the app has to deal with. If we do not first check for an available connection, we do need to be able to handle the exceptions that will be thrown when the connection fails.

 Sending data over a network that is unavailable will throw an exception. The network should be verified first or the exceptions caught and handled correctly.

Even if there is a connection available, we need to first check to see whether this request will cause problems for the user in other areas. For example, if the user is using mobile data, we should not download large files, and if we need to do so, it should be confirmed with the user.

We can control when requests are made, and we should ensure that our app can adjust according to the network type, speed, or limits. Data could be requested at a lower resolution, or less frequently, when there is a slower connection. When the connection is faster or has more bandwidth, we could prefetch data.

 Data requests made by the app should adjust according to the available connection.

There's more...

When we start a download, there may be an instance when the network goes down. We can subscribe to various events and then pause the download, instead of the app crashing. To do this, we register a `BroadcastReceiver()` method with the `ConnectivityAction` instance.

See also

▸ The *Consuming REST services with HttpClient* recipe

▸ The *Handling network state changes* recipe

Handling network state changes

If we are busy transferring data to or from our device, we need to respond appropriately if the network goes down or if it changes from Wi-Fi to mobile data for some reason.

How to do it...

In order to receive events from the ConnectivityManager instance, we register a BroadcastReceiver instance with the current activity or service:

1. When we want to access the state of the network, we have to request permission from Android first:

```
[assembly: UsesPermission(
   Manifest.Permission.AccessNetworkState)]
```

2. After obtaining permission, we create an instance of BroadcastReceiver that will handle network events:

```
private class NetworkReceiver : BroadcastReceiver {
   public override void OnReceive(
      Context context, Intent intent) {
   }
}
```

3. In the OnReceive() method, we handle the network events:

```
var manager = ConnectivityManager.FromContext(context);
var networkInfo = manager.ActiveNetworkInfo;
if (networkInfo != null && networkInfo.IsConnected) {
   // we are connected, so resume a download
}
else {
   // no connection, so pause the download
}
```

4. Once we have our receiver, we register it with the activity or service, filtering by the `ConnectivityAction` action intent:

```
var filter = new IntentFilter(
   ConnectivityManager.ConnectivityAction);
receiver = new NetworkReceiver();
RegisterReceiver(receiver, filter);
```

5. We also have to make sure that we unregister it when we no longer need it:

```
if (receiver != null) {
   UnregisterReceiver(receiver);
}
```

How it works...

Network connections are unstable and change frequently, especially on a mobile device where the device may have settings changed or physically moved around. The user may move out of range of a hotspot, run out of data, or move from one cell tower to another. Our app needs to handle these changes without impacting the user too much.

In order to handle system events such as network events, we use a `BroadcastReceiver` instance.

 Broadcast receivers are used by Android to send messages across apps.

Implementing a `BroadcastReceiver` instance is easy, all we have to do is implement the `OnReceive()` method. This method is invoked when the receiver gets a message from a source, such as from another app or the operating system.

If a broadcast is detected and matches the intent filter, the `OnReceive()` method is invoked on the broadcast receiver. When a broadcast is received, we can check the network state and then adjust our app accordingly.

The broadcast receiver can be registered with the `AndroidManifest.xml` file or at runtime. When we register the receiver in the manifest file, the app will receive incoming broadcasts even if it is not running. If we only need to respond when the app is in the foreground; it is better to register the receiver at runtime to reduce system load.

 Broadcast receivers can be registered with the `AndroidManifest.xml` file or at runtime.

Registering receivers at runtime is done by invoking the `RegisterReceiver()` method with an `IntentFilter` instance, and the `BroadcastReceiver` instance that will respond to the actions in that filter. When the system broadcasts the action, it will not only instantiate our receiver but will also invoke the `OnReceive()` method.

If we register a receiver at runtime, we need to be sure to unregister it when it is no longer in use. If we register it in the `OnResume()` method of the activity, we should unregister it in `OnPause`. We won't receive broadcasts when the app is paused, so unregistering it reduces unnecessary system overhead.

 If a receiver is registered when the activity is resumed, it should be unregistered when the app is paused to reduce system overhead.

There's more...

If our app does not need fine control over how a file is downloaded, we can make use of the `DownloadManager` instance. This provides a simple interface for managing downloads.

See also

▶ The *Obtaining a network state* recipe

▶ The *Using DownloadManager* recipe

Using DownloadManager

If we wish to download files or resources but do not need fine control over the actual download, we can hand the task over to the `DownloadManager` instance.

How to do it...

We can use the `DownloadManager` instance to initiate, cancel, and query downloads:

1. As with normal HTTP requests, we need to request permission to access the Internet:

   ```
   [assembly: UsesPermission(Manifest.Permission.Internet)]
   ```

2. Then, we get hold of `DownloadManager` so that we can work with it:

   ```
   var manager = DownloadManager.FromContext(this);
   ```

3. Once we have the manager, we can start downloads using the `Enqueue()` method with a `DownloadManager.Request` instance:

   ```
   var request = new DownloadManager.Request(Uri.Parse(uri));
   long downloadId = manager.Enqueue(request);
   ```

4. We can also specify whether we only want the download to progress on Wi-Fi, mobile data, or both by using the `DownloadNetwork` flags enumeration:

```
request.SetAllowedNetworkTypes(DownloadNetwork.Wifi);
```

5. If we want to cancel a download, we pass the download ID to the `Remove()` method:

```
var removed = manager.Remove(downloadId);
```

6. To obtain the progress or state of a download, we pass an instance of `DownloadManager.Query` to the `InvokeQuery()` method:

```
var query = new DownloadManager.Query();
query.SetFilterById(downloadId);
ICursor cursor = manager.InvokeQuery(query);
```

7. Once we have the cursor, we can query the result just as we would with a content provider:

```
if (cursor.MoveToFirst()) {
  var statusIndex = cursor.GetColumnIndex(
    DownloadManager.ColumnStatus);
  var soFarIndex = cursor.GetColumnIndex(
    DownloadManager.ColumnBytesDownloadedSoFar);
  var totalIndex = cursor.GetColumnIndex(
    DownloadManager.ColumnTotalSizeBytes);

  int status = (DownloadStatus)cursor.GetInt(statusIndex);
  double soFar = cursor.GetDouble(soFarIndex);
  double total = cursor.GetDouble(toitalIndex);
  string progress = (soFar / total).ToString("0.00 %");
}
```

If we want to be notified when the download is completed, is canceled, or fails, we register a `BroadcastReceiver` instance with the activity or service:

1. We need to create an instance of `BroadcastReceive` that will handle the download event:

```
private class DownloadReceiver : BroadcastReceiver {
  public override void OnReceive(
    Context context, Intent intent) {
    long downloadId = intent.GetLongExtra(
      DownloadManager.ExtraDownloadId, 0);
  }
}
```

2. Once we have the download ID, we can query the `DownloadManager` instance as we normally would:

```
var manager = DownloadManager.FromContext(context);
var query = new DownloadManager.Query();
query.SetFilterById(downloadId);
ICursor cursor = manager.InvokeQuery(query);
if (cursor.MoveToFirst()) {
  // handle the download
}
```

3. In order to register the receiver with the activity or service, we use the `RegisterReceiver()` method:

```
var filter = new IntentFilter(
  DownloadManager.ActionDownloadComplete);
receiver = new DownloadReceiver();
RegisterReceiver(receiver, filter);
```

4. And we must make sure that we unregister it when we no longer need it:

```
if (receiver != null) {
  UnregisterReceiver(receiver);
}
```

We can also display the Android Downloads app, if our app downloads files that can be accessed by the user directly:

1. If we want to open the native Downloads app, we use an `Intent` instance:

```
var intent = new Intent();
intent.SetAction(DownloadManager.ActionViewDownloads);
StartActivity(intent);
```

How it works...

If we have an app that downloads large files, we can use the `DownloadManager` instance. The `DownloadManager` instance is useful because it will manage our downloads for us, for example by retrying downloads after the network connection is lost or the device is restarted. It will also broadcast an action when the download is completed.

 The `DownloadManager` instance can be used to manage the download process, including the handling of network issues, and broadcast an action when it has completed.

Once we have the `DownloadManager` instance, we can start queuing up downloads using the `DownloadManager.Request` type and the `Enqueue()` method. The request is constructed with a URI, but can have several additional properties set.

We could set the download to be invisible to the user by passing `false` to the `SetVisibleInDownloadsUi()` method, or we can specify on which types of network the download can run via the `SetAllowedNetworkTypes()` method.

 Downloads can be hidden from the Downloads app as well as prevented from displaying progress notifications.

When a download is queued, the `Enqueue()` method will return an ID for the download. We can use the ID to find out the progress or state of the download. If we want to query the status of a download, we construct a `DownloadManager.Query` instance and set the filter via the `SetFilterById()` or `SetFilterByStatus()` methods.

Once we have a query, we can get results by invoking the `InvokeQuery()` method on the download manager. Similar to querying a `ContentProvider()` method, we will receive an `ICursor` instance that we can use. With the cursor, we read the progress, status, any errors, and paths associated with a download.

Information on a download is returned through an `ICursor` instance, similar to results from `ContentProvider`.

If we want to be notified when a download is complete, we can create a `BroadcastReceiver` instance that will respond to the `ActionDownloadComplete` broadcast. This broadcast will contain the ID of the download in the extras of the intent, which we can use to update our app.

See also

▸ The *Handling network state changes* recipe

Accessing Bluetooth

Data sometimes needs to be transferred to another device, but to one where there is no network infrastructure. We may therefore want to integrate Bluetooth into our app to transfer data or to interact with various devices that cannot be accessed via the Internet or a local network.

How to do it...

To interact with the various Bluetooth services, we need the `BluetoothAdapter` instance:

1. As with most hardware services, we need to request permission to access Bluetooth:

```
[assembly: UsesPermission(Manifest.Permission.Bluetooth)]
```

2. If we want to directly control the Bluetooth hardware, we need to specify an additional permission:

```
[assembly: UsesPermission(
   Manifest.Permission.BluetoothAdmin)]
```

3. Once we have the permissions we need, we obtain the `BluetoothAdapter` instance:

```
var bluetooth = BluetoothAdapter.DefaultAdapter;
if (bluetooth == null) {
  // device does not support Bluetooth
}
else {
  State state = bluetooth.State;
}
```

4. If Bluetooth is not enabled, we can request the user to enable it:

```
const string RequestToEnableBluetooth = 1; // any ID
if (!bluetooth.IsEnabled) {
  var intent = new Intent(
    BluetoothAdapter.ActionRequestEnable);
  StartActivityForResult(intent, RequestToEnableBluetooth);
}
```

5. Once the Bluetooth activity has started and finished, we will get a callback to the `OnActivityResult()` method:

```
protected override void OnActivityResult(
  int requestCode, Result resultCode, Intent data) {
    base.OnActivityResult(requestCode, resultCode, data);
    if (requestCode == RequestToEnableBluetooth) {
    bool success = resultCode == Result.Ok;
  }
}
```

6. Once we have Bluetooth enabled, there are several things we can do with the adapter, such as getting a list of paired devices:

```
var pairedDevices = bluetooth.BondedDevices;
foreach (var device in pairedDevices) {
  var name = device.Name;
}
```

7. We can also start listening for new Bluetooth devices:

```
bool started = bluetooth.StartDiscovery();
```

8. Once we have a device that we want, we can stop listening:

```
if (bluetooth.IsDiscovering) {
  bool canceled = bluetooth.CancelDiscovery();
}
```

9. If we want to make this device discoverable to other devices, we can request it for a specified time interval:

```
int interval = 300; // seconds
var intent = new Intent(
  BluetoothAdapter.ActionRequestDiscoverable);
intent.PutExtra(
  BluetoothAdapter.ExtraDiscoverableDuration,
  interval);
StartActivity(intent);
```

If we want to listen for changes to the Bluetooth state or to be notified when a new device is found, we register a broadcast receiver with the activity or service:

1. For this, we need the receiver that will handle events that we are interested in:

```
private class BluetoothReceiver : BroadcastReceiver {
  public override void OnReceive(
    Context context, Intent intent) {
    string action = intent.Action;
    if (action == BluetoothAdapter.ActionStateChanged) {
      var newState = (State)intent.GetIntExtra(
        BluetoothAdapter.ExtraState, 0);
    }
    if (action == BluetoothAdapter.ActionScanModeChanged) {
      var newScanMode = (ScanMode)intent.GetIntExtra(
        BluetoothAdapter.ExtraScanMode, 0);
    }
    if (action == BluetoothDevice.ActionFound) {
```

```
        var newDevice = intent.GetParcelableExtra(
          BluetoothDevice.ExtraDevice) as BluetoothDevice;
      }
    }
  }
```

2. We can then register the receiver for each action we are interested in:

```
receiver = new BluetoothReceiver();
RegisterReceiver(receiver,
  new IntentFilter(BluetoothAdapter.ActionStateChanged));
RegisterReceiver(receiver,
  new IntentFilter(BluetoothAdapter.ActionScanModeChanged));
RegisterReceiver(receiver,
  new IntentFilter(BluetoothDevice.ActionFound));
```

3. Finally, we have to be sure to unregister it when we no longer need it:

```
if (receiver != null) {
  UnregisterReceiver (receiver);
}
```

How it works...

Bluetooth is a wireless technology for transmitting and receiving data over short distances. There are three classes of Bluetooth radios, each with a different range. Typically, Class 3 radios have a very short range of less than one meter, Class 2 radios have a range of 10 meters, and Class 3 radios about 100 meters.

More information on how Bluetooth works can be found on the official Bluetooth website: `http://www.bluetooth.com/Pages/Basics.aspx`.

We can use the Android Bluetooth API to scan for and connect to other Bluetooth devices, as well as to send data to other devices. But before we start using the Bluetooth adapter, we need to request permission to do so from Android.

 In order to control the Bluetooth adapter, we need admin permission.

If we want to interact with the Bluetooth adapter, we need to obtain the current adapter by using the `DefaultAdapter` property on the `BluetoothAdapter` type. We need to first verify that there is a Bluetooth adapter, and if there is one, that it is enabled.

We can request that the user enable the adapter by starting an activity with the `ActionRequestEnable` action intent. This will display a popup requesting permission for the app to enable Bluetooth.

Once we have the adapter, we can view the paired devices as well as scan for other devices. We use the `StartDiscovery()` method to scan for devices, and we make the device discoverable using the `ActionRequestDiscoverable` action intent.

A device will only be discovered by other devices if that device has been made discoverable. Before scanning for devices, it may be worth querying the collection of paired devices to see if the device is already known.

 A device may already be known, so querying the collection of paired devices may be more advantageous than starting the discovery scan.

When we want to discover other devices, we initiate the scan with the `StartDiscovery()` method and then listen for an `ActionFound` action intent using a broadcast receiver. The scan interval is usually short, around 12 seconds.

We can also make the device discoverable by starting an activity with the `ActionRequestDiscoverable` action intent. A device can be made discoverable for a slightly longer period than a scan. A value between 0 and 3,600 seconds can be specified by the `ExtraDiscoverableDuration` intent extra. By default, and for any value outside those bounds, the device will become discoverable for 120 seconds.

Similar to listening for network state changes, we can listen for events from the Bluetooth adapter. We are able to listen to several events, including when the Bluetooth state has changed, when the scan mode has changed, or when a new device has been discovered. In each type of broadcast, we can access the relevant information in the extras of the intent.

There's more...

In addition to normal Bluetooth, the device may also support **Bluetooth Low Energy** (**BLE**). BLE is available on Android versions 4.3 and above, and has lower power consumption compared to classic Bluetooth. BLE is used for devices that have low power requirements such as proximity sensors or health and fitness monitors.

To check to see if a device has BLE, we can ask the `PackageManager` instance:

```
bool hasBLE = PackageManager.HasSystemFeature(
    PackageManager.FeatureBluetoothLe);
```

Once we have determined that the device supports BLE, we can then use slightly different mechanisms to scan, connect, and communicate. Instead of `StartDiscovery`, we would invoke `StartLeScan`, and instead of the usual RFCOMM channel, we connect to a GATT server.

See also

▸ The *Obtaining network state changes* recipe

▸ The *Transferring data via Bluetooth* recipe

▸ The *Receiving NFC events* recipe

Transferring data via Bluetooth

We can transfer data to another device directly without having to use the Internet or any network infrastructure outside another device. Bluetooth allows one device to directly communicate with another device.

How to do it...

We can set up our app to listen for Bluetooth devices that we can communicate with:

1. As with normal Bluetooth access, we need to have the apropriate permissions, such as `Bluetooth` and `BluetoothAdmin`, before we can transmit data via Bluetooth:

```
[assembly: UsesPermission(Manifest.Permission.Bluetooth)]
[assembly: UsesPermission(Manifest.Permission.BluetoothAdmin)]
```

2. Before we start the listener, we need to have a name that will be used to register it with the system:

```
const string ServiceName = "XamarinCookbookBluetooth";
```

3. Before two apps can communicate, they need to know about each other. This is achieved by providing a generated UUID that will be used by both devices:

```
const string Uuid = "25c0d296-0e78-4849-b70b-86f01f415add";
```

4. We start the listener with the `ListenUsingRfcommWithServiceRecord()` method on the Bluetooth adapter, passing the service registration name and the UUID for this app:

```
BluetoothServerSocket serverSocket = null;
BluetoothSocket serverClientSocket = null;
try {
  serverSocket =
    bluetooth.ListenUsingRfcommWithServiceRecord(
      ServiceName, UUID.FromString(Uuid));
  while (serverClientSocket == null) {
    serverClientSocket = await serverSocket.AcceptAsync();
  }
}
```

```
catch (IOException ex) {
  // there was an error, such as no devices found
}
```

5. Once a device is found, we can stop the listener and get hold of the communication streams:

```
if (serverClientSocket != null) {
  serverSocket.Close();
  var device = serverClientSocket.RemoteDevice;
  try {
    inputStream = socket.InputStream;
    outputStream = socket.OutputStream;
  }
  catch (IOException ex) {
    // handle errors
  }
}
```

Setting up the app to connect to another device that is listening is much the same, except we request to connect to a specific device:

1. First, we need to get hold of the device we wish to connect to:

```
BluetoothDevice paired = bluetooth.BondedDevices.First();
```

2. Before we try and connect, we must make sure to cancel any discovery, as this slows down the connection and we already have a device:

```
bluetooth.CancelDiscovery();
```

3. Then we request a connection, providing the specific UUID for the app we wish to talk to:

```
BluetoothSocket clientSocket = null;
clientSocket = paired.CreateRfcommSocketToServiceRecord(
  UUID.FromString(Uuid));
await clientSocket.ConnectAsync();
```

4. Once a device is connected, we can get hold of the communication streams, just like the server did:

```
try {
  inputStream = clientSocket.InputStream;
  outputStream = clientSocket.OutputStream;
}
catch (IOException ex) {
  // handle errors
}
```

On both the server listener and the client, we can transfer data back and forth using the two streams:

1. We can start reading the data off the input stream:

```
byte[] bytes = new byte[1024];
while (true) {
  try {
    var size = await inputStream.ReadAsync(
      bytes, 0, bytes.Length);
    var stringRead = Encoding.UTF8.GetString(
      bytes, 0, size);
  }
  catch (IOException ex) {
    // handle errors
  }
}
```

2. To send data, we just write to the output stream:

```
var stringToSend = "Hello World!";
var bytes = Encoding.UTF8.GetBytes(stringToSend);
try {
  await outputStream.WriteAsync(bytes, 0, bytes.Length);
}
catch (IOException ex) {
  // handle errors
}
```

How it works...

In order to send data from one device to another, both devices need to have an open stream. One device will send data, and the other will listen for incoming data. Also, both devices need to use an UUID that represents the connection from the client. The server listens for an incoming connection with a particular UUID and then accepts it, if it is the expected one.

The UUID is app-specific in that it is controlled by the app. Some apps may randomly generate UUIDs each time, and others may have a hardcoded value. This UUID can be randomly generated by the app, or specified by some other source, such as a new UUID for each major app version.

 In order to connect two devices, both the server and the client need to use the same UUID while connecting.

More information on how Bluetooth actually transfers data can be found on the official Bluetooth website: `http://www.bluetooth.com/Pages/How-It-Works.aspx`.

The server, or the listener, starts listening for incoming connections via the `ListenUsingRfcommWithServiceRecord()` method on the Bluetooth adapter. This method returns a `BluetoothServerSocket` with which we try and accept an incoming connection using the `AcceptAsync()` method. As soon as an incoming client connection is accepted, the method returns a `BluetoothSocket` instance, which represents an open connection.

Once we have an open connection to the client, we can stop listening for more connections by invoking the `Close()` method on the `BluetoothServerSocket` instance. We can then query the open client connection for the device by using the `RemoteDevice` property as well as get the communication streams.

The connection has two streams, one for incoming data, from the `InputStream` property, and one for outgoing data, from the `OutputStream` property. Both are basic `Stream` types that support byte-based communication.

> Before connecting to a server, the client should cancel any ongoing device discovery as it may negatively impact connection performance.

If we want to connect to a listening server, we first need a device to which we want to connect. Once we have the device, either after a discovery or from an existing pair, we invoke the `CreateRfcommSocketToServiceRecord()` method on the `BluetoothDevice` instance. This method returns a `BluetoothSocket` instance, which represents a connection to the server. In order to start communicating, we have to open the connection using the `ConnectAsync()` method.

Once the connection to the server is opened, we can obtain the two streams just as we did with the server. Again, the `InputStream` instance represents the incoming data channel and the `OutputStream` represents the outgoing data channel.

> Reading from and writing to the Bluetooth streams involves only the usual .NET stream operations, either directly or through a serializer.

Reading data from the input stream is simply a matter of continuously reading the data out of the `InputStream` instance. To do this, we can invoke the `ReadAsync()` method, with a buffer, and wait for a response. As soon as enough data is read, either when the buffer is full or when there is no more to read, the method will return with the number of bytes read. We can then convert those bytes into a stream. We could also read the data using a `Stream` instance by passing the actual stream to a deserializer or any reader that accepts a `Stream` instance such as `XDocument.Load()`.

Sending data to the other device is simply a matter of writing bytes to the `OutputStream` instance. We could write directly using the `WriteAsync()` method or we could use a serializer, such as `XDocument.Save()`, which accepts a `Stream` instance.

There's more...

Just as we can communicate via Bluetooth, we can communicate via NFC, which is a shorter range communication technology.

See also

▶   The *Accessing Bluetooth* recipe

▶   The *Sending data via NFC* recipe

Receiving NFC events

Sometimes we may wish to make use of NFC, a very short range communication technology, to transfer data or to interact with NFC tags.

Getting ready

To develop for NFC, we need to have a device that includes NFC hardware.

How to do it...

We can query the `NfcAdapter` instance for the status of the hardware as well as to be notified when a new tag is detected:

1. As with the other hardware features, we need permission to access NFC services:

    ```
    [assembly: UsesPermission(Manifest.Permission.Nfc)]
    ```

2. Additionally, we need to specify that we are going to be using the NFC device feature. If our app cannot run without NFC, we set the `Required` property to `true`:

    ```
    [assembly: UsesFeature(
      PackageManager.FeatureNfc, Required = true)]
    ```

    However, if our app runs fine on a device without NFC, we set the `Required` property to `false`:

    ```
    [assembly: UsesFeature(
      PackageManager.FeatureNfc, Required = false)]
    ```

3. Now that we have permission, we can get the `NfcAdapter` instance:

```
adapter = NfcAdapter.GetDefaultAdapter(this);
```

4. If NFC is enabled and the app is in the foreground, we can start listening for NFC events using the `EnableForegroundDispatch()` method:

```
if (adapter != null && adapter.IsEnabled) {
  var tagDetected = new IntentFilter(
    NfcAdapter.ActionTagDiscovered);
  var pendingIntent = PendingIntent.GetActivity(
    this, 0, new Intent(this, GetType()), 0);
  adapter.EnableForegroundDispatch(
    this, pendingIntent, new[]{ tagDetected }, null);
}
```

5. When the app goes into the background, we need to disable the listener:

```
adapter.DisableForegroundDispatch(this);
```

6. As soon as the device detects an NFC device or tag, it will notify our app via the `OnNewIntent()` method. We will receive the type of technology detected via the `Tag` extra:

```
protected override void OnNewIntent(Intent intent) {
  var tag = intent.GetParcelableExtra(
    NfcAdapter.ExtraTag) as Tag;
  if (tag != null) {
    string[] techs = tag.GetTechList();
  }
}
```

7. We can access the actual data in the tag or device message via the `NdefMessages` extra:

```
var ndefMessages = intent.GetParcelableArrayExtra(
  NfcAdapter.ExtraNdefMessages);
if (ndefMessages != null) {
  foreach (var msg in ndefMessages.Cast<NdefMessage>()) {
    foreach (var record in msg.GetRecords()) {
      byte[] typeBytes = record.GetTypeInfo();
      byte[] payloadBytes = record.GetPayload()
      var type = Encoding.UTF8.GetString(typeBytes);
      var payload = Encoding.UTF8.GetString(payloadBytes);
    }
  }
}
```

How it works...

Like Bluetooth, NFC is a wireless communication technology for use over short distances. However, in the case of NFC, the distance is less than 10 centimeters. Unlike Bluetooth, which uses radio transmissions, NFC uses electromagnetic radio fields to communicate. More information on NFC and how it works can be found on the official NFC website: `http://www.nearfieldcommunication.org`.

We can use the Android NFC API to do several things, including reading or writing to passive tags and communicating with other devices.

Like any other hardware feature we want to use, we have to request permission to do so. There is the usual NFC permission that we need to request as well as an additional feature that we have to specify. The feature is used by the package manager to let the store know that we may require a device that supports NFC. The feature can be set to `required` or `optional`.

 If an app specifies that the NFC feature is optional, it has to support devices without NFC hardware.

Before we can interact via NFC, we have to obtain the `NfcAdapter` instance from the current context. Once we have the adapter, we start listening for NFC tags or devices using the `EnableForegroundDispatch()` method. We provide the `ActionTagDiscovered` action filter to this method and a `PendingIntent` instance that holds an `Intent` instance to return to our activity. We could specify any activity here.

Once the listener is started, we need to make sure we stop it as soon as the app leaves the foreground; otherwise, an exception will be thrown. We can cancel the NFC listener by invoking the `DisableForegroundDispatch()` method.

 We start listening for NFC when the activity is in the foreground, and we stop listening when the activity is paused.

Because we specified that the listener should return to our activity, the `OnNewIntent()` method is invoked, along with the `Intent` instance we specified in the `PendingIntent` instance, as soon as a tag is detected.

 The `Intent` instance contains extras describing the NFC tag, including the technologies and the messages embedded within.

The `Intent` instance will contain the NFC extras that we can use to read the tags and message. If we request the `ExtraTag` extra from the intent, we will obtain the `Tag` instance that initiated the event. We can use this `Tag` instance to read various details out as well as to write to the tag.

We can also read any of the messages stored in the tag using the `ExtraNdefMessages` extra. This extra is an array of `NdefMessage` types, each of which contains one or more `NdefRecord` types. On each record, we can get type information, such as the MIME type, from the `GetTypeInfo()` method. We can also get the actual payload using the `GetPayload()` method.

There's more...

Some tags support being written to, and we can do this by creating `NdefMessage` and `NdefRecord` instances. We can also use these messages to send data to another device.

See also

- ▸ The *Accessing Bluetooth* recipe
- ▸ The *Writing NFC tags* recipe
- ▸ The *Transferring data via NFC* recipe

Writing NFC tags

We can use NFC tags for many things, such as storing tiny amounts of data, typically ranging from a few bytes to a few megabytes, or using it to interact with other devices.

How to do it...

If we want to write to a tag, we need to obtain the tag and create a message to write:

1. In order to write to a `Tag` instance, we need to start listening for NFC tags:

```
var adapter = NfcAdapter.GetDefaultAdapter(this);
if (adapter != null && adapter.IsEnabled) {
  var tagDetected = new IntentFilter(
    NfcAdapter.ActionTagDiscovered);
  var pendingIntent = PendingIntent.GetActivity(
    this, 0, new Intent(this, GetType()), 0);
  adapter.EnableForegroundDispatch(
    this, pendingIntent, new[]{ tagDetected }, null);
}
```

2. Once the listener has started, we can wait for the tag to be discovered and passed to the `OnNewIntent()` method:

```
protected override void OnNewIntent(Intent intent) {
  var tag = intent.GetParcelableExtra(
    NfcAdapter.ExtraTag) as Tag;
}
```

3. Once we have obtained the `Tag` instance from the extras in the `OnNewIntent()` method, we can start writing by creating the message. In this case, a custom data tag will be created for our custom MIME type:

```
var payload = Encoding.UTF8.GetBytes("Xamarin Cookbook!");
string mimeType =
"application/vnd.xamarincoockbook.nfcrecipe";
var mimeBytes = Encoding.UTF8.GetBytes(mimeType);
var record = new NdefRecord(
  NdefRecord.TnfMimeMedia,
  mimeBytes,
  new byte[0],
  payload);
var message = new NdefMessage(new[] { record });
```

4. Now that we have our message, we can attempt to write to the tag:

```
var ndef = Ndef.Get(tag);
await ndef.ConnectAsync();
await ndef.WriteNdefMessageAsync(message);
ndef.Close();
```

5. If this fails for some reason, it could be that the tag is not formatted, so we can try formatting the tag with the message:

```
var format = NdefFormatable.Get(tag);
await format.ConnectAsync();
await format.FormatAsync(message);
format.Close();
```

How it works...

NFC tags can be read by Android and can perform many actions such as opening apps, changing settings, or starting services. NFC tags require no power as the radio is powered solely by the RF field of the device. Not only do they not require power, but passive NFC tags are tiny, lightweight, and paper thin.

NFC tags can be written using a special format, NDEF messages, or custom formats. Android has the best support for tags written in the NDEF format. NDEF data is encapsulated inside a message, an `NdefMessage` instance, which contains one or more records, `NdefRecord`. Each record must be formed according to the type of record we want to create.

 The same NDEF messages used to write to a tag can be used to send data to another device.

Each message can have multiple records, but the first record is used to determine how to interpret all the records. Thus, the first record should contain several fields:

- **Type Name Format** (**TNF**), which describes how to interpret the `Variable Length Type` field, which could be a URI, a custom type, or a well-known type.

- **Type**, which describes the type of record. If the tag is marked as a well-known type, this field is used to specify the **Record Type Definition** (**RTD**) such as URI or text.

- **ID**, which provides a unique identifier for the tag itself.

- **Payload**, which contains the actual data of the tag.

Once we have created a properly formatted NDEF message, we can write it to the tag. In order to do this, we have to first obtain the `Ndef` instance from a tag. The `Ndef` instance provides access to NDEF content and operations.

With the `Ndef` instance, we can start writing to the tag. Before we start, we have to open a connection. To do this, we invoke the `ConnectAsync` method. After the connection is opened, we can write the data to the tag using the `WriteNdefMessageAsync` method. When writing has completed, we need to close the connection in order to free up any resources that may have been used. This is done via the `Close` method.

If, for some reason, the write fails, it may be due to the fact that the tag itself is incorrectly formatted. If this is the case, we can format the tag with our message. As with writing a tag, we need to obtain the formatter, the `NdefFomatable` type, from the tag.

Once we have the formatter, we can perform operations on the tag. As with the write process, we have to connect to the tag using `ConnectAsync`. Then, instead of writing, we format the tag via the `FormatAsync` method. Once the format has completed, we must close the connection to the tag with the `Close` method.

 Regardless of whether the tag is being written to or formatted, the connection needs to be opened before operations are performed and then closed after operations have completed.

There's more...

If our app is targeted at Android version 4.0 and above, we can write tags to launch other apps. To do this, we write a special type of `NdefRecord` instance to the tag, an Android Application Record:

```
NdefRecord.CreateApplicationRecord("com.xamarincookbook.example");
```

When a tag is scanned with this record, Android will try and launch the app. If the app is not installed, Android will open the Play Store at the app's page.

See also

▶ The *Receiving NFC events* recipe

▶ The *Transferring data via NFC* recipe

Transferring data via NFC

Chunks of data can be transferred from one device to another with NFC, using the same messages used when writing to tags.

How to do it...

If we want to send messages from a device, we need to register a message with the NFC push system. We could create a custom message, as in the previous recipe, but here we will just send an HTTP URI to another device:

1. If we are targeting Android version 2.3 and above, we need to manually create the correct NDEF message payload:

```
byte httpType = 0x01; // 'http://www.'
var theUri = Encoding.UTF8.GetBytes("xamarin.com");
var payload = new byte[theUri.Length + 1];
payload[0] = httpType;
Array.Copy(theUri, 0, payload, 1, theUri.Length);
```

2. Once we have the payload, we create the message:

```
var record = new NdefRecord(
  NdefRecord.TnfWellKnown,
  NdefRecord.RtdUri.ToArray(),
  new byte[0],
  payload);
var message = new NdefMessage(new[] { record });
```

3. If we are targeting Android version 4.0 and above, it is far easier to create the record:

```
var uri = "http://www.xamarin.com";
var record = NdefRecord.CreateUri(uri);
var message = new NdefMessage(new[] { record });
```

Now that we have the message, we need to let Android know that it needs to send it:

1. If we are targeting Android version 2.3 and above, we have to register the message with the NFC adapter when the app is in the foreground:

```
adapter.EnableForegroundNdefPush(this, message);
```

2. When the app leaves the foreground, we need to disable it:

```
adapter.DisableForegroundNdefPush(this);
```

3. Android version 4.0 and above does things a bit differently. We set the message once and let Android take over:

```
adapter.SetNdefPushMessage(message, this);
```

4. If we want the message to be more dynamic, we can create the message on the fly using the `NfcAdapter.ICreateNdefMessageCallback` interface on our activity:

```
public class MainActivity : Activity,
  NfcAdapter.ICreateNdefMessageCallback
{
  public NdefMessage CreateNdefMessage(NfcEvent e)
  {
    var message = ...
    return message;
  }
}
```

5. We then register this with the adapter as well:

```
adapter.SetNdefPushMessageCallback(this, this);
```

6. We can also be notified when the app has sent a message through the `NfcAdapter.IOnNdefPushCompleteCallback` interface:

```
public class MainActivity : Activity,
  NfcAdapter.ICreateNdefMessageCallback
{
  public void OnNdefPushComplete(NfcEvent e)
  {
    // message sent
  }
}
```

7. Finally, we register this with the adapter:

```
adapter.SetOnNdefPushCompleteCallback(this, this);
```

How it works...

Sending data to another device using NFC is a two-step process: first, we create the message, and then we register the message with the NFC adapter. This very simply makes the device an NFC tag that can be read by another device.

The way we register a message was changed in Android version 4.0 from a manual process to one that is more automatic. If we are targeting Android version 2.3, we need to register the message with the NFC adapter by using the `EnableForegroundNdefPush()` method. If we are targeting Android version 4.0 and above, we use the `SetNdefPushMessage()` method.

Messages can only be sent from an app when the app is in the foreground. If the app is paused, the message is removed (manually for Android version 2.3 and below and automatically for Android version 4.0 and above). To manually remove the message on Android version 2.3, we use the `DisableForegroundNdefPush()` method.

Android version 4.0 also introduces several other enhancements in the form of callbacks. If we want our message to be created at the time the data is to be transferred, we register a type that implements the `NfcAdapter.ICreateNdefMessageCallback` interface with the adapter. This is done instead of using the `SetNdefPushMessage()` method. When the message is needed, the `CreateNdefMessage()` method is invoked and we return the message we want to transmit to the other device.

There is also a callback for when the message has been transferred. Similarly, we register a type that implements the `NfcAdapter.IOnNdefPushCompleteCallback` interface using the `SetOnNdefPushCompleteCallback` method. When the message has been sent, the `OnNdefPushComplete()` method is invoked.

For both callbacks, we can just implement the interfaces on the actual activity. This allows us to easily handle NFC operations.

Obtaining location coordinates and addresses

Many devices have the ability for us to obtain the location of the user in a very precise manner. Android provides a few means to access the location, including using the network or using **Global Positioning System** (**GPS**).

How to do it...

If we are designing an app that requires the user's location, such as finding things nearby, we can use `LocationManager` to get the user's current location:

1. If we are only interested in using the network provider, we only need to ask for permission to use coarse location:

    ```
    [assembly: UsesPermission(
        Manifest.Permission.AccessCoarseLocation)]
    ```

2. If we want to use GPS, we need to use the fine location permission instead:

```
[assembly: UsesPermission(
  Manifest.Permission.AccessFineLocation)]
```

3. Once we have permission for location requests, we need to get `LocationManager`:

```
manager = LocationManager.FromContext(this);
```

4. We can check to see whether a specific provider, such as GPS, is enabled:

```
manager.IsProviderEnabled(
  LocationManager.GpsProvider);
```

5. We can also take the user to the settings in order to enable the location services:

```
var intent = new Intent(
  Settings.ActionLocationSourceSettings);
StartActivity(intent);
```

6. Before we start requesting new locations, we can use the cached location:

```
var cached = manager.GetLastKnownLocation(
  LocationManager.GpsProvider);
```

7. We need to provide a destination for the location results when requesting the location, so we implement the `ILocationListener` interface:

```
public class MainActivity : Activity, ILocationListener
{
  public void OnLocationChanged(Location location)
  {
  }
  public void OnProviderDisabled(string provider)
  {
  }
  public void OnProviderEnabled(string provider)
  {
  }
  public void OnStatusChanged(
    string provider,
    Availability availability,
    Bundle extras)
  {
  }
}
```

8. Once we receive a location, the `OnLocationChanged` method will be invoked and we can access the various location properties:

```
double latitude = location.Latitude;
double longitude = location.Longitude;
```

9. Once we have implemented the interface, we can start requesting updates. If our app only requires a single location request, such as to just get a one-off location, we can use the `RequestSingleUpdate` method:

```
manager.RequestSingleUpdate(
   LocationManager.GpsProvider, this, null);
```

10. We can also register for a continuous stream of updates using the `RequestLocationUpdates` method:

```
manager.RequestLocationUpdates(
   LocationManager.GpsProvider, 0, 0, this);
```

11. We can also request to get updates from multiple providers at the same time:

```
manager.RequestLocationUpdates(
   LocationManager.NetworkProvider, 0, 0, this);
```

12. We can then find the best location provider to use:

```
var criteria = new Criteria();
var provider = manager.GetBestProvider(criteria, false);
```

13. No matter how we register for updates, we can stop listening as well:

```
manager.RemoveUpdates(this);
```

We can also work backwards. If we have location coordinates, we can request information about what is at that location using the `Geocoder` instance:

1. Before we start making requests, we need to be sure that `Geocoder` is available on the device:

```
var isPresent = Geocoder.IsPresent;
```

2. If `Geocoder` is available, we can make a request based on latitude, longitude, and the number of results that we want by using the `GetFromLocationAsync()` method:

```
var geocoder = new Geocoder(this);
var resultCount = 1;
var addresses = await geocoder.GetFromLocationAsync(
   currentLocation.Latitude,
   currentLocation.Longitude,
   resultCount);
```

3. This method returns a collection of `Address` objects that represent places at the given coordinates:

```
Address address = addresses.FirstOrDefault();
StringBuilder builder = new StringBuilder();
for (int i = 0; i < address.MaxAddressLineIndex; i++) {
   var line = address.GetAddressLine(i);
   if (!string.IsNullOrWhiteSpace(line))
      builder.AppendLine(line);
}
string addressLines = builder.ToString();
```

4. As well as requesting the address lines, we can obtain various bits of information directly:

```
string houseNumber = address.SubThroughfare;
string roadName = address.Throughfare;
string suburb = address.SubLocality;
string city = address.Locality;
```

How it works...

`LocationManager` provides a uniform way to access a device's physical location from various providers such as cell towers, Wi-Fi, GPS data from other apps and services, and the GPS device itself. Different providers provide varying degrees of accuracy as well as differing power requirements.

GPS is the most accurate but also requires the most power. The network provider, which uses the cell towers and Wi-Fi, is less accurate but requires less power. Less accurate providers can be used if the app does not require a constant stream of updates or needs to consume minimal battery.

In order to access the location services, we need to ask for permission. There are two levels of permissions, fine and coarse. Fine location permission is required for the GPS provider and the passive provider, which uses GPS data collected by other apps. Coarse location permission is used when using the cellular and Wi-Fi location data.

Before requesting location data, we need to be sure that the provider is available and is enabled. We can request that the user enable certain providers if it is needed. Enabling location services can be achieved by showing the settings activity.

When listening for location data, we subscribe to the updates with an interface. In order to catch the updates, we implement the `OnLocationChanged()` method. This method will be invoked each time there is a new location from one of the location providers. The `Location` parameter contains several properties which we can use to determine the coordinates and many other location attributes as well as the accuracy and time of the particular result.

We can request updates in two ways: as a single response or as a continuous stream of new location updates. If our app only requires the location once-off or infrequently, we can use the `RequestSingleUpdate()` method. This will only request a single location result. If we need a stream of updates, we use the `RequestLocationUpdates()` method.

Both methods require a provider to use when requesting updates. We can request updates from multiple providers using the same receiver as each new location will contain details on where the update came from.

If we are requesting a single update, we supply the provider, the callback, and the thread we wish to invoke the callback on. If we want to use the current thread, we pass `null`. Similarly, when requesting a stream of updates, we provide the same parameters, but with an additional two. The first additional parameter specifies how frequently, in milliseconds, to request a new update; passing a zero will return them as fast as possible. The second specifies how far, in meters, the device needs to have moved before updating the location.

If we want to find out what provider is the best available, we can pass an instance of `Criteria` to the `GetBestProvider()` method. This method tries to find the best provider that matches the given criteria, excluding those that the app does not have permission for. We can also specify what the criteria are for selecting a provider using the various properties on the `Criteria` type. Some of these properties include `Accuracy` and `Power` as well as `AltitudeRequired` and `SpeedRequired`.

Once we have the location we need or want to cancel updates, we can use the `RemoveUpdates` method to stop listening on a particular `ILocationListener` instance.

We can get an accurate location from the sensors, but sometimes we need to get some idea of what addresses are at or near that location. To do this, we use `Geocoder`.

`Geocoder` can provide a collection of `Address` types that represent the physical addresses that are found near the provided location. There are two ways which we can request addresses: by specific location coordinates using the `GetFromLocationAsync()` method or by a string location name using `GetFromLocationNameAsync()`.

There's more...

Android provides an additional location provider through Google Play Services: Fused Location Provider is an optional alternative to the standard Android Location Service that automatically handles changes in provider status inside our app. It selects the best provider at any given moment. It also provides the ability to create location-aware apps that use geo-fencing.

More information on using Fused Location Provider can be found at: `http://developer.xamarin.com/guides/android/platform_features/maps_and_location/location/`.

We can also embed a map directly into our app. This can be used to provide a visual representation of the device's location as well as enable us to place markers on the map showing the locations of various objects.

More information on including maps in an app can be found at: `http://developer.xamarin.com/guides/android/platform_features/maps_and_location/maps/part_2_-_maps_api`.

One of the requirements for using an embedded map is that we need a Google Maps API key. More information on how to obtain one for our app can be found at: `http://developer.xamarin.com/guides/android/platform_features/maps_and_location/maps/obtaining_a_google_maps_api_key/`.

6
Using Background Tasks

In this chapter, we will cover the following recipes:

- ▶ Asynchronous tasks
- ▶ Starting services
- ▶ Stopping services
- ▶ Handling simultaneous service requests
- ▶ Starting services automatically
- ▶ Communicating with running services
- ▶ Critical tasks

Introduction

Multitasking is what computers do, and they do it amazingly well. In the case of mobile apps, the user expects the app to always be responsive even if a complex task is being executed.

Most devices are fast enough to execute tasks as needed, but sometimes those tasks take longer than a few milliseconds. If that task was to be executed on the main, or UI thread, then the UI would freeze.

Users demand that not only an app be responsive when executing long-running tasks, but also that animations and transitions run smoothly. In such a case, the task has to be moved into the background so that the app continues to give the impression that it is waiting for the user, when in fact, it is working hard.

Some tasks are not work happing but rather managing the tasks being run by others. This can include playing music or downloading a file. The app has already handed the task over to the operating system, and all that the user cares about is starting a new app or task.

The device must remain responsive for the user while continuing the previous task in the background, but it should still listen for the user to jump back into the previous task. In the case of a file download, the user may decide that it is no longer needed and cancel the download. The state should be restored and the task should be canceled without a delay. After all this, the user will probably switch to another app.

The user is not as fast as a computer, but they will notice immediately if there are any delays. As the computer is able to multitask at high speed, there is no real reason as to why an app should freeze for any amount of time.

Asynchronous tasks

All apps need to perform tasks that may take longer than a few milliseconds. If a task blocks the UI thread for longer than a few seconds, Android will terminate it, crashing the application.

How to do it...

If we want to do work in the background, we use a new thread. To do this, we make use of the **Task Parallel Library** (**TPL**) and the `async/await` keywords:

1. The first thing that is needed is the method that we wish to execute:

   ```
   public async Task DoWorkAsync() {
     await Task.Run(() => {
       // some long running task
     });
   }
   ```

2. We then invoke it like a normal method, but just with the `await` keyword:

   ```
   await DoWorkAsync();
   ```

3. We can also attach it to an event:

   ```
   doWork.Click += async (sender, args) => {
     await DoWorkAsync();

   }
   ```

4. We can also override the `void` methods by simply inserting the `async` keyword before the return type:

```
protected override async void OnCreate(Bundle bundle) {
    base.OnCreate(bundle);
    await DoWorkAsync();
}
```

5. If the method needs to return a value, we use `Task<>`:

```
public async Task<bool> DoWorkAsync() {
    await Task.Run(() => {
        // some long running task
    });
    return true;
}
```

6. We invoke the method as usual, storing the actual value returned:

```
var success = await DoWorkAsync();
```

7. If we want to update the UI from a background thread, we have two methods that we can use. If we have an activity, we use the `RunOnUiThread()` method:

```
Activity.RunOnUiThread(() => {
    // UI interaction
});
```

8. Or if we have a view, we use the `Post()` method:

```
View.Post(() => {
    // UI interaction
});
```

How it works...

One of the most important areas to consider when creating the UI of an app is how it will perform on the device. No matter how great we design the UI, if it freezes or hangs, the Android OS may terminate the app or the user will uninstall it. This is because Android is continually updating the UI and handling events. If we were to perform a long-running task, the UI would have to wait for our task to complete.

 If a long-running task is executed on the UI thread, the UI thread will have to wait until the task is complete before it can refresh the views. This results in the app freezing.

The most common causes of a frozen UI are network or I/O operations. If we are opening a file, then we can do so on a background thread. Although this operation is very quick, it may not be quick enough for the app or user. By moving the task into the background, the file can be opened in often less than a second but with no chance of the UI blocking.

In the case of network operations, such as downloading an image thumbnail, moving the task into the background will allow the user to scroll through a list view at high speed. As the images are downloaded, they can be displayed without causing the list to freeze until the download is complete.

To prevent the UI freezing, we use threads or do the work in the background. There are several ways to do this but the easiest and simplest is to let the compiler do all the work for us. When we do this, we make use of the TPL and the `async` and `await` keywords. We mark methods as asynchronous using the `async` keyword. Then, when we invoke the asynchronous method, we use the `await` keyword.

When we use these keywords, the compiler will rewrite our code during the build process to actually execute the method on a new thread. This is a great way to keep our code clean as well as the app performing optimally.

 The compiler rewrites the code when using `async` and `await`. This allows the code to be neater and easier to maintain.

Using the `async` and `await` keywords doesn't automatically create a new thread unless we specify what to execute on a new thread. We can await the `Task.Run` method to execute a block of code in the background, or we can await another asynchronous method. When the awaited code is to be executed, a new thread is created and used. When the execution is finished, it is returned to the caller and back to the caller's thread.

Unlike the synchronous methods, if our method is to return a value, we have to use the generic `Task<>` return type. This is because, although we are returning a value, the compiler is writing additional code that requires additional members from our method. If our asynchronous method does not return a value, we use the `Task` return type.

So, instead of simply returning the value, such as `bool`, we wrap it in the generic `Task<bool>` tag. And, instead of `void`, we have a `Task` return type. When we use the `await` keyword, the compiler rewrites the code to extract the returned value, which we then use.

There is a special case in which we can await tasks within a `void` method. For events, this usually does not matter as the sender usually does not care what happens. For events that may require a handled notification, we must set the properties before starting the background work.

Another special case is when overriding a method that returns `void`. As we cannot change the return type, we have to work around it by ensuring that we invoke the base method before awaiting any tasks. If we do not, then the method will return immediately without invoking the base method, which, in the case of Android lifecycle events, is not valid.

If we want to update the UI from within a block of code that is executing on another thread, we cannot do so from that thread. All UI operations must be performed on the UI thread. Android provides two means of doing this, using an activity or the view itself.

> The UI cannot be updated from a background thread as the UI is not thread-safe.

We can update the UI from another thread if we have access to the activity that holds the view, using the `RunOnUiThread()` method defined in the activity itself. Alternatively, we can use the `Post()` method or the `PostDelayed()` method, defined on a view. These methods accept an `Action` instance, or a block of code, which is then executed on the UI thread.

It is important to remember that the lifetime of a background thread is not related to the lifetime of the caller. If an activity starts a new thread and then the activity is destroyed, the thread will continue to execute in the background. This may cause undesired results or crash the app. Thus, when creating a thread, it should be terminated when the caller is no longer available. To avoid running into problems, we can use threads for shorter tasks and services for longer tasks.

> Background threads can be used for short tasks, but services should be used for longer tasks.

There's more...

We do have the option to use .NET threads or the thread pool along with the Android `AsyncTask` instance. However, this involves new types and more complex code:

```
private class DownloadFilesTask : AsyncTask<Uri, int, long> {
  protected override long DoInBackground(params Uri[] uris) {
    // on BACKGROUND thread
    foreach (var uri in uris) {
      if (IsCancelled)
        break;
    }
    return uris.Length;
  }
  protected override void OnProgressUpdate(params int[] progress)
  {
```

```
      // on UI thread
    }
    protected override void OnPostExecute(long result) {
      // on UI thread
    }
  }
```

And then to execute this logic, we will do the following:

```
new DownloadFilesTask().Execute(url1, url2, url3);
```

See also

▸ The *Starting services* recipe

▸ The *Communicating with running services* recipe

Starting services

Sometimes, we have to execute a task that must continue to run even if the user switches to another app or activity.

How to do it...

To be able to execute a task, even if the user switches away, we use a `Service` instance:

1. First, we need an instance of `Service`, and in most cases, we can use an `IntentService` instance:

   ```
   [Service]
   public class XamarinService : IntentService {
     protected override void OnHandleIntent(Intent intent) {
       // some long-running task
     }
   }
   ```

2. In order to begin execution, we invoke the `StartService()` method on the `Context` type:

   ```
   StartService(new Intent(this, typeof(XamarinService)));
   ```

3. We can pass data to the service when we start it by adding data to the intent:

   ```
   var intent = new Intent(this, typeof(XamarinService));
   intent.PutExtra("MyKey", "MyValue");
   StartService(intent);
   ```

4. Additionally, in the service, we can retrieve the values from the intent's extras:

```
string value = null;
if (intent.HasExtra("MyKey"))
  value = intent.GetStringExtra("MyKey");
```

How it works...

Some tasks take fairly long to execute or may be a continuous execution. If normal threads are used, they are not terminated and will be leaked if the activity is killed or paused.

 Running threads are not automatically terminated and will leak when the activity is killed.

Services are used as they are independent of other app components and have their own lifecycle. They can be used to perform tasks and the various activities can interact with them. Services stop automatically when they complete the task, or they can be stopped by another component.

Some of the most common tasks performed by services are network or I/O operations. By delegating downloads or file processing to a background service, the user and the app are free to continue working. When the task has completed, the service can inform the user, who can then decide to continue the last task.

Another task can be to play music. The service can be started with a playlist and then left to go on ahead. When the user wants to control playback, messages can be sent to the service. This frees up the app for navigation and filtering, without having to worry about playing audio. The same goes for the service, which now no longer has to worry about any UI operations and can focus on its task.

Services inherit from the `Service` type either directly or indirectly. For most simple cases of executing a task in the background, we can use the `IntentService` instance. This type of service starts from an `Intent` instance and runs the task in a new thread in the background. As soon as the task is complete, the service is terminated.

This type of service is the best option if we don't need the service to handle multiple requests simultaneously. If multiple requests come in, they are queued up and executed one at a time. If the service is required to be able to handle simultaneous requests, we should inherit from the base `Service` type.

 The `IntentService` instance processes requests sequentially, unlike the base `Service` type, which processes requests simultaneously.

All services must include the `[Service]` attribute as this declares the service with the `AndroidManifest.xml` file. This is then registered by the Android OS so that we can start the services using the `StartService()` method or the `BindService()` method. If we want to prevent the service from being accessed by other apps, we can explicitly set the `Exported` attribute property to `false`.

We override the `OnHandleIntent()` method to perform the task. This happens on a new thread so we don't have to start our own. As soon as the task has completed and we exit the method, the service is terminated. If there are other requests in the queue, the process is repeated.

To start a service, we need to invoke the `StartService()` method on the `Context` type, such as the `Activity` or `BroadcastReceiver` instances. We pass an `Intent` instance that defines the service to start as well as any extra pieces of data we wish to pass to the service. Data is passed via the extras mechanism of the `Intent` instance through the `PutExtra()` method on the intent itself. In the service, we can extract the extra data from the intent using the various `GetXxxExtra()` methods.

> Data can be passed to the service through the extras on the intent when starting the service.

There's more...

The `IntentService` instance does not process start requests simultaneously, but rather queues them and executes them one at a time. To handle simultaneous execution, we need to use the base `Service` type.

See also

▸ The *Stopping services* recipe

▸ The *Handling simultaneous service requests* recipe

Stopping services

As with most tasks, sometimes we have to stop doing them. This may be because it is no longer necessary or because there are problems.

How to do it...

In order to stop a `Service` instance, an instance needs to be executing a task, otherwise the command will be ignored. Stopping a service can be done using a reference to the `Context` instance or from within the service:

1. We first need a `Service` instance, such as an `IntentService` instance:

```
[Service]
public class XamarinService : IntentService {
  private bool stopping = false;
  protected override void OnHandleIntent(Intent intent) {
    // some long-running task
    while (!stopping) {
    }
  }
}
```

2. Then, we can start it as follows:

```
StartService(new Intent(this, typeof(XamarinService)))
```

3. Now, we can stop it in a very similar manner using the `StopService()` method on the `Context` type:

```
StopService(new Intent(this, typeof(XamarinService)));
```

4. We can also stop the service from inside the service using the `StopSelf()` method:

```
StopSelf();
```

5. If we use either the `StopService` or `StopSelf` instance, the `OnDestroy()` method is invoked on the service, which we use to clean up the service and stop any running tasks:

```
public override void OnDestroy() {
  stopping = true;
  base.OnDestroy();
}
```

How it works...

As a service is not tied to the lifecycle of activities or other app components, we have to start and stop them manually.

It is important that services are stopped in order to free up memory and other resources.

Services can be stopped in two ways, from within the service itself using the `StopSelf()` method or from an external component using the `StopService()` method on a `Context` instance. Some service types, such as the `IntentService` instance, will automatically stop themselves when they no longer have any task to perform. Services which inherit from the base `Service` type do not automatically stop, and we have to stop them manually.

If the service handles the simultaneous execution of requests, we need to ensure that we do not stop the service if there are other requests running. When we handle requests in this instance, we are provided a start ID, which we can use to keep track of the service that is running. This ID is a sequential number representing the order in which the requests came in.

See also

> ▸ The *Starting services* recipe

> ▸ The *Handling simultaneous service requests* recipe

Handling simultaneous service requests

We may require a single service to be able to handle multiple requests from multiple sources simultaneously.

How to do it...

If we want a service to be able to handle multiple requests simultaneously, we inherit from the `Service` type, which provides the required features:

1. We first need a type that inherits from `Service`:

```
[Service]
public class XamarinService : Service {
  public override StartCommandResult OnStartCommand(
    Intent intent, StartCommandFlags flags, int startId) {
    return StartCommandResult.Sticky;
  }
  public override IBinder OnBind(Intent intent) {
    return null;
  }
}
```

2. Now, we can create a method that handles multiple requests:

```
private int started = 0;
private async void ProcessRequest() {
  started++;
  await Task.Run (() => {
    // do the work for this particular request
    // ...
    StopSelf (startId);
  });
  started--;
  if (started == 0)
    StopSelf();
}
```

3. Each time the `OnStartCommand()` method is invoked, we can start a new batch of work:

```
ProcessRequest();
```

4. Then, we can start the service multiple times if required:

```
StartService(new Intent(this, typeof(XamarinService)));
```

How it works...

When we need our service to handle multiple requests simultaneously, we need to inherit from the base `Service` type. Instead of the requests being queued and executed one at a time, each request reaches the `OnStartCommand()` method immediately.

When handling an `Intent` instance in the `OnStartCommand()` method, we can decide to do whatever we want. Usually, the task can be started in this method. But, where this differs from a `ServiceIntent` instance is the creation of a new thread. The `ServiceIntent` instance creates a new thread and executes the `OnHandleIntent()` method on that new thread. The base `Service` instance does not do this, but rather executes on the UI thread. We have to manually create a new thread for execution.

 The `OnStartCommand()` method executes on the UI thread. Unlike the `OnHandleIntent()` method, a new thread must be created manually.

The `OnStartCommand()` method returns a `StartCommandResult` instance value that specifies what the system is to do in the event that the service is terminated before the execution is complete. We can request that the service should not be restarted, or we can request that the service is restarted with or without the original intent:

Return value	Effect	Use
NotSticky	This does not restart the service if it is terminated unless there are more intents to still be delivered.	When the app can simply restart any unfinished jobs.
Sticky	This restarts the service, but uses a `null` intent if there are no more intents to deliver.	When the service is not performing tasks but rather waiting for incoming jobs.
RedeliverIntent	This restarts the service with the last intent.	When the service is performing a task that needs to be immediately retried.

If the service is performing specific tasks, it is important that the service is stopped using `StopSelf()` when all the tasks are complete. We have to keep track of when services start and finish and then stop the service when the work is done. We can make use of the `startId` instance provided by the `OnStartCommand()` method and pass that to `StopSelf()`. However, we still have to ensure that we do not invoke `StopSelf()` with the most recent ID while some tasks are still being processed. If we do, the service will be terminated anyway and the threads will be leaked.

The `OnBind()` method is not required to be implemented and can safely return `null`. This method is used when connecting to the service directly. There is more information on this in the *Communicating with running services* recipe.

We can start the service multiple times, and multiple threads will be created from the thread pool. Each thread will perform the task and then stop. Once all the tasks have finished, the service should be terminated.

See also

▶ The *Starting services* recipe
▶ The *Communicating with running services* recipe

Starting services automatically

We might have a long-running task that we need to execute when the device starts. This may be needed to set up some service or configuration for other services.

How to do it...

When we want to perform a task when the device starts up, we can start a service when we receive the `ActionBootComplete` intent action:

1. As subscribing to the boot events is a privileged action, we have to request special permission to do so:

   ```
   [assembly: UsesPermission(
     Manifest.Permission.ReceiveBootCompleted)]
   ```

2. Before we can start our task, we need a `Service` instance that will perform the actual task:

   ```
   [Service]
   public class XamarinService : IntentService {
     protected override void OnHandleIntent(Intent intent) {
       // some startup task
     }
   }
   ```

3. Once we have the service and permission, we need to listen for the boot events using a `BroadcastReceiver` instance:

   ```
   [BroadcastReceiver]
   [IntentFilter(new []{ Intent.ActionBootCompleted })]
   public class ServiceStarter : BroadcastReceiver {
     public override void OnReceive(
       Context context, Intent intent) {
       var serviceIntent = new Intent(
         context, typeof(XamarinService));
       context.StartService(serviceIntent);
     }
   }
   ```

4. Finally, to prevent the user from having to reboot the device just to start using the app, we manually check whether the service has run when the app is launched:

   ```
   var intent = new Intent(this, typeof(XamarinService));
   StartService(intent);
   ```

How it works...

If we want to perform any task as soon as the device starts up, for example to start a service or to execute a configuration or security task, we need to register a broadcast receiver with the Android OS.

Before we can register for the boot notification, we need to request permission to do so. This is done by requesting the `ReceiveBootCompleted` permission. Another important aspect to realize is that the app has to be launched manually by the user at least once before the receiver is allowed to receive the intent. Also, if the user force stops the app from the device settings, they will have to relaunch the app before the receiver is registered.

 The app has to have been launched at least once before the receiver is allowed to be registered for boot intents.

In order to listen for the `ActionBootCompleted` intent, we need to create a `BroadcastReceiver` instance that filters the `ActionBootCompleted` action. As soon as the device has finished booting, it will broadcast the intent and we will be able to perform a task.

As a `BroadcastReceiver` instance usually executes the `OnReceive()` method on the UI thread, we need to execute the task on a new thread. However, we cannot use asynchronous tasks in a broadcast receiver, because as soon as the `OnReceive()` method is returned, the receiver is terminated, and if there are any threads, they will be leaked. Thus, we should use a service with a broadcast receiver.

 As the broadcast receiver does not support long-running or asynchronous tasks, services can be started to perform those tasks.

As the intent is broadcasted when the device is booted, we need to ensure that even if the user does not reboot the device, we still perform the tasks when the user launches the app. For example, if we want to start a service when the device is booted, we have to ensure that if the app is launched without rebooting, we start the service manually.

 The app must be capable of its launch without the user having to restart the device beforehand.

See also

▶ The *Starting services* recipe
▶ The *Critical services* recipe

Communicating with running services

Sometimes, we have a long-running task in a service, but it needs to communicate with our app. This can be needed to send data to the service or to be notified of an event from the service.

How to do it...

To communicate with a service, we need a connection. We use the connection to get a binder, which holds a reference to the service. Let's take a look at the following steps:

1. Although not entirely necessary for very simple services, we will want an interface that defines the public interface of the service:

```
public interface IXamarinService {
  event EventHandler SomeEvent;
  void SomeInstruction();
}
```

2. Next, we create an instance of `IBinder`, or rather `Binder`, which holds a reference to the running service:

```
public class XamarinBinder : Binder {
  public IXamarinService Service { get; private set; }

  public XamarinBinder(IXamarinService service) {
    Service = service;
  }
}
```

3. Now that we have the `binder` instance, we can create the actual service implementing the service interface. To support connections, we return an instance of the binder in the `OnBind()` method:

```
[Service]
public class XamarinService : Service, IXamarinService {
  public event EventHandler SomeEvent;
  public void SomeInstruction() {
  }
}
```

4. To support incoming connections, we return an instance of the binder in the `OnBind()` method:

```
public override IBinder OnBind(Intent intent) {
  return new XamarinBinder(this);
}
```

5. Now, we can implement the service logic in the `OnStartCommand()` method, which will start the task on a new thread, returning immediately with `NotSticky` so that the service will be stopped automatically when the task is done:

```
public override StartCommandResult OnStartCommand(
    Intent intent, StartCommandFlags flags, int startId) {
    // do some work on a new thread
    // ...
    return StartCommandResult.NotSticky;
}
```

6. Once we have the service that supports binding, we need a connection that implements the `IServiceConnection` interface:

```
public class XamarinConnection
    : Java.Lang.Object, IServiceConnection {
    private XamarinBinder binder;
    public void OnServiceConnected(
    ComponentName name, IBinder service) {
        binder = service as XamarinBinder;
        var handler = Connected;
        if (handler != null)
            handler(this, EventArgs.Empty);
    }
    public void OnServiceDisconnected(ComponentName name) {
        var handler = Disconnected;
        if (handler != null)
            handler(this, EventArgs.Empty);
        binder = null;
    }
    public event EventHandler Connected;
    public event EventHandler Disconnected;
    public IXamarinService Service {
        get {
            if (binder != null && binder.Service != null)
                return binder.Service;
            return null;
        }
    }
}
```

7. We start the service, although the service is not required, as follows:

```
var intent = new Intent(this, typeof(XamarinService));
StartService(intent);
```

8. Whether or not the service is started, we can bind to it as follows:

```
var connection = new XamarinConnection();
BindService(intent, connection, Bind.AutoCreate);
```

9. We should ensure that we unbind from the service if the activity stops:

```
UnbindService(connection);
```

10. If we want to attach events to the service, we can subscribe to them when the connection is made:

```
connection.Connected += delegate {
   connection.Service.SomeEvent += OnSomeEvent;
};
connection.Disconnected += delegate {
   connection.Service.SomeEvent -= OnSomeEvent;
};
```

11. And, we can also invoke methods on the service:

```
var service = connection.Service;
if (service != null) {
   service.SomeInstruction();
}
```

How it works...

Once we have started a service, we may wish to set up communication with it. This may be to receive progress notifications or request a specific operation while it is performing the tasks. To do this, we can connect to the service using an `IBinder` instance and an `IServiceConnection` instance.

Usually, we would inherit our service from the base `Service` type and provide a public interface for the service. We can use the `service` object directly instead of an interface, but we would not be able to control how the service is used.

 An interface can be used to define the public interface of the service. This will prevent accidental or intentional misuse of the members on the service.

After we have, optionally, created an interface that defines the public aspects of the service, we create a binder. We can use the `IBinder` interface, but then we would have to implement all the methods on that interface. Thus, we use the `Binder` type, which provides a standard implementation of all the methods. For most local services, we do not even use the methods, but rather just provide our own means of obtaining a reference to the running service.

From the service, we override the `OnBind()` method and return an instance of our binder. We can create a new instance each time or return the same instance each time.

We use an implementation of the `IServiceConnection` interface when subscribing to a service, there are two methods we need to implement. The first is the `OnServiceConnected()` method, which is invoked when a connection to the running service is established. In this method of the connection, we are provided the binder that we returned from the `OnBind()` method of the service. We can then use this binder and get hold of the actual service.

The other method is the `OnServiceDisconnected()` method. This is invoked when a connection to the service is lost, typically when the hosting process has crashed or is terminated. The connection object is not destroyed and will reconnect when the service becomes available again. If we subscribe to any events on the service when we connect, we need to unsubscribe from them when the service is destroyed so that resources can be disposed of.

When a service is destroyed, the `OnServiceDisconnected()` method is invoked on any open connections. The connection objects are not destroyed, and as soon as the service is re-created, the `OnServiceConnected()` method is invoked on those connections.

We can connect, or bind, to a service whether it has started or not using the `BindService` instance on the `Context` type. If we have not started the service, it will be created and started. However, the `OnStartCommand()` method will not be invoked as no intent would have been received. But, as the service has started, we can still invoke methods on that service and subscribe to events.

A service does not have to be started before it can be bound. If it is not started, it will be.

Once we have a connection to the service, we can obtain the service from the binder that was provided to the connection. Once we have the service, we can directly invoke methods or subscribe to events as we would do for any object.

To unbind from a service, we pass the open connection to the `UnbindService()` method on the `Context` type. This disconnects the connection from the service and we will no longer receive a notification if the service is started or stopped. If the service wasn't started with `StartService`, it is now available to be terminated at any time by the Android OS. However, this does not mean that it will be terminated immediately.

Disconnecting from a bound service does not mean that it will be destroyed.

There's more...

Using a separate connection object is not required. Instead of a separate object, the activity can be used instead. Thus, when connecting to a service, we pass the activity to the `BindService()` and `UnbindService()` methods.

See also

- ▸ The *Starting services* recipe
- ▸ The *Handling simultaneous service requests* recipe

Critical services

If we are running a task and it needs to complete as soon as possible, we can prevent the device's CPU from going to sleep. This allows the task to finish without interruption.

How to do it...

To prevent the CPU from going to sleep, we can use a wake lock:

1. We will need to ensure that the **Xamarin Support Library v4** NuGet or component is installed into the project if we are going to be using the `WakefulBroadcastReceiver` type.

2. Before we can prevent the CPU from going to sleep with a wake lock, we need permission to do so:

   ```
   [assembly: UsesPermission(Manifest.Permission.WakeLock)]
   ```

3. The recommended way to get hold of a wake lock is to use an instance of `WakefulBroadcastReceiver` and invoke the `StartWakefulService()` method:

   ```
   [BroadcastReceiver]
   public class CriticalReceiver : WakefulBroadcastReceiver {
     public override void OnReceive(
     Context context, Intent intent) {
       var serviceIntent = new Intent(
         context, typeof(CriticalService));
       StartWakefulService(context, serviceIntent);
     }
   }
   ```

4. The service will then perform the task and invoke the `CompleteWakefulIntent()` method:

```
[Service]
public class CriticalService : IntentService {
  protected override void OnHandleIntent (Intent intent) {
    try {
      // perform the task
    }
    finally {
      WakefulBroadcastReceiver.CompleteWakefulIntent(
        intent);
    }
  }
};
```

5. If the receiver needs to be executed manually, we can do so with the `SendBroadcast()` method on the activity:

```
SendBroadcast(new Intent(this, typeof(CriticalReceiver)));
```

6. There is also another way to obtain a wake lock, which is using the `PowerManager` instance and requesting a lock with the `NewWakeLock()` method:

```
var manager = PowerManager.FromContext(this);
var wakeLock = manager.NewWakeLock(
  WakeLockFlags.Partial, "WakeLockTag");
wakeLock.Acquire();
try {
  // perform the task
}
finally {
  wakeLock.Release();
}
```

How it works...

Some tasks are critical and need to be finished as soon as possible and as fast as possible. Normally, if the device is left idle, the screen and then the CPU turn off. Turning off various pieces of hardware is a great way to preserve battery life, but it also prevents some important tasks from completing until the CPU is awoken by the user.

If we have a task that is important to finish in a timely fashion, we can prevent the CPU from turning off by obtaining a wake lock. This is done by either using the recommended way of a `WakefulBroadcastReceiver` instance or by manually acquiring a wake lock from the `PowerManager` instance.

Using a `WakefulBroadcastReceiver` instance is very useful when the task comes from push notifications, as this will wake the CPU so that the message can be handled before going back to sleep. We just have to add the **Xamarin Support Library v4** NuGet or component into our project, and then instead of inheriting from `BroadcastReceiver`, we inherit from the `WakefulBroadcastReceiver` type. This will automatically acquire a wake lock and we just have to implement the task we want to perform.

As the `WakefulBroadcastReceiver` instance is just an extended `BroadcastReceiver` instance, we cannot execute long-running or asynchronous tasks. If we wish to perform a task, we start that task in a service using the static `StartWakefulService()` method. We pass an `Intent` instance to this method, which specifies the service to start. Once the service has completed, we invoke the static `CompleteWakefulIntent()` method on the `WakefulBroadcastReceiver` type.

It is important to release the wake lock and to do it as soon as possible to avoid battery drain. In the case of exceptions, wrapping the execution of the task in a `try/finally` block will ensure that even if a problem occurs, the wake lock is released. This is important because even if the user presses the power button when a wake lock is being held, the CPU will not go to sleep.

> The task should be wrapped in a `try/finally` block to ensure that the wake lock is always released. This ensures that there will be no unnecessary battery consumption due to an exception.

If the task does not need to be in a broadcast receiver or a service, we can acquire a wake lock directly from the `PowerManager` instance. This is simple to implement by first obtaining the `PowerManager` instance through the `FromContext()` method. Then, we request a new wake lock using the `NewWakeLock()` method. This method takes two parameters, the wake lock type and the tag that is used in debugging.

There are several types of wake locks, some of which keep the screen on. If we want to keep just the CPU awake, we use the `Partial` value of the `WakeLockFlag` enumeration.

Once we have the wake lock, we have to acquire the actual lock by invoking the `Acquire()` method. After invoking this method, the device's CPU is guaranteed not to turn off until we invoke the `Release()` method. As the wake is not released until explicitly instructed, it is best to wrap the task in a `try/finally` block to ensure that the wake lock will always be released.

There's more...

Some critical services don't need to run continuously, but rather once every few minutes. We can do this by setting up an alarm, and in this case, a repeating alarm, to broadcast an intent for our broadcast receiver:

```
var intent = new Intent(this, typeof(CriticalReceiver));
intent.PutExtra(CriticalService.DataKey, "Using alarm manager.");
var pending = PendingIntent.GetBroadcast(
  ApplicationContext, 123, intent, 0);
var manager = AlarmManager.FromContext(this);
manager.SetRepeating(AlarmType.RtcWakeup, 0, 30*1000, pending);
```

When the alarm triggers, it will wake the device and broadcast the intent. The broadcast receiver will then acquire a wake lock and start the service.

7
Notifying Users

In this chapter, we will cover the following topics:

- ▸ Toasts
- ▸ Alert dialogs
- ▸ Alert fragments
- ▸ Embedded alert fragments
- ▸ Selection alerts
- ▸ The notification builder
- ▸ Ongoing notifications
- ▸ Custom notification views
- ▸ Push notifications

Introduction

A notification is something that draws someone's attention to let them know that something has happened. Notifications exist in the real world as well as in the digital world. Without notifications the user would have to keep checking to see if something has happened, and since most probably nothing has, the whole exercise becomes a waste of time.

By relying on something to let the user know about an event, the user is free to work on other things. Notifications must be easy to recognize and must be distinguishable from other notifications. However, it is important that notifications don't become a distraction. Too many notifications can become a hindrance to productivity. If the notification is overpowering, the user will be forced to stop what they are doing.

In contrast, some notifications cannot be ignored and require a user's immediate attention and action. These types of notifications are very annoying as they usually appear at the worst of times, but they are also very critical. Sometimes a decision has to be made, and there is no avoiding it.

One of the features of a good notification is that it lets the user know that something has happened but does so in a subtle way. The user is aware of it but can choose to ignore it.

Toasts

Sometimes we have to provide a small notification to the user to tell them that something has happened. At the same time, we don't want to interrupt the user's task in any way. That's where toast notifications come in. We can use toast notifications to display subtle notifications in our app.

How to do it...

We can create toast notifications with the `Toast` type as follows:

1. A simple text toast is created through the `MakeText()` method, as shown here:

```
using (var toast = Toast.MakeText(
this, "This is a toast...", ToastLength.Short)) {
  toast.Show();
}
```

2. There are a few aspects we can customize using the various setter methods:

```
using (var toast = Toast.MakeText(
this, "This is another toast...", ToastLength.Short)) {
  toast.SetGravity(GravityFlags.Center, 0, 0);
  toast.SetMargin(24, 24);
  toast.Show();
}
```

3. We can also specify an entire view to use instead of the default text view through the `View` property:

```
using (var toast = new Toast(ApplicationContext))
using (var image = new ImageView(this)) {
  image.SetImageResource(Resource.Drawable.Icon)
  toast.Duration = ToastLength.Short;
  toast.View = image;
  toast.Show();
}
```

How it works...

Often an app needs to inform the user that something has happened, but the occurrence is not important enough to merit a disruption or interruption of normal use. If we want to let the user know about something, we can display a small text message somewhere in case the user is interested.

Usually, these types of notifications do not require any response from the user and thus have no intractable elements. For example, if the user is saving some settings, we don't need to pop up a dialog to inform the user that the settings have been saved. We would use a small notification that can be ignored.

We do this by using the toast notification system. One of the simplest ways is to simply invoke the `MakeText()` method on the `Toast` type, through which we obtain a toast. To display it, we invoke the `Show()` method on the result.

The `MakeText()` method requires the context, the text message, and the duration of the toast. For additional properties, we can use the various setter methods. For example, the `SetGravity()` and `SetMargin()` methods specify where on the screen and how large the toast will be.

If we really need more advanced toasts, we can instantiate a `Toast` type through the constructor. With this object, we specify a custom view with the `View` property. This could be a simple view, such an `ImageView` instance, or it could be an entire view structure that was inflated from a resource.

Regardless of what is displayed, we have to remember that the toast cannot be interacted with and is timed. Also, it needs to be small and not invade the user's current task.

 Toasts should be small and not require any action. They should be easy to consume as they will soon disappear.

There's more...

Toasts can be displayed from anywhere as they don't require a **User Interface** (**UI**) to be present. That means that they can be shown from a service or broadcast receiver. However, they have to be displayed from the UI thread.

If we are working in the background, we can show a toast by using the **Task Parallel Library** (**TPL**). First, we need to capture the UI scheduler when we are in the UI thread, say in the `OnStartCommand()` method of a service:

```
uiScheduler = TaskScheduler.FromCurrentSynchronizationContext();
```

Then, when we want to show the toast from the background, we start a `Task` instance using this scheduler:

```
new Task(() => {
   // show toast
}).Start(uiScheduler);
```

Alert dialogs

In many apps, we will require some input from the user or a decision to be made. The decision may require a response before the app can continue.

How to do it...

If we want a decision to be made, we can use a pop-up dialog. This is achieved by using the `AlertDialog.Builder` type:

1. Alerts are easy to create using the `AlertDialog.Builder` type:

   ```
   using (var dialog = new AlertDialog.Builder(this)) {
      dialog.SetTitle("Alert Title");
      dialog.SetMessage("Alert message text here...");
      dialog.Show();
   }
   ```

2. We can also add buttons to the alert by using the `SetPositiveButton()`, `SetNegativeButton()`, or `SetNeutralButton()` methods:

   ```
   dialog.SetPositiveButton("Yes", delegate {
      // do something cool here
   });
   dialog.SetNegativeButton("No", delegate {
      // do something uncool here
   });
   ```

3. Custom views can also be used with alerts through the `SetView()` method:

   ```
   var layout = LayoutInflater.Inflate(
      Resource.Layout.DialogLayout, null);
   dialog.SetView(layout);
   ```

How it works...

An alert dialog is a pop-up window that appears and prompts the user to make a decision or select from a series of options. It does not fill the screen but is a modal window, meaning that although the user has to make a decision before proceeding, the current context hasn't switched away. Alert dialogs are a specific dialog type, usually used to display a three-button decision platter or a list of selectable items, but they can also have a totally custom layout.

> Alert dialogs interrupt user activity and require a response, so they should be used sparingly.

In order to create a dialog, we use the constructor of the `AlertDialog.Builder` type. Once we have an instance, we can provide a title using the `SetTitle()` method and provide a message using the `SetMessage()` method. The title is optional and should not be used if the dialog only displays a simple question.

If we want to provide the user with a choice using a set of buttons, we use the `SetPositiveButton()`, `SetNegativeButton()`, and `SetNeutralButton()` methods. Each method allows us to specify a button caption and a delegate that can be used to attach code to the button tap.

Each button type has a preferred purpose. The positive button should be used to accept or to continue with an action, and the negative button should be used to cancel the operation. The neutral button is used to provide an option that allows the user to neither accept nor cancel an operation. Such an action could be to postpone the operation.

We can also customize the dialog entirely by replacing the view with a custom layout. This is done by inflating a layout, or creating one, and assigning it to the dialog with the `SetView()` method. This allows for far greater flexibility and can be used to create more advanced dialogs.

> The Android support libraries also provide an `AlertDialog` type, which is styled using the material design.

We can also make use of the Android support library to style our dialogs using the new material design. This dialog functions in exactly the same way as the native dialog, only with a modern theme. By using the `AlertDialog` type in the `Android.Support.V7.App` namespace, our dialogs will be styled to match the `AppCompatActivity` and `Fragment` themes.

There's more...

There are also two other types of dialogs: `DatePickerDialog` and `TimePickerDialog`. These dialogs have a predefined UI that allows the user to select a date or time.

Dialogs can be used directly, but they should be used with a `DialogFragment` instance. This fragment is specially designed as a container for the dialog and provides all the control needed for creating and displaying dialogs.

Alert fragments

Traditional alert dialogs do not conform the lifecycle events when using fragments such as correctly handling back button presses or device rotations.

Getting ready

If we are going to support Android versions prior to 3.0, we will have to install the **Xamarin Support Library v7 AppCompat** NuGet or component into our project.

How to do it...

Using a dialog in a `DialogFragment` instance ensures that the dialog correctly handles the lifecycle events. We override the `OnCreateDialog()` method to create the dialog:

1. To create an alert fragment, we inherit from `DialogFragment` and override the `OnCreateDialog()` method. In this method, we create and return the dialog:

   ```
   public class AlertFragment : DialogFragment {
     public override Dialog OnCreateDialog(Bundle savedState)
     {
       using (var alert = new AlertDialog.Builder(Activity)) {
         dialog.SetTitle("Alert Title");
         dialog.SetMessage("Alert message text here...");
         return alert.Create();
       }
     }
   }
   ```

2. When it is going to be displayed in an activity, we create an instance of the fragment:

   ```
   AlertFragment frag = new AlertFragment();
   ```

3. Finally, we invoke the `Show()` method on the fragment to display it:

   ```
   frag.Show(SupportFragmentManager, "AlertFragment");
   ```

4. If we are only supporting Android versions 3.0 and above, we can use this:

   ```
   frag.Show(FragmentManager, "AlertFragment");
   ```

How it works...

Dialogs can be used directly, but when using fragments they should be used with a `DialogFragment` instance. These fragments are designed to work with dialogs. They follow the lifecycle of fragments but contain all that is needed for creating and displaying dialogs.

Using a `DialogFragment` instance allows us to embed the dialog into an activity just like any other fragment. This gives us the extra flexibility to support embedding or popping up a dialog depending on the screen size or any other criteria.

 Dialogs should be used with a `DialogFragment` instance to better integrate with the fragment lifecycle of modern Android apps.

In order to use dialog fragments, we have to inherit from the more specific `DialogFragment` instance, instead of `Fragment`, and override the `OnCreateDialog()` method. In this method, we create the dialog as we would without fragments, but instead of invoking `Show`, we return the actual dialog from the `Create()` method.

When we want to display the dialog in a `DialogFragment` instance, we invoke the `Show()` method that is on the fragment, rather than the one on the dialog. We pass the `FragmentManager` instance along with a tag to the `Show()` method. The tag is used by the underlying fragment transaction.

There's more...

As the `DialogFragment` instance is just an extension of `Fragment`, we can interact with the containing `Activity` instance just as we would when overriding the base `Fragment` instance. For example, we can interact with the activity when the fragment is attached to the activity. We can capture the instance of the activity by overriding the `OnAttach()` method. When something happens in the dialog fragment, we can invoke methods or set properties on the activity.

See also

▶ *Chapter 2*, *Showing Views and Handling Fragments*, the *Creating and using fragments* recipe

Embedded alert fragments

Sometimes, we want more control over how the dialogs are displayed. We may want the dialog to be a popup on a tablet, but to be displayed as a full page on a phone.

Getting ready

If we are going to support Android versions prior to 3.0, we will have to install the **Xamarin Support Library v7 AppCompat** NuGet or component into our project.

How to do it...

We can use the `DialogFragment` instance to display either a pop-up dialog or embed it into the activity fragment navigation by using the following steps:

1. If we want to embed a dialog into the view, we cannot use the alert builder but we have to use normal layouts. Therefore, we inflate a layout in the `OnCreateView()` method of the `DialogFragment` instance:

```
public class AlertFragment : AppCompatDialogFragment {
  public override View OnCreateView(
    LayoutInflater inflater,
    ViewGroup container,
    Bundle savedInstanceState) {
      var view = inflater.Inflate(
        Resource.Layout.DialogLayout, container, false);
      return view;
    }
}
```

2. If we need to add additional features, such as a title for the dialog, we can override the `OnCreateDialog()` method:

```
public override Dialog OnCreateDialog(Bundle savedState) {
  var dialog = base.OnCreateDialog(savedState);
  dialog.SetTitle("Cool Dialog");
  return dialog;
}
```

3. To display the dialog as a pop-up window, we use the `Show()` method on the fragment:

```
var fragment = new AlertFragment();
fragment.Show(SupportFragmentManager, "AlertFragment");
```

4. To embed the fragment into a view, we follow the typical fragment steps:

```
var fragment = new AlertFragment();
SupportFragmentManager
    .BeginTransaction()
    .SetTransition(FragmentTransaction.TransitFragmentOpen)
    .Replace(Resource.Id.content, fragment)
    .AddToBackStack(null)
    .Commit();
```

How it works...

As Android devices have a wide variety of screen sizes, creating a UI involves designing for any issues that may arise in a single design. On a small-screen device, such as a mobile phone, a pop-up dialog may not be the best use of screen estate. We can make use of the flexibility of a `DialogFragment` instance to have the dialog appear as a fullscreen fragment.

Because the `DialogFragment` instance is an extension of a `Fragment` instance, we still have all the inherited functionality. We also get the added functionality of the view being rendered in a pop-up dialog. However, if we want to be able to embed the dialog into the normal fragment navigation, we cannot use the `AlertDialog.Builder` instance, or any `Dialog` instance, to create the UI.

While creating pop-up dialogs using the `DialogFragment` instance, the theme that is applied is that of the core operating system. So, when running on the older Android versions with the support libraries, the dialog will look out of place. To rectify this, we rather inherit from an extension of the base `DialogFragment` type, the `AppCompatDialogFragment` type. This type will ensure that the dialog matches the theme of the app.

 While using the support library, the `AppCompatDialogFragment` type should be used if the `AlertDialog.Builder` type is not being used to build the popup.

As with all fragments, we inflate or create the UI in the `OnCreateView()` method. When we override the `OnCreateView()` method, we are only creating the UI for the main content of the dialog.

If we are creating a pop-up dialog, we may have to change or remove some window features such as the title. To do this, we override the `OnCreateDialog()` method. In this method, we first call the base method that provides the dialog. We then use this to change the dialog in the way we require.

The `OnCreateDialog()` method is only invoked when the fragment is going to be displayed as a pop-up dialog.

If we add the fragment to the activity using the `FragmentTransaction` instance, the fragment will be embedded and will act as a normal fragment. If we invoke the `Show()` method on the fragment, it will appear as a pop-up dialog.

There's more...

We can also combine both methods of embedded fragments and pop-up dialogs by creating the dialog separately. We can override the `OnCreateView()` method for when the fragment is embedded and override the `OnCreateDialog()` method for when the dialog is a popup.

In the `OnCreateView()` method, we inflate or create the view layout, but in the `OnCreateDialog()` method, we use the `AlertDialog.Builder` instance instead of calling the base method. We can also use the inflated UI in the dialog by invoking the `SetView()` method with the result from the `OnCreateView()` method. By doing this, we can provide the most flexible means of displaying the dialog, depending on how the dialog is presented.

Selection alerts

Sometimes we have to ask the user to select one or more items from a larger collection. This may be necessary as normal dialogs only have up to three buttons, but a fully customized UI is unnecessary.

How to do it...

To provide a list of items in a dialog, we can specify the items in much the same way as a simple message:

1. If we need to provide the user with a selection of items in a dialog, we can also use the `AlertDialog` instance and the `SetItems()` method:

```
string[] items = new string[] { ... }
using (var dialog = new AlertDialog.Builder(this)) {
    dialog.SetTitle("Alert Title");
    dialog.SetPositiveButton("Close", delegate {
    });
    dialog.SetItems(items, (s, e) => {
        int index = e.Which;
    });
    dialog.Show();
}
```

2. We can also use data adapters in a dialog, through the `SetAdapter()` method:

```
var adapter = new ArrayAdapter(
   this, Android.Resource.Layout.SimpleListItem1, items);
dialog.SetAdapter(adapter, (s, e) => {
   var index = e.Which;
});
```

3. If we want to support a single-select radio button list, we use the `SetSingleChoiceItems()` method:

```
int selected = -1;
dialog.SetSingleChoiceItems(items, selected, (s, e) => {
   selected = e.Which;
});
```

4. We use the `SetMultiChoiceItems()` method if we want to support a multi-select checklist:

```
bool[] selected = new bool[items.Length];
dialog.SetMultiChoiceItems(items, multiChecked,
   (s, e) => {
      int index = e.Which;
      bool isChecked = e.IsChecked;
      selected[index] = isChecked;
   });
```

How it works...

Using a dialog to display a list is very useful if switching context is to be avoided. A list in a dialog provides great flexibility, such as providing an option to select multiple items or none at all.

There are three types of lists that can appear in a dialog. First, there is the traditional single-select dialog that will hide when an item is selected. Then, there is the radio list, which also allows the user to select a single item. This list differs from the traditional list in two ways: the dialog has to be dismissed manually, and the dialog allows us to specify which item is selected when it appears. Finally, there is the check list, which is very similar to the radio list but allows multiple items to be selected.

 The list view in a dialog can be populated from a `string` array, an adapter, a cursor, or a resource.

There are several ways to populate the list in the dialog. We could use an array resource, a `string` array, a `ListAdapter` instance, or a `Cursor` instance. The traditional list dialog uses the `SetItems()` method to specify an array or resource, the `SetAdapter()` method for a `ListAdapter` instance, and the `SetCursor()` method for a `Cursor` instance. All these methods allow us to provide the list as well as a delegate that will get invoked when the user selects an item.

If we want to use the radio list, we use the `SetSingleChoiceItems()` method. This method allows us to specify the item collection, the index of the initially selected item, and the delegate that will be invoked when an item is selected. If `-1` is provided for the selected index, nothing will be selected initially.

If we want to use the check list, we use the `SetMultiChoiceItems()` method. We can specify the item collection, an array with the initially selected indexes, and the delegate that will be invoked when an item is checked or unchecked. The selected items are determined by a `bool` array, which will contain `true` at every index that should be selected. If `null` is provided instead of an array, nothing will be selected initially. The `bool` array must be the same size as the item collection.

 The list view in a dialog can be a single select or multiselect.

In all the methods, the delegate will receive an `EventArgs` method that will contain details about which item was selected. The `EventArgs` method contains a `Which` property representing the index of the item that was selected. Additionally, the `SetMultiChoiceItems()` method provides an extra property, `IsChecked`, which holds a value representing whether the item was checked or unchecked.

 The delegate is fired each time the user selects an item, not when the dialog is dismissed.

The notification builder

Some tasks take a long time, or events may occur when the user is not using our app. Because some tasks take a long time, we run them in the background. As a result, we need to let the user know when a task is complete, or that some extra information is needed.

Getting ready

If we are going to support Android versions prior to 3.0, we will have to install the **Xamarin Support Library v4** NuGet or component into our project.

How to do it...

If an event occurs when the user is not using our app, we can let the user know about it by using a `Notification` instance from the following steps:

1. Create the notification using the `NotificationCompat.Builder` instance:

```
var builder = new NotificationCompat.Builder(this)
    .SetSmallIcon(Android.Resource.Drawable.StatNotifySync)
    .SetContentTitle("Simple Notification")
    .SetContentText("Hello World!")
    .SetAutoCancel(true);
```

2. Or, if only supporting Android versions 3.0 and above, use the `Notification.Builder` instance:

```
var builder = new Notification.Builder(this)
    .SetSmallIcon(Android.Resource.Drawable.StatNotifySync)
    .SetContentTitle("Simple Notification")
    .SetContentText("Hello World!")
    .SetAutoCancel(true);
```

3. Before we display the notification, we need the `NotificationManager` type and an ID used to reference this notification once displayed:

```
const int notificationId = 123;
var manager = NotificationManager.FromContext(this);
```

4. Now we create the actual notification using the `Build()` method and display it using the `Notify()` method of the `NotificationManager` type:

```
manager.Notify(notificationId, builder.Build());
```

Often, we will want to navigate the user to a specific activity in our app, and for this we add a content intent to the notification:

1. To launch our activity when we tap the notification, we create a `PendingIntent` instance that holds the `Intent` instance to launch the activity:

```
var intent = new Intent(
    this, typeof(NotificationActivity));
var pendingIntent = PendingIntent.GetActivity(
    this, 0, intent, PendingIntentFlags.UpdateCurrent);
```

2. We then assign this pending intent to the notification by using the `SetContentIntent()` method:

```
builder.SetContentIntent(pendingIntent);
```

If we want to provide a back stack for when the user presses the back button once the notification activity is shown, we can do so using the `TaskStackBuilder` type:

1. First, we need to let Android know what to go back to, and we do this by setting the `ParentActivity` property of the `[Activity]` attribute for our notification activity:

   ```
   [Activity(..., ParentActivity = typeof(MainActivity))]
   ```

2. If we are supporting versions of Android below 4.1, we also need to add a `[MetaData]` attribute:

   ```
   [MetaData(
       "android.support.PARENT_ACTIVITY",
       Value = "com.xamarincookbook.MainActivity")]
   ```

3. We have to make sure that we also register our parent activity with the same name as the value of the metadata:

   ```
   [Register("com.xamarincookbook.MainActivity")]
   ```

4. Finally, we can create the back stack to the `Intent` instance using the `AddNextIntentWithParentStack()` method of the `TaskStackBuilder` type:

   ```
   var intent = new Intent(
       this, typeof(NotificationActivity));
   var backStack = TaskStackBuilder.Create(this)
       .AddNextIntentWithParentStack(intent);
   var pendingIntent = backStack.GetPendingIntent(
       0, (int)PendingIntentFlags.UpdateCurrent);
   ```

How it works...

Some tasks take a long time and the user will switch to another app while such a task is running. When the task is finished, we may want to let the user know. Or an event may occur in the background while the user is using another app. Regardless of what the user is doing, we can use a `Notification` instance to display information in the system status bar.

When the user decides that they want to respond to the notification, they can tap it and it will launch right into the activity that relates to the notification. The whole notification could be used as the entry point, with buttons that provide additional actions.

 Notifications are used to display information in the notification area and allow the user to respond whenever they want to, if at all.

Almost all notifications provide an action, even if it is just to launch the app or an activity in the app. To do this, we use a `PendingIntent` instance, which holds the actual `Intent` instance that we wish to trigger. The `PendingIntent` instance can hold any `Intent` instance with any amount of extras or back stacks that will be required to get the user directly to the desired point. We can attach the intent using the `SetContentIntent()` method of the builder.

Setting the intent is not required, but is both expected and recommended because the user expects that something will happen after tapping the notification. However, if action buttons are used, the intent does not have to be attached to the actual notification but to the action buttons.

Although optional, an intent is used to launch the app from the notification.

To create the actual `Notification` instance, we use the `NotificationCompat.Builder` instance, or if we are only supporting Android versions 3.0 and above, we use `Notification.Builder`. We construct an instance of the builder and use the many setter methods to create the structure of the notification.

There are three required properties of a notification: the icon, set by `SetSmallIcon`; the title, set by `SetTitle`; and the detail text, set by `SetContentText`. The user also expects that the notification will be removed from the status bar when it is tapped. We could remove this manually, but we can do this automatically by passing `true` to the `SetAutoCancel()` method.

Using auto-cancel removes the need for any extra code to cancel the notification when it is tapped.

When we are ready to display the notification, we use the `NotificationManager` instance. To obtain the actual notification that is to be displayed, we invoke the `Build()` method on the builder. We then invoke the `Notify()` method on the manager with both an ID and the notification. The ID allows us to locate, update, or remove a notification once it has been displayed, if need be.

Unless the notification takes the user to a special activity, we should also specify a back stack on the intent. Without a back stack, the notification will launch the activity, and when the user presses back, the activity will close and return the user to exactly where they were. By specifying a back stack, we can allow the user to navigate upwards, just as if they had entered the app from the home screen.

The advantage of a back stack is that the navigation path through the app is maintained regardless of the entry point.

The back stack is created by setting the parent activity for the notification activity. We do this by adding attributes to the notification activity, which describe how to get to the parent activity. Typically, we would provide the type of the parent activity for the ParentActivity property of the [Activity] attribute. Because we are supporting versions of Android prior to 4.1, we also add a [MetaData] attribute. This attribute has a string value of the full name of the parent activity as it appears to Android. In order to know what the compiler will use as the name, we need to specify exactly what we want. By adding a [Register] attribute to the parent activity, we can control what the name will be. We then use this name in our notification activity's metadata.

Both the ParentActivity property of the [Activity] attribute and a [MetaData] attribute must be applied to support the back stack on all versions of Android.

When creating the back stack, we use the TaskStackBuilder type. This type has been around since Android version 3.0, but we use the type from the support library instead. If we do not, the app will crash on older Android versions. Both types work the same, and we use the AddNextIntentWithParentStack() method to attach the intents for both the destination activity and its parents. One difference is that on Android versions prior to 3.0, the back stack is ignored.

The support library provides the TaskStackBuilder type so the app does not crash, but it does not add any functionality.

Once we have built our back stack, we get the PendingIntent instance using the GetPendingIntent() method. We can then pass this pending intent to the notification builder using the SetContentIntent() method.

There's more...

We can also add many features to the notification, such as action buttons using the AddAction() method. To do this, we provide an icon, some text, and a PendingIntent instance. The PendingIntent instance is triggered when the user has tapped a button and we then respond when we receive it. We can also add various extra features such as tickers and vibrations, as well as more information to notifications. All these features can be added using the various setter methods on the Builder object.

Ongoing notifications

Some notifications are used to display a task that is underway and may even include information on progress or state.

Getting ready

If we are going to support Android versions prior to 3.0, we will have to install the **Xamarin Support Library v4** NuGet or component into our project.

How to do it...

To show progress in a notification, we can use a progress bar and update the notification as progress is made:

1. Most ongoing notifications are not going to be dismissed when tapped, so instead of using `SetAutoCancel()` method, we use `SetOngoing()` method:

   ```
   var notification = new NotificationCompat.Builder(this)
       .SetSmallIcon(Android.Resource.Drawable.StatNotifySync)
       .SetContentTitle("Simple Notification")
       .SetContentText("Starting Work!")
       .SetOngoing(true);
   ```

2. We can also have a progress bar in the notification. This could be indeterminate:

   ```
   notification.SetProgress(0, 0, true);
   ```

3. Or the progress bar could display a specific value:

   ```
   notification.SetProgress(100, 27, false);
   ```

4. We can update notifications simply by notifying the `NotificationManager` instance with the same notification ID:

   ```
   manager.Notify(notificationId, notification.Build());
   ```

5. If, for some reason, we have to cancel the notification and remove it from the status bar, we use the `Cancel()` method with the notification ID:

   ```
   manager.Cancel(notificationId);
   ```

How it works...

Because tasks take some time to complete, we may want to report the progress or the state of the task. Notifications provide a few means of showing such progress. We could use a normal text message to display the state, or we could use a progress bar to show the progress.

To display a progress bar, we use the `SetProgress()` method. The progress bar can either have a specific progress or be indeterminate. For a specific progress, we specify the maximum and progress values along with `false`. For indeterminate progress, we pass 0 to both the maximum and progress parameters, but `true` for indeterminate.

> A progress bar could be indeterminate, such as before real progress is made, or have a specific value.

To prevent the notification from being dismissed by the user, we do not specify the `SetAutoCancel()` method as `true`, but rather the `SetOngoing()` method. This will prevent the notification from being dismissed by the user, even when they swipe the notification out of the notification drawer.

> The notification can be prevented from being dismissed, even manually, by passing `true` to the `SetOngoing()` method.

To update the notification once displayed, we simply have to invoke the `Notify()` method again. We must pass the same notification ID; otherwise, a new notification will be created. Every time the notification changes, we invoke the `Notify()` method.

> The same ID must be used for updating notifications; otherwise, a new notification will be created.

Once the task has completed, we can update the notification with a dismissible notification, or we can manually remove the notification from the notification drawer. Cancelation is done by invoking the `Cancel()` method on the `NotificationManager` instance, providing the ID of the notification that we want to cancel.

Custom notification views

Sometimes notifications created by the builder just don't provide enough flexibility compared to what is required. Sometimes notifications created by the builder just don't provide enough flexibility or customization. As a result, an entirely custom notification layout is needed to provide this level of customization.

Getting ready

If we are going to support Android versions prior to 3.0, we will have to install the **Xamarin Support Library v4** NuGet or component into our project.

How to do it...

We can use `RemoteViews` with a layout file to provide a custom layout for a notification:

1. We can also display an entirely custom view in a notification. To do this, we create a `RemoteViews` object, passing the resource ID of the layout:

```
var view = new RemoteViews(
    PackageName, Resource.Layout.NotificationLayout);
```

2. We can then update the various sub views using the various setter methods, such as `SetTextViewText()`, `SetProgressBar()`, and `SetImageViewResource()`:

```
view.SetTextViewText(Resource.Id.title, "Title Text");
view.SetProgressBar(Resource.Id.progress, 100, 25, false);
view.SetImageViewResource(
    Resource.Id.state, Resource.Drawable.state);
```

3. Once we have the view, we can create the `Intent` instance for the notification:

```
var intent = new Intent(this, typeof(MainActivity));
var pendingIntent = PendingIntent.GetActivity(
    this, 0, intent, PendingIntentFlags.UpdateCurrent);
```

4. Then we can create the notification using the builder:

```
var notification = new NotificationCompat.Builder(this)
    .SetSmallIcon(Android.Resource.Drawable.StatNotifySync)
    .SetAutoCancel(true)
    .SetContentIntent(pendingIntent)
    .SetContent(view);
```

5. Finally, we display the notification:

```
manager.Notify(CustomId, notification.Build());
```

6. We can update the notification by updating the `RemoteViews` object and notifying the `NotificationManager` instance:

```
view.SetTextViewText(Resource.Id.title, "Updated!");
manager.Notify(SimpleId, notification.Build());
```

How it works...

Some notifications require a custom layout, especially if they have to present advanced data. The notification builder provides many features, but sometimes this is not flexible enough to present the required data to the user.

To display a custom layout, we first define the layout in a resource file just like any other layout. However, not all view elements can be used easily as the views are not exposed publicly. The views are accessed by various setter methods instead of directly. Views such as `TextView` and `ImageView` can be used, but custom views with complex properties or methods cannot be modified.

To build the notification view, we construct an instance of `RemoteViews`, providing a package name and the layout resource ID in that package. Usually, we will use the current package name and a resource in our app.

Custom notification layouts are just normal layouts inflated in a notification.

We can update the notification view and set any properties using the methods on the `RemoteViews` object. The values set are stored and then applied when the notification is presented. There are various methods that are available, such as `SetTextViewText()` or `SetProgressBar()`, that make updating certain types of views easy. Properties are set by providing the view ID and the value. There are also the type setter methods, such as `SetString()` and `SetInt()`, that can be used to set arbitrary properties of a view.

Elements of the layout are updated by their IDs through the `RemoteViews` object.

To create the notification, we still create an instance of the notification builder, but the difference now is to set the content. Instead of setting the title or content text, we rather just set the `SetContent()` method with the `RemoteViews` object.

At the time of writing, there is a bug in the Android support library, which prevents the custom view from loading on Android versions prior to 3.0. A workaround is to set the content view on the built notification:

```
var notification = notificationBuilder.Build();
if (Build.VERSION.SdkInt < BuildVersionCodes.Honeycomb) {
  notification.ContentView = remoteViews;
}
```

To update the notification, we just need to update the `RemoteViews` object and invoke the `Notify()` method again.

There's more...

We can also create notifications using `RemoteViews` directly without having to use the notification builder or the Android support library. This is similar to using the builder, but instead of creating an instance of the builder, we construct an instance of `Notification`. We then set the various properties on the notification, such as `Title`, `Icon`, `ContentIntent`, and `ContentView`.

Although possible, this is often unnecessary and introduces complications. One such complication is that the notification will not be synchronized with any paired wearables.

Push notifications

There may be times where we create an app that needs to receive messages or events from a remote server. Instead of polling the server for updates, we want the server to let our app know directly.

Getting ready

Push notifications allow a remote server to send a message directly to a specific device. To implement push notifications, we will need a project number and an API key from the **Google Developers Console** (`https://cloud.google.com/console`):

1. First, we have to set up a project on the Google Developers Console if we do not have one already. When logged in, click on **Create Project** and enter a project name and ID:

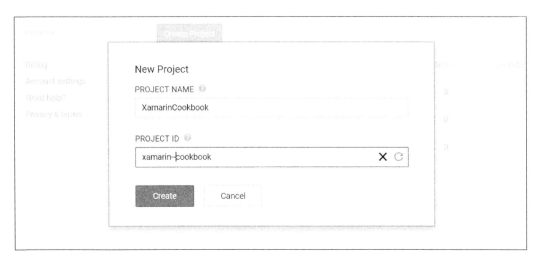

The Create Project dialog

2. Once we have created or selected an existing project, we need to make a note of the **Project Number**. This is used to be able to receive messages:

The Project Number

3. Select the **APIs** option under the **APIs & auth** section in the left-hand menu and make sure that the **Google Cloud Messaging for Android** option is on:

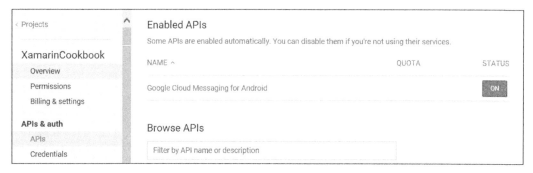

Enabling Google Cloud Messaging for Android

4. Then, select the **Credentials** option under the **APIs & auth** section from the left-hand menu. In the **Public API access** section, click on **Create New Key** and then on **Server Key**:

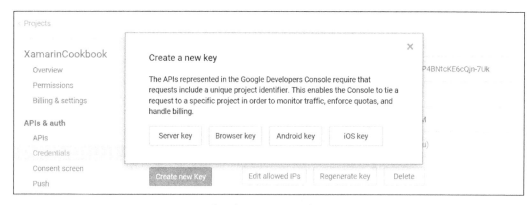

Creating a new server key

5. Enter the server's IP address—for testing we will use 0.0.0.0/0—and click on **Create**:

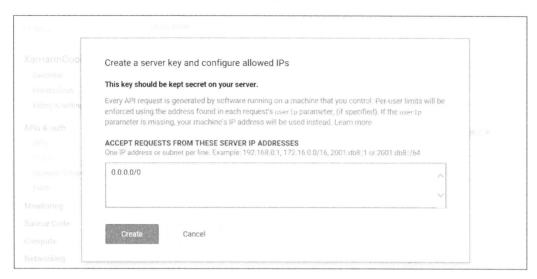

Entering the servers IP address

6. On the new page, under the **Public API access** section, make a note of the API key. This is used to send messages with Google Cloud Messaging:

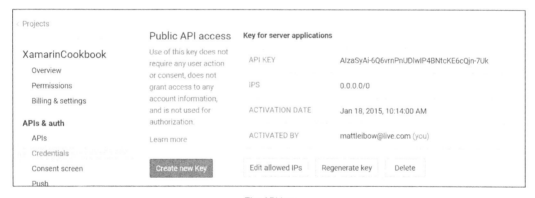

The API key

How to do it...

After we have obtained the required keys, we can start implementing the client. The client registers with the cloud service and then is able to receive push notifications:

1. We will need to ensure that the Xamarin Google Play Services - **Google Cloud Messaging** (**GCM**) NuGet or component is installed into the project. This library contains the code needed to interact with Google Cloud Messaging.

2. We will need several permissions in order to use push notifications:

    ```
    [assembly: UsesPermission(Manifest.Permission.Internet)]
    [assembly: UsesPermission(Manifest.Permission.GetAccounts)]
    [assembly: UsesPermission(Manifest.Permission.WakeLock)]
    [assembly: UsesPermission(
      "com.google.android.c2dm.permission.RECEIVE")]
    ```

3. There is also a special permission that we have to add, and this is the app package name with `.permission.C2D_MESSAGE` appended. Instead of hardcoding the package name, we use the `@PACKAGE_NAME@` value:

    ```
    [assembly: UsesPermission(
      "@PACKAGE_NAME@.permission.C2D_MESSAGE")]
    ```

4. There are several things we need. The first is to make sure that Google Play Services is available on the device:

    ```
    private bool CheckPlayServices() {
      var play = GoogleApiAvailability.Instance;
      var result = play.IsGooglePlayServicesAvailable(this);
      if (result == ConnectionResult.Success)
        return true;

      if (play.IsUserResolvableError(result)) {
        play.GetErrorDialog(this, result, 0)).Show();
      }
      else {
        Finish();
      }
      return false;
    }
    ```

5. Next, using the project number from the Google Developers Console, we get our token from Google Play Services. Once we have obtained a token, we might want to send it to a server that will be sending messages to our app:

    ```
    private Task<string> GetRegistrationAsync() {
      return Task.Run(() => {
        string token = null;
        try {
          var instanceId = InstanceID.GetInstance(this);
          token = instanceId.GetToken(
            "PROJECT_NUMBER",
            GoogleCloudMessaging.InstanceIdScope);
          // send the token to the server that sends messages
        }
        catch (Exception ex) {
    ```

```
        // handle/log the error and let the user try again
      }
      return token;
    });
}
```

6. When we load our activity, we can check for Google Play Services and then load the registration in the `OnCreate()` method:

```
if (CheckPlayServices()) {
  registrationId = await GetRegistrationAsync();
}
```

7. To make sure that the app doesn't launch if Google Play Services is not installed, we can request the user installs it each time the app is resumed in `OnResume`:

```
CheckPlayServices();
```

Now that we have the connection set up and the device registered with the cloud service, we need to get the receiver in place so that we can actually receive incoming messages:

1. We create a `GcmReceiver` instance that will receive incoming push notifications. It doesn't do anything except allow us to attach attributes:

```
[BroadcastReceiver(
  Permission = "com.google.android.c2dm.permission.SEND",
  Exported = true)]
[IntentFilter(
  new []{
    "com.google.android.c2dm.intent.RECEIVE",
    "com.google.android.c2dm.intent.REGISTRATION" },
  Categories = new[]{ "@PACKAGE_NAME@" })]
public class NotificationReceiver : GcmReceiver {
}
```

2. The receiver will redirect any messages to a service for processing. The service inherits from `GcmListenerService` and has a specific intent filter. We can then process the message in the `OnMessageReceived()` method:

```
[Service]
[IntentFilter(new []{
  "com.google.android.c2dm.intent.RECEIVE })]
public class NotificationService : GcmListenerService {
  public override void OnMessageReceived(
  string from, Bundle data) {
    // process the data bundle
    var message = data.GetString("cookbook_message");
  }
}
```

Sometimes the token becomes invalid, for example if the server or Google decide to refresh the tokens. When this happens, our app will be notified:

1. To handle token refresh events, we create an interface that inherits from the `InstanceIDListenerService` type:

```
[Service]
[IntentFilter(
new []{ "com.google.android.gms.iid.InstanceID" })]
public class InstanceIdService : InstanceIDListenerService
{
  public override void OnTokenRefresh() {
    var instanceId = InstanceID.GetInstance(this);
    var token = instanceId.GetToken(
      "PROJECT_NUMBER",
      GoogleCloudMessaging.InstanceIdScope);
  }
}
```

In order for a device to receive messages, they have to be sent from our server to the cloud service. There are several ways to do this, but here we use HTTP requests:

1. We can send a message to the cloud service using JSON, specifying a message and a device registration token:

```
var server = "https://android.googleapis.com/gcm/send";
var message = string.Format(
  "{{" +
  "  \"registration_ids\": [ \"{0}\" ]" +
  "  \"data\": {{" +
  "    \"cookbook_message\": \"Hello World!\"" +
  "  }}" +
  "}}", registrationId);
var bytes = Encoding.UTF8.GetBytes(message);
var request = WebRequest.CreateHttp(server);
request.Method = "POST";
request.ContentType = "application/json";
request.ContentLength = bytes.Length;
var stream = await request.GetRequestStreamAsync();
stream.Write(bytes, 0, bytes.Length);
stream.Close();
```

2. We have to authorize the request using the API key we got from the Google Developers Console:

```
request.Headers.Add(
  HttpRequestHeader.Authorization, "key=API_KEY");
await request.GetResponseAsync();
```

How it works...

Push notifications are very useful for many types of apps. They allow a remote server to send a message directly to the phone and our app, without the app having to continually poll the server. The app registers with GCM and waits for the cloud service to send messages. Once a message is received, the service broadcasts the message, which the app can then handle.

 Sending messages to a device is not done directly but rather through GCM.

A server that wants to send a message to a device actually sends the message to GCM but specifies which device should receive it. Once GCM receives the message, it is relayed to the actual device.

The advantage of using GCM is that our app does not have to query the server or maintain connections to the server. If each app tried to connect to servers just to check if there was a message, the battery would drain quickly. Using a centralized connection, the service can open and maintain connections instead of each app. This also reduces much of the code that would be needed to maintain connections to a server as well as actually maintaining an actual server for the device to connect to.

 Using GCM reduces the number of open connections, thus reducing battery usage.

As there is a lot of work going on underneath, we have to include the Google Play Services library to do the work for us. This library contains all the logic needed to interact with GCM on an Android device.

Along with this library, we have to request several permissions for the app. First, we will need the `Internet` and `GetAccounts` permissions. Because we are going to use GCM to receive messages, we need the `com.google.android.c2dm.permission.RECEIVE` permission. As the device may be asleep when a message comes through, we need the `WakeLock` permission so that we can wake the device to process the incoming message.

Finally, we need to request an app-specific permission. This permission is the package name appended with `.permission.C2D_MESSAGE`. Instead of hardcoding the package name, we make use of the `@PACKAGE_NAME@` value. This value is then replaced at compile time with the actual package name.

Before we can interact with GCM, we have to first make sure that Google Play Services is installed on the device. This is a separate package from the Play Store that we can ask the user to install. First, we make sure that Google Play Services is installed by invoking the `IsGooglePlayServicesAvailable()` method on the `GoogleApiAvailability` instance. The result is a description of the error. If everything is in place, the result will be `ConnectionResult.Success`. Sometimes there is an issue that the user can fix, such as when the services are disabled or not installed. We check for this using the `IsUserResolvableError()` method. If this method returns `true`, we can display a dialog that will allow the user to rectify the problem. We get the dialog as a result of the `GetErrorDialog()` method. If there is any other problem, we can either close the app or allow the user to use the app without GCM, depending on what is required or supported.

 The Google Play Services package needs to be installed from the store before push notifications can be used. However, on most devices it is already installed.

If there are no errors and everything is installed, we can register with GCM and obtain an instance token that identifies the instance of the app on a device. To do this, we first need an instance of the `InstanceID` type, which we obtain by invoking the `GetInstance()` method. With the result, we can invoke the `GetToken()` method. This method requires that we have a valid Project Number, and, because we are going to be using the messaging APIs; we specify the `GoogleCloudMessaging.InstanceIdScope` method as the scope. The result of this method is a string instance token for the device. The Project Number is obtained from the Google Developers Console. As this is an input and output operation across a network, we must run this on a background thread.

 Registration for push notifications must happen on a background thread as the method does not return immediately.

Once we have registered, we need to send the token to whatever server will be sending notifications to our app. In the case of this example, the server will be the device. Our device will now receive any messages from the GCM server. However, in order to be able to handle these messages, we have to create a broadcast receiver. Because the device may be sleeping when a message is received, we use a `GcmReceiver` instance to ensure that the message is handled before going back to sleep.

 The device may be asleep when a push notification is received.

The receiver is usually very simple and just passes the incoming intent on to a service. But in order for the receiver to receive messages, we have to specify what messages we want to receive. We use the `[BroadcastReceiver]` attribute to specify that this receiver only accepts broadcasts from GCM services. To do this, we set the `Permission` property to `com.google.android.c2dm.permission.SEND`. Finally, we have to let the system know we are only interested in messages sent to this app from the GCM server. In order to ignore other messages, we specify an `[IntentFilter]` attribute with the action set to `com.google.android.c2dm.permission.SEND` and the `Categories` property set to the app package name.

 Specific permissions and filters are used on the receiver to ensure that the app can and only will receive messages sent to that specific app.

Once a message is received, it will get redirected to a service that has the `com.google.android.c2dm.intent.RECEIVE` intent filter. The easiest way to handle these messages is to create a service that inherits from the `GcmListenerService` type. We can read the message using the bundle provided to the `OnMessageReceived()` method. How the message is processed depends on how the message was structured when it was sent.

The `InstanceID` type is used to get a token when implementing push notifications, but this token may change over time, although often not frequently. Tokens may be reset, and when this happens, our app must request a new token. By creating a service that inherits from `InstanceIDListenerService` and has the `com.google.android.gms.iid.InstanceID` intent filter, we can handle this.

One of the ways to send a message to the GCM server is to use the HTTP server located at the address `https://android.googleapis.com/gcm/send`. We can send a JSON message to this server using an HTTP POST request:

```
{
    "registration_ids": ["DEVICE_REGISTRATION_ID"],
    "data": {
      "JSON-KEY": "JSON-VALUE"
    }
}
```

The HTTP message needs to be authorized with the API key from the Google Developers Console. The `key=API_KEY` value is used in the authorization header. This is because all servers will send messages to the same server, so they are distinguished using the authorization header.

There's more...

Push notifications can be used to reduce the number of times an app needs to communicate with a server. If all messages are sent directly to the device, there will be no need to check for messages on the server. However, if the device goes offline, for example if it is turned off, there is a limit to how many messages will be stored. Currently, the limit is 100 messages. If the limit is reached, all the stored messages are discarded and replaced with a special message that indicates a full sync is needed.

It is important to remember that only a tiny amount of data can be sent via push. Currently, the maximum message size is 4 KB. To send larger messages, we can send a message that indicates that the app should sync its data.

8
Interacting with Other Apps

In this chapter, we will cover the following recipes:

- ▸ Starting app components
- ▸ Launching other apps
- ▸ Obtaining data from activities
- ▸ Using BroadcastReceivers
- ▸ Scheduling tasks
- ▸ Making phone calls
- ▸ Intercepting phone calls
- ▸ Sending SMS messages
- ▸ Receiving SMS messages

Introduction

No app is developed or run in a vacuum. All users will have multiple apps installed on their devices, and we can take advantage of that to make our apps great.

If our app is an encyclopedia for a specific topic, we may want to share something. We can create mini Twitter, Facebook, and Google+ activities to interact with these social networks. We can create mini e-mail and SMS sections to support sharing in those formats. Alternatively, we can just use the user's favorite app that is installed on their device.

Using other apps that the user has installed on their device allows us to write smaller and more specific apps. We can then focus on our app and let the other developers improve their apps. This leads to a generally better app ecosystem. Also, if we use the app that the user prefers, we make our app friendlier to that user.

We may want our app to respond to system events and then change the way we work. For example, if the device loses connectivity, we can pause downloads and wait for the connection to return. If the battery runs low, we can make our app download fewer resources and maybe try stopping some background tasks. If the device reports an incoming call, we can pause the music or video so that the sound does not interfere with the call.

Responding to changes in the system allows the app to improve the user experience as the system changes. This leads to an app that makes the user feel like it is working with them to achieve a common goal.

Starting app components

All apps have several components that make up the app. These can be screens, chunks of work, and listeners that wait for an event to happen somewhere.

How to do it...

There are three basic components to any app: the `Activity`, the `Service`, and the `BroadcastReceiver` component:

1. The most common and most visible component is the `Activity` component:

```
[Activity]
public class DestinationActivity : Activity {
  protected override void OnCreate(Bundle savedState) {
    base.OnCreate(savedState);
  }
}
```

2. To start or display an activity, we simply invoke the `StartActivity()` method, as follows:

```
var intent = new Intent(this, typeof(DestinationActivity));
StartActivity(intent);
```

3. The next component that we use is a `Service`, or the chunk of work:

```
[Service]
public class DestinationService : IntentService {
  protected override void OnHandleIntent(Intent intent) {
  }
}
```

4. Similar to activities, we start a `Service` using the `StartService()` method:

```
var intent = new Intent(this, typeof(DestinationService));
StartService(intent);
```

5. Finally, there is the `BroadcastReceiver`, which is a listener for global events:

```
[BroadcastReceiver]
public class DestinationReceiver : BroadcastReceiver {
  public override void OnReceive(
  Context context, Intent intent) {
  }
}
```

6. The broadcast receiver can be started or reached using the `SendBroadcast()` method, as follows:

```
var intent = new Intent(this, typeof(DestinationReceiver));
SendBroadcast(intent);
```

Data can be passed to each of the components using the intents that are used to start them:

1. To attach data to an `Intent` instance, we make use of the extras feature:

```
intent.PutExtra("SomeKey", "Some String Value");
intent.PutExtra("AnotherKey", 123);
```

2. Once in a component, we can access the data using the various getter methods:

```
if (Intent.HasExtra("SomeKey")) {
  var text = Intent.GetStringExtra("SomeKey");
}
if (Intent.HasExtra("AnotherKey")) {
  var integer = Intent.GetIntExtra("AnotherKey");
}
```

How it works...

Each of the three main app components is used for very specific tasks. The `Activity` represents a single screen in an app. The activities are loosely bound to each other to create the visual aspect of an app. The `Service` represents a long-running, background task that can still run when the activities are terminated. The `BroadcastReceiver` is registered with the system and then waits for a specific event or message to be sent out.

 Usually, a `BroadcastReceiver` will simply start a `Service`, which does the actual work.

Activities, services, and broadcast receivers are registered with the Android system using various attributes. Activities require the `[Activity]` attribute, services require the `[Service]` attribute, and broadcast receivers require the `[BroadcastReceiver]` attribute.

> Attributes can be applied to the app components instead of manually updating the `AndroidManifest.xml` file.

Each component can be started directly using various methods found on the `Context` type. Activities are displayed using the `StartActivity()` method. However, if a result is desired from an activity, we use the `StartActivityForResult()` method instead. Services are started using the `StartService()` method. Broadcast receivers are initiated from either the `SendBroadcast()`, `SendOrderedBroadcast()`, or `SendStickyBroadcast()` methods.

When starting any app component, we provide an `Intent` instance. This intent holds the information that lets the Android system know which component to start and what data is required for it to start.

> An `Intent` instance can hold any extra data that needs to be passed to the app component that is going to be started.

In order to pass data into a component when it is started, we add the data to the intent. Data is added using the extras mechanism. Each piece of simple data is added as a `key-value` pair through the `PutExtra()` method. The data is usually primitive data types or arrays of primitive data types, but there is the option to add `IParcelable` objects such as another `Bundle` instance.

When we wish to retrieve data from the intent, we make use of the getter methods. These methods are named in the form `Get<Type>Extra`. For example, to obtain a string or an integer, we use the `GetStringExtra()` or `GetIntExtra()` methods respectively.

There's more...

When intents specify the exact type of the component to start, we call them **explicit intents**. These intents are usually used to start components within the app.

If we want to launch a component in another app, we cannot use explicit intents. This is because we may not know the fully-qualified name of the component or the user may not have installed the particular app. To get around this, we use implicit intents. These intents specify a general action and then hand it off to the system. This allows either the user, or the system, to specify a particular app to use with that action.

Explicit intents are created using a specific type to start a specific component. Implicit intents are created to initiate a general action.

Launching other apps

Often, we have to integrate our apps with existing apps on the user's device. This is simply because we will never be able to cover all the possible actions a user may wish to perform.

How to do it...

Using `Intents`, we can launch specific activities in other apps:

1. We can start other activities, such as the default map app, using the `ActionView` intent and a URI, as follows:

```
var uri = Uri.Parse("geo:37.797786,-122.401855");
var intent = new Intent(Intent.ActionView, uri);
StartActivity(intent);
```

2. Some activities require that a type be specified instead of a URI; which is done as shown here:

```
var intent = new Intent(Intent.ActionSend);
intent.SetType("text/plain");
intent.PutExtra(
   Intent.ExtraEmail, new[]{"user@example.com"});
intent.PutExtra(
   Intent.ExtraSubject, "Email Subject");
intent.PutExtra(
   Intent.ExtraText, "Email message text here...");
StartActivity(intent);
```

3. If the user has selected a default app for a particular intent, for example when the user chooses to always open pictures in a specific app, the app chooser will not be displayed. We can force the chooser to always be displayed using the following lines of code:

```
Intent intent = ...;
var chooser = Intent.CreateChooser(intent, "Open...");
StartActivity(chooser);
```

4. If we want to get a list of all the available activities for an intent, we use the `QueryIntentActivities()` method:

```
Intent intent = ...;
IList<ResolveInfo> activities =
PackageManager.QueryIntentActivities(intent, 0);
foreach (var activity in activities) {
  var name = activity.ActivityInfo.Name;
}
```

We can also make our activities available in the chooser for other apps to launch:

▶ To make our app visible, we add the `[IntentFilter]` attribute to our activity and set the `DataScheme` property to the scheme of the data URI:

```
[IntentFilter(
  new []{ Intent.ActionView },
  DataScheme = "geo",
  Categories = new[]{ Intent.CategoryDefault })]
```

▶ There is also an option to launch activities with an intent MIME type, which is filtered with the `DataMimeType` property:

```
[IntentFilter(
  new []{ Intent.ActionSend },
  DataMimeType = "text/plain",
  Categories = new[]{ Intent.CategoryDefault })]
```

▶ If we want to launch from an intent with both a MIME type and a data URI, we filter with both properties:

```
[IntentFilter(
  new []{ Intent.ActionSend },
  DataScheme = "geo",
  DataMimeType = "text/plain",
  Categories = new[]{ Intent.CategoryDefault })]
```

How it works...

Sometimes, we have to send data to, or open an activity from, another app. As we may not know the exact fully qualified name of the activity, or the user may be using an alternative app to handle the action, we have to use a more generic intent. These intents specify a generic action such as "share data" or "show map coordinates". The Android system searches through the list of registered activities to find the ones that can handle the intent. This type of intent is called an **implicit** intent.

Implicit intents specify a general action and the Android system displays a list of activities that are able to handle that action.

Some implicit intents are created with an action and a URI to be used with the action. An example of an action can be viewing or editing a specified URI. For example, when viewing a map coordinate, we specify the view intent action and then specify the geolocation as the URI.

Another form of implicit intent is to specify the action and the MIME type of the data we wish to view or edit. An example of an action can be sharing some data with a specific type. For example, we can share plain text data using the MIME type "text/plain" or share image data using the "image/jpeg" MIME type.

The data URI can be specified either in the constructor or using the `SetData()` method. To specify a MIME type, we use the `SetType()` method. If we want to specify both the URI and the MIME type, we use the `SetDataAndType()` method. The Android system uses these pieces of data to obtain a list of activities that support interaction with that intent.

 Implicit intents can start activities using a data URI, a MIME type, or both.

Once the system has obtained a list of all the activities that can interact with the intent, it may display the chooser to the user. The chooser allows the user to specify the actual activity that they wish to use. If there is only one activity, or the user has specified a default activity, the system will automatically launch that one. To always display the chooser, we wrap the real intent in a chooser intent, and then display that chooser intent instead of the real intent. The chooser intent is created from the actual intent along with a title, which is to be displayed on the chooser dialog. We use the static `CreateChooser()` method on the `Intent` type.

 The activity chooser will not be displayed if either a default app is selected for the intent or none of the apps can handle the intent.

If there are no activities that support the intent, then an `ActivityNotFoundException` exception will be thrown. We can either catch this exception or first verify that an activity does exist for the intent. To do this, we query the package manager using the `QueryIntentActivities()` method. The result is a collection of information regarding the available activities.

We may want one of our activities to appear in the chooser for other apps to launch. We may be creating an app that can handle map coordinates or an app that displays images. To let the Android system know that our app can be used in this manner, we use the `[IntentFilter]` attributes on the types that we wish to make available.

To let Android know that an activity should appear in the chooser, the [IntentFilter] attribute should be applied with parameters specifying what intents it can handle.

The intent filter describes which intents are able to launch this activity. When applying this attribute, we are required to specify the action that can launch this activity. Along with the action, we can specify which URI scheme starts this activity using the DataScheme property. Also, we can specify what MIME type is supported using the DataMimeType property. We can use either one or both of these properties to further restrict the intents that can launch this activity.

Finally, we can specify the category that is associated with the component. Categories are used to provide information about what kind of component should handle the intent. If we want our activity to appear in the chooser, we must specify the CategoryDefault category. Another category that can be used to allow a web browser to launch the activity is the CategoryBrowsable category. If we apply the CategoryLauncher category, the activity will appear in the top-level list of apps. This is automatically applied to activities when we set the MainLauncher property of the [Activity] attribute.

There's more...

We can specify custom icons and descriptions for activities that appear in the chooser dialog by setting the Icon and Label parameters on the [IntentFilter] attribute. This is especially useful when a single activity has multiple entry points based on different requirements.

For example, if a single activity can be used to view or to share a data element, we may wish to specify two intent filters. This way we can provide a customized icon and label that more accurately describes the action associated with the entry in the chooser.

Obtaining data from activities

We may want to show the user a new screen in order to obtain some feedback before the current task can be completed.

How to do it...

Starting an activity so that we can get feedback is done through the StartActivityForResult() method:

1. First, we start the activity using the StartActivityForResult() method:

```
var intent = new Intent(this, typeof(ResultsActivity));
StartActivityForResult(intent, 1234);
```

2. Then, when that activity is finished, we handle the result in the
   `OnActivityResult()` method:

```
protected override void OnActivityResult(
int requestCode, Result resultCode, Intent data) {
  base.OnActivityResult(requestCode, resultCode, data);

  if (requestCode == 1234) {
    if (resultCode == Result.Ok) {
      var value = data.GetStringExtra ("Key");
    }
    else {
      // canceled
    }
  }
}
```

3. In the new activity, we specify the result data to be passed back to the calling activity
   through the `SetResult()` method:

```
var result = new Intent();
result.PutExtra("Key", "Some Value");
SetResult(Result.Ok, result);
Finish();
```

How it works...

Sometimes, we require feedback from an activity that was just displayed. To get this feedback, we have to launch the activity while letting the Android system know that we wish to be notified of the outcome of the user's actions.

Similar to launching activities just to display another screen, we create an intent that will launch the activity. But, instead of calling `StartActivity`, we invoke the `StartActivityForResult()` method along with an integer code. This code will be used to associate the start operation with the result of the new activity.

 The `StartActivityForResult()` method should not be used to start activities that do not return a result.

The user can then select an option or perform an operation on the second activity. Once the user has returned from the second activity, we will be notified of this in the first activity. In order to respond to these notifications, we override the `OnActivityResult()` method.

In this method, we are provided with three pieces of data that we use to determine what happened in the activity that was just closed. The first piece is the request code, or the code that was specified when starting the activity. It is the value that was passed to the `StartActivityForResult()` method. We use this to associate the result logic with the initial logic.

> The request code value provided by the `OnActivityResult()` method when an activity is closed is the value that was passed to the `StartActivityForResult()` method when that activity was started.

The next piece of data is the result code. This represents a value showing whether the activity was successful, canceled, or an error occurred. If the result code is `Ok`, then the operation was successful and data was returned. If the result code is `Canceled`, then either the user canceled the operation or an error occurred.

Finally, the last piece of data represents an intent that was specified by the second activity. This intent can be used to hold any data we wish either in the `Data` property or in the various extras.

> The result code and the intent are values passed back from the closed activity.

If we want to create an activity that can be used in this manner, we just need to set the result code and, optionally, an intent before the activity is terminated. This is done by passing a result code and an intent to the `SetResult()` method.

This is usually followed by the `Finish()` method to let the Android system know that the activity should now be terminated. If no result is specified before the activity is terminated, then the result is automatically set to `Canceled`.

> If no result is set before the activity is closed, the result that the caller will receive is a `Canceled` value.

Using BroadcastReceivers

There may be several instances when we would want to listen for the occurrence of events as they occur on the running Android system.

How to do it...

To listen for broadcast system events, we make use of a `BroadcastReceiver` instance:

1. To listen for events, we need an instance of `BroadcastReceiver`:

```
public class WorkReceiver : BroadcastReceiver {
  public override void OnReceive(
  Context context, Intent intent) {
  }
}
```

2. Often, broadcast receivers don't do much except starting a service, which does the work on a background thread:

```
var service = new Intent(context, typeof(WorkService));
context.StartService(service);
```

Once we have a broadcast receiver, we need to register it with the Android system. There are three ways to do this:

▶ We can automatically register the receiver when the app is installed using the `[BroadcastReceiver]` attribute:

```
[BroadcastReceiver]
[IntentFilter(new []{ "xamarincookbook.Work" })]
```

▶ We can also manually register the receiver using the `RegisterReceiver()` method when we need to start listening:

```
receiver = new WorkReceiver();
var filter = new IntentFilter("xamarincookbook.Work");
RegisterReceiver(receiver, filter);
```

▶ And then we can unregister it when we are finished:

```
UnregisterReceiver(receiver);
```

▶ Regardless if it was installed automatically or manually, we can broadcast an intent to these receivers using the `SendBroadcast()` method:

```
var intent = new Intent("xamarincookbook.Work");
SendBroadcast(intent);
```

If we are going to be listening for messages that are only broadcast from within our app, we can use the `LocalBroadcastManager` instance:

1. The `LocalBroadcastManager` instance is available in the **Xamarin Support Library v4** NuGet or component, so we have to install that first.

2. Similar to manually registered receivers, we register the receiver with the local broadcast manager:

    ```
    receiver = new WorkReceiver();
    var filter = new IntentFilter("xamarincookbook.Work");
    var manager = LocalBroadcastManager.GetInstance(this);
    manager.RegisterReceiver(receiver, filter);
    ```

3. We can unregister the receiver when we are finished:

    ```
    var manager = LocalBroadcastManager.GetInstance(this);
    manager.UnregisterReceiver(receiver);
    ```

4. However, we have to broadcast a message through the local broadcast manager instead of the global broadcast manager:

    ```
    var intent = new Intent("xamarincookbook.Work");
    var manager = LocalBroadcastManager.GetInstance(this);
    manager.SendBroadcast(intent);
    ```

How it works...

A `BroadcastReceiver` instance is essentially an app component that listens for a specific global event to occur. Such events can be a change in Wi-Fi state, battery level, or the device booting up. Regardless of the event, broadcast receivers are very simple and only live as long as it takes to complete the execution of the `OnReceive()` method.

The `OnReceive()` method should be as short as possible and, and as a result, any long-running task should be assigned to a service instead of being executed directly. As soon as the method has completed, the receiver is marked as finished and ready to be disposed of. This is important when running asynchronous tasks. As the method will probably return before the background task has completed, the thread may be leaked or terminated unexpectedly.

> A `BroadcastReceiver` instance only lives as long as it takes for the `OnReceive()` method to return. Any running threads will be leaked.

We can register the receiver automatically when the user installs the app. This is especially useful for events that we want to listen for, even when the app is not running. To do this, we apply the `[BroadcastReceiver]` attribute to the receiver. Then, we apply the `[IntentFilter]` attribute to inform the Android system about the broadcast messages that we are waiting for.

However, this may not be necessary as we might only be listening for a message for a short period of time. This can be while downloading a file, or when we are interested in pausing the download when the user is no longer connected to Wi-Fi. In this case, we can dynamically register the receiver using the `RegisterReceiver()` method.

When we do this, we do not apply the attributes, but instead pass an instance of the receiver along with an instance of `IntentFilter` to the `RegisterReceiver()` method. We need to keep a reference to the receiver so that we can unregister it when we are finished.

 A single instance of a broadcast receiver can be registered multiple times, each time with a different intent filter.

As soon as we no longer require the receiver to listen for messages, we unregister it by passing the instance of the receiver to the `UnregisterReceiver()` method. When we unregister a receiver, all registrations of that receiver are removed.

 A broadcast receiver that is registered in the `OnResume()` method of an activity should be unregistered in the `OnPause()` method.

If we are only listening for internal broadcasts, we can further cut down on system resources by registering with the `LocalBroadcastManager`. This implementation is more efficient, but we can only respond to internally broadcast messages.

In order to use the `LocalBroadcastManager`, we have to install the Android Support v4 library. This is found in either the **Xamarin Support Library v4** NuGet or Component.

When we want to register a receiver with the local manager, we have to first obtain an instance of the manager using the static `GetInstance()` method. Once we have an instance, we can invoke the `RegisterReceiver()` and `UnregisterReceiver()` methods just as would invoke them on the `Context` type.

 Unregistering receivers when they are not needed helps reduce the impact on system resources.

Finally, we can broadcast messages using the `SendBroadcast()` method. We simply pass an intent to this method, and each of the registered receivers will receive them. We can also add any data to the intent using the extras mechanism. When the receiver responds to the message, it can obtain the values from the intent.

If we have registered the receiver using the local broadcast manager, we have to broadcast the intents using the manager. Receivers registered with the local broadcast manager will not receive globally broadcast intents and globally registered receivers will not receive locally broadcast messages.

Using the `LocalBroadcastManager` to broadcast intents increases app security as data that is broadcast never leaves the app.

Scheduling tasks

Some tasks need to be performed at a particular time in the future, some may even be required to recur.

How to do it...

We can schedule tasks for the future using the `AlarmManager` instance:

1. As scheduling tasks involves running code when the app is closed by the user, we have to get permission to do this:

   ```
   [assembly: UsesPermission(Manifest.Permission.SetAlarm)]
   ```

2. Then, we need a broadcast receiver that will receive a notification when the alarm is triggered:

   ```
   [BroadcastReceiver]
   [IntentFilter(new[] { "xamarincookbook.Alarm" })]
   public class AlarmReceiver : BroadcastReceiver {
     public override void OnReceive(
     Context context, Intent intent) {
       // alarm has triggered
     }
   }
   ```

3. When we want to schedule a task, we set an alarm for a specific time and then provide an intent that should be broadcast when the time expires:

   ```
   var ringTime = JavaSystem.CurrentTimeMillis() +
   (long)TimeSpan.FromSeconds(5).TotalMilliseconds;
   var intent = new Intent("xamarincookbook.Alarm");
   var alarm = PendingIntent.GetBroadcast(this, 0, intent, 0);
   var manager = AlarmManager.FromContext(this);
   manager.Set(AlarmType.RtcWakeup, ringTime, alarm);
   ```

How it works...

Sometimes, there is a need for a specific task to be performed after an interval, either once or repeatedly. This may be to check for data updates or to synchronize settings. To create a task that will execute later in the future, we use the `AlarmManager` instance.

Before we can use the `AlarmManager` instance, we need to request the `SetAlarm` permission. Next, we create a broadcast receiver that will be used to receive an intent once the alarm is triggered. The intent action that we specify in the intent filter is the action that will be broadcast once the alarm is triggered.

In order to schedule an alarm, we have to first obtain an instance of the manager using the static `FromContext()` method on the `AlarmManager` type. To set an alarm, we invoke the `Set()` method. This method takes three parameters, the type of alarm, the time, and the intent to broadcast when the alarm is triggered.

We specify that we want to use real time and we want to wake the device using the `RtcWakeup` alarm type. As the alarm may be triggered when the device is asleep, the manager holds a wake lock until the `OnReceive()` method is complete. This guarantees that the device will wake when the alarm is triggered and may go back to sleep as soon as it is finished executing.

> If the `AlarmType` does not specify that it will wake the device, the intent will wait until the device is woken before broadcasting the intent. This may not be desired if the intent needs to be broadcast at a specific time.

Then, we specify the alarm time in the number of milliseconds since the Unix epoch. In order to calculate the alarm time, we first obtain the current time as the number of milliseconds since the Unix epoch by using the static `CurrentTimeMillis()` method on `JavaSystem`. We then add to that the number of milliseconds between the current time and the desired time.

> Unix, or Java, time starts from January 1, 1970, but .NET or C# time starts from January 1, 2001.

The last parameter is the `PendingIntent` instance that holds the `Intent` instance that will be broadcast when the alarm expires.

There is also the option to repeat the operation after a certain interval. To do this, we can use the `SetRepeating()` method instead of the `Set()` method. This will allow us to specify an additional parameter, which is the number of milliseconds between alarm triggers.

> When using the repeating alarm, the interval must be greater than or equal to 60 seconds. If not, the interval will be adjusted. For shorter intervals, an exact alarm can be used, with a manual reschedule.

There's more...

There are two main types of alarms: real time and boot time. Each type has an option to wake the device when the alarm is triggered. The real time clock uses the current system time of the device and the boot time starts from the time the device is booted.

To specify real time, we use the `Rtc` or `RtcWakeup` instances, and to specify boot time, we use `ElapsedRealtime` or `ElapsedRealtimeWakeup`.

The wake-up variants specify that the device should wake up and execute the broadcast. If this is not necessary, the manager will wait until the device is woken before broadcasting. If the device is not woken, the broadcasts are not queued up, and when the device finally wakes, only one broadcast will be sent.

Making phone calls

Our app may need to initiate a phone call from within the app without the user having to leave the current context.

How to do it...

To initiate a call directly from within our app, we use an `Intent` instance:

1. We first need to ensure that the device has telephony features. There are two ways to do this; one way is to use attributes:

   ```
   [assembly: UsesFeature(
       Android.Content.PM.PackageManager.FeatureTelephony)]
   ```

   Alternatively, we can check for the telephony feature using the `HasSystemFeature()` method at runtime:

   ```
   var hasTelephony = PackageManager.HasSystemFeature(
       Android.Content.PM.PackageManager.FeatureTelephony);
   if (hasTelephony) {
       // do something
   }
   ```

2. If we are running on a device with telephony features, we still need to request permissions to start phone calls:

   ```
   [assembly: UsesPermission(Manifest.Permission.CallPhone)]
   ```

3. Finally, we can make the phone call using the `ActionCall` action intent:

```
var number = "0123456789";
var intent = new Intent(Intent.ActionCall);
intent.SetData(Uri.Parse("tel:" + number));
StartActivity(intent);
```

How it works...

We may want to allow the user to start a call directly from our app, and we can do this very easily. This is useful if we want the app to start calling immediately without the user having to press the call button on the phone's dialer.

As some devices, such as Wi-Fi tablets, do not actually have telephony features, we need to ensure that the device has the desired features first. There are two ways to check for the availability of specific features.

We can ensure that the app cannot be installed on a device without telephony features. For this, we use the `[UsesFeature]` attribute, which will add an entry into the `AndroidManifest.xml` file. Alternatively, we can check for the availability of specific features at runtime using the `HasSystemFeature()` method on the `PackageManager` type.

 To prevent an app from being installed on a device without a certain feature, the `[UsesFeature]` attribute is used. If the app can still function without the feature, the `HasSystemFeature()` method can be used at runtime.

We first need to request permission to start calls directly as this may cost the user. So, we request the `CallPhone` permission.

To place the call, all we need to do is create an intent with the `ActionCall` intent action. We then specify the number using the `SetData` mechanism. When we call `StartActivity`, the phone will begin calling the number.

If multiple phone apps exist on the device, such as Skype and the default dialer, the chooser will be displayed. If there are multiple apps, but the user has selected a default, then the default will be used automatically.

There's more...

If we want to call numbers from our app, without getting the `CallPhone` permission but only a confirmation from the user to receive the call, we can open the dialer.

To open the dialer we use the `ActionDial` intent action instead of `ActionCall`. This will display the dialer with the telephone number already entered, but this will not start the call.

Intercepting phone calls

An app might need to keep track of, or be notified of, incoming and outgoing phone calls.

How to do it...

In order to intercept incoming and outgoing phone calls, we listen for broadcasts:

1. First, we require the permissions to intercept phone calls:

```
[assembly: UsesPermission(
  Manifest.Permission.ReadPhoneState)]
[assembly: UsesPermission(
  Manifest.Permission.ProcessOutgoingCalls)]
```

2. Next, we need to create a broadcast receiver that can handle phone state changes and call events:

```
[BroadcastReceiver]
[IntentFilter(new[] {
  TelephonyManager.ActionPhoneStateChanged,
  Intent.ActionNewOutgoingCall })]
public class PhoneCallReceiver : BroadcastReceiver {
  public override void OnReceive(
  Context context, Intent intent) {
  }
}
```

3. Now, in order to intercept incoming calls, we listen for phone state changes:

```
if (intent.Action ==
TelephonyManager.ActionPhoneStateChanged) {
  var number = intent.GetStringExtra(
    TelephonyManager.ExtraIncomingNumber);
  if (!string.IsNullOrEmpty(number)) {
    // incoming call
  }
}
```

4. We can also intercept outgoing calls by listening for the `ActionNewOutgoingCall` intent action:

```
if (intent.Action == Intent.ActionNewOutgoingCall) {
  var number =
  intent.GetStringExtra(Intent.ExtraPhoneNumber);
  if (!string.IsNullOrEmpty(number)) {
    // outgoing call
  }
}
```

How it works...

If we wish to be notified when a call is made or there is a new incoming call, we can listen for these events using a broadcast receiver.

 It will be useful to first verify that the telephony features are supported on the device before attempting to use them.

Before we can interact with the phone aspects of the device, we have to request permission to do so. We will need the `ReadPhoneState` permission if we want to be notified of incoming calls, and we will need the `ProcessOutgoingCalls` permission if we want to be notified of outgoing calls.

Now, we can create the broadcast receivers that will handle the phone events. We can create two separate receivers, each listening for a specific broadcast, but this is not required. When creating a receiver that listens for multiple messages, we can combine the intent actions in the array passed to the `[IntentFilter]` attribute.

 Broadcast receivers can listen for multiple intents if they are registered using multiple action intents with the intent filter.

We should listen for the `TelephonyManager.ActionPhoneStateChanged` intent if we want to be notified of incoming calls and the `Intent.ActionNewOutgoingCall` intent if we want to be notified of outgoing calls.

The `TelephonyManager.ActionPhoneStateChanged` action is broadcast for various reasons as the phone state changes, but we are only interested in the event if the `ExtraIncomingNumber` extra is there. The existence of this extra means that there is an incoming call.

 If the incoming call is from a private number, the value of the extra will be a negative integer.

To intercept outgoing calls, we respond to the `Intent.ActionNewOutgoingCall` intent action. When we receive this action, we can obtain the phone number using the `ExtraPhoneNumber` extra.

There's more...

We can cancel an outgoing call by setting the `ResultData` property of the broadcast receiver to `null`. And, we can change the number that is called by setting the `ResultData` property of the broadcast receiver as the new number. This, however, only applies to normal numbers. Emergency numbers cannot be manipulated or canceled.

Sending SMS messages

We may be creating an app that requires the user to send an SMS message to a specific number.

How to do it...

To send an SMS message, we make use of the `SmsManager` instance:

1. Before we can work with the `SmsManager` instance, we require a permission:

   ```
   [assembly: UsesPermission(Manifest.Permission.SendSms)]
   ```

2. To send the SMS, we only require a single method—`SendTextMessage`:

   ```
   var number = "0123456789";
   var message = "SMS Message Text...";
   var manager = SmsManager.Default;
   manager.SendTextMessage(number, null, message, null, null);
   ```

If we need to verify that the message was sent successfully, we can use intents that will be broadcast with the operation status:

1. First, we have to send the message providing the intents that will be broadcast when the message is sent and delivered:

   ```
   var sentIntent = PendingIntent.GetBroadcast(
      this, 0, new Intent("xamarincookbook.Send"), 0);
   var deliveredIntent = PendingIntent.GetBroadcast(
      this, 0, new Intent("xamarincookbook.Delivered"), 0);
   manager.SendTextMessage(
      number, null, message, sentIntent, deliveredIntent);
   ```

2. We then create a broadcast receiver that will listen for these intents:

   ```
   public class SmsSentReceiver : BroadcastReceiver {
     public override void OnReceive(
     Context context, Intent intent) {
       if (intent.Action == "xamarincookbook.Send") {
         var sendSuccess = ResultCode == Result.Ok;
       }
   ```

```
      if (intent.Action == "xamarincookbook.Delivered") {
        var deliverySuccess = ResultCode == Result.Ok;
      }
    }
  }
}
```

3. The broadcast receiver can be registered dynamically as it will only be needed for a short while:

```
receiver = new SmsSentReceiver();
RegisterReceiver(
  receiver, new IntentFilter("xamarincookbook.Send"));
RegisterReceiver(
  receiver, new IntentFilter("xamarincookbook.Delivered"));
```

4. The broadcast receiver can then be unregistered when the message has been delivered successfully:

```
UnregisterReceiver(receiver);
```

How it works...

Sending SMS messages can be done from within an Android app without user intervention.

 Like phone calls, working with SMS messages requires that the device supports the telephony features.

To send SMS messages, we first need to request the `SendSms` permission. This is required because sending an SMS message involves a cost for the user.

Once we have the permission, we can then obtain an instance of the `SmsManager` instance. We then pass the destination number and message to the `SendTextMessage()` method.

 To confirm that a message was delivered to a recipient, an intent can be provided to the `SendTextMessage()` method. When the message is delivered, the intent will be broadcast.

The second last parameter of the `SendTextMessage()` method is a `PendingIntent` instance that will be broadcast if the message is successfully sent out or if there is an error in sending. The `ResultCode` will either be `Ok` if it is successful, or another value if there is an error.

To confirm that the SMS is delivered to the recipient, we provide a `PendingIntent` instance to the last parameter. This intent will be broadcast when the message has been delivered.

There's more...

If the message is going to be too long for a single message, we can use the `DivideMessage()` method on the `SmsManager` instance to break the message up into fragments.

The fragments are then sent to a recipient using the `SendMultipartTextMessage()` method. We pass the collection of fragments along with a collection of pending intents that should be broadcast as each fragment is sent and delivered.

Receiving SMS messages

Our app may be using SMS messages to verify the phone number that the user has specified. If we want to do this, we may want to listen for an incoming SMS message.

How to do it...

To listen for incoming SMS messages, we will use a broadcast receiver:

1. First, we will need a permission to receive SMS messages:

   ```
   [assembly: UsesPermission(Manifest.Permission.ReceiveSms)]
   ```

2. Next, we will need a broadcast receiver that listens for incoming messages:

   ```
   [BroadcastReceiver]
   [IntentFilter(
     new[] { "android.provider.Telephony.SMS_RECEIVED" })]
   public class SmsReceiver : BroadcastReceiver {
     public override void OnReceive(
     Context context, Intent intent) {
     }
   }
   ```

3. Finally, we process the incoming intent and read the SMS message:

   ```
   if (intent.HasExtra("pdus")) {
     var smsArray =
       (Java.Lang.Object[])intent.Extras.Get("pdus");
     string address = "";
     string message = "";
     foreach (var item in smsArray) {
       var sms = SmsMessage.CreateFromPdu((byte[])item);
       message += sms.MessageBody;
       address = sms.OriginatingAddress;
     }
   }
   ```

How it works...

Listening for incoming SMS messages is useful, especially as we can use them to verify the existence of a device. We can have an app requires that the user to have a valid mobile number. It can request that a server sends an SMS to the device, and when the message is received, allow the user to log in.

Before we can listen for incoming SMS messages, we require the `ReceiveSms` permission.

We can receive events for incoming SMS messages if we register a broadcast receiver for the `android.provider.Telephony.SMS_RECEIVED` intent action.

When the device receives an SMS message, we can read the message out of the `pdus` extra. The extra contains an array of one or more message parts. Each part is an array of bytes that can be used to create a `SmsMessage` object instance.

 The incoming SMS intent represents a single message, but each intent may contain multiple parts of the message.

Once we have created a `SmsMessage` instance using the static `CreateFromPdu()` method, we can then read various properties to obtain information on each part.

As the message may be broken up into parts, we have to concatenate the message text obtained from the `MessageBody` property. We can use the `OriginatingAddress` property to obtain the number that the message was sent from.

There's more...

If, for some reason, we do not wish to display the SMS notification on the device, we can stop the broadcast from being propagated to the default SMS app.

To do this, we use the `InvokeAbortBroadcast()` method on the receiver. This will prevent the message from reaching the default SMS app, therefore, we need to be very careful when doing this.

We may have to ensure that our app receives the SMS before the default app, otherwise the abort operation will do nothing. To ensure this, we set the `Priority` property in the `[IntentFilter]` attribute as `IntentFilterPriority.HighPriority`.

9

Presenting Multimedia

In this chapter, we will cover the following recipes:

- ▸ Playing audio
- ▸ Playing audio in the background
- ▸ Managing the audio volume
- ▸ Recording an audio
- ▸ Playing a video
- ▸ Custom video controls
- ▸ Using the camera
- ▸ Creating a camera app
- ▸ Handling high-resolution images
- ▸ Drawing on the canvas of a View
- ▸ Drawing on the canvas of SurfaceView

Introduction

Multimedia is one of the most commonly used mechanisms for attracting users to mobile apps and games. No matter how great an app, if it is not designed well, it will not be well received by the users. Users not only want to be amazed by great designs, but they also want to be entertained.

Adding audio and sound effects to a game really makes the game seem more complete. By simply adding feedback sound effects, the app seems to be responding more rapidly. Sound effects can range from short sounds when a button is tapped to a looping background track while the app is open. Even game menus have sounds, and although it should not be overdone, sounds add depth to many types of apps.

Not only sound, but also visual effects and feedback. By simply displaying a small change when the user interacts with an onscreen element, the user already feels that the app is responding. Visual enhancements can go all the way to including videos. Almost all content can be described by static text and images, but a video provides a far greater means to present data, as well as to draw a user into an app. Videos can range from a simple looping background all the way to longer, more detailed videos.

If the user wants to be entertained, making use of the camera allows the user to interact with the real world through the device. This can range from taking a photo and adding a message and effects all the way to providing an augmented reality experience. Allowing the user to capture a moment and then adding to it or sharing it supports the reason why social networks exist. People want to be able to interact with others, and, by taking the user's world and showing it on the device with more information, in real time, further makes the device and the app more real. This information can simply be real world information, such as mapping or face recognition, all the way to games that require the user to move in the real world in order to be able to move in the game.

One of the most common form of multimedia, after videos, is games. Games provide the user with a greater experience as compared to a video. The user is immersed in an entire world, where they are in control. This immersion allows the user to be a part of an alternate reality. As a result of this experience, users will continue to buy games so they can remain in the virtual world and do things that may be impossible in the real world.

Playing audio

Many apps, especially games, have sounds. This can just be a feedback sound or one that enhances the navigation or interaction of the game. Games usually have background music playing on a loop.

How to do it...

The `MediaPlayer` type is used to play a sound from a content provider, a URI or a resource:

1. To play a sound from included resources or a `Uri` instance, we use the static `Create()` method on `MediaPlayer`:

```
var mediaPlayer = MediaPlayer.Create(
    this, Resource.Raw.SoundResource);
```

2. Then, because we need to be able to clean up after the sound is finished, we subscribe to the `Completion` event and release the player:

```
mediaPlayer.Completion += delegate {
    mediaPlayer.Release();
    mediaPlayer = null;
};
```

3. To begin playing, either from a paused or prepared state, we invoke the `Start()` method:

```
mediaPlayer.Start();
```

4. Finally, we can control the player using the `Pause()` and `Stop()` methods:

```
mediaPlayer.Pause();
mediaPlayer.Stop();
```

If we want to stream sound from an asset or a remote URI, we construct a new `MediaPlayer` object, which sets various options before starting:

1. For more control over how and what is played, we use the `MediaPlayer` constructor:

```
var mediaPlayer = new MediaPlayer();
```

2. Before we can play sound, we have to specify what type of sound will be played. The most common is `Music`, so lets execute the following code to add sound in our project:

```
mediaPlayer.SetAudioStreamType(Stream.Music);
```

3. We can play a file out of the app assets by passing the `FileDescriptor` to the `SetDataSource()` method:

```
var fd = Assets.OpenFd("SoundAsset.mp3");
mediaPlayer.SetDataSource(
    fd.FileDescriptor, fd.StartOffset, fd.Length);
fd.Close();
```

Alternatively, we could play a file from a content provider or remote URI using the `SetDataSource()` method as well:

```
var uri = "http://example.org/audio.mp3");
mediaPlayer.SetDataSource(uri);
```

4. Again, we may want to clean up the player when the playback is complete, if we aren't going to use it again:

```
mediaPlayer.Completion += delegate {
    mediaPlayer.Release();
    mediaPlayer = null;
};
```

5. In case of any errors, we will have to reset the player before we can use it again:

```
mediaPlayer.Error += delegate {
  mediaPlayer.Reset();
};
```

6. Before the audio can be played, it has to be prepared. As this takes some time, it has to be done on a separate thread, using the `PrepareAsync()` method. When the preparation is complete, the playback can be started:

```
mediaPlayer.Prepared += delegate {
  mediaPlayer.Start();
};
mediaPlayer.PrepareAsync();
```

7. If we are already on another thread, we can just invoke the synchronous `Prepare()` method and then use the `Start()` method to begin the playback:

```
mediaPlayer.Prepare();
mediaPlayer.Start();
```

How it works...

If we want to play audio, we make use of the `MediaPlayer` type, which provides all the tools needed to play media. Media can be streamed from local sources, such as the file system, and remote sources, such as internet streaming.

 The `MediaPlayer` type can play both video and audio from either local or remote sources.

For the most simplest of cases, we can just make use of the convenient static `Create()` method overloads. This method will automatically prepare the player, and once the method returns, we can start playing the audio. The `Create()` method can load and prepare local audio, for example a packaged resource or a URI, such as that from a content provider or the file system.

 The `Create()` method will automatically prepare the media player.

The `MediaPlayer` object is quite expensive and should be disposed of as soon as we are finished with it. We let the system know that it should clean up the resources by invoking the `Release()` method. If we are creating a sound that will be played once, we can attach an event handler to the `Completion` event, which will allow us to clean up as soon as the event is fired. If the player is stopped before the end of the file, the `Completion` event will not be triggered, and we will have to release the player ourselves.

We can control the player through the various methods available. The most basic is `Start`, which will start the player, and `Stop`, which will stop the playback. If we stop the playback, we will have to prepare the player before we can start playing again. If we invoke the `Pause()` method, playback is paused and can be resumed by the `Start()` method without having to prepare the player.

 If the player is stopped, the `Completion` event will not be triggered and the player will have to be prepared again before resuming.

If we want to jump to a specific location in the playback, we can use the `SeekTo()` method. This method is asynchronous and moves the playback to the specified millisecond location. If we want to be notified about the completion of the seek, we can subscribe to the `SeekCompleted` event. Seeking is asynchronous as we may have to wait for the buffer to load enough data before playing.

 The `SeekTo()` method is asynchronous as the media may be streaming over a network.

To have greater control over what, and how, audio is played, we can use the default `MediaPlayer` constructor. This provides us with a player that is not already set up and ready to play. If we use the constructor, we will have to set the audio type using the `SetAudioStreamType()` method. The audio stream type can be, but is not limited to, `Stream.Music`, `Stream.Alarm`, or `Stream.Notification`, depending on what we will play. For most cases, `Stream.Music` will be used.

Creating the `MediaPlayer` instance through the constructor allows us to play files from stream-based locations, such as the assets or a remote URL. To play a file from the assets, we can open the `FileDescriptor` instance and then pass it to the `SetDataSource()` method. Similarly, we can pass either a string or an `Uri` instance to the `SetDataSource()` method to specify what should be played.

 The default constructor does not prepare the player and has to be done manually.

As there may be a problem during the execution of asynchronous methods, we can subscribe to the `Error` event. This allows us to receive notifications when an error occurs. If there is an error, the player goes into an invalid state and will have to be reset using the `Reset()` method before we can perform any other operations.

Before we can play the audio, we have to prepare the player. We can do this either asynchronously or synchronously. If we prepare the player synchronously, it will block the current thread. If the player is streaming from a remote source, this may take some time; thus, it should always be done on a separate thread.

If we prepare the player asynchronously, it will not block the UI and will trigger the Prepared event on completion. We can use this event to start the audio playback immediately, or we can delay the playback until a later time. To prepare asynchronously, we invoke the PrepareAsync() method, and to prepare synchronously, we invoke the Prepare() method.

 Preparing the player may take some time, especially if the source is on a network. Thus, PrepareAsync should always be used on the UI thread.

There's more...

The SoundPool instance can also be used for small audio clips. It can repeat or play several sounds simultaneously. Sounds are loaded asynchronously, but should not exceed 1 MB.

Sounds are loaded using the Load() method, which returns an ID that is used by the Play() method to start the playback of that sound. The Play() method returns another ID, which we use to control the playback through the Pause() and Resume() methods.

Playing audio in the background

Sometimes, we may want to be able to play audio in the background after the user has closed the app. We may be creating a media player app, or we may just want to allow various media to be played without requiring an activity to be displayed on the screen.

How to do it...

We can play audio in the background if we play it from a Service instance:

1. First, we will create a service that will be responsible for playing music. Here, we have methods that will be expanded in the following code snippet:

```
[Service]
public class MediaService : Service {
  public const string ActionPlay = "ActionPlay";
  public const string ActionPause = "ActionPause";
  public const string ActionStop = "ActionStop";

  private MediaPlayer mediaPlayer;
  private bool isPrepared = false;

  public override void OnDestroy() {
    base.OnDestroy();
    CleanUpPlayer();
  }
  public override StartCommandResult OnStartCommand(
```

```
    Intent intent, StartCommandFlags flags, int startId) {
      switch (intent.Action) {
        case ActionPlay:
          StartPlaying();
          break;
        case ActionPause:
          PausePlaying();
          break;
        case ActionStop:
          StopPlaying();
          CleanUpPlayer();
          break;
      }
      return StartCommandResult.Sticky;
    }
    public override IBinder OnBind(Intent intent) {
      return null;
    }
```

2. When the activity starts, we can launch the service using the `StartService()` method:

```
StartService(new Intent(this, typeof(MediaService)));
```

3. When we want to control the player, we can send intents to the service using the `StartService()` method with an intent action:

```
StartService(new Intent(MediaService.ActionPlay,
  null, this, typeof(MediaService)));
StartService(new Intent(MediaService.ActionPause,
  null, this, typeof(MediaService)));
StartService(new Intent(MediaService.ActionStop,
  null, this, typeof(MediaService)));
```

Once we have our service created, we need to go ahead and implement the various methods that control the underlying `MediaPlayer` instance:

1. When we want to play the music, we need to create a `MediaPlayer` instance. We do this in our `StartPlaying()` method:

```
if (mediaPlayer == null) {
  isPrepared = false;
  mediaPlayer = new MediaPlayer();
  // ... set up the media player ...
  mediaPlayer.Prepared += delegate {
    isPrepared = true;
    mediaPlayer.Start();
  };
  mediaPlayer.PrepareAsync();
```

```
}
else if (isPrepared && !mediaPlayer.IsPlaying) {
  mediaPlayer.Start();
}
```

2. To pause music, we can just use the `Pause()` method. We do this in our `PausePlaying()` method:

```
if (isPrepared) {
  mediaPlayer.Pause();
}
```

3. If we want to stop the player, we can also simply invoke the `Stop()` method. This is done in our `StopPlaying()` method:

```
if (isPrepared) {
  mediaPlayer.Stop();
}
```

4. Finally, we should implement the `CleanUpPlayer` instance to free resources:

```
if (mediaPlayer != null) {
  mediaPlayer.Release();
  mediaPlayer = null;
}
isPrepared = false;
```

The Android system may decide that our service is not important as it is only running in the background, and it may terminate the service. We can avoid this in two ways, wake locks or foreground services.

Way 1:

1. We can tell the media player to acquire a wake lock while it is playing music, preventing the CPU from going to sleep. We do this through the `SetWakeMode()` method:

```
mediaPlayer.SetWakeMode(
    ApplicationContext, WakeLockFlags.Partial);
```

2. In order to use the wake locks, we need to request for a permission to do so:

```
[assembly: UsesPermission(Manifest.Permission.WakeLock)]
```

3. If we are streaming audio over Wi-Fi, we can also acquire a `WifiLock` instance, which will prevent the Wi-Fi hardware from going to sleep:

```
manager = WifiManager.FromContext(ApplicationContext);
wifiLock = manager.CreateWifiLock(WifiMode.Full, "tag");
```

4. We then release the lock when the playback stops or pauses:

```
wifiLock.Release();
```

Way 2:

1. Also, we can specify that our service should be treated as a foreground component. For this, we pass a `Notification` instance to the `StartForeground()` method:

```
var context = ApplicationContext;
var activity = new Intent(context, typeof(MainActivity));
var pending = PendingIntent.GetActivity(
   context, 0, activity, PendingIntentFlags.UpdateCurrent);
var notification = new NotificationCompat.Builder(context)
   .SetSmallIcon(Android.Resource.Drawable.IcMediaPlay)
   .SetContentTitle("Music Player Sample")
   .SetContentText("Playing music...")
   .SetOngoing(true)
   .SetContentIntent(pending)
   .Build();
StartForeground(MediaNotificationId, notification);
```

2. We may want to move the service into the background when the music is paused, but we may not want to remove the notification. This is done using the following line of code:

```
StopForeground(false);
```

3. When the music stops, we can move the service into the background and remove the notification:

```
StopForeground(true);
```

How it works...

There may be cases where we would like to play audio across activities or fragments, especially if we are creating a media player app. To do this, we can play the audio from a background service and is fairly similar to playing audio in an `Activity` attribute. This is required if we want the audio to continue even when the user has closed the app or if another app is in use.

 A `MediaPlayer` instance should be released when an `Activity` attribute is paused. To continue playing audio, even when the app is closed, a `Service` instance is used.

The main thing that needs to be done is to create a service that will handle requests to control the playback. We inherit from `Service` and implement the control methods in the `StartCommandResult()` method and the cleanup in `OnDestroy`.

In the `StartCommandResult()` method, we can interact with our `MediaPlayer` object as we would from an `Activity` instance. For a `MediaPlayer` service, we might want to specify `Sticky` or `RedeliverIntent` to ensure that the service is restarted if the system decides to stop it. Similar to releasing a player when the activity is paused, we would want to release the `MediaPlayer` instance in the `OnDestroy()` method.

As the service actually runs on the main thread, we can start a new thread that does the work. The service will just receive an `Intent` instance and pass it on to the thread which would control the player. Or, we can take advantage of the asynchronous methods of the media player, such as `PrepareAsync()` and `SetDataSourceAsync()`. Setting up a media player in a service is exactly the same as in an activity, except that it is not limited to the life of an activity.

[The service that controls a media player can either create a new thread to prepare the player or make use of the asynchronous methods.]

We use `Intents` to control the media player in the service. The action can specify what we would like to do and then make use of the extras to provide information needed to do it. For example, if we were creating a media player app, we can send the play intent action and provide the track ID in the extras. Another example is if the user has updated the playback type from loop all audio to loop a single track, we can use a more general settings action, but then provide the actual type of action as an extra.

[Android may stop background services when the device goes to sleep, so a media player service should be moved to the foreground.]

As the service runs as a background process, the Android may decide to stop services when the device goes to sleep. This is a result of an attempt of the Android system to preserve the battery life when not in use. As a media player should not stop playing when the screen is turned off, we need to let the system know that we want our service to be treated as if it was a foreground app even when the device is sleeping.

To do this, we first have to tell the `MediaPlayer` instance to acquire a wake lock when music is playing. This is easy to do and we just need to let the player know what wake lock to use. As wake locks are a privileged feature, we need to ensure that we requested the `WakeLock` permission for the app.

Then, to specify that the player should acquire a wake lock, we pass the app context and the wake lock type to the `SetWakeMode()` method on the player. The wake lock is automatically managed by the player and it will acquire a wake lock when audio begins playing. As soon as the playback stops due to a pause, stop, or when the audio reaches the end, the wake lock is released.

[Wake locks are automatically managed by the media player, and only held while there is media playback.]

If we are streaming audio over Wi-Fi, we can also acquire a `WifiLock` to prevent the Wi-Fi hardware from going to sleep and stopping the playback. This is simple to do and we only need the `WifiManager` instance, which we get from the app context. Once we have the manager, we invoke the `CreateWifiLock()` method, passing the lock type and a tag used for debugging purposes. When the playback stops or is paused, we can then `Release()` the lock to conserve battery life.

 Unlike wake locks, Wi-Fi locks have to be managed manually.

Even if we hold a wake lock and a Wi-Fi lock, the Android system may still determine that the service can be stopped. This is because although the service holds locks, it is still in the background. This may occur if the user starts some activity that requires a lot of resources, and as the service is in the background, it is considered to be less important than the foreground activity.

 Android may stop a background service even if it holds wake locks.

To avoid our service being treated as a background service, we can move it to the foreground. Foreground services require a user-visible notification that is displayed while the service remains in the foreground. Notifications used with foreground services are just normal notifications and are created as we would create any notification. We can also update these notifications to display the service progress. To move the service into the foreground, we pass the notification that will be shown and a notification ID to the `StartForeground()` method.

 When the service is in the foreground, it will almost never be stopped by the Android system.

To move a service out of the foreground, such as when audio is finished, stopped, or paused, we can use the `StopForeground()` method. This method requires a `bool` value. If we specify `true`, the notification that was passed to `StartForeground()` will be removed. If we specify `false`, the notification will remain, but it will be automatically removed when the service is destroyed.

There's more...

When we are playing audio in a service, we must ensure that our app does not interfere with any other app that wants to play audio. When our app is not in the foreground, other apps take priority. To allow other apps to take priority, we make use of the audio focus features of the `AudioManager` instance.

Managing the audio volume

When we play music, for example in a media player or game, we need to be able to control the volume based on what the user is doing. For example, if the user receives a call, the music should be paused. If there is an alarm, the volume should drop.

How to do it...

We can respond to various system requests to reduce the volume of media. One instance of this is when the headphones are removed, we may wish to pause the playback so as to avoid unexpected loud sounds:

1. If we want to pause music when the headphones are removed, we can respond to the `ActionAudioBecomingNoisy` instance broadcast and pause the playback:

```
[BroadcastReceiver]
[IntentFilter(
  new[]{ AudioManager.ActionAudioBecomingNoisy })]
public class MediaReceiver : BroadcastReceiver {
  public override void OnReceive(
  Context context, Intent intent) {
    context.StartService(new Intent(
      MediaService.ActionPause, null, context,
      typeof(MediaService)));
  }
}
```

Also, we can respond to requests from other apps to reduce the sound volume, or request other apps reduce their volume for our app:

1. We can listen for audio focus changes by registering with the `AudioManager` instance. First, the `AudioManager.IOnAudioFocusChangeListener` interface needs to be implemented, allowing us to be notified of focus changes:

```
public class MediaService : Service,
AudioManager.IOnAudioFocusChangeListener {
  public void OnAudioFocusChange(AudioFocus focusChange) {
  }
}
```

2. Next, we will need a reference to the `AudioManager` instance:

```
manager = AudioManager.FromContext(ApplicationContext);
```

3. Then, when we start playing music, we pass the interface implementation to the `RequestAudioFocus()` method on `AudioManager`. We use the `AudioFocus.Gain` value to indicate that we want to gain focus, as follows:

```
var request = manager.RequestAudioFocus(
    this, Stream.Music, AudioFocus.Gain);
if (request != AudioFocusRequest.Granted) {
    // handle any failed requests
}
```

4. Similarly, we can release audio focus by passing the same interface implementation to the `AbandonAudioFocus()` method, as follows:

```
var abandon = manager.AbandonAudioFocus(this);
if (abandon != AudioFocusRequest.Granted) {
    // handle any failed requests
}
```

5. As soon as another app, such as the dialer during an incoming call, requests focus, we can respond through the `OnAudioFocusChange()` method:

```
switch (audioFocus) {
    case AudioFocus.Gain:
        mediaPlayer.SetVolume(1.0f, 1.0f);
        break;
    case AudioFocus.Loss:
        StopPlaying();
        CleanUpPlayer();
        break;
    case AudioFocus.LossTransient:
        PausePlaying();
        break;
    case AudioFocus.LossTransientCanDuck:
        mediaPlayer.SetVolume(0.25f, 0.25f);
        break;
}
```

How it works...

Playing audio, whether in the background or in the foreground, needs to work with other apps on the device as well as with the users in their environments.

An example of working with the user is to ensure that the audio stays at the same level with regards to the environment. If the user is using headphones, the actual environment has no sound as all the sound is contained inside the headphones. When the user removes the headphone jack, the environment should not suddenly receive additional loud audio from the device. We can do this by stopping the playback when the Android system determines that the current state of audio will affect the environment. To be notified of such events, we have to listen for the `ActionAudioBecomingNoisy` broadcast.

> The `ActionAudioBecomingNoisy` broadcast can be used to pause the playback if the headphones are removed from the device, preserving the audio level of the environment.

In the case of working with other apps on the device, we can ensure that the user is notified, or the user's attention is shifted from our activity to one that is more important. An example would be to shift the user's attention to an incoming call or an important notification.

This is done by requesting and listening for requests to shift audio focus. Shifting audio focus means that when there is a more important audio that needs to be played, we either lower the volume of our audio or we stop our audio completely. Determining whether we can lower the volume, or if we should just stop the playback is determined by the type of audio focus requested.

To start receiving audio focus messages, we first need to request focus. When we request focus, we need to provide the `AudioManager` instance with an implementation of the `IOnAudioFocusChangeListener` interface. We pass this to the `RequestAudioFocus()` method along with two other parameters. The second parameter specifies the type of audio that will be affected by the focus shift. The last parameter specifies the type of focus that is to be obtained. There are several focus types:

Type	Description	Example Usage
Gain	This gets focus for an unknown duration	Music
GainTransient	This gets focus for a short period	Driving directions
GainTransientMayDuck	This gets focus for a short period, but the other audio does not have to stop, only lower their volume	Notifications
GainTransientExclusive	This gets focus for a short period, and the system will not play any sounds	Speech recognition

If we request the `Gain` audio focus, the other apps will stop their audio as we might be requesting focus for a long time. By requesting `GainTransient` or `GainTransientExclusive`, other apps will stop their audio, but still hold onto their resources as we would be releasing the focus shortly. By requesting `GainTransientExclusive`, the system will also stop its audio. When we request `GainTransientMayDuck`, other apps will simply lower their volume so that ours can be heard more clearly.

If we have focus, we should release the focus once we have completed our playback, for example, when the player is stopped or paused by the user. Releasing focus is done using the `AbandonAudioFocus()` method and allows the other apps to resume or continue with whatever they were doing before we requested focus.

The `IOnAudioFocusChangeListener` interface has a single method, `OnAudioFocusChange`, which will receive one of the incoming audio focus request `types`:

Focus Request Type	Description
`Gain`	This indicates that we have received audio focus
`Loss`	This indicates that we have lost audio focus for an unknown duration
`LossTransient`	This indicates that we have lost audio focus for a short period
`LossTransientMayDuck`	This indicates that we have lost audio focus, but we may just lower our volume

If we receive the `Loss` audio focus message, we should stop and release the player resources as we may not get the focus back for a long time. When we receive the `LossTransient` message, we can just pause the player as we may resume in a very short period of time. The `LossTransientMayDuck` message means that we can continue to play but at a lower volume. We can lower the volume of our player by passing a value in the `1.0` to `0.0` range to the `SetVolume()` method, with `1.0` representing full volume.

There's more...

Requesting focus is very useful if will be recording audio or video. We don't want the sound from the device to override the incoming sound from the microphone. Also, if we are going to make use of the text-to-speech features, we don't want the music to hinder the listener's ability to understand what is being read out.

Recording an audio

There may be several reasons to record an audio in an app. We could be processing the audio for speech recognition or we could just be making a game that requires some phrase from the user.

How to do it...

Our app can record audio using the `MediaRecorder` type, which can capture audio from a variety of sources and in various formats:

1. Recording any part of the user's surroundings, such as the audio, requires a permission:

   ```
   [assembly: UsesPermission(Manifest.Permission.RecordAudio)]
   ```

2. To record audio, we need a `MediaRecorder` instance with the audio source set to the microphone:

   ```
   var recorder = new MediaRecorder();
   recorder.SetAudioSource(AudioSource.Mic);
   ```

3. Then, we must specify in the format in which we want to persist the audio file:

   ```
   recorder.SetOutputFormat(OutputFormat.ThreeGpp);
   recorder.SetAudioEncoder(AudioEncoder.Default);
   ```

4. Next, we specify where to save the audio file using the `SetOutputFile` method:

   ```
   var path = FilesDir.AbsolutePath;
   path = Path.Combine(path, "Recording", "audio.3gp");
   recorder.SetOutputFile(path);
   ```

5. Finally, we start the recorder after preparing it:

   ```
   recorder.Prepare();
   recorder.Start();
   ```

6. In order to stop the recorder, use the following line of code:

   ```
   recorder.Stop();
   ```

7. If we aren't going to use the recorder again, we will free any resources that are used:

   ```
   recorder.Release();
   recorder = null;
   ```

How it works...

Recording an audio is useful when creating an app that will send voice messages, or if the app has to perform speech or music analysis.

The actual process of recording an audio is very simple and only has a few steps. Before we record an audio, we will require the `RecordAudio` permission. If we have the permission, setting up the recorder is done in just three steps.

The first is to specify the locations of the audio source. Using the `SetAudioSource()` method, we can specify that the audio should be captured from various sources. These sources include the microphone, which can be specified using the `Mic` value, the camera microphone using the `Camcorder` value, or even a voice call using the `VoiceCall` value.

Next, we specify the type of audio that we are going to record, and this is a combination of the format and the encoder. The format is set using the `SetOutputFormat()` method and can be MPEG4 using `Mpeg4`, 3GPP using `ThreeGpp`, or another format from the available options. The encoder is set using the `SetAudioEncoder()` method, and it can be AAC, using the `Aac` value, or one of the other encoders. Both the format and encoder allow us to specify `Default`, which allows the system to decide the best values. The audio source has to be set prior to setting the output audio format.

 Android version 5.0 supports recording an Ogg Vorbis audio in a WebM container using the `Webm` output format and the `Vorbis` audio encoder.

Finally, we specify the save location of the recorded file. This can be a `string` or a `FileDescriptor` with the desired location of the audio file. This is done by passing the desired location to the `SetOutputFile()` method.

 The location should be set after setting the output audio format.

Once we have set up our recorder, we can start the recording process. The first thing we do is to prepare the recorder, which gets the recorder ready using the specified options. Once the recorder is prepared, we can start the record process using the `Start()` method.

We can stop the recording at any time using the `Stop()` method. Before we can reuse the recorder, we will have to reset it. If no data was actually recorded before it was stopped, the `Stop()` method will throw a `RuntimeException` exception. We can catch this exception and then clean up any empty files.

The `Stop()` method will throw an exception if no data was recorded, allowing the empty files to be removed.

After stopping the recorder, if we aren't going to use it again, we should release it so that resources can be freed. If the activity goes into the background, we should stop and release the recorder in the `OnPause()` or `OnStop()` methods.

 We can use the `MediaRecorder` instance in a `Service` to record audio across activities.

There's more...

When recording an audio, we have great control over what and how the audio is recorded.

We can specify the number of audio channels using the `SetAudioChannels()` method, the encoding bitrate using the `SetAudioEncodingBitRate()` method, and the sampling rate using the `SetAudioSamplingRate()` method.

We can also specify duration for which the recording has to be done using the `SetMaxDuration()` method, and we can specify how large the file can be using the `SetMaxFileSize()` method.

If we specify the maximums, the recorder will raise the `Info` event upon reaching them. If a maximum file size was specified, the `What` property will be `MaxFilesizeReached`, otherwise, it will be `MaxDurationReached`.

 When the `Info` event is received, it is not guaranteed that the recording has actually finished yet.

Playing a video

Videos allow complex information to be presented to a user. This can just be a background, or it can be an information animation. Regardless of the exact reason, videos can enhance apps.

How to do it...

One of the simplest ways to display a video is to use a `VideoView` instance, which wraps an underlying `SurfaceView` and a `MediaPlayer`:

1. The first thing we add to the layout is a `VideoView` instance, using either code or the layout resources:

```
<VideoView
    android:layout_width="match_parent"
    android:layout_height="wrap_content"
    android:layout_gravity="center"
    android:id="@+id/videoView" />
```

2. If we are using a layout resource, we get hold of the `VideoView` from the layout:

```
var videoView =
    FindViewById<VideoView>(Resource.Id.videoView);
```

3. Once we have the `VideoView` property, we can set the source of the video. This can either be from a remote source, or from a local resource, such as one of the app resources:

```
var path = string.Format(
    "android.resource://{0}/{1}",
    PackageName,
    Resource.Raw.big_buck_bunny);
videoView.SetVideoPath(path);
```

4. Next, we may want to display the onscreen video controls, such as the play and pause buttons. If we want this, we set a `MediaController` instance:

```
videoView.SetMediaController(new MediaController(this));
```

5. Now that everything is set, we can play the video using the `Start()` method:

```
videoView.Start();
```

6. If we want to skip to a position in the video, we can use the `SeekTo()` method:

```
videoView.SeekTo(position);
```

When the activity is recreated for some reason, for example following a rotate, we have to ensure that the player is returned to its previous position. These set of steps shows one way in which to preserve the playback position following an activity re-creation:

1. To save the current position, we override the `OnSaveInstanceState()` method and add the video player's state to the `Bundle` object:

```
outState.PutBoolean("isPlaying", videoView.IsPlaying);
outState.PutInt("position", videoView.CurrentPosition);
```

2. Then, in `OnCreate`, we restore the state from the `Bundle` object:

```
if (savedInstanceState != null) {
   if (savedInstanceState.GetBoolean("isPlaying", false)) {
      var pos = savedInstanceState.GetInt("position", 0);
      videoView.SeekTo(pos);
   }
}
```

3. We also have the option to prevent Android from destroying and recreating the activity using the `ConfigurationChanges` property of the `[Activity]` attribute:

```
[Activity(
   ..., ConfigurationChanges = ConfigChanges.Orientation)]
```

How it works...

The ability to play a video in an app is very useful. We can just be providing a beautiful snippet as a background or header, or we can be playing a longer video as part of the app's core functionality.

Similar to playing audio, playing video is also straightforward. Instead of creating a `MediaPlayer` object, we use a `VideoView` control. The control can be created and added from code or it can be placed in the layout resource files.

Once we have the video view, we can set it up to play the video. All we need to do is set the location to the actual video that we want to play. To do this, we pass a string path to the `SetVideoPath()` method or a URI to the `SetVideoURI()` method. This location can be a local path, such as a resource or the local filesystem, or a remote path to a server. If we are using a URI, we can even provide additional headers in the request to the server.

 The `VideoView` can play a video from either local or remote sources.

As soon as we set the video source, the underlying media player will be automatically prepared. This means that we can invoke the `Start()` method as soon as we wish to. The playback can be controlled using the `Pause()`, `Resume()`, and `StopPlayback()` methods. We can also use the `SeekTo()` method to jump to a specific location in the video.

 The `VideoView` is automatically prepared when the video source is set, allowing playback to begin immediately.

We may choose to present media controls on a `VideoView` but are not required to do so. These controls will allow the user to directly control the playback. They include: a seek bar, a play/pause button, and skip buttons. If the video is streamed, a buffer progress will also be shown. To display these controls, we can provide the view with an instance of `MediaController` using the `SetMediaController()` method.

 A `MediaController` instance does not have to be set in order to play a video. If one is not provided, playback cannot be controlled by the user.

If a `VideoView` goes into the background or is destroyed, it will not restore its state when it is recreated, we have to do this manually. The simplest way is to record the states, for example `IsPlaying` and `CurrentPosition`, when the view is about to be destroyed. We can do this in the `OnSaveInstanceState()` or `OnPause()` methods, and then when the view is reconstructed, we can restore the state in the `OnRestoreInstanceState()` or `OnCreate()` methods.

If the device is rotated, the activity is usually destroyed and recreated. This presents a problem as the video will have to be prepared again and this may cause a delay in the playback. This is even more a problem when the video comes from a remote source, as it will have to buffer again.

Another way to get around this is to ensure that the activity is not destroyed when the device orientation changes. We add the `ConfigChanges.Orientation` flag to the `ConfigurationChanges` property on the `[Activity]` attribute. By setting this property, the activity is not destroyed, but it also means that the usual orientation-specific layouts will not be switched automatically. We will now have to take care of this ourselves in the `OnConfigurationChanged()` method of the activity.

There's more...

Before we start seeking to a position in the video, we need to ensure that the source supports seeking in that direction. We can check for support using the `CanSeekForward()` and `CanSeekBackward()` methods.

Custom video controls

The `VideoView` is great for displaying videos with a basic set of controls; however, we may require more flexibility and control over how the video is played.

How to do it...

We can play a video onto a `SurfaceView` using a `MediaPlayer` instance if we need fine control over what we can do or if we want custom video controls:

1. First, when using a `SurfaceView` instance, we need to implement the `ISurfaceHolderCallback` interface, ensuring that we keep track of the surface:

```
public class MainActivity :
  Activity, ISurfaceHolderCallback {
  private ISurfaceHolder surfaceHolder;
  public void SurfaceChanged(
    ISurfaceHolder holder, Format format,
  int width, int height) {
  }
  public void SurfaceCreated(ISurfaceHolder holder) {
    surfaceHolder = holder;
  }
  public void SurfaceDestroyed(ISurfaceHolder holder) {
    surfaceHolder = null;
  }
}
```

2. Then, in the `OnCreate()` method, we want to get hold of the `ISurfaceHolder` instance using the `Holder` property of the `SurfaceView` instance:

```
var holder = surfaceView.Holder;
holder.SetType(SurfaceType.PushBuffers);
```

3. Next, we pass the instance of `ISurfaceHolderCallback` to the `AddCallback()` method:

```
holder.AddCallback(this);
```

4. Before we have a playing surface, we can start setting up our `MediaPlayer` instance that will play the video:

```
mediaPlayer = new MediaPlayer();
mediaPlayer.SetDataSource(this, videoUri);
mediaPlayer.SetAudioStreamType(Stream.Music);
```

5. When the surface is created, we pass it to the media player using `SetDisplay`:

```
mediaPlayer.SetDisplay(surfaceHolder);
```

6. We will also want to subscribe to the `VideoSizeChanged` event, which will provide us with the video size:

```
mediaPlayer.VideoSizeChanged += (sender, e) => {
  surfaceHolder.SetFixedSize(e.Width, e.Height);
};
```

7. To begin playing, we prepare the player asynchronously and then start the playback:

```
mediaPlayer.Prepared += (sender, e) => {
  mediaPlayer.Start();
};
mediaPlayer.PrepareAsync();
```

8. Finally, we need to ensure that when the activity is paused, we release the resources used by the media player:

```
if (mediaPlayer != null) {
  mediaPlayer.Release();
  mediaPlayer = null;
}
```

9. If the surface is destroyed or created while the video is playing, we can assign the new surface, or `null` surface, to the player:

```
if (mediaPlayer != null) {
  mediaPlayer.SetDisplay(surfaceHolder);
}
```

Once our video is playing in the surface view, we can add the video controls. Here, we will toggle visibility when the surface is tapped:

1. First, we will need a `Handler` instance that will do the work of managing the visibility of the video controls:

```
const int WhatHideControls = 1;
handler = new Handler(message => {
  if (message.What == WhatHideControls) {
    videoController.Visibility = ViewStates.Gone;
  }
});
```

2. We will attach logic that will show the controls when the surface is tapped, and add a message in the `Handler` instance to hide them after a few seconds:

```
const int HideTimeout = 5000;
surfaceView.Click += delegate {
  videoController.Visibility = ViewStates.Visible;
  handler.SendEmptyMessageDelayed(
    WhatHideControls, HideTimeout);
};
```

3. Then, when the surface is tapped again, it should hide the controls, ensuring that it removes any existing messages in the `Handler` instance:

```
handler.RemoveMessages(WhatHideControls);
videoController.Visibility = ViewStates.Gone;
```

4. Before we show the controls, we need to ensure that we update the controls to match the media player's state:

```
if (mediaPlayer.IsPlaying) {
  playPauseButton.SetImageResource(
    Android.Resource.Drawable.IcMediaPause);
}
else {
  playPauseButton.SetImageResource(
    Android.Resource.Drawable.IcMediaPlay);
}
```

5. If we want to update the progress in the controls, we can add a new message to the `Handler` instance that fires every second:

```
const int WhatProgress = 2;
if (message.What == WhatProgress) {
  if (mediaPlayer != null && mediaPlayer.IsPlaying) {
    var pos = mediaPlayer.CurrentPosition;
    var next = 1000 - (pos % 1000);
    progressBar.Progress = pos;
    handler.SendEmptyMessageDelayed(WhatProgress, next);
  }
  else {
    progressBar.Progress = 0;
  }
}
```

6. Then, when the controls are going to be shown, we start updating the progress by adding the update message to the `Handler` instance:

```
progressBar.Max = mediaPlayer.Duration;
handler.SendEmptyMessage(WhatProgress);
```

How it works...

We can play a video in a `VideoView` instance, but this is fairly limited in what we can do. We can create a custom media controller, but it is still limited by the small API exposed by the `VideoView` instance. If we want to create a more advanced player, we will have to create it from scratch.

This is not as difficult as it may initially appear to be, as there are only three main parts to the view. There is the underlying `MediaPlayer` instance that will render a video on a `SurfaceView` instance and be controlled by a set of buttons or other controls.

Using a `MediaPlayer` instance to play a video is the same as when playing audio, except that the display surface needs to be set using the `SetDisplay()` method.

In order to play a video, we will need an instance of `MediaPlayer`. We work with this in a very similar manner to playing an audio. The only difference is that as the player will be rendering a video, we need to let it know about the surface it can render onto. We do this by passing the surface to the `SetDisplay()` or `SetSurface()` method. As the video size may not be the same as the surface size, we can use the `VideoSizeChanged` event to be notified of when the video size is known or changed. Other than those two extra members, we set up the data source and audio stream as we would for a normal audio file.

 The `VideoSizeChanged` event is used to obtain the dimensions of the video being played.

To actually display the video, we will have to set up and use a `SurfaceView` instance. A `SurfaceView` instance is a special kind of view that provides a dedicated drawing surface to another object. The actual drawing is done using the `SurfaceView` instance's `ISurfaceHolder`, which is obtained from the `Holder` property. We do not directly control the creation and destruction of a surface, but rather listen for an event that lets us know that the surface is ready for drawing.

To start using the surface, we need to obtain the `ISurfaceHolder` implementation from the `SurfaceView` instance, using the `Holder` property. Then, we pass an implementation of the `ISurfaceHolderCallback` interface to the `AddCallback()` method of the holder. On devices running Android versions below 3.0, we must also specify the type of surface using the `SetType()` method. For videos, we just use the `SurfaceType.PushBuffers` value.

 A surface is not created on demand, but rather constructed when a `SurfaceView` instance becomes visible.

When the surface is ready, the `SurfaceCreated()` callback method is invoked with a reference to a valid surface holder instance. We keep a reference to this surface holder and use it to display the video. At some point, such as when the app is paused, the surface may be destroyed. This will result in the `SurfaceDestroyed()` callback method being invoked. When this happens, the surface is no longer available for drawing and we should update the media player's display surface.

Once we receive the surface, we can pass it on to the media player using the `SetDisplay()` method. Doing this will result in the player rendering the video in the view. If the surface is destroyed, we can remove the surface from the player by passing `null` to `SetDisplay`. This will cause the video to stop, but the audio will continue playing. To stop the audio, we will have to stop or pause the player.

[When the media player is provided a `null` display, the video
will not be visible, but the audio will continue playing.]

If we are going to create a custom video player, we will need to provide the user with a means to control the playback. To do this, we can create a view, which contains the various controls that will overlay the video. One option to show the controls is to wait for the user to tap the video, after which the controls will be shown. After a few seconds, we can hide the controls and only show the video.

To update the controls with the video progress or buffer options, we need to query the media player each time. There are no events on the player, so we will have to check every second or more. An easy way to do this is to make use of a `Handler` type, which is a queue that allows us the scheduling of the messages to be handled on a particular thread. We can use this mechanism to schedule a message to update the various controls every second.

[A `Handler` type can be used to queue messages to be
actioned by another thread either immediately or after a delay.]

Using a handler is very simple and all we have to do is create an instance of the `Handler` type. The constructor allows us to pass in a delegate that will be executed when a message needs to be handled. Messages can be handled immediately after it is sent to the handler, or after some delay. When the delegate is executed, we are provided with the `Message` instance that was queued. We can use this message to perform any action based on the data in the message. One of the most important pieces of information in a `Message` instance is the `What` data, which is a custom ID that we use to identify what the message is about.

We can enqueue a message in the `Handler` instance either with an empty message or with a populated message. To send an empty message, we can use the `SendEmptyMessage()` method and pass in the `What` value. To post a more complex message, we can first create one using the `Obtain()` method on the `Handler`. The result is a `Message` instance that we populate and then enqueue using the `SendMessage()` method.

If we want to enqueue a message that should be dequeued at a point in the later future, we can send a delayed message. This is the same as sending a normal message, but we use the `SendEmptyMessageDelayed()` and `SendMessageDelayed()` methods instead. These methods take an additional parameter—the delay in milliseconds before the message is actually dequeued.

To remove a message, regardless of how it was enqueued, we can pass the `What` value to the `RemoveMessages()` method. This will dequeue all the messages with the specified `What` value, but will not execute the `Handler` delegate.

Using the camera

Making use of the camera allows the user to interact with the real world through the device. This can range from taking a photo and adding a message and effects all the way to providing an augmented reality experience.

How to do it...

If our app requires a photo, we can make use of the camera to record an image. However, we need to first ensure that there is a camera available on the device for us to use:

1. If our app requires the camera and cannot function without it, we can enforce this by specifying that there must be a camera on the device in the features:

    ```
    [assembly: UsesFeature(PackageManager.FeatureCamera)]
    [assembly: UsesFeature(PackageManager.FeatureCameraFront)]
    ```

2. If the feature is not required, we can indicate that it is optional by adding the `Required` property to the `[UsesFeature]` attribute:

    ```
    [assembly: UsesFeature(..., Required = false)]
    ```

3. Then, we can check when the app starts if the feature is available and adjust functionality accordingly:

    ```
    if (!PackageManager.HasSystemFeature(
    Android.Content.PM.PackageManager.FeatureCamera) {
      // we don't have a rear camera
    }
    ```

4. Finally, as we are going to rely on the existence of a camera app, we need to check whether it exists:

    ```
    var activities = PackageManager.QueryIntentActivities(
       new Intent(MediaStore.ActionImageCapture),
       PackageInfoFlags.MatchDefaultOnly);
    if (activities.Count == 0) {
      // handle no camera apps
    }
    ```

Once we know there is a camera app on the device, we need a place for the photos to be stored by the camera:

1. As we can't ask another app to store photos into our app sandbox, we have to use a shared location, such as the external storage photos directory:

    ```
    var root = Environment.GetExternalStoragePublicDirectory(
       Environment.DirectoryPictures);
    ```

2. We can then get the location of the file that we will use to store the photo:

```
root = new Java.IO.File(root, "XamarinCookbook");
if (!root.Exists()) {
  root.Mkdirs();
}
var imageFile = new Java.IO.File(root, "image.jpg");
```

3. As we need to use a `Uri` instance to specify the location, we convert the `File` into a Uri instance using the `FromFile()` method:

```
var imageUri = Android.Net.Uri.FromFile(imageFile);
```

Now that we know we have a camera app and a place to store the photo, we can launch the camera:

1. First, we will start the camera using the `MediaStore.ActionImageCapture` intent action:

```
const int TakePhotoCode = 1;
var intent = new Intent(MediaStore.ActionImageCapture);
intent.PutExtra(MediaStore.ExtraOutput, imageUri);
StartActivityForResult(intent, TakePhotoCode);
```

2. We will then override the `OnActivityResult()` method of the activity to handle the response:

```
if (requestCode == TakePhotoCode) {
  if (resultCode == Result.Ok) {
    // display the picture found at imageUri
  }
  else {
    // photo intent was canceled
  }
}
```

Recording videos using an intent is just as easy; all we need is a different intent action:

1. To start the camera app to record video, we use the `MediaStore.ActionVideoCapture` intent action:

```
var intent = new Intent (MediaStore.ActionVideoCapture);
intent.PutExtra(MediaStore.ExtraOutput, videoUri);
StartActivityForResult (intent, TakeVideoCode);
```

2. Then, in `OnActivityResult()`, we can read the video file as we would for an image:

```
if (requestCode == TakeVideoCode) {
  if (resultCode == Result.Ok) {
    // display the video found at videoUri
  }
```

```
    else {
      // video capture intent was canceled
    }
  }
}
```

How it works...

The camera is a very powerful piece of hardware on a user's device. It can capture a moment that was powerful enough to compel that person to take a photo in the first place. Adding the ability to capture, share, store, or react to a moment of the user's life can make our app even more personal.

We don't have to go on to create a brand new camera app; instead, we can just use the existing camera app and ask it to take a photo for us. To do this, we use the normal way of communicating between activities using an `Intent` instance with the `StartActivityForResult()` and `OnActivityResult()` methods.

Not everything has to be recreated, making use of other apps installed on the device allows the user to install preferred applications to do a specific task.

Before trying to access the camera app, we have to ensure that there is a camera on the device and that there is a camera app installed. Usually, if there is a camera, the device manufacturer will have made sure there is a camera app installed. But, the user might have uninstalled it for some reason.

The first check is to ensure that there is an actual camera on the device. To prevent our app from appearing in Google Play if the user is using a device without a camera, we can make use of the feature filtering support of Google Play. We use the `[UsesFeature]` attribute to indicate what feature the app requires, and in the case of a camera, we can specify `FeatureCamera` and/or `FeatureCameraFront` to indicate that we require a camera.

Before using some hardware, it should be verified that the device includes it.

If the app does not require a camera, but rather it is optional, we can specify this using the `Required` property on the `[UsesFeature]` attribute. If we set this to `false`, we will have to check at runtime for a camera. We can check for features at runtime using the `HasSystemFeature()` method of the `PackageManager` class. We obtain the current package manager from the `PackageManager` property of an `Activity` or `Service`. Similar to the attribute, we use `FeatureCamera` and/or `FeatureCameraFront` as a parameter when checking for the existence of a camera.

If the camera is only accessed using an `Intent` instance, then the app does not require the camera permissions.

Once we know there is a camera on the device, we can check whether there are any camera apps on the device. To do this, we query the `PackageManager` class for a list activities that support the camera intent. To launch a camera app, we create an `Intent` instance with the `ActionImageCapture` action. We then pass this intent to the `QueryIntentActivities()` method of the package manager, which will return a list of all the activities that can take a photo. If there are any items in the list, we know that there is at least one camera app.

 Before starting an activity with an intent, it should be verified that there is an app on the device that can handle it.

Now that we know the device has a camera and at least one camera app, we can ask one of these activities to take a photo. This requires setting up an intent that will start an activity. The only thing we need is to specify where the camera app should place the file for us to read. As the camera app cannot access our app's private content and we cannot access the camera's private content, we have to specify a shared location.

Usually, we can use the result of `GetExternalStoragePublicDirectory`, with the `DirectoryPictures` parameter. This will provide us with a location to the public location of all photos. We then pass a `Uri` instance of that location as an extra on the intent, with a key of `ExtraOutput` and the value being the `Uri`.

 To start the camera app to take a photo, the `ActionImageCapture` intent action is used; for videos, the `ActionVideoCapture` intent action is used.

To start the camera app, we pass the `Intent` instance, along with a code to identify the action, to the `StartActivityForResult()` method. The camera app will launch and allow the user to take a photo. Once the user takes a photo, the camera will close and take us back to our app. We are informed about this through the `OnActivityResult()` method, which we override.

In the `OnActivityResult()` method, we can use the request code to identify the camera action, which will be the value passed to the `StartActivityForResult()` method. Also, to determine whether the user took a photo or canceled the camera, we use the result code. If the user took a photo, the result code will be `Ok` and we can then handle reading the image. The image will be located at the same location that we specified when creating the `Intent` instance.

Recording a video is exactly the same, but instead we specify a different intent action. In the case of a video, we use the `ActionVideoCapture` intent action. We then set the location extra and pass the intent to the `StartActivtyForResult()` method. In the `OnActivityResult()` method, we can read the video file if the result is `Ok`.

Creating a camera app

Sometimes the basic camera intents aren't enough, or we are creating an augmented reality game, and we want to process the images as the camera streams them.

How to do it...

To create a camera app, or some other app that displays a live preview from the camera hardware, we need to set up several things similar to playing a video, we must implement the `ISurfaceHolderCallback` interface, which will manage the live preview:

1. As with using intents to start the camera, we need to check for the existence of a camera on the device. Additionally, we will need to request permission to manage the camera, as follows:

    ```
    [assembly: UsesPermission(Manifest.Permission.Camera)]
    ```

2. Next, we will need a surface to display the camera preview, and to do this, we will need an instance of the `ISurfaceHolderCallback` interface:

    ```
    public class MainActivity :
      Activity, ISurfaceHolderCallback {
      private ISurfaceHolder surfaceHolder;
      public void SurfaceChanged(
        ISurfaceHolder holder, Format format,
        int width, int height) {
      }
      public void SurfaceCreated(ISurfaceHolder holder) {
        surfaceHolder = holder;
      }
      public void SurfaceDestroyed(ISurfaceHolder holder) {
        surfaceHolder = null;
      }
    }
    ```

3. Then, we pass this instance as the callback of the `SurfaceView` instance's `Holder` property:

    ```
    var holder = surfaceView.Holder;
    holder.SetType(SurfaceType.PushBuffers);
    holder.AddCallback(this);
    ```

Now that we have our surface for the preview, we can get hold of the cameras and start setting one of them up:

1. We need to get hold of the cameras on the device so that we can use one of them:

```
var cameraCount = Camera.NumberOfCameras;
var cameras = new Camera.CameraInfo[cameraCount];
var backIndex = 0;
for (int index = 0; index < cameraCount; index++) {
  cameras[index] = new Camera.CameraInfo();
  Camera.GetCameraInfo(index, cameras[index]);
  if (cameras[index].Facing == CameraFacing.Back) {
    backIndex = index;
  }
}
```

2. We then need to open the camera so that we can get the preview. We should do this on a background thread as it may take some time to complete:

```
await Task.Run(() => {
  try {
    camera = Camera.Open(backIndex);
  }
  catch (Exception ex) {
    // handle the camera being used
  }
});
```

3. Now that we have our camera, we can get the supported preview sizes:

```
var parameters = camera.GetParameters();
var previewSizes = parameters.SupportedPreviewSizes;
```

4. Next, we tell the camera to use the size with the best resolution:

```
var best = previewSizes[0];
parameters.SetPreviewSize(best.Width, best.Height);
camera.SetParameters(parameters);
```

Now we can set up the camera to preview onto our new surface either after the camera is opened or after the surface is created:

1. Once we have the preview sizes, we need to resize the surface to avoid stretching the preview:

```
var scale = Math.Min(
  container.Width / (float)best.Width,
container.Height / (float)best.Height);
var width = best.Width * scale;
var height = best.Height * scale;
surfaceHolder.SetFixedSize((int)width, (int)height);
```

2. Next, we have to let the camera know where to display the preview:

```
camera.SetPreviewDisplay(surfaceHolder);
```

3. Then, we tell the camera to start the preview:

```
camera.StartPreview();
```

The next step is to manage the camera after the destruction of either the surface or the actual activity:

1. When the surface is destroyed, we can just stop the preview in `SurfaceDestroyed()` as we will be starting it when a new surface is created:

```
camera.StopPreview();
```

2. When the activity is paused, we should release the camera as soon as we can:

```
camera.StopPreview();
camera.Release();
camera = null;
```

To implement the logic to take a photo, we will need to implement two `Camera` interfaces:

1. To take a photo, we will need an implementation of the `Camera.IPictureCallback` interface:

```
public class MainActivity : Camera.IPictureCallback {
  public void OnPictureTaken(byte[] data, Camera camera) {
  }
}
```

2. In the `OnPictureTaken()` method, we can save the bytes to a file or process them in some way:

```
File.WriteAllBytes(imagePath, data);
```

3. We have to ensure that we start the preview again as taking a photo stops the preview:

```
camera.StartPreview();
```

4. If we want to play a shutter sound, we need an instance of the `Camera.IShutterCallback` interface:

```
public class MainActivity : Camera.IShutterCallback {
  public void OnShutter() {
    // an empty method plays the default shutter sound
  }
}
```

5. To actually take a photo, we invoke the `TakePicture()` method on the camera, the first parameter being the shutter callback and the last being the picture taken callback. If we pass a `null` value for the shutter callback, no sound will be played:

```
camera.TakePicture(this, null, this);
```

To record a video, we use a `MediaRecorder` instance and set various parameters to indicate what camera and audio to record.

1. As we are going to record audio, we will have to request an additional permission:

```
[assembly: UsesPermission(Manifest.Permission.RecordAudio)]
```

2. To allow the recorder to access the camera, we have to allow the camera to be shared with the recorder:

```
camera.Unlock();
```

3. Then, we create a `MediaRecorder` instance and set the audio and video source to be the camera:

```
recorder = new MediaRecorder();
recorder.SetCamera(camera);
recorder.SetAudioSource(AudioSource.Camcorder);
recorder.SetVideoSource(VideoSource.Camera);
recorder.SetProfile(
   CamcorderProfile.Get(CamcorderQuality.High));
```

4. Next, we specify where to create the video file:

```
recorder.SetOutputFile("video.mp4");
```

5. We have to ensure that we tell the recorder to preview on the surface:

```
recorder.SetPreviewDisplay(surfaceHolder.Surface);
```

6. Finally, we can prepare the recorder and start the recording:

```
recorder.Prepare();
recorder.Start();
```

7. To stop the recorder, either by user request or when the activity is paused, we invoke the `Stop()` method:

```
recorder.Stop();
recorder.Reset();
recorder.Release();
recorder = null;
```

8. Once we are finished with the recorder, we need to lock the camera again:

```
camera.Reconnect();
```

How it works...

If we want to take a photo, we can use the default camera app. But, this app may not provide the required functionality that we need. We can be creating an actual camera app, or an app that provides augmented reality with real-time image effects or image overlays. Alternatively, it can be to provide image analysis, such as a QR reader or face detection.

Using the default camera app prevents us from modifying or overlaying the preview image in real-time, as we are only presented with the final captured image. If we need to access the real-time camera stream, we can request the data directly from the camera and display it on a surface.

As we are accessing the camera hardware directly, we need to request the `Camera` permission. If we are going to record videos, we need to request the additional `RecordAudio` permission to record the audio as well.

 When using intents to take photos, the `Camera` permission is not required. When controlling the camera hardware, permission is required.

Once we have the permission to use the camera, we need to set up a surface to render the camera's preview. For this, we can use a `SurfaceView` instance. To set up the surface, we can request the `ISurfaceHolder` instance using the `Holder` property on the `SurfaceView` instance. Like when setting up to play a video, we need to add a callback that we use to monitor the life of the surface. The callback implements the `ISurfaceHolderCallback` interface and provides methods that relate to the life of a surface. We will stop the preview if the surface is destroyed, and start it again when it is created.

After the surface is set up, we need to set up the camera that we are going to use. Before we can use a camera, we need to get hold of the cameras on the device. To get the cameras, we use the `Camera` type. We can iterate over the cameras on the device using the `NumberOfCameras` property and the `GetCameraInfo()` method. The `NumberOfCameras` property returns the number of cameras available on the device. The `GetCameraInfo()` method is a method that allows us to obtain information about a particular camera.

We use the `GetCameraInfo()` method with a `Camera.CameraInfo` object instance. To obtain information about a single camera, we pass the index of the camera we want the information on and a `CameraInfo` object that will be populated with the information. To find a specific camera, we can use the `Facing` property, which can be either `Back` or `Front`.

In order to begin using the camera, we have to open it. To do this, we pass the index of the camera we wish to use to the `Open()` method. This gives us exclusive access to the camera hardware, but if another app has opened the camera, this method will throw a `RuntimeException` exception. As the camera can only be opened once, as soon as our activity is paused, we must release the camera using the `Release()` method. If we do not release the camera, no other app will be able to use it.

When opening a camera, it may take some time on some devices. Thus, a background thread should be used to avoid blocking the UI thread.

Now that we have the camera open, we need to start the preview on our surface. Before we start the preview, we have to resize the surface to the aspect ratio of the camera preview to avoid the preview stretching. We also have to specify the desired size of the preview to the camera. We cannot use any arbitrary size but only the one that is supported by the camera.

To get the supported sizes, we first get the camera parameters using the `GetParameters()` method. We then query the `Parameters` object for the sizes using the `SupportedPreviewSizes` property. This will provide a list of supported sizes, in descending order of size, which we use to select a specific size. The `Parameters` object has a `SetPreviewSize()` method, which allows us to specify a width and height of a preview size from the list. To actually set the preview size, we assign the `Parameters` instance back to the camera using the `SetParameters()` method.

 Only a size from the `SupportedPreviewSizes` property can be used when setting the camera preview size, other sizes may result in an exception.

When the surface becomes available, or when the camera is opened, we have to let the camera know that it should preview on the surface. First, we must ensure that the surface aspect ratio is the same as that of the camera preview to avoid the preview stretching. Then, we pass the surface to the `SetPreviewDisplay()` method of the open camera. Finally, we start the preview using the `StartPreview()` method.

As the preview only works when there is a surface, as soon as it is destroyed, we must stop the preview. We do this using the `StopPreview()` method. When the activity is paused, we need to release the camera as it is a shared resource that we can only hold when our app is in the foreground. We can open the camera again once our app has resumed.

 The camera can only be held when the activity is in the foreground. As soon as the activity is paused, the camera should be released.

If we want to take a photo, all we need is an instance that implements the `Camera.IPictureCallback` interface. We then pass this instance as the last parameter of the `TakePicture()` method. This is an asynchronous method that will return immediately, but the callback method will only be invoked once the image has been captured. The callback method, `OnPictureTaken()`, gives us access to a byte array that represents the image. We can either process or save the image to disk.

The image data that is provided, when using the last parameter, is the compressed JPEG data. If we use the second parameter, we will obtain the raw image data from the camera sensor. We can use either one or both, of the picture callbacks to obtain the image data. If we do not wish to provide a callback for a particular type, we can pass `null` instead.

 To play the shutter sound, an instance of `Camera.IShutterCallback` must be passed to `TakePicture`.

By default, the capture process does not play a shutter sound. To get a sound to play, we specify a callback that will fire on the shutter operation. This callback must implement the `Camera.IShutterCallback` interface. We can leave the callback method, `OnShutter()`, empty if we wish to play the default camera shutter sound. This method is not guaranteed to be called exactly when the photo is captured, but as soon as possible after the capture. Typically, the shutter sound will play after the capture was triggered, but before the image data is available. We pass the shutter callback instance as the first parameter of the `TakePicture()` method.

 The camera preview must be started before capturing an image. Once an image has been captured, the preview must be started again as taking a photo stops the preview.

If we want to record a video, we use a `MediaRecorder` instance. Before we can record, we have to ensure that we have the `RecordAudio` permission as well as the `Camera` permission. Then, in order for the recorder to be able to access the camera, we have to unlock it. We do this using the `Unlock()` method. This is required as the camera is a shared resource, and once opened, cannot be accessed by anything else.

 Unlocking the camera allows the recorder to be able to access the camera hardware.

Once the camera is unlocked, we can set up the `MediaRecorder` instance. First, we set the camera that the recorder will use, then we set the audio and video source. The audio source must be `Camcorder` and the video source must be `Camera`. Next, we specify a profile to use, which can be `High` or `Low`. This is obtained using the `Get()` method on the `CamcorderProfile` type. Then, we set the output file location and the preview surface. The preview surface must be the same surface that was specified when setting the preview surface on the camera. Finally, we prepare the recorder and start it.

As soon as we want to stop recording, we invoke the `Stop()` method. Then, we must reset the recorder using the `Reset()` method. Next, we must release the resources held by the recorder using the `Release()` method. Finally, we must lock the camera again using the `Reconnect()` method. This prevents access to the camera from other apps while we are using it.

The camera must be unlocked using `Unlock` before recording, and locked again using `Reconnect` when recording is finished.

There's more...

With Android version 5.0, an entire new namespace was created for working with cameras. This namespace is `Android.Hardware.Camera2`. Cameras are accessed using the `CameraManager` and `CameraDevice` types. Photos are captured using a `CameraCaptureSession` instance.

Although this new API is much more powerful, it is only available to devices running Android version 5.0 and above. Although the old API is deprecated, it is still supported and fully functional. This is very useful if we are going to support older devices.

Handling high-resolution images

Working with images often requires the app to be able to load very large images. Photos are especially large due to modern cameras producing high resolution images from excellent camera hardware.

How to do it...

We can easily load images from files, resources, or remote sources using the `BitmapFactory` type:

1. All we need in order to load a bitmap is the path or stream and one of the decode methods, such as `DecodeStreamAsync`:

```
using (var stream = Assets.Open("bigimage.png"))
using (var bitmap = await
BitmapFactory.DecodeStreamAsync(stream)) {
   imageView.SetImageBitmap(bitmap);
}
```

As images can be quite large, both in resolution and in memory size, it is often better to reduce them using subsampling:

1. When using subsampling, we need to provide extra options to the decode methods. This requires the use of the `BitmapFactory.Options` type:

```
var options = new BitmapFactory.Options();
```

2. Once we have the options, we can set various properties. If we want to load just the dimensions of the image, we can request the following:

```
options.InJustDecodeBounds = true;
```

3. If the `InJustDecodeBounds` property is set to `true`, decoding the image only loads the image dimensions, not the actual image data:

```
using (var stream = Assets.Open("bigimage.png")) {
   await BitmapFactory.DecodeStreamAsync(stream));
}
```

4. Once the decoding has finished, we can access the image dimensions using the `OutWidth` and `OutHeight` properties:

```
var height = options.OutHeight;
var width = options.OutWidth;
```

5. To reduce the image size when loading the actual data, we make use of the `InSampleSize` property. This takes any value in powers of two:

```
options.InSampleSize = 4;
```

6. If we are reusing the same options instance, we need to remember to set the `InJustDecodeBounds` property to `false` as we want to load the image data:

```
options.InJustDecodeBounds = false;
```

7. Then to load the image, we can make use of the same decode method, but this time, we keep a reference to the returned decoded `Bitmap` instance:

```
Bitmap bitmap;
using (var stream = Assets.Open("bigimage.png")) {
   bitmap = await BitmapFactory.DecodeStreamAsync(stream);
}
```

8. Finally, we can assign the bitmap to an `ImageView` instance or draw it onto a `Canvas` instance:

```
imageView.SetImageBitmap(bitmap);
```

Images take up large amounts of memory on a device, and may even cause the device to run out of memory altogether. To avoid this, we have to dispose of the resources as soon as we no longer need them:

1. If we are no longer going to reference the image from .NET, we can dispose the handle:

```
bitmap.Dispose();
```

2. When we are finished with the image, and we never going to display it again, we can dispose the actual image data:

```
bitmap.Recycle();
```

3. If we want to replace an image inside an `ImageView` instance, we can also dispose of the old image currently displayed:

```
var old = imageView.Drawable as BitmapDrawable;
imageView.SetImageBitmap(null);
if (old != null) {
   old.Bitmap.Recycle();
}
```

How it works...

Working with images often requires the app to be able to load very large images. Photos are especially large due to modern cameras producing high resolution images from excellent camera hardware. If we try and load images with very high resolutions, especially if there are multiple images to load, we may cause the device to run out of memory.

Although the device may have a large amount of memory, only a small amount is allowed to be used by the app. Some devices, especially the older ones, only permit a maximum of 24 MB per application.

 Images require a fairly large amount of memory and may quickly consume the memory available to the app.

Additionally, even the images with small file sizes still consume large amounts of memory. This is due to file compression, which results in the image being decompressed into memory. Even though this limitation is not always a problem, we can have issues when developing an image-intensive app, such as an image gallery. There would be no point in loading a 3 MB file, which might decompress into 30 MB, if we were just going to show a 100 x 100 pixel thumbnail. The memory cost and processor usage would be wasted.

Subsampling allows the app to decode a large image file but only load a reduced image with a smaller memory size. To make use of subsampling, we use the `BitmapFactory` and `BitmapFactory.Options` types.

 Android provides a way to load a reduced image using subsampling.

When loading bitmaps, we are usually able to make use of the various decode methods, such as `DecodeStreamAsync`, `DecodeFileAsync`, or `DecodeResourceAsync`. When loading subsampled images, we still use these methods, but we use the overload that takes a `BitmapFactory.Options` instance. Providing options to the decode method allows us to specify a subsampling size.

> A new `BitmapFactory.Options` instance is obtained using the default constructor.

Before subsampling, we probably would want to check the size of the original image. There is no point in reducing the size of the image if it is already smaller than what we want it to be. To query the size of an image without having to decode the entire image, we set the `InJustDecodeBounds` property to `true` on the options instance. If we were going to decode a stream, we would use the `DecodeStreamAsync()` method and pass the stream as the first parameter and the options as the second. When the method returns, the `OutWidth` and `OutHeight` properties on the options instance will contain the image's width and height, respectively. We can use these values to calculate an optimal sampling value.

> Setting the `InJustDecodeBounds` property to `true` results in only the image dimensions and MIME type being loaded, not the image data.

We can use the image width and height to calculate the optimal subsampling size in powers of two. Once we have a size, we set the `InSampleSize` property to that value, ensuring that we have set the `InJustDecodeBounds` instance back to `false`. When the decode method returns, it will have loaded a subsampled, or smaller, version of the image that takes up far less space in memory. This is especially useful when we want to load many images into a list view. We can quickly load many large images and only consume a small amount of memory.

However, even the smaller images take up space, and if not disposed correctly, they will eventually use all the available space. In the case of a list view, this can quickly happen if the user scrolls faster than the garbage collector, which is often the case. As Xamarin.Android involves using two garbage collectors, one for .NET and one for Java, we need to ensure that we allow both to work optimally.

> The bitmap data only exists in the Java world, and .NET only retains a reference to it. Disposing the .NET handle does not dispose the actual bitmap data, only the handle.

If we are going to assign an image to an `ImageView` instance or some other Java type, after which we won't need to access the bitmap data again, we can tell the .NET collector that it can collect the .NET handle. This is done by calling the `Dispose()` method on the object. This will release the bitmap data into the Java world. If we ever want to access the bitmap data again, we will have to query Java for a new reference. For example, to access the bitmap in an `ImageView` instance, we would use the `Drawable` property on the `ImageView` instance.

> The `Recycle()` method is used to destroy the bitmap data, allowing the Java garbage collector to clean up.

If we are going to need to reference the image again, we can retain a reference, but we need to ensure that we let the Java collector know when it can collect it. This is done by making use of the `Recycle()` method. We need to ensure that we aren't using the image anywhere when recycling the bitmap, as whatever tries to display the image after the image was recycled will throw an exception.

Drawing on the canvas of a View

Sometimes using the animation and shape APIs are not enough to create the image or app that we want to create. This may be to create a game or draw a complex image.

How to do it...

Drawing to a canvas can be easily done by creating a new view that derives from `View`, and then overriding the `OnDraw()` method:

1. First, we will need our custom `View` instance that implements the constructors that allow us to instantiate the view from either code or a layout file:

```
public class CustomView : View
{
  public CustomView(Context context)
    : base(context) {
  }
  public CustomView(Context context, IAttributeSet attrs)
    : base(context, attrs) {
  }
  public CustomView(
    Context context, IAttributeSet attrs, int defStyle)
    : base (context, attrs, defStyle) {
  }
}
```

2. Next, we override the `OnDraw()` method. This method draws the actual frame and will be called each time the view needs refreshing:

```
protected override void OnDraw(Canvas canvas) {
  base.OnDraw(canvas);
}
```

3. Drawing on a canvas requires a `Paint` object, and as this is expensive to create, we create it only once in a field:

```
private Paint paint = new Paint();
```

4. To avoid objects appearing too large or too small on different devices, we make use of the `Density` property of the `DisplayMetrics` object:

```
float density = Resources.DisplayMetrics.Density;
```

Now, we can start the actual drawing process. We specify a series of operations on the `Canvas` object, which is passed into the `OnDraw()` method:

1. As we will be reusing the `Paint` object each time we draw, we can reset any properties using the `Reset()` method:

```
paint.Reset();
```

2. As drawing round shapes may result in jagged edges, we can enable anti-aliasing:

```
paint.AntiAlias = true;
```

3. To start off drawing, we could paint or clear the entire view using a single color:

```
canvas.DrawColor(Color.CornflowerBlue);
```

4. If we want to draw a shape, such as a solid green circle, we set the properties on the `Paint` object, and then use the `DrawCircle()` method:

```
paint.SetStyle(Paint.Style.Fill);
paint.Color = Color.DarkGreen;
canvas.DrawCircle(centerX, centerY, radius*density, paint);
```

5. We can draw a border on the circle at the setting by the paint style to `Stroke` and then redrawing the circle:

```
paint.SetStyle(Paint.Style.Stroke);
paint.StrokeWidth = 2*density;
paint.Color = Color.Black;
canvas.DrawCircle(centerX, centerY, radius, paint);
```

6. We can also draw text, in this case, centered and at the top, on the screen:

```
paint.TextAlign = Paint.Align.Center;
paint.SetStyle(Paint.Style.Fill);
paint.TextSize = 20*density;
Rect measureRect = new Rect();
paint.GetTextBounds(text, 0, text.Length, measureRect);
var textHeight = measureRect.Height();
canvas.DrawText(text, Width / 2f, textHeight, paint);
```

7. If we are making a game, we can request that the view be updated again as soon as possible using the `Invalidate()` method:

```
Invalidate();
```

How it works...

Sometimes using the animation and shape APIs are not enough to create the image or app that we want to create. This may be required to create a game or draw a complex image. To draw a custom image, we make use of a `View` instance and its `Canvas` attribute. This is especially useful for games or apps that need to update a portion of the screen, or the entire screen, very frequently.

This is easy to do as all it requires is that we inherit from `View` and override the `OnDraw()` method. This method is provided a `Canvas` instance onto which we draw our graphics. Each time that Android determines that the view needs to be redrawn, this method will be called.

 Android will only redraw a `View` instance when it determines that it has changed. To force a redraw as soon as possible, the `Invalidate()` method can be invoked.

We can also request that the view be redrawn by invoking the `Invalidate()` method on the `View` instance. This will cause the entire view to be refreshed and redrawn. If we only want a partial area to be redrawn, we can pass the rectangle bounds to an overload. The `Invalidate()` method must be called from the UI thread; all other threads must use the `PostInvalidate()` methods.

If we were going to make a game, we could update the game state and then draw the game out onto the canvas provided by the `OnDraw()` method. Then, we can request a new update of the view by invoking `Invalidate` from the `OnDraw()` method. This will create the update-draw loop required in some games.

 Most, if not all, drawing operations onto a `Canvas` require a `Paint` instance.

A `Paint` instance holds the information of how to draw the particular request, and it ultimately controls what the resulting image will look like. The paint object also provides a few extra properties that allow us to enhance the drawing, such as antialiasing using through the `AntiAlias` property.

Creating an instance of `Paint` is quite expensive and should probably be done once and reused for all drawing operations. To prevent previous property values of `Paint` being accidentally used, we can reset the entire object to its initial state using the `Reset()` method.

When drawing on a canvas, we need to keep in mind that different devices have different screen densities. This is essential if we want images to appear with similar sizes on all devices. On devices with high densities, everything will appear much smaller than expected, and possibly too small for the user to work with. We can obtain the screen density using the `Density` property on the `DisplayMetrics` instance returned by the view's `Resources` property. We can use this property to multiply our calculations by in order to get similar sized images, even on devices with very high densities.

 Because devices have different screen densities, drawing operations should account for higher density screens to avoid things appearing too small.

Once we have our `Paint` instance and the `Canvas`, we can start drawing our image. Every time the `OnDraw()` method is called, we are provided with a blank, transparent canvas to draw on. To prevent other controls or views from showing through, we can clear the canvas using the `DrawColor()` method. This method accepts a color, which will then be used to fill the entire canvas.

The only thing left to do is to draw our image onto the canvas. This takes place by setting the paint properties and then drawing something. For example, to draw a solid green circle, we first set the paint to fill using the `SetStyle()` method with the `Paint.Style.Fill` value. Then, we set the color using the `Color` property and use the `Color.DarkGreen` value. As `Color` is a type, we are not limited to the predefined colors, but can construct any color we wish.

Now, we can draw the actual circle using the `DrawCircle()` method of the canvas. All the draw methods take parameters of the image we want to draw and then the paint instance, in this case, the center's *X* and *Y* coordinates, the radius of the circle, and finally the `Paint` instance. We need to remember to multiply the radius by the screen density to avoid the circle being tiny on high density devices.

To draw a circle outline, instead of a filled circle, we can use the `SetStyle()` method on `Paint` and pass in `Paint.Style.Stroke`. Then, we call the same `DrawCircle()` method passing the same parameters. As the paint object has changed properties, the result will be different. If we want to draw a circle with a border, we first draw the solid circle, then draw the circle stroke.

There are many methods for drawing geometric shapes, such as `DrawRect()` and `DrawPath()`, as well as methods for drawing whole images such as `DrawBitmap()` or `DrawPicture()`. We can also write text using the `DrawText()` method. Drawing text is very much the same as drawing anything, but we should remember to first set the font size using the `TextSize` property. Again, we need to remember to multiply the screen density. There is also the `TextAlign` property that enables us to align text to the left, right, or center of drawing a rectangle.

The origin of a rectangle is at the top-left corner, that of a circle is at the center, and for text is, it is at the baseline. The baseline is below the text, but above the descent.

Often, we would like to position text more precisely, such as below or above an object. As text is not positioned from the usual top-left corner, but rather from the baseline, we have to ensure that we take into account the fact that most of the text will be above the specified coordinates.

We can measure the size of the text bounding box using the `GetTextBounds()` method of `Paint`. Measuring a string, or portion of a string, allows us to position the text and take into consideration the different origin. The text measurements are taken using the styles and properties set on the `Paint` object.

There's more...

We can make use of the ability to draw on a `Canvas` instance when making an app or game that provides augmented reality. We can overlay the `SurfaceView` instance used by the camera with a transparent `View` instance. Then, we process the camera image stream and draw onto the `View` instance, providing the illusion that we are drawing onto the camera stream, or rather revealing something that was otherwise hidden in the real world.

Drawing on the canvas of a SurfaceView

Even after inheriting from `View` for custom drawing code, we are limited to Android's determination and frequency to actually redraw the view.

How to do it...

Drawing on a `View` instance requires that the drawing occurs within the UI update cycles as well as on the UI thread. This provides limitations that can be avoided by drawing on a `SurfaceView` instance from another thread:

1. In order to draw on a `SurfaceView` instance, we need a `Surface` instance to draw on. Thus, we need to know when the surface is created and destroyed:

```
public class MainActivity :
   Activity, ISurfaceHolderCallback {
   private ISurfaceHolder surfaceHolder;
   public void SurfaceChanged(
      ISurfaceHolder holder, Format format,
   int width, int height) {
   }
   public void SurfaceCreated(ISurfaceHolder holder) {
      surfaceHolder = holder;
   }
   public void SurfaceDestroyed(ISurfaceHolder holder) {
      surfaceHolder = null
   }
}
```

2. Then, we need to get hold of the `ISurfaceHolder` instance when the activity is created:

```
var holder = surfaceView.Holder;
holder.AddCallback(this);
```

3. Once we have a surface to draw on, we can start a new thread to draw on the `Canvas` as frequently as we need:

```
cancellation = new CancellationTokenSource();
var token = cancellation.Token;
Task.Run(() => {
   while (!token.IsCancellationRequested) {
      // ... draw on the canvas ...
   }
}, cancellation.Token);
```

4. In order to obtain a canvas, we use the `LockCanvas()` method. We can then draw as usual. When we are finished, we must ensure that we write the `Canvas` instance to the `Surface` instance using the `UnlockCanvasAndPost()` method:

```
Canvas canvas = null;
try {
   canvas = holder.LockCanvas();
```

```
      // ... draw as normal with the canvas ...
    }
    catch (Exception ex) {
      // handle errors
    }
    finally {
      if (canvas != null) {
        holder.UnlockCanvasAndPost(canvas);
      }
    }
```

5. When the surface is destroyed, we must stop the draw thread:

```
cancellation.Cancel();
```

How it works...

If we want to create a game or app that requires high performance and frequent updates to a view, we can simply inherit from `View` and override the `OnDraw()` method. However, we are limited to Android's determination and frequency to update the view. Invoking `Invalidate()` does not guarantee that the view will be immediately refreshed. Also, we can only draw on the canvas from the UI thread.

 The `Invalidate()` method does not guarantee that the `View` will immediately be redrawn, rather it is a request to redraw as soon as possible.

If we want to have a dedicated thread and surface for drawing on, we must use a `SurfaceView` instance instead. Drawing on a surface is very similar to drawing on a view in that we execute the same logic for drawing on a `Canvas`, but differs in where we get the `Canvas` from. When we inherit from a `View` instance, we override the `OnDraw()` method and make use of the canvas argument. When we draw on a `Surface` instance, we request a canvas from the `ISurfaceHolder` instance.

Just like when we want to render a video or camera preview, we need a `Surface` instance to draw on, we can either add a `SurfaceView` instance to the layout, or we can inherit from `SurfaceView` and add an instance of the new type to the layout. We then need an instance of the surface holder, which we obtain from the `Holder` property of the surface. We attach an implementation of `ISurfaceHolderCallback`, which will provide us with the actual surface holder.

As usual, when working with surfaces, we need to keep a reference of the holder from the `SurfaceCreated()` method and ensure that we stop the drawing in the `SurfaceDestroyed()` method.

One of the main features of drawing on a surface is the ability to draw from a thread other than the UI thread.

When we have a surface holder, we can request a canvas using the `LockCanvas()` method. We can only request, and lock, one canvas instance at a time. If `LockCanvas()` is invoked again before the canvas is released, this method will throw an exception. To release the canvas, and at the same time draw the canvas onto the surface, we invoke the `UnlockCanvasAndPost()` method with the canvas returned by the `LockCanvas()` method.

If we were making a game, or some app that required high-performance updates, we would start a new thread and initiate a loop that would continuously update and draw on the canvas acquired from the surface holder.

There's more...

Instead of drawing 2D images on a canvas, we can draw in 3D using OpenGL. OpenGL ES is a graphics library that support for high-performance 2D and 3D graphics. Instead of drawing on a `SurfaceView` instance, we draw on a `GLSurfaceView` instance, which inherits from `SurfaceView`, through a renderer. We use `GLSurfaceView.Renderer` to draw a frame instead of a canvas. Drawing with OpenGL is very different to drawing on a canvas, only similar in that drawing occurs on a surface instead of a `View` instance. However, for 3D games, OpenGL must be used.

We can also draw in 3D using a framework that uses OpenGL. An example would be to make use of MonoGame. This is a game engine that makes it easier to make games as well as provide cross-platform support. Games written using MonoGame can usually run without much, if any, modification on iOS, Windows Phone, Windows, Mac OS X, and Linux.

10
Responding to the User

In this chapter, we will cover the following recipes:

- ▶ Responding to simple touches
- ▶ Responding to scroll gestures
- ▶ Responding to manipulation gestures
- ▶ Detecting rotate gestures
- ▶ Responding to custom user gestures
- ▶ Listening to sensor data
- ▶ Listening for sensor triggers
- ▶ Discovering the environment
- ▶ Detecting device shakes

Introduction

Apps would not be useful if there was no way for either the user or the system to input data. The very definition of an app is to fulfil a purpose for the user, and the only way to let the app know what to do is to provide it with input. Almost all apps require some input, ranging from word processors with hundreds of key strokes and mouse clicks to screensavers, which close as soon as the mouse moves. All apps take input, process it, and output the result in some form.

For modern mobile devices, the primary form of input is touch, and on some devices, there is only one hardware button, the power button. Initially, Android devices were built with keypads, but now, almost all devices are built with a large touchscreens.

A touchscreen is actually very limited, because they can only respond to input when a user actually touches the screen. This makes processing the touch events the real source of input. Depending on the pressure the user applies, how many fingers the user uses, and how the user moves those fingers, we can determine what the user is doing.

If the user taps a single finger to the screen for a few milliseconds, it is a simple tap. If the user presses and holds for a few seconds, then it is a long press. When the user presses and drags a finger across the screen, it can be a scroll. If the user places multiple fingers on the screen, there is a whole new set of events that need to be processed. But that is not all, because mobile devices are so portable, they can actually be moved in their environment, providing another source of input data. The multitude of sensors built into the device allow the app to detect whether the device is being moved, rotated, shaken, or even that the user is walking with it. There are also many sensors to detect what is happening around the device. This provides yet another source of input data. These sensors can detect the amount of light or even the air pressure around the device.

In the same way that touch events are processed to provide the real input, the sensor data also needs to be processed to determine what the user is doing with the device. The touchscreen and the sensor simply provide raw data to the app, which then processes it into useful input data.

With all these forms of input, the mobile device ends up having far more sources of input than the typical desktop computer. This allows mobile apps to be more natural and more exciting to use. This allows us as developers to create great user experiences when designing apps.

Responding to simple touches

One of the primary means for the user to interact with the device is through touch. Often, this is the only way as there is no keyboard or mouse, and other methods might be unavailable or undesirable.

How to do it...

All views provide access to the two most common forms of touch input: single taps and long presses. We respond to these events using either listeners or event handlers:

1. We respond to taps using the `Click` event:

```
view.Click += (sender, e) => {
  // the user tapped the view
};
```

2. In the same way, we respond to long presses using the `LongClick` event. To prevent the `Click` event from also being triggered, we ensure that the `Handled` property of the `EventArgs` is set to `true`:

```
view.LongClick += (sender, e) => {
  // the user long-pressed on the view
  e.Handled = true;
};
```

Both the `Click` and `LongClick` events can also be subscribed to using listeners:

1. To use a listener with the `Click` event, we ensure that we implement the `View.IOnClickListener` interface:

```
public class MyView : View, View.IOnClickListener {
  public void OnClick(View view) {
    // the user tapped the view
  }
}
```

2. To subscribe using the listener, we make use of the `SetOnClickListener()` method:

```
SetOnClickListener(this);
```

3. Similarly, the `LongClick` events can also be subscribed to using listeners. To do this, we implement the `View.IOnLongClickListener` interface:

```
public class MyView : View, View.IOnLongClickListener {
  public bool OnLongClick(View view) {
    // the user long-pressed the view
    return true;
  }
}
```

4. Again, we set the listener using the `SetOnLongClickListener()` method:

```
SetOnLongClickListener(this);
```

How it works...

There are many ways to interact with apps running on a device. One of the most common ways is touch. Most Android smartphones are built with large, touchscreens which are the primary source of input.

Touch input can range from simple, single taps all the way to multifinger gestures. The simplest and most common are single taps and longpresses. Both forms are very easy to implement, requiring only logic to be attached to the `Click` event, for single taps, and the `LongClick` event, for longpress gestures.

Both events will fire as soon as the user completes the touch, but in the case of a long-press, we have to ensure that we let the event system know that we are handling a longpress instead of a single tap.

 A long-press is just a tap, but with a longer contact duration.

We let the system know that we are handling the long-press by setting the value of the `Handled` property on the `LongClickEventArgs` parameter of the `LongClick` event to `true`. If we do not do this, the `Click` event will also be raised, possibly resulting in unexpected behavior.

Both the `Click` and `LongClick` events can also be handled using Java-style listeners. The listener interface for the `Click` event is `View.IOnClickListener` and `View.IOnLongClickListener` for the `LongClick` event. Instances of classes implementing the interfaces are passed to the `SetOnClickListener()` and `SetOnLongClickListener()` methods.

Because the events actually use the listeners under the covers, attaching a handler to the event will disconnect the listeners. Also, assigning a listener to the view will detach the events. As a result, only one form of handler can be used at a time.

 Either the C#-style events or the Java-style listeners can be used, but not both at the same time.

There's more...

Sometimes, we need more advanced touch events, such as the number of fingers on the screen and their position on the screen. We get all the touch data by overriding the `OnTouchEvent()` method and accessing the `MotionEvent` argument:

```
public class MyView : View {
  public override bool OnTouchEvent(MotionEvent e) {
    return base.OnTouchEvent(e);
  }
}
```

Every time a touch event is triggered, we can access the data related to the touch using the `MotionEvent` argument. This instance contains data such as the number of fingers touching the screen, in the `PointerCount` property, and the location of each finger, through the `GetX()` and `GetY()` methods. We use the `ActionMasked` property to determine what raised the event. Possible reasons for touch events could be that a finger was either added, removed, or moved over the screen.

We can use this data to interpret gestures such as zoom, rotate, or drag. Here, we store all the fingers in a dictionary, along with their position on the screen:

```
var pointerIndex = e.ActionIndex;
var pointerId = e.GetPointerId(pointerIndex);
switch (e.ActionMasked) {
  case MotionEventActions.Down:
  case MotionEventActions.PointerDown:
    pointers[pointerId] =
    new PointF(e.GetX(pointerIndex), e.GetY(pointerIndex));
  break;
  case MotionEventActions.Move:
  for (int i = 0; i < e.PointerCount; i++) {
    var id = e.GetPointerId(i);
    pointers[id] = new PointF(e.GetX(i), e.GetY(i));
  }
  break;
  case MotionEventActions.Up:
  case MotionEventActions.PointerUp:
  case MotionEventActions.Cancel:
    pointers.Remove(id);
  break;
}
```

Responding to scroll gestures

There are many more ways for a user to interact with the device when using a single finger. These interactions include scrolling, flinging, and various kinds of tapping.

How to do it...

To receive the events from the gesture detector, we must implement the nested interface in the `GestureDetector` type and pass the instance to the gesture detector:

1. For most gestures, we implement the `IOnGestureListener` interface. As we are going to implement scrolling and flicking, we return `true` for the `OnDown()`, `OnFling()`, and `OnScroll()` methods. Because we are not concerned with the screen taps, we return `false` for the `OnSingleTapUp()` method:

```
public class MyView : View,
  GestureDetector.IOnGestureListener {
    public bool OnDown(MotionEvent e) {
      return true;
    }
```

```
public bool OnFling(MotionEvent e1, MotionEvent e2,
float velocityX, float velocityY) {
  return true;
}
public bool OnScroll(MotionEvent e1, MotionEvent e2,
float distanceX, float distanceY) {
  return true;
}
public void OnLongPress(MotionEvent e) {
}
public void OnShowPress(MotionEvent e) {
}
public bool OnSingleTapUp(MotionEvent e) {
  return false;
}
}
```

2. Once we have implemented the interface, we will need an instance of
   `GestureDetector`:

   ```
   gestureDetector = new GestureDetector(Context, this);
   ```

3. Then, we need to override the `OnTouchEvent()` method of the view to pass the
   events to the gesture detector:

   ```
   public override bool OnTouchEvent(MotionEvent e) {
     var handled = gestureDetector.OnTouchEvent(e);
     return handled || base.OnTouchEvent(e);
   }
   ```

Now, we start implementing the logic that should be executed when the gesture detector
detects a scroll or fling:

1. If we want to support a fling action, we will need a `scroller` instance, which is used
   to track scrolling. This can either be a `Scroller` instance or an `OverScroller`:

   ```
   scroller = new OverScroller(Context);
   ```

2. Next, we implement the `OnFling()` method to pass the fling event values to the
   `scroller` instance, along with the current scroll offset, view bounds, and, if we are
   using the `OverScroller`, the maximum over-scroll amount:

   ```
   public bool OnFling(MotionEvent e1, MotionEvent e2,
   float velocityX, float velocityY) {
     scroller.Fling(
       (int)ScrollX, (int)ScrollY,
       (int)-velocityX, (int)-velocityY,
       minimumX, maximumX,
   ```

```
      minimumY, maximumY,
   overscrollAmount, overscrollAmount);
   return true;
}
```

3. To actually scroll the view, we need to override the `ComputeScroll()` method and invoke the `ScrollTo()` method:

```
public override void ComputeScroll() {
  base.ComputeScroll();
  if (scroller.ComputeScrollOffset()) {
    ScrollTo(scroller.CurrX, scroller.CurrY);
  }
}
```

4. To implement scrolling as the user drags a finger across the screen, we implement the `OnScroll()` method:

```
public bool OnScroll(MotionEvent e1, MotionEvent e2,
float distanceX, float distanceY) {
  scroller.ForceFinished(true);
  var offsetX = (int)(ScrollX + distance);
  offsetX = Clamp(minimumX, offsetX, maximumX);
  var offsetY = (int)(ScrollY + distance);
  offsetY = Clamp(minimumY, offsetY, maximumY);
  ScrollTo(offsetX, offsetY);
  return true;
}
```

How it works...

Using only a single tap or long-press for touch input may not be enough. Often, the device screen is smaller than the content to be displayed, resulting in the requirement for the content to be scrolled. We can scroll through the content on the screen either by dragging the content or by performing a fling gesture.

Adding support for scrolling content is built into many of the views; however, sometimes custom views are created and scrolling needs to be added. We do this by making use of a gesture detector, which raises events when a scroll of fling gesture is detected.

To implement a `GestureDetector` object, we first need to implement the `IOnGestureListener` interface. Some of the methods in this interface return a `bool` value. This value lets the event chain know about what events are handled and what events should be bubbled up to the parent or other gesture detectors.

If `false` is returned from the `OnDown()` method, the gesture detector does not process any further events. If `true` is returned, then the gesture detector will process the event and then invoke the other methods, depending on what the user does. In a similar fashion, the `OnScroll()` and `OnFling()` methods should return `true` if the event was handled so that the event chain can be correctly processed.

 The `OnDown()` method should return `true` before the gesture detector starts processing further events.

Once the interface is implemented, we pass the instance to a new `GestureDetector` object. Then, we override the `OnTouchEvent()` method of the view and pass the `MotionEvent` instance to the gesture detector. This allows the gesture detector to process the events and make a decision on whether there was a tap, scroll, fling, or some other gesture.

The `MotionEvent` instance is passed to the `OnTouchEvent()` method of the gesture detector, which will then return a `bool` value indicating whether the view should continue to process events or not. If the method returns `false`, we should allow the view to process its own events by invoking the base `OnTouchEvent()` method.

When implementing a fling gesture, we need to handle the cases when the fling results in the content being over scrolled when too much force is applied. This is not required and we can stop scrolling as soon as the boundary of the content is reached; however, this often looks unnatural.

 A fling gesture can overscroll the content, before returning the content to the correct position. A scroll gesture should stop as soon as the content is on the screen.

Regardless of whether over-scrolling is desired or not, we use a `scroller` instance to translate a fling gesture into a series of scroll gestures. This is because once the user performs a fling, no further fingers are going to be on the screen to send scroll events.

A fling gesture is processed by passing the velocity of the fling and the boundaries of the view to an instance of either a `Scroller` instance or an `OverScroller` instance. In the case of the `OverScroller`, we need to pass in a value indicating how far the view can over-scroll.

Then, we need to override the `ComputeScroll()` method of the view. This method is used by the parent view to request that the view update its `ScrollX` and `ScrollY` properties. When this method is invoked, we ask the `scroller` instance if there is a scroll currently being performed using the `ComputeScrollOffset()` method. This method will return `true` if a scroll needs to be performed. In that case, we request for the view to be scrolled on its own using the `ScrollTo()` method passing in the new scroll values from the `scroller` instance. These values are obtained using the `CurrX` and `CurrY` properties.

When implementing the drag-to-scroll gesture, we do so by simply requesting that the view scroll to the new coordinates. If there is currently a scroll underway from a fling gesture, we should cancel it first using the `ForceFinished()` method. This will result in the scroll being stopped at the current position. When scrolling a view, we need to ensure that we do not over-scroll the content.

There's more...

The gesture detector also provides a means to detect whether a single tap or a double tap has been performed. If we know we are not going to be listening to double taps at all, we can respond to single taps in the `OnSingleTapUp()` method of the `IOnGestureListener` interface:

```
public bool OnSingleTapUp(MotionEvent e) {
  // handle single tap
  return true;
}
```

If we want to respond to double taps as well, we have to implement the `IOnDoubleTapListener` interface. Because we are interested in completed single taps and double taps, we return `true` for the `OnDoubleTap()` and `OnSingleTapConfirmed()` method:

```
public class MyView : View,
GestureDetector.IOnDoubleTapListener {
  public bool OnDoubleTap(MotionEvent e) {
    // handle double tap
    return true;
  }
  public bool OnDoubleTapEvent(MotionEvent e) {
    return false;
  }
  public bool OnSingleTapConfirmed(MotionEvent e) {
    // handle single tap
    return true;
  }
}
```

Then, we let the gesture detector know that we are listening for the double tap events using the `SetOnDoubleTapListener()` method:

```
gestureDetector.SetOnDoubleTapListener(this);
```

Responding to manipulation gestures

In some cases, an object needs to be manipulated on the screen. This can be done using the stretch action, and the most natural way to do this is to simply use a two-finger pinch gesture.

How to do it...

Adding support for pinch-to-zoom is just a matter of passing the touch events to an instance of `ScaleGestureDetector` and implementing the `IOnScaleGestureListener` interface:

1. To support the pinch-to-zoom gesture, we need to first implement the `ScaleGestureDetector.IOnScaleGestureListener` interface:

```
public class MyView : View,
ScaleGestureDetector.IOnScaleGestureListener {
  public bool OnScaleBegin(ScaleGestureDetector detector) {
    return true;
  }
  public bool OnScale(ScaleGestureDetector detector) {
    return true;
  }
  public void OnScaleEnd(ScaleGestureDetector detector) {
  }
}
```

2. Then, we create an instance of the `ScaleGestureDetector` type:

```
scaleDetector = new ScaleGestureDetector(Context, this);
```

3. Next, we need to override the `OnTouchEvent()` method to pass the event to the scale gesture detector:

```
public override bool OnTouchEvent(MotionEvent e) {
  var handled = scaleDetector.OnTouchEvent(e);
  return handled || base.OnTouchEvent(e);
}
```

4. Finally, we can implement the `OnScale()` method to handle the actual gesture:

```
public bool OnScale(ScaleGestureDetector detector) {
  scale *= scaleDetector.ScaleFactor;
  return true;
}
```

How it works...

Just as a user can touch the screen with one finger, gestures can be performed using multiple fingers. This creates an entirely new set of gestures that can now be performed. Some of these gestures can be pinches and twists, which are used to zoom or rotate respectively.

Using multitouch gestures allows the user to interact with the device in a more natural manner, and the app translates those gestures into the action that the user is trying to achieve.

> Often, multitouch gestures are more natural for the user than other forms of touch input.

Once such gesture is the pinch-to-zoom gesture. This is performed by making use of a `ScaleGestureDetector` instance.

At the time of implementing the `GestureDetector` object, we need to implement the `IOnScaleGestureListener` interface. We then pass the implementation of the interface to a new instance of `ScaleGestureDetector`.

The `OnScaleBegin()` and `OnScale()` methods on the interface should return `true` when we are handling the event. When the user starts the scale gesture, the `OnScaleBegin()` method is invoked. If we return `false` here, the scale gesture will be canceled. This is useful if there is only a small region of the view that should be scaled. This allows us to make a decision to start a scale gesture if the user is touching the appropriate region.

> The `OnScaleBegin()` method should return `true` to continue the gesture, and `false` to cancel it.

To process the touch events, we override the `OnTouchEvent()` method of the view and pass the `MotionEvent` argument to the `OnTouchEvent()` method of the gesture detector. This allows the gesture detector to invoke the various methods when a scale gesture is detected. Like with the simple gesture detector, the result of the gesture detector's `OnTouchEvent()` method is used to determine whether the base `OnTouchEvent()` method of the view should be invoked.

Once a scale gesture has commenced, the `OnScale()` method will be invoked every time the user moves their fingers across the screen. In this method, we can obtain the values from the gesture detector using the various properties. The most important of these is the `ScaleFactor` property, which is the amount scaled since the last time the method was invoked. The others include the `FocusX` and `FocusY` properties, which represent the focal point coordinates between the fingers, and the `CurrentSpan` property, which represents the linear distance between the two fingers.

Detecting rotate gestures

A common gesture for manipulating objects on the screen is to use the twist or rotate gesture. This is often more natural than entering a rotation value or dragging a cursor.

How to do it...

Another multifinger gesture that is very common is the rotate gesture. For a two-finger rotate, we can do something very similar to what we would do when implementing the `ScaleGestureDetector` instance. However, we do have to create a `RotateGestureDetector` instance ourselves as this is not currently provided by the framework. We will create `RotateGestureDetector` by preforming the following steps:

1. First, we need an interface that represents our gesture detector's events:

    ```
    public interface IOnRotateGestureListener {
      bool OnRotateBegin(RotateGestureDetector detector);
      void OnRotate(RotateGestureDetector detector);
      void OnRotateEnd(RotateGestureDetector detector);
    }
    ```

2. Then, we create the gesture detector type:

    ```
    public class RotateGestureDetector {
      private float oldX2, oldY2, oldX1, oldY1;
      private int pointerId1, pointerId2;
      private IOnRotateGestureListener listener;

      public RotateGestureDetector(
      IOnRotateGestureListener listener) {
        this.listener = listener;
        pointerId1 = -1;
        pointerId2 = -1;
      }

      public bool IsInProgress { get; private set; }
      public float Angle { get; private set; }
      public float FocusX { get; private set; }
      public float FocusY { get; private set; }

      public bool OnTouchEvent(MotionEvent e) {
        return true;
      }
    }
    ```

Once we have the structure in place, we can now implement the logic that will process the touch events from the view. It is important to ensure that we return the correct `bool` value when we handle the event to let any other gesture detectors know that it has been handled:

▸ After the interface has been defined, we implement the `OnTouchEvent()` method so that we can process the rotate gesture:

```
public bool OnTouchEvent(MotionEvent e) {
  var pointerIndex = e.ActionIndex;
  var pointerId = e.GetPointerId(pointerIndex);

  switch (e.ActionMasked) {
  case MotionEventActions.Down:
    pointerId1 = pointerId;
    pointerId2 = -1;
    IsInProgress = false;
    break;
  case MotionEventActions.PointerDown:
    if (pointerId1 != -1 && pointerId2 == -1) {
      pointerId2 = pointerId;
      var index1 = e.FindPointerIndex(pointerId1);
      var index2 = e.FindPointerIndex(pointerId2);
      oldX1 = e.GetX(index1);
      oldY1 = e.GetY(index1);
      oldX2 = e.GetX(index2);
      oldY2 = e.GetY(index2);

      FocusX = (oldX1 + oldX2) / 2f;
      FocusY = (oldY1 + oldY2) / 2f;
      Angle = 0;

      if (listener != null) {
        IsInProgress = listener.OnRotateBegin(this);
      }
    }
    break;
  case MotionEventActions.Move:
    if (IsInProgress) {
      float newX2, newY2, newX1, newY1;
      var index1 = e.FindPointerIndex(pointerId1);
      var index2 = e.FindPointerIndex(pointerId2);
      newX1 = e.GetX(index1);
      newY1 = e.GetY(index1);
      newX2 = e.GetX(index2);
```

```
            newY2 = e.GetY(index2);

            FocusX = (newX1 + newX2) / 2f;
            FocusY = (newY1 + newY2) / 2f;

            var oldA = Math.Atan2(oldY1 - oldY2, oldX1 - oldX2);
            var newA = Math.Atan2(newY1 - newY2, newX1 - newX2);
            var angle = (float)(oldA - newA);
            Angle = angle * 180.0f / (float)Math.PI;

            oldX1 = newX1;
            oldY1 = newY1;
            oldX2 = newX2;
            oldY2 = newY2;

            if (listener != null) {
              listener.OnRotate(this);
            }
          }
        }
        break;
      case MotionEventActions.Up:
      case MotionEventActions.PointerUp:
        if (IsInProgress) {
          if (pointerId == pointerId1) {
            pointerId1 = pointerId2;
            pointerId2 = -1;
          }
          else if (pointerId == pointerId2) {
            pointerId2 = -1;
          }
          if (pointerId1 == -1 || pointerId2 == -1) {
            IsInProgress = false;

            if (listener != null) {
              listener.OnRotateEnd(this);
            }
          }
        }
        break;
    }
    return true;
  }
```

Now that we have completed our rotate gesture detector, we can use it to perform a rotation:

1. Just like we did when implementing the scale gesture detector, we must implement the `IOnRotateGestureListener` interface:

```
public class MyView : View, IOnRotateGestureListener {
  public bool OnRotateBegin(RotateGestureDetector detector)
  {
    return true;
  }
  public void OnRotate(RotateGestureDetector detector) {
  }
  public void OnRotateEnd(RotateGestureDetector detector) {
  }
}
```

2. Then, we create an instance of `RotateGestureDetector`:

```
rotateDetector = new RotateGestureDetector(this);
```

3. Next, we need to override the `OnTouchEvent()` method to pass the event to the rotate gesture detector:

```
public override bool OnTouchEvent(MotionEvent e) {
  var handled = rotateDetector.OnTouchEvent(e);
  return handled || base.OnTouchEvent(e);
}
```

4. Lastly, in the `OnRotate()` method, we can read the rotation angle since the last update:

```
public void OnRotate(RotateGestureDetector detector) {
  rotation = (rotation + detector.Angle) % 360f;
}
```

How it works...

Using touch as input is one of the easiest forms of input. Whether it be a stretch, twist, or fling, the user will always find it easier to actually interact with the objects on the screen.

Android provides many of the common forms of gesture detection, but not everything that may be needed has been added to the framework. However, there is no reason why we cannot create custom gesture detectors to make it easier for the user to work with our app.

 Custom gesture detectors can be created to add functionality to an app when a native gesture detector is not available.

We can implement touch event processing in many ways, but following the patterns of the Android framework makes it easier to reuse the code in other apps as well as to make it easier to maintain in the future.

Custom gesture detectors are simple to create, requiring an interface that defines the events of the gesture detector, and the gesture detector itself. The gesture detector receives all the touch events from the view, which are processed. When the gesture actually occurs, the appropriate method on the interface is invoked.

[Gesture detectors consist of an interface defining the events and the gesture detector type.]

In the case of our rotate gesture detector, as soon as the user places two fingers on the screen, we initiate the rotate gesture. As the user moves their fingers across the screen, we calculate the size of the angle that the fingers have moved in. The angle is calculated from the lines formed from the location of the two fingers on the screen. When the user lifts a finger off the screen, we complete the rotate gesture.

Like with the scale gesture detector, we implement the interface on our view and create an instance of the RotateGetureDetector instance. Then, we override the OnTouchEvent() method, passing the touch event data to the gesture detector. This will result in the interface methods being invoked when a rotate gesture is detected.

We can prevent the rotate gesture from being performed for some reason by returning false from the OnRotateBegin() method. This is useful when we want to allow objects to be rotated on the screen, but only when both fingers are actually touching the object.

Responding to custom user gestures

There are other types of gestures that the user can perform, such as drawing letters or other shapes. These gestures may be more complex than a twist or drag, so we cannot just rely on simple finger tracking, but rather we need shape recognition.

How to do it...

We can store, recognize, and visualize shape gestures using a GestureLibrary instance:

1. We access a particular GestureLibrary by requesting one through the GestureLibraries type:

   ```
   GestureLibrary library =
     GestureLibraries.FromPrivateFile(this, "gestures");
   ```

2. When we want to load the gestures, or refresh the library, we invoke the `Load()` method:

```
library.Load();
```

3. Then, we can list all the gestures in the library using the `GestureEntries` property:

```
string[] entries = library.GestureEntries.ToArray();
```

4. To read the data about a specific gesture, we use the `GetGestures()` method:

```
Gesture gesture = library.GetGestures("my gesture")[0];
```

5. With the gesture, we can visualize the pattern as a `Bitmap` instance:

```
var bitmap = gesture.ToBitmap(100, 100, 0, Color.Yellow);
```

6. We can also visualize the gesture strokes as a `Path` instance:

```
var path = gesture.ToPath();
```

If we want to create a new gesture, we can make use of the `GestureOverlayView` instance and save the gesture to the library:

1. First, we add a `<android.gesture.GestureOverlayView>` element to the layout:

```
<android.gesture.GestureOverlayView
    android:id="@+id/overlay"
    android:layout_width="match_parent"
    android:layout_height="match_parent" />
```

Then we can access the overlay using the `FindViewById()` method:

```
var overlay =
    FindViewById<GestureOverlayView>(Resource.Id.overlay);
```

Alternatively, we can create and add a `GestureOverlayView` from code:

```
var overlay = new GestureOverlayView(this);
```

2. To prevent the drawn gesture from disappearing as soon as the user has finished, we can set the `GestureStrokeType` to `Multiple`:

```
overlay.GestureStrokeType = GestureStrokeType.Multiple;
```

3. After the user has drawn the gesture on the overlay, we can save the gesture to the library:

```
gestureLibrary.AddGesture("name", overlay.Gesture);
gestureLibrary.Save();
```

4. To allow a new gesture to be drawn, we can clean up the overlay:

```
overlay.Clear(false);
```

When we want to respond to a user's gesture, we can place a `GestureOverlayView` parameter on the UI and wait for the user to draw on it:

1. To respond to a gesture that the user has drawn, we can attach a handler to the `GesturePerformed` event:

    ```
    overlay.GesturePerformed += (sender, e) => {
    }
    ```

2. Then, we check the gesture against the library:

    ```
    var recognitions = gestureLibrary.Recognize(e.Gesture);
    ```

3. In the result, we can find the best guess:

    ```
    var guess = recognitions.FirstOrDefault(r => r.Score > 1);
    ```

How it works...

Simple gesture recognition involves tracking the movement of one or more fingers across the device screen. This data is used to update the screen or manipulate objects in real time. These gestures are limited to the data that is provided every few milliseconds and usually doesn't track the entire gesture.

More advanced gestures require the entire gesture to be performed before it can be processed. These types of gestures are delayed and do not perform any direct manipulations. However, feedback to the user may be required in the form of a path being traced onto the screen.

 Some gestures are more complex and require the entire gesture to be drawn before it can be processed.

Android provides an easy way to both record and recognize gestures through the `GestureLibrary` type. A `GestureLibrary` type can be obtained through one of the methods on the `GestureLibraries` type, either from a raw resource of from a file on the file system.

When we have created the gesture library instance, we load or reload the gestures into memory using the `Load()` method. And, if we update the library, we can persist the changes using the `Save()` method.

 Both the `Load()` and `Save()` methods need to be invoked manually in order to load and save the gesture library, respectively.

Once loaded, we can list the gestures loaded using the `GestureEntries` property, or query specific gestures using the `GetGestures()` method. After we have queried a specific gesture, we can make use of the various methods to convert a gesture into a visual `Path` or `Bitmap` parameters.

In order to build up the library of gestures, we can either load an existing library file, or we can create and add new gestures to the library. Regardless of how gestures are created, we add them to the library using the `AddGesture()` method. We pass the gesture, along with a name, to this method. After adding gestures, we need to ensure that we save the library.

> Adding multiple gestures with the same name can improve the chances of the drawn gesture being correctly recognized.

Gestures can be created by building a collection of timestamped coordinates. A series of `GesturePoints` are added to a `GestureStroke` instance, which in turn are added to a gesture.

Another means of creating gestures is via the `GestureOverlayView` instance. When displayed, the user can trace the gesture, which we can then read and save into a library. Some gestures require multiple strokes, thus we need to set the `GestureStrokeType` property to `Multiple`. This prevents the view from clearing the surface as soon as the user lifts all their fingers off the view.

> When adding the `GestureOverlayView` instance to the `.axml` file, the fully qualified name, `android.gesture.GestureOverlayView`, must be used as it is not part of the usual `Android.Widget` namespace.

Now that we have a collection of gestures in a gesture library, we need to be able to recognize user gestures. This is done by passing the gesture to be recognized to the `Recognize()` method of the library. The `Recognize()` method returns a collection of scored predictions or matches.

Each prediction is provided a score or match rating, and the match collection is ordered by score from the highest match to the lowest. Predictions with scores above 1.0 indicate good matches, and scores below 1.0 are poor matches. However, any threshold can be used to determine the desired match.

> Gesture predictions with a score of above 1.0 usually indicate good matches.

When using the `GestureOverlayView` instance to draw gestures, there are several events that we can subscribe to. One of the most common events is `GesturePerformed`, which is raised as soon as the view detects that the user has finished drawing a gesture.

There's more...

The `GestureOverlayView` instance can also be used to overlay regular views, and detect gestures when the user interacts with those views. As the `GestureOverlayView` instance is simply a `FrameLayout` instance, child views can be added to it in the same way views are added to other layouts.

As child views also will be processing events, we need to ensure that as soon as the gesture overlay view detects a gesture, it prevents the child views from processing touch events. This is done by setting the `EventsInterceptionEnabled` property to `true`. This is useful when the child view is a scrollable view, as the `GestureOverlay` view prevents the scrollable view from scrolling during gestures.

If the child view is scrollable, we need to indicate to the gesture overlay view what direction the view scrolls in. We do this by setting the `Orientation` property to the child view scroll direction. This allows scroll gestures to be correctly recognized as scrolling and not a custom gesture.

Listening to sensor data

Just as touching a device screen is input, so is rotating and moving the actual physical device in its environment. Most devices are built with several sensors that can be used to read the state of the device in its environment.

How to do it...

We can access all the available sensors and the sensor data on the device through the `SensorManager` type:

1. The instance of the `SensorManager` type is obtained from the current context:

   ```
   var manager = SensorManager.FromContext(this);
   ```

2. Once we have the manager, we check whether a particular sensor exists, and return the instance of it using the `GetDefaultSensor()` method:

   ```
   var type = SensorType.Accelerometer;
   var accelerometer = manager.GetDefaultSensor(type);
   if (accelerometer == null) {
     // handle no acceleromenter
   }
   ```

3. In order to be able to receive sensor data, we must implement the `ISensorEventListener` interface:

   ```
   public class MyActivity : Activity, ISensorEventListener {
     public void OnAccuracyChanged(
       Sensor sensor, SensorStatus accuracy) {
   ```

```
    }
    public void OnSensorChanged(SensorEvent e) {
    }
}
```

4. To start receiving data from a sensor, we register it along with the listener instance and data update rate via the `RegisterListener()` method:

```
manager.RegisterListener(
    this, accelerometer, SensorDelay.Fastest);
```

5. Once we are finished with the sensor, we unregister the listener:

```
manager.UnregisterListener(this);
```

The data from sensors can be used for many different purposes, ranging from making decisions to drawing on the screen. For example, we can make use of the accelerometer data in the `OnSensorChanged()` method to create a level or plumb line:

1. First, we will need fields to hold data across events:

```
private float rotationX;
private float rotationY;
```

2. Then, we will filter the raw event data to prevent rapid fluctuations of the values:

```
const float Filter = 0.05f;
var x = e.Values[0];
var y = e.Values[1];
rotationX = (x * Filter) + (rotationX * (1f - Filter));
rotationY = (y * Filter) + (rotationY * (1f - Filter));
```

3. Now that we have the filtered values, we can convert this into a 2D angle:

```
var rotation2d = (float)Math.Atan2(rotationY, rotationX);
var degrees = -rotation2d * (180f / (float)Math.PI);
```

4. Finally, we can apply the rotation to a view:

```
levelView.Rotation = degrees + 90f;
```

How it works...

Many devices are built with multiple sensors. This can range from accelerometers and gyroscopes to proximity sensors and step counters. All of these sensors constantly stream data of where and how the device is situated in the environment. All this data can be used to both enhance as well as provide core functionality to an app.

For example, the accelerometer and gyroscope can be used to create a game that allows the user to control a player based on how the device is rotated. Or, the step counter sensor can be used to provide data to a health or fitness app.

However, not all devices have all the sensors. Before a sensor can be used by our app, we need to ensure that it exists on the device and that we can access the data. This is done using the `SensorManager` instance. Once we have obtained the instance of the sensor manager, we are able to query the existence of a particular sensor using the `GetDefaultSensor()` method.

Not all devices may have a particular sensor, thus checks need to be performed before using it.

The `GetDefaultSensor()` method returns either the sensor that was requested or `null` if the device does not support that sensor. As sensors are queried by type, there may be multiple versions of a sensor by different vendors. If this is the case, we can use the `GetSensorList()` method instead. This will provide a collection of sensors that match the requested sensor type.

There may be multiple versions of a sensor type on a device.

We can find out about a particular sensor using the various properties on the `Sensor` type. These properties include the `Version` and `Vendor` properties, as well as the characteristics of the sensor, such as `Power` for the power requirements.

Once we have the desired sensor, we can start reading the data stream. To do this, we need to implement the `ISensorEventListener` interface, and register it with the sensor manager. Registering for data requires that we provide the sensor manager with the listener, sensor, and sampling rate of the `RegisterListener()` method.

After the listener is registered, we will receive the sensor data in the `OnSensorChanged()` method. This method receives the data from the sensor, which includes the accuracy, time, and the actual data values. The values from the sensor are provided via the `Values` property on the `SensorEvent` type. This property is an array of type `float`, and the elements vary across sensor types.

The number of values provided by the `OnSensorChanged()` method may vary from sensor to sensor.

For example, the accelerometer sensor has three elements, the first being the force along the x axis, the second being the force along the y axis, and the third being the force along the z axis. The step counter sensor only has one element, which is the number of steps taken since the device boot.

As the `OnSensorChanged()` method may be invoked at a high rate, we should avoid blocking its return. If filtering or processing of the data is required, we should move it out from the current method and into another method. Also, when registering the listener, we can possibly select a lower rate of data if a high rate is not required. This will preserve both battery and system resources.

 The `OnSensorChanged()` method should not block its return.

As having a listener registered to a sensor consumes battery, we should unregister the sensor as soon as it is no longer needed. We do this by passing the listener to the `UnregisterListener()` method. If the sensor is used to update the UI, then as soon as the activity leaves the foreground, we can unregister it in the `OnPause()` method and reregister it in the `OnResume()` method.

Listening for sensor triggers

Some sensors do not provide a continuous stream of data, but rather raise an event when something happens.

How to do it...

To use trigger-based sensors, we also make use of the sensor manager. Unlike stream-based sensors, we inherit from the `TriggerEventListener` type:

1. First, we need the instance of the `SensorManager` type:

   ```
   var manager = SensorManager.FromContext(this);
   ```

2. Next, we get a reference to the sensor. If the sensor is `null`, then it is not available on the device:

   ```
   var type = SensorType.SignificantMotion;
   var motion = manager.GetDefaultSensor(type);
   if (motion == null) {
     // handle no significant motion sensor
   }
   ```

3. Then, we create inherit from the `TriggerEventListener` type:

   ```
   private class MyListener : TriggerEventListener {
     public override void OnTrigger(TriggerEvent e) {
       // handle significant motion
     }
   }
   ```

4. We create an instance of this trigger event listener:

```
listener = new MyListener();
```

5. Once we have the listener, we register it with the sensor manager along with the sensor:

```
manager.RequestTriggerSensor(listener, motion);
```

6. When we no longer need the trigger, we unregister it:

```
manager.CancelTriggerSensor(listener, motion);
```

How it works...

Devices have many sensors, some providing a stream of data to apps and others providing data when certain events occur. These events might be triggered when the user takes a step or when the user moves to a new location.

These sensors work by only enabling when a listener is attached, then as soon as the event it raised, the trigger is invoked and the listener detached. In order for the trigger to be invoked when the event occurs again, we need to reregister the listener.

 Trigger-based sensors automatically unregister when the event occurs.

Just like when accessing all other sensors, we need to use the `SensorManager` instance. Once we have obtained the sensor manager, we need to ensure that the particular sensor exists on the device. As with all sensors, we use the `GetDefaultSensor()` method to do this.

Once we have the sensor, we need an instance of the `TriggerEventListener` type. Unlike other sensors, this is not an interface to be implemented. Instead, it is a type that we inherit from and override the `OnTrigger()` method.

 Trigger-based sensors do not require the implementation of an interface but rather an instance of a type inheriting from `TriggerEventListener`.

The `OnTrigger()` method has a single `TriggerEvent` argument, which provides access to the timestamp of the event and the actual sensor data. The sensor data is provided in the form of a float array property named `Values`.

When we want to register the listener with the sensor, we pass an instance of the listener and the sensor to the `RequestTriggerSensor()` method on the sensor manager. As soon as the event is raised, the `OnTrigger()` method will be invoked and the listener automatically unregistered. If the trigger needs to be invoked again, it will have to be reregistered.

Once we no longer need the sensor to invoke our trigger, we can cancel the listener by passing both the listener and the sensor to the `CancelTriggerSensor()` method on the sensor manager.

Discovering the environment

Not all sensors are used to access the state of the device. Some are used to describe the world in which the device exists.

How to do it...

The environment sensors are the same as most of the sensors, in that they require an implementation of the sensor event listener interface to be registered with the sensor manager:

1. As with all sensors, we have to use the `SensorManager` instance to access the sensor:

   ```
   var manager = SensorManager.FromContext(this);
   ```

2. When we have the sensor manager, we obtain the specific sensor:

   ```
   var type = SensorType.Light;
   var light = manager.GetDefaultSensor(type);
   if (light == null) {
     // handle no significant motion sensor
   }
   ```

3. Next, we implement the `ISensorEventListener` interface:

   ```
   public class MyActivity : Activity, ISensorEventListener {
     public void OnAccuracyChanged(
     Sensor sensor, SensorStatus accuracy) {
     }
     public void OnSensorChanged(SensorEvent e) {
     }
   }
   ```

4. Then, we implement the `OnSensorChanged()` method to read the single value from the sensor:

   ```
   var lx = e.Values[0];
   ```

5. To start receiving events, we register the listener along with the desired update rate:

   ```
   manager.RegisterListener(
     this, accelerometer, SensorDelay.Fastest);
   ```

6. Once we are finished with the sensor, we unregister it:

   ```
   manager.UnregisterListener(this);
   ```

How it works...

Touch describes how the user interacts with the device and sensors describe how the device exists in the world. But, another form of input that we can utilize is the data from the actual environment that the device is in. This data can be the amount of light in the environment or the air pressure, moisture, and temperature.

The four sensors currently available are the relative ambient humidity sensor, the illuminance sensor, the ambient pressure sensor, and the ambient temperature sensor. There are actually two temperature sensors: the `Temperature` sensor type and the `AmbientTemerature` instance. The first sensor measures the actual device CPU temperature and the second measures the ambient temperature near the device.

 There are two temperature sensors—one measures the temperature of the CPU and the other measures the air temperature.

Although these sensors are not as common as the others, such as the accelerometer, we can still use these to enhance an app. The light or illuminance sensor is the most commonly available sensor in most devices, because it is used to control the display brightness.

Although they are functionally the same as the other sensors, the environment sensors only return a single sensor value from the `Values` property on the `SensorEvent` argument. Also, this value does not require filtering to reduce noise, and it can be consumed directly from the event.

 Environment sensors only have a single sensor value, which does not need filtering.

Detecting device shakes

A fairly common gesture that can be implemented using sensors is the shake gesture. This can be used to shuffle cards in a game or tracks in a playlist.

How to do it...

To detect a shake, we will need to record the data from the accelerometer and determine whether a shake has occurred:

1. First, we implement the `ISensorEventListener` interface, and register it with the manager:

```
var manager = SensorManager.FromContext(this);
var type = SensorType.Accelerometer;
```

```
var accelerometer = manager.GetDefaultSensor(type);
manager.RegisterListener(
    this, accelerometer, SensorDelay.Fastest);
```

2. Then, we will need a few fields that will store the values across the accelerometer events:

```
private int lastUpdate;
private float lastX;
private float lastY;
private float lastZ;
```

3. As we are also going to process shakes, we will need a field to hold the shake related data:

```
private int lastShake;
```

4. In the `OnSensorChanged()` method, we ensure that we only process the events after a reasonable interval of time has passed:

```
const int EventTimeLimit = 100;
var current = System.Environment.TickCount;
var updateDelta = current - lastUpdate;
if (updateDelta < EventTimeLimit) {
    return;
}
```

5. Then, we calculate the distance by which the device has moved to detect a shake gesture:

```
const int ShakeThreshold = 350;
var x = e.Values[0];
var y = e.Values[1];
var z = e.Values[2];
var delta = x + y + z - lastX - lastY - lastZ;
var speed = Math.Abs(delta) / updateDelta * 1000;
if (speed > ShakeThreshold) {
    lastShake = current;
    // there was a shake
}
```

6. We ensure that we update the fields with the latest values from the sensor so that we can start checking for another shake:

```
lastUpdate = current;
lastX = x;
lastY = y;
lastZ = z;
```

How it works...

Just like we can process touch events to detect touch gestures, we can process sensor data to detect device gestures. One gesture can be that when the user shakes the device, we shuffle tracks in a playlist or move on-screen objects.

 Encapsulating touch or device gesture detection logic allows the logic to be reused across apps and helps reduce maintenance efforts.

If we want to implement a shake detector, we make use of the accelerometer, and track the amount of change the device experiences every few milliseconds. If the direction changes rapidly, then the user is shaking the device.

The way we detect this is by storing the old accelerometer values and then comparing the new values. When the difference between the values over a time period reaches a certain threshold, then we record a shake.

There's more...

We can extend this model to only record a shake gesture after a few shakes have already occurred. This reduces the chance of incorrectly detecting a shake if the user makes a sudden movement. To do this, we count the number of shakes every time the device is shaken, and after a certain number of times, we actually record the shake.

First, we change the shake detection logic to rather count the shakes, reporting only after it reaches a certain number:

```
const int ShakesRequired = 3;
if (speed > ShakeThreshold) {
  lastShake = current;
  shakeCount++;
  if (shakeCount > ShakesRequired) {
    // there was a shake
    shakeCount = 0;
  }
}
```

To prevent the number of shakes from growing continuously, we can reset the counter after a short period of no shakes:

```
const int ShakeTimeLimit = 500;
if (shakeDelta > ShakeTimeLimit) {
  shakeCount = 0;
}
```

11
Connecting to Wearables

In this chapter, we will cover the following recipes:

- ► Introducing wearable notifications
- ► Customizing wearable notifications
- ► Creating wearable apps
- ► Creating always-on wearable apps
- ► Creating dynamic always-on wearable apps
- ► Communicating with wearables
- ► Building watch faces
- ► Configuring watch faces

Introduction

Whether it is something that makes life a little easier or just for fun, everybody enjoys cool gadgets and small things. Wearables are all the rage with many companies trying to produce watches and bands in various forms.

Whether a wearable is an enhanced watch, a fitness band, or a fully digital watch with app support, all the wearables have one thing in common—they provide users an enhanced experience and are easily worn on the wrists.

Most devices worn on the wrist are watches and, even with modern mobile phones, watches remain the primary mobile timekeeping means. They are light, fashionable, and reliable. Wearables can be deemed to be devices that not only keep these basic requirements, but also provide additional features.

Wearables not only display the accurate time, but they also provide a constant stream of current, relevant, and useful information. Thus, the information is relevant to the user's current location, time, and environment.

Wearables often extend a mobile phone's experience, such as providing a user with notifications from the mobile device or letting users easily view any of the upcoming events.

With all the great aspects of the many wearables, these tiny devices are now becoming more and more prevalent and will continue to become so in the future. Similar to the time when mobile phones first became commonplace, wearables will soon be on everyone's wrist. By preparing apps for the future now, developers can equip themselves to help the user's experience reach to an entirely new level.

Introducing wearable notifications

Wearable devices are very useful for apps as they allow users to read notifications without having to reach for a handheld.

Getting ready

To make use of notifications on a wearable, we need to have the **Android Support Library v4 Component** or the **Xamarin.Android.Support.v4 NuGet** installed on our handheld project.

How to do it...

We can make notifications automatically appear on a wearable if we manage our app's notifications using the `NotificationCompat` type:

1. To display typical notifications on a wearable, we will build and display them using the `NotificationCompat` and `NotificationManagerCompat` types:

```
var notification = new NotificationCompat.Builder(this)
  .SetSmallIcon(Android.Resource.Drawable.StatSysDownload)
  .SetContentTitle("Wearable Notifications")
  .SetContentText("This is a notification from a device.")
  .SetContentIntent(pendingIntent)
  .Build();
var manager = NotificationManagerCompat.From(this);
manager.Notify(NotificationId, notification);
```

2. If we have specified a style for the notification, the wearable notification will also adhere to this style:

```
var expandedStyle = new NotificationCompat.BigTextStyle();
expandedStyle.BigText("This is the extended text...");
var notification = new NotificationCompat.Builder(this)
   ...
   .SetStyle(expandedStyle)
   .Build();
```

3. If we want to display buttons on the notification on both handheld and wearable, then we will use the `SetAction()` method of the notification builder:

```
var action = new NotificationCompat.Action.Builder(
   iconResource, "Open Maps", pendingIntent)
   .Build();
var notification = new NotificationCompat.Builder(this)
   ...
   .AddAction(action)
   .Build();
```

How it works...

When an Android wearable device is connected to a handheld device, the handheld device automatically synchronizes notifications to this wearable. This allows users to read notifications without having to reach for the handheld. This hands-free ability is what makes this wearable device such a great convenience. Although not as powerful as a handheld, the wearable can often provide an overall improved user experience.

To provide notifications on the wearable, no extra code or configuration is required. All that needs to be done is to show the notification using the `NotificationCompat` type. This `type()` functions exactly similar to the `Notification` type and supports all the Android versions from Android 2.0.

To show a notification, we will create it using the `NotificationCompat.Builder` type. Once we have set all the properties, we will build it using the `Build()` method. Then, to show the built notification, we will pass it to the `Notify()` method on the `NotificationManagerCompat` type.

In addition to displaying notifications, we can customize their appearance using various styles and actions. Each component of the notification is rendered differently and more appropriately on each type of device. Whether it is the handheld or wearable, the notification will be displayed in an easy-to-consume manner.

Customizing wearable notifications

Notifications displayed on the wearable offer a hands-free experience for using apps; however, it is often desirable to provide the user with a wearable-specific experience.

How to do it...

Notifications from a handheld device can be easily displayed on wearables, but we can also provide special features for notifications that will only appear on a wearable:

1. We can customize the appearance of notifications using extenders, such as `NotificationCompat.WearableExtender` for wearable devices:

```
var background = BitmapFactory.DecodeResource(
  Resources, Resource.Drawable.notificationBackground);
var extender = new NotificationCompat.WearableExtender()
  .SetHintHideIcon(true)
  .SetBackground(background);
```

2. We can also use extenders to provide specific action buttons for the wearable, instead of just using the actions from a handheld:

```
var icon = Android.Resource.Drawable.IcDialogDialer;
var action = new NotificationCompat.Action(
  icon, "Make Call", pendingIntent);
extender.AddAction(action);
```

3. To apply the customizations of the extenders, we will attach the extender using the `Extend()` method:

```
var notification = new NotificationCompat.Builder(this)
  ...
  .Extend(extender)
  .Build();
```

4. Then, we can show the notification normally, and the extender will render the additional content on the wearable:

```
var manager = NotificationManagerCompat.From(this);
manager.Notify(NotificationId, notification);
```

5. Once we have created the notification, we can read the extended values through the same extender type:

```
var extender =
  new NotificationCompat.WearableExtender(notification);
var isIconHidden = extender.HintHideIcon;
```

How it works...

Android automatically synchronizes notifications to the wearable, which is often enough. However, we can provide an improved experience for the wearable using the `NotificationCompat.WearableExtender` type.

The `WearableExtender` type can be used to provide wearable-specific features and functionality to synchronized notifications.

This type provides the means to override and customize the default notification functionality and appearance on the wearable device. Usually, the notification has an app icon in the corner of the notification, but we may wish to use a different look for our app.

If we create an instance of the `WearableExtender` type, we can use it to modify the notification. We will use the `SetHintHideIcon()` method to let the wearable know not to render the icon. Then, we set a background behind the content card using the `SetBackground()` method. In addition to removing the icon, we can also change its position or use an icon that is different from the app icon.

The bitmap that we use with the `SetBackground()` method should have a resolution of 400 × 400 for non-scrolling backgrounds and 640 × 400 for scrolling backgrounds. These images should be placed in the `drawable-nodpi` resource folder. Other image resources for wearable notifications, such as icons, should be placed in the `drawable-hdpi` resource folder.

When using the `WearableExtender` type, a custom set of actions can be provided for the wearable.

Another method to override functionality is to provide a different set of actions for the wearable. When not providing actions via the extender, all the actions on the notification are available on the wearable. We may want to provide a more useful set of actions designed for a hands-free device. One such improvement would be to provide a reply by typing a response on the handheld; but on the wearable, we would provide a reply by a voice input.

To provide custom actions on a wearable, we can create the action using the `NotificationCompat.Action` type. Then, instead of adding the action to the notification, we add the action to the wearable extender using the `AddAction()` method.

If the actions are added to the `WearableExtender` type, they replace all actions for the wearable, resulting in a different set of actions for each device.

There's more...

Notifications using `RemoteViews` are stripped of custom layouts, and the wearable will only display the text and icons. However, we can create the appearance custom notifications by creating an app that runs on the wearable device.

If the standard notification styles don't provide the required features or appearance, we can display a custom activity with a custom layout. Then, we can request for the wearable to issue a notification and set the activity as the display intent.

 Notifications displayed from the wearable are not synchronized to the handheld, but notifications on the handheld are synchronized to the wearable.

We can use normal mechanisms to display a notification from a wearable because the wearable is actually just a smaller Android device. Displaying a notification from the wearable is the same as displaying a notification on the handheld.

Creating wearable apps

Synchronizing notifications to the wearable provides an easy means to extend an app to the wearable; however, sometimes, an entirely customized or fully-featured wearable experience is required.

Getting ready

All the wearable apps require an app to first be installed on the handheld. Here, we can assume that we have an existing project to which we are adding a wearable companion. Although, automatically installed when creating a new Android Wear project, we do need to have the **Xamarin.Android.Wear NuGet** installed in the wearable project.

How to do it...

Wearable apps require a companion app on the handheld. Usually, we already have an existing app to which we can simply add a new wearable app:

1. In the open solution, right-click on the solution node, select **Add**, and then select **Add New Project...**.
2. In the wizard that appears, create a new `Android Wear App` project just as we would for any other app. The only thing that we need to do is to ensure that the **Identifier** field exactly matches that of the companion app.

Once the wearable app is created, we need to add it as a project reference to the handheld companion app:

1. To do this, right-click on the `References` folder under the handheld app project, and select **Edit References…**.

2. In the dialog that appears, select the **Projects** tab, check the box next to the wearable app project, and then click on **OK**.

Once the project references are set up, we can run the app on the handheld and the wearable:

1. Set the configuration to **Release**, and run the handheld app.

2. After the app has been installed on the handheld, the OS will begin copying the wearable app to the wearable device.

3. In a few moments, the wearable will get a notification that a new app has been installed.

Because some devices have round screens and others have square, we need to be able to specify different layouts for each screen type:

1. In the `Main.axml` layout file, we will create a proxy layout using `WatchViewStub`, and use the `rectLayout` and `roundLayout` attributes to specify the real layout to load depending on the screen type:

    ```
    <android.support.wearable.view.WatchViewStub
      xmlns:android="http://schemas.android.com/apk/res/android"
      xmlns:app="http://schemas.android.com/apk/res-auto"
      android:id="@+id/watch_view_stub"
      android:layout_width="match_parent"
      android:layout_height="match_parent"
      app:rectLayout="@layout/RectangleMain"
      app:roundLayout="@layout/RoundMain" />
    ```

2. Then, we can create the different `RectangleMain.axml` and `RoundMain.axml` layout files for the app in the layout folder:

    ```
    <LinearLayout
      xmlns:android="http://schemas.android.com/apk/res/android"
      android:orientation="vertical"
      android:layout_width="fill_parent"
      android:layout_height="fill_parent"
      <Button
        android:id="@+id/myButton"
        android:layout_width="match_parent"
        android:layout_height="match_parent"
        android:text="Click Me!" />
    </LinearLayout>
    ```

3. Finally, we can access various controls in the `LayoutInflated` event of `WatchViewStub`:

```
protected override void OnCreate(Bundle bundle) {
    // load normally
    base.OnCreate(bundle);
    SetContentView(Resource.Layout.Main);

    // wait until the stub loads the real layout
    var id = Resource.Id.watch_view_stub;
    var stub = FindViewById<WatchViewStub>(id);
    stub.LayoutInflated += delegate {
        // now we can access the button
        var buttonId = Resource.Id.myButton;
        var button = FindViewById<Button>(buttonId);
    };
}
```

How it works...

An Android Wear app is the most powerful method to provide a wearable experience for Android users. These apps are fully-featured Android apps that run on a wearable device with only a few differences.

One of the most notable things is the design and usability. Although running on Android, the wearable has a much smaller screen size as well as more limited hardware. Due to these limitations, wearable apps are often reduced in functionality and complement the handheld apps.

 Android Wear devices are much smaller and less powerful, and thus, these apps are usually not as comprehensive.

Wearable apps are not distributed via Google Play directly, but are embedded within a handheld app. To install an app on the wearable, the handheld must have the wearable app package embedded as a raw resource. When the app is installed on the handheld, Android copies the embedded package onto the wearable.

When creating a wearable app, we just need to select the `Android Wear App` project template. This template is very similar to the normal app template, but has a few extra packages installed by default. We can, in fact, create a normal app and use it as a wearable app, but as we are starting out, using the template is simpler.

Wearable apps are exactly the same as the handheld apps, and follow the same app lifecycles.

One extra difference is that instead of a single layout file, it provides the proxy layout via the `WatchViewStub` type. This is not required and can usually just be replaced with the normal layout files. The `WatchViewStub` type is a special view that loads another layout depending on the screen shape. The two typical screen shapes are square and round, and often the layout has to be slightly adjusted for each.

When we use the `WatchViewStub` type, instead of handling the initialization logic in the `OnCreate()` method, we attach it to the `LayoutInflated` event. Then, when the view is initialized by Android, this event is fired, allowing us to perform the remainder of the initialization logic. Using the `WatchViewStub` type is, in fact, similar to what would happen when creating different layout resources for different device configurations.

 Wearable apps can either use special adaptive layouts or separate layouts via the `WatchViewStub` layout.

Once we have the wearable app project created (or if we chose to use a normal app project), we can then set it as a wearable app for the main app. We can do this by simply adding it as a project reference, just as we would for any other library project. The difference happens during the compile time when the compiler packages the app. Instead of including the wearable app as a reference, it adds it as a wearable app resource. No extra logic is required; and when the handheld app is deployed to a device, the wearable app is deployed to the wearable.

 Android apps become wearable apps when they are added as project references to another Android app.

When debugging wearable apps, we can simply deploy the wearable app directly to the wearable device via a USB cable. This is simple to do and usually works; however, if the wearable device does not support a USB debugging, we can forward the ports used to debug the wearable through the Android Wear app.

More information on forwarding the port can be found on the Google website, available at `http://developer.android.com/training/wearables/apps/bt-debugging.html`.

There's more...

Sometimes, the layouts for the round and square screens are so similar that creating multiple screens using the `WatchViewStub` type is not even necessary. We can make use of various other views that will adjust depending on the screen type. One such view is the `BoxInsetLayout` view:

```
<android.support.wearable.view.BoxInsetLayout
xmlns:android="http://schemas.android.com/apk/res/android"
  xmlns:app="http://schemas.android.com/apk/res-auto"
  android:background="@drawable/background"
  android:layout_height="match_parent"
  android:layout_width="match_parent">
  <FrameLayout
    android:id="@+id/frame_layout"
    android:layout_width="match_parent"
    android:layout_height="match_parent"
    app:layout_box="bottom" />
</android.support.wearable.view.BoxInsetLayout>
```

Whatever we place inside the `FrameLayout` view will automatically receive the correct padding to ensure that the content is not outside of the visible screen area. Sometimes, the views are so simple we can just use one of the pre-defined template layouts, such as the `CardFragment` instance. This is a special `Fragment` instance that renders content in the `Card` format:

```
var cardFragment = CardFragment.Create(
  "The Title",
  "This is a nice description for the cool title.");
FragmentManager.BeginTransaction()
  .Add(Resource.Id.frame_layout, cardFragment)
  .Commit();
```

There are a few other views that can be used to automatically adjust its appearance depending on the wearable's screen. Other views include the `CardScrollView` view and the `CardFrame` instance. For other layout types, there is the `WearableListView` type with `WearableListItemLayout` view for each item, or the `GridViewPager` instance. There are also many activities such as the `ConfirmationActivity` instance.

Creating always-on wearable apps

The ability to create fully-featured apps for Android wearables is a great way to provide a hands-free experience. However, to preserve battery, Android will quickly put the device to sleep, resulting in the experience being lost.

How to do it...

Sometimes, we want to be able to display content on the screen, even when the wearable goes to sleep or enters the ambient mode:

1. The first thing that we need to do is add the wake lock permission requirement. We need to add this to both, wearable and handheld, as the wearable cannot have any permission that the handheld does not have:

   ```
   [assembly: UsesPermission(Manifest.Permission.WakeLock)]
   ```

2. Next, in the wearable app, we need to specify that we are going to be using the wearable library if it is available:

   ```
   [assembly: UsesLibrary(
     "com.google.android.wearable", false)]
   ```

3. Now, we can begin implementing the always-on activity. Instead of inheriting from `Activity`, we can inherit from `WearableActivity`:

   ```
   public class MainActivity : WearableActivity
   ```

4. Then, we can request to be notified when the ambient mode changes, by invoking the `SetAmbientEnabled()` method:

   ```
   protected override void OnCreate(Bundle bundle) {
     base.OnCreate(bundle);
     SetAmbientEnabled();
   }
   ```

5. Finally, we can override the `OnEnterAmbient()` and `OnExitAmbient()` methods to perform the desired actions when the ambient mode changes:

   ```
   public override void OnEnterAmbient(Bundle ambientDetails) {
     base.OnEnterAmbient(ambientDetails);
   }
   public override void OnExitAmbient() {
     base.OnExitAmbient();
   }
   ```

6. We can detect whether the device is in ambient mode using the `IsAmbient` property:

   ```
   boo linAmbientMode = IsAmbient;
   ```

7. There is also a special method that will trigger once every minute so that we can update the UI when in ambient mode:

   ```
   public override void OnUpdateAmbient() {
     base.OnUpdateAmbient();
   }
   ```

How it works...

Sometimes, we create an app that we would like to use to display data on the screen, even after the device goes to sleep. This is most useful for a watch face; but it is also used in other apps, such as a fitness app. It is unnecessary for the device to be running at full power if the screen is going to be updated only in every few seconds or even minutes.

These types of apps are useful when only we want to allow the user to always be able to see the information, but when we do not want to keep the device awake all the time. When the device is awake, battery gets consumed. So having an app that can run in low-power ambient mode preserves battery as well as functioning as an always-on display.

> The ambient mode is a low-power mode that allows an app to run when the device goes to sleep, but with more limited capacity.

The first thing that needs to be done is to get the permission of keeping the display awake. However, only the wearable app, and not the handheld, requires the permission. The handheld app must have the same or more permissions than the wearable app, because the wearable app cannot exceed the permissions of the handheld app. If we forget to add the permission to the handheld, the wearable app will not be installed.

> A wearable app can only have a subset of the permissions of the handheld app.

To be able to use the always-on activity on the wearable, we must specify that we are going to use the `com.google.android.wearable` library. If we want our app to be installed on the wearables running Android versions prior to version 5.1, we need to specify that the library is not required by passing `false` as the second parameter. If the device is not running the appropriate version of Android or does not support the ambient mode, then the activity will function as a normal activity.

For utilizing the activity that is aware of the ambient mode, our activity should inherit from `WearableActivity` instead of `Activity`. This type provides features that inform us about when the devices enter or leave the ambient mode. To be notified of these events, we need to request that the activity to runs in ambient mode. We do this by invoking the `SetAmbientEnabled()` method in `OnCreate`.

As soon as the device enters the ambient mode or goes to sleep, the activity's `OnEnterAmbient()` method will be invoked. Conversely, when the device leaves the ambient mode or wakes up, the `OnExitAmbient()` method is invoked. We can override these methods to handle the transitions, allowing our app to adjust. If we need to verify that we are in the ambient mode, we can easily do so using the value of the `IsAmbient` property.

When in the ambient mode, the activity will invoke the `OnUpdateAmbient()` method once in a minute so that we can update the screen with information for the user. Although, we can update the screen more frequently using alarms, we should not exceed an update once every ten seconds.

> When in the ambient mode, the device should not be woken up more than once in every 10 seconds.

When updating the screen in the ambient mode, we should reduce the amount of processing and colors displayed to reduce the battery consumption. Usually, we would specify a black background and minimal white graphics or text. Since the ambient mode does not receive events, we can disable any kind of interactive element.

Creating dynamic always-on wearable apps

An always-on app provides the user with the ability to view information at any time, without having to wake the device; however, the visible information may become stale if the actual information changes more frequently than once in a minute.

How to do it...

We may need to update the content on the wearable more frequently than once in a minute; thus, we can schedule an alarm to trigger an update outside the one-minute interval:

1. We will need the wake lock permission on both, the handheld and wearable:

   ```
   [assembly: UsesPermission(Manifest.Permission.WakeLock)]
   ```

2. If we want to support older wearables, we will need to set the wearable library as optional:

   ```
   [assembly: UsesLibrary(
       "com.google.android.wearable", false)]
   ```

3. Next, we need to inherit it from `WearableActivity`:

   ```
   public class MainActivity : WearableActivity
   ```

4. We are going to use the alarm manager to send us an `Intent` instance, which we will respond to by updating the UI. As the intent will try to launch a new instance of our activity, we will specify that we only want a single instance of our activity using the `LaunchMode` property of the `[Activity]` attribute on our activity:

   ```
   [Activity(..., LaunchMode = LaunchMode.SingleInstance)]
   ```

Now that the activity is set up, we schedule the alarm for several seconds in the future when we are in the ambient mode:

1. In `OnCreate`, we request ambient mode notifications by invoking the `SetAmbientEnabled()` method:

   ```
   SetAmbientEnabled();
   ```

2. As we need to schedule an alarm, we get an instance of `AlarmManager`:

   ```
   alarmManager = AlarmManager.FromContext(this);
   ```

3. Because we are just going to request that the alarm sends an `Intent` instance to our activity, we create the `PendingIntent` instance for the alarm manager:

   ```
   var alarmIntent = new Intent(
     ApplicationContext, typeof(MainActivity));
   alarmPendingIntent = PendingIntent.GetActivity(
     ApplicationContext,
     0,
     alarmIntent,
     PendingIntentFlags.UpdateCurrent);
   ```

4. Now, we create a method to schedule our once-off alarm to fire several seconds in the future. We use the `IsAmbient` property to ensure that we only schedule the alarm when in the ambient mode:

   ```
   private void ScheduleAlarm() {
     if (IsAmbient) {
       long alarmInterval = 15 * 1000; // 15 seconds
       long time = JavaSystem.CurrentTimeMillis();
       long delay = alarmInterval- (time % alarmInterval);
       long trigger = time + delay;
       alarmManager.SetExact(
         AlarmType.RtcWakeup, trigger, alarmPendingIntent);
     }
   }
   ```

5. When we enter the ambient mode, we schedule the alarm:

   ```
   public override void OnEnterAmbient(Bundle ambientDetails)
   {
     base.OnEnterAmbient(ambientDetails);
     ScheduleAlarm();
   }
   ```

6. After the alarm manager sends the intent, we will receive it in the `OnNewIntent()` method. As this type of alarm is a once-off alarm, we will have to reschedule when it fires:

```
protected override void OnNewIntent(Intent intent) {
    base.OnNewIntent(intent);
    Intent = intent;
    if (IsAmbient) {
        // update the ambient UI
    }
    ScheduleAlarm();
}
```

7. When we leave the ambient mode, we must make sure to cancel the alarm:

```
public override void OnExitAmbient() {
    base.OnExitAmbient();
    alarmManager.Cancel(alarmPendingIntent);
}
```

8. We need to do the same for `OnDestroy` so that we cancel the alarm when the user exits the app:

```
protected override void OnDestroy() {
    base.OnDestroy();
    alarmManager.Cancel(alarmPendingIntent);
}
```

Although, this is all that is needed to update the UI every few seconds while in the ambient mode, we can add a further improvement to take into consideration the default one-minute update provided by the framework:

▶ To avoid unnecessary wake operations, we can move the scheduled alarm to the next interval:

```
public override void OnUpdateAmbient() {
    base.OnUpdateAmbient();
    // update the ambient UI
    ScheduleAlarm();
}
```

How it works...

Although, the Android Wear provides the `WearableActivity` type to allow us to neatly create always-on apps, the default update interval of one minute may not be frequent enough. This maybe the case for a fitness app or some other app where we want the user to be able to glance at the information, which is updated fairly rapidly.

Creating a more dynamic always-on app is more of an extension of a typical always-on app. We still require the activity inherit from `WearableActivity`, and we do need other various events that this type brings. What we add is a timer or alarm that triggers additional updates more frequently. Because we are still creating a traditional always-on app, we still need to specify the wake lock permission and the `com.google.android.wearable` library requirement. Also, we must request that the activity be allowed to enter the ambient mode using the `SetAmbientEnabled()` method in `OnCreate`.

The simplest method to update the screen could just be to relaunch the activity. We can do this as Android provides us with a means to skip the actual launch if the activity is already visible, which will be the case. To prevent multiple instances of our activity, we can set the `LaunchMode` property on the `[Activity]` attribute to `LaunchMode.SingleInstance`. Then, when the alarm fires, a new activity will not be created, but just the `OnNewIntent()` method will be invoked on the existing activity.

 If an activity is set to only exist as a single instance, any attempt to start a new instance will get redirected to the `OnNewIntent()` method of this activity.

In `OnCreate`, we set up the `AlarmManager` instance using the static `FromContext()` method. And, as we don't need a dynamic intent, we can create the `PendingIntent` instance that will hold the `Intent` instance to launch our activity.

When the wearable enters the ambient mode, the `OnEnterAmbient()` method will be invoked. Here, we will schedule the pending intent for several seconds into the future. We should make sure that we do not wake the device up more frequently than once in every 10 seconds. Waking up the device requires much more power than keeping the device awake. So, if we need the screen to get updated more frequently, we should rather not allow the device to enter the ambient mode.

 When in the ambient mode, the device should not be woken up more than once every 10 seconds, but should rather acquire a normal wakelock to prevent the device from going to sleep altogether.

To avoid unnecessary events, we should ensure that the device is in the ambient mode using the `IsAmbient` property, before we schedule the alarm. Then, we must schedule an exact alarm for several seconds into the future. We can't use a repeating alarm as Android does not permit a more frequent alarm than once in a minute. Also, we must ensure that we use the `RtcWakeup` alarm type so that the device will wake up when the alarm fires.

For intervals that are shorter than one minute, an exact alarm must be scheduled instead of a repeating alarm.

When the device wakes, the OnExitAmbient() method will be invoked. To ensure that the alarm does not fire unnecessarily, we cancel it using the same pending intent that we used to schedule the alarm with. To prevent the activity from being relaunched when the user exits our app, we must make sure to cancel the alarm in the OnDestroy() method.

The OnNewIntent() method is invoked when the alarm fires. What actually happens is that the alarm fires and Android tries to launch the activity intent contained in the pending intent. When it sees that the activity is already visible, it then just invokes the OnNewIntent() method.

The first thing we can do is to update the Intent property of the activity to be the intent we just received. Then, we can update the screen with the information that we want to present to the user. Just before we allow the device to go back to sleep, we need to re-schedule the alarm as an exact alarm is only a once-off alarm.

One additional thing we can do to further optimize the app is to ensure that we don't allow the alarm to fire too soon after Android invokes the OnUpdateAmbient() method. The OnUpdateAmbient() method is still invoked every minute, because we have just added an additional mechanism to wake the device. In this method, we can update the screen and reschedule the alarm, just as we would in the OnNewIntent() method.

Communicating with wearables

Wearable apps provide a great way to extend handheld devices; however, sometimes, a wearable is not powerful enough to perform a task on its own, or it needs information from the handheld.

Getting ready

As we are going to be communicating between the devices using Google Play services, we need to install the **Xamarin.GooglePlayServices.Wearable** NuGet before we start.

How to do it...

Apps running on wearables can communicate with apps running on the handheld devices using the Google Play services. To implement data communication between the handheld and the wearable, we can actually use the same code:

1. We are going to make use of the Google Play services' Data API to synchronize data between the devices. First, we need to implement the `IDataApiDataListener` interface in our activity:

```
public class MainActivity : Activity, IDataApiDataListener {
  public void OnDataChanged(DataEventBuffer dataEvents) {
  }
}
```

2. Then, we need to create an instance of the Google Play services' API client, usually in the `OnCreate()` method of the activity. We use various callbacks to add and remove the Data API listener:

```
apiClient = new GoogleApiClientBuilder(this)
  .AddConnectionCallbacks(bundle => {
    // attach the data listener
    WearableClass.DataApi.AddListener(apiClient, this);
  }, cause => {
    // detach the listener
    WearableClass.DataApi.RemoveListener(apiClient, this);
  })
    .AddOnConnectionFailedListener(result => {
      // handle errors
  })
  .AddApi(WearableClass.API)
  .Build();
```

3. Now that we have the client, we can initiate the connection to the backing service by invoking the `Connect()` method of the client. This is typically done in the `OnResume()` method of the activity when we are in the foreground:

```
protected override void OnResume() {
  base.OnResume();

  apiClient.Connect();
}
```

4. To ensure that we clean up when the user exits our app, we remove the Data API listener and disconnect it from the services in the `OnPause()` method:

```
protected override void OnPause(){
  if (apiClient != null &&apiClient.IsConnected) {
    WearableClass.DataApi.RemoveListener(apiClient, this);
  apiClient.Disconnect();
  }

  base.OnPause();
}
```

Once we are connected, we can start updating our app's data using the Data API. These updates are then synchronized with the handheld and wearable:

1. Data is synchronized using a set of key-value pairs at a virtual location. We need to specify a string key for the data member, and a string path to the entire data object:

```
private const string CountKey ="keys.count";
private const string CounterPath = "/games/counter";
```

2. To create the data request that will be sent over the Data API, we make use of the `DataMap` and `PutDataMapRequest` types:

```
var mapRequest = PutDataMapRequest.Create(CounterPath);
mapRequest.DataMap.PutInt(CountKey, count);
```

3. Then, we send the new `DataMap` instance over the Data API using the `PutDataItemAsync()` method:

```
var dataRequest = mapRequest.AsPutDataRequest();
var dataApi = WearableClass.DataApi;
await dataApi.PutDataItemAsync(apiClient, dataRequest);
```

4. As soon as the data has synchronized, we will receive an event on the other device via the `OnDataChanged()` method of the `IDataApiDataListener` interface:

```
public void OnDataChanged(DataEventBuffer dataEvents) {
  if (dataEvents.Status.IsSuccess) {
    // get the value from the event
    foreach (var dataEvent in dataEvents) {
      if (dataEvent.Type == DataEvent.TypeChanged) {
        var item = dataEvent.DataItem;
        if (item.Uri.Path == CounterPath) {
          var map = DataMapItem.FromDataItem(item).DataMap;
          count = map.GetInt(CountKey);
          break;
        }
      }
```

```
    }

    // make sure we update on the UI thread
    RunOnUiThread(() => {
      // update the UI
    });
  } else {
    // handle errors
  }
}
```

5. When we start the app for the first time after the connection has succeeded, we might want to get hold of the existing data:

```
var dataApi = WearableClass.DataApi;
var dataItems = await dataApi.GetDataItemsAsync(apiClient);
foreach (var item in dataItems) {
  if (item.Uri.Path == CounterPath) {
    var dataMap = DataMapItem.FromDataItem(item).DataMap;
    count = dataMap.GetInt(CountKey);
    break;
  }
}
```

How it works...

Creating a wearable app is a great way to extend the handheld and provide an additional user experience. However, the device is often much more limited in hardware, most certainly so with regards to the screen size.

One of the great ways we can extend the handheld experience, but without losing on the power of the handheld, is by establishing communication between the devices. By communicating with a handheld, the wearable is able to offload any intensive or complex tasks to a more capable device.

 Wearable apps can communicate with their handheld counterparts in many ways.

The devices can communicate using several methods, and one of the easiest and most common methods is to synchronize the data, such as app settings or user preferences. This type of communication or synchronization uses the Google Play services' Data API.

The Data API not only synchronizes data between the wearable and handheld, but also with the cloud and any other devices connected to the cloud. To use the Data API in an Android wearable app, we must first install the **Xamarin.GooglePlayServices.Wearable** NuGet, which will install the prerequisites.

By storing the data on the cloud, our app can preserve its data when the user gets new devices, as well as provide a persistent storage option for the app data. Another benefit of cloud storage is that if the wearable loses its connectivity temporarily, the wearable can retrieve the data from the cloud when it reconnects.

> Google Play services synchronize data with all the connected devices, both those connected directly and those connected through the cloud.

To communicate between devices, we need to set up the Google API client. This client manages the connections and events, providing a simple, listener-based notification system. In addition to the Data API events, we are notified of connection events, such as when the connection is established or if it goes down temporarily.

The Data API has an event to notify listeners when new data is synchronized or changed on one of the devices. Since we want to know when the handheld or wearable changes the data, we must implement the `IDataApiDataListener` interface. It is not necessary to create a new object for this, and therefore, the current activity can be used.

The `IDataApiDataListener` interface has a single method—`OnDataChanged()`. This method is invoked as soon as the client is informed about another device changing the data. If the wearable is connected via Bluetooth, then the data and events come through the Bluetooth stack. Other devices receive events through the cloud, possibly over Wi-Fi.

> The `IDataApiDataListener` interface is used when listening for making changes to the data.

Before we can transfer data, we need to connect to the Google Play services. To create the client, we instantiate a new `GoogleApiClientBuilder` instance.

Because we care about the connection status, we need to pass two delegates to the `AddConnectionCallbacks()` method. The first method is invoked when the client connection succeeds. Here, we make sure to attach our `IDataApiDataListener` interface instance to the Data API. The second delegate is invoked when the connection is suspended. In this delegate, we make sure to detach our interface instance so that no memory is leaked.

The other connection event method is the `AddOnConnectionFailedListener()` method. This method allows us to attach a delegate that will be invoked if the connection fails.

The Google Play services client uses callbacks to notify about connection status changes.

Finally, before we create the client instance, we specify that we are going to be using the wearable APIs for communication with the wearable. We do this by passing the value of the `API` property of the `WearableClass` to the `AddApi()` method. The `WearableClass` type contains various properties that are used to access various APIs used for communication with wearables. The `API` property contains a token used by the client to set up the wearable APIs.

After a client has been connected, we can use the `DataApi` property of the `WearableClass` type to access the data APIs for wearables. The `DataApi` property returns an instance of the `IDataApi` interface, which we can use to attach and detach the listeners relating to the wearable Data API.

The `WearableClass` type contains various properties that are used to communicate with wearables.

The `IDataApi` interface has several methods, but we only need the `AddListener()` and `RemoveListener()` methods. We pass the current client and the `listener` instance to each of these methods, making sure to attach the listener when the client connects, and detaching it when the connection is suspended.

We invoke the `Connect()` method of the client in `OnResume`, as we want to connect only when our activity is in the foreground. Conversely, we invoke the `Disconnect()` method when we leave the foreground or when the `OnPause()` method is invoked. We should detach the listener before we disconnect so that we do not leak any memory.

Once we are connected, we can start sending data to the service. The service will then process and synchronize the data to various devices and the cloud. The easiest way to manage the data is using the `DataMap` type. A `DataMap` instance is stored at a specific path and consists of key-value pairs. There are various `put` and `get` methods, such as `PutString` and `GetString`, which are used to store and retrieve data.

Even though we are using the `DataMap` type to store our data, the Data API expects the `DataItem` types. When storing and retrieving data, the `DataMap` type is serialized and deserialized into a `DataItem` type, which stores the `DataMap` type as a byte array.

The Data API handles the `DataItem` types, which are deserialized into and serialized from the `DataMap` types.

When we want to store a new data map, we create an instance of `PutDataMapRequest` using the static `Create()` method. The `PutDataMapRequest` instance is a container type for a `DataMap` instance and the path to the data map. To access or update the data map that will be stored, we use the `DataMap` property.

The `Create()` method requires that we specify the path where we are going to store the data map. The path is similar to a Unix-based, file-system path. It uses forward slashes and must begin with a forward slash. Although similar to a file system, it is not actually stored at this location on the local file system.

 The `PutDataMapRequest.Create()` method requires that the path start with a forward slash.

Before we can synchronize our data map, we must obtain the data item from our `PutDataMapRequest` using the `AsPutDataRequest()` method. This method returns another container object, a `PutDataRequest` instance, which now contains the serialized byte array that was once a `DataMap` type.

We can now pass the new `PutDataRequest` instance to the `PutDataItemAsync()` method of the Data API, along with an open API client. We can verify that the operation was successful using the result of this method, which returns an `IDataApiDataItemResult` instance. This type contains both the data item that was saved and the status of the operation. The data item is obtained through the `DataItem` property and the status through the `Status` property.

After the data is passed to the Data API, it will be passed on to any attached wearables or other devices. Because we attached an instance of `IDataApiDataListener` to the Data API, the `OnDataChanged()` method of this listener will be invoked. The data has been received on another thread, so we have to make sure that when we update the UI, we do so on the UI thread. We can easily do this by using the `RunOnUiThread()` method.

 The `OnDataChanged()` method of the `IDataApiDataListener` instance is invoked on a background thread, thus all UI operations must be forwarded to the UI thread.

The `OnDataChanged()` method has one argument—a `DataEventBuffer` instance. This type inherits from `IEnumerable<IDataEvent>` with an additional `Status` property. We can iterate through the `IDataEvent` items and process them accordingly by taking advantage of LINQ.

Each `IDataEvent` item has a `Type` property, which is either `DataEvent.TypeChanged` or `DataEvent.TypeDeleted`. Since we only process data that has not been deleted, we will first check the `Type` property. Another property that is used to identify the data is the `Uri` property, which contains the path that was specified when the data was created. If there are multiple sources of data, which might be the case in some apps, we must first verify that it is the data we are expecting.

Once we have determined that we are going to process the item, we can read the associated data using the `DataItem` property. This property has a type of `IDataItem`, which contains the serialized `DataMap` instance.

As a result of using a `DataMap` type to synchronize data, we have to convert the `IDataItem` type back into `DataMap`. This is done using the `DataMapItem` type. This type has a static `FromDataItem()` method, which accepts an `IDataItem` instance and returns a `DataMapItem` instance. This type also has a `Uri` property that we could read, but, as we have already read the value from the `IDataItem` type, we can move on to the `DataMap` property.

The `DataMap` property returns the deserialized `DataMap` instance that was originally passed to the Data API from another device. We can now read the data map using the various `get` methods, such as `GetString()` or `GetBoolean()`. Each `get` method has two overloads: one that returns a system default, if no value is found for the specified key; and another that returns a provided default.

When our app starts, we want to be able to read any previously synchronized data. Instead of waiting for the data to be sent over the Data API, we can request the current data that uses the `GetDataItemsAsync()` method of the wearable Data API. The return type of this method is `DataItemBuffer`, which inherits from `IEnumerable<IDataItem>` with an additional `Status` property. We can use the `Status` property to determine if the request was successful, and then iterate through the result. Similar to items obtained from a `DataEventBuffer` instance, we read the `Uri` property and convert each item into a `DataMap` property. Then, we process the data map accordingly.

There's more...

In any case where we don't want to synchronize the data, but rather send it directly to another device, we can use the Message API instead of the Data API.

1. We need to make sure that we implement the `IMessageApiMessageListener` interface on the activity:

```
public class MainActivity :
Activity, IMessageApiMessageListener {
  public void OnMessageReceived(IMessageEvent messageEvent) {
  }
}
```

2. Then, we add the `listener` instance to the Message API:

```
WearableClass.MessageApi.AddListenerAsync(client, this);
```

3. In order to communicate, we need a node to communicate with. We can use the `GetConnectedNodesAsync()` method to fetch all the connected nodes, making sure that the node is available for communication using the `IsNearby` property:

```
await WearableClass.NodeApi.GetConnectedNodesAsync(client);
var node = result.Nodes.FirstOrDefault(n => n.IsNearby);
```

4. For sending data to another device, we pass the node ID, along with the path and data, to the `SendMessageAsync()` method:

```
var bytes = BitConverter.GetBytes(count);
await WearableClass.MessageApi.SendMessageAsync(
  client, node.Id, CounterPath, bytes);
```

5. On another device, the `OnMessageReceived()` method will be invoked, and we can read the data using the `GetData()` method:

```
public void OnMessageReceived(IMessageEvent messageEvent) {
  var bytes = messageEvent.GetData();
  if (bytes != null && bytes.Length> 0) {
    count = BitConverter.ToInt32(bytes, 0);
  }
}
```

Building watch faces

Android wearables are far more than just watches, but they still need to perform the basic task of presenting the user with the current time.

Getting ready

Although, automatically installed when creating a new Android Wear project, we do need to have the **Xamarin.Android.Wear** NuGet installed in the wearable project.

How to do it...

Creating a watch face consists of creating two parts. The first is the rendering engine, which inherits from one of the `WatchFaceService.Engine` types, and the other is `WatchFaceService`, which manages it:

1. We need to specify the permissions for both the handheld and wearable apps. The handheld does not require any activities, but just requires the permissions to be set:

```
[assembly: UsesPermission(Manifest.Permission.WakeLock)]
[assembly: UsesPermission(
  "com.google.android.permission.PROVIDE_BACKGROUND")]
```

2. For our watch face, we use `CanvasWatchFaceService.Engine` as our base type. In the constructor, we keep a reference to `CanvasWatchFaceService` because we will need it for creating the watch face:

```
class WatchFaceEngine : CanvasWatchFaceService.Engine {
  private readonly CanvasWatchFaceService service;
  public WatchFaceEngine(CanvasWatchFaceService service)
  : base (service) {
    this.service = service;
  }
  public override void OnCreate(ISurfaceHolder surface) {
    base.OnCreate(surface);
  }
  public override void OnTimeTick() {
    base.OnTimeTick();
  }
  public override void OnVisibilityChanged(bool visible) {
    base.OnVisibilityChanged(visible);
  }
  public override void OnAmbientModeChanged(bool isAmbient) {
    base.OnAmbientModeChanged(isAmbient);
  }
  public override void OnSurfaceChanged(
  ISurfaceHolder holder, Format format,
  int width, int height) {
    base.OnSurfaceChanged(holder, format, width, height);
  }
  public override void OnDraw(Canvas canvas, Rect bounds) {
    base.OnDraw(canvas, bounds);
  }
}
```

3. In the constructor, we set up a `Handler` instance to trigger at every second so that we can draw the second hand:

```
private const int MessageId = 123;
private const long Interval = 1000;

tickHandler = new Handler(message => {
  var timerEnabled = IsVisible&&!IsInAmbientMode;
  if (message.What == MessageId&&timerEnabled) {
  Invalidate();
    long time = Java.Lang.JavaSystem.CurrentTimeMillis();
    long delay = Interval - (time % Interval);
    tickHandler.SendEmptyMessageDelayed(MessageId, delay);
  }
});
```

4. Because we are going to be painting every second, we initialize the `Paint` instances in the `OnCreate()` method to reduce the overhead:

```
hourPaint = new Paint();
hourPaint.SetARGB(255, 200, 200, 200);
hourPaint.StrokeWidth = 5.0f;
hourPaint.AntiAlias = true;
hourPaint.StrokeCap = Paint.Cap.Round;
minutePaint = new Paint();
minutePaint.SetARGB(255, 200, 200, 200);
minutePaint.StrokeWidth = 3.0f;
minutePaint.AntiAlias = true;
minutePaint.StrokeCap = Paint.Cap.Round;
secondPaint = new Paint();
secondPaint.SetARGB(255, 200, 200, 200);
secondPaint.StrokeWidth = 4.0f;
secondPaint.AntiAlias = true;
secondPaint.StrokeCap = Paint.Cap.Round;
```

5. Also in the `OnCreate()` method, we set the `WatchFaceStyle` instance for our watch face, using a reference to the watch face service:

```
var style = new WatchFaceStyle.Builder(service)
  .SetCardPeekMode(WatchFaceStyle.PeekModeShort)
  .SetBackgroundVisibility(
    WatchFaceStyle.BackgroundVisibilityInterruptive)
  .SetShowSystemUiTime(false)
  .Build();
SetWatchFaceStyle(style);
```

6. Every minute, Android will automatically invoke the `OnTimeTick()` method, so we can simply request for the view to be redrawn:

```
Invalidate();
```

7. In the `OnVisibilityChanged()` and `OnAmbientModeChanged()` methods, we need to request for the face to be redrawn, as well as making sure the second-hand timer is enabled or disabled, depending on the visibility and ambient values:

```
Invalidate();
tickHandler.RemoveMessages(UpdateMessageId);
if (IsVisible&&!IsInAmbientMode) {
  tickHandler.SendEmptyMessage(UpdateMessageId);
}
```

8. Before we draw, the `OnSurfaceChanged` view may be invoked indicating that the drawing surface has changed, so we can adjust our drawing parameters there:

```
centerX = width / 2f;
centerY = height / 2f;
secondHandLength = centerX * 0.875f;
minuteHandLength = centerX * 0.75f;
hourHandLength = centerX * 0.5f;
```

9. Finally, in the `OnDraw()` method, we draw the watch face onto the screen, drawing as little as possible in the ambient mode:

```
// background color
if (IsInAmbientMode) {
  canvas.DrawColor(Color.Black);
}
else {
  canvas.DrawColor(Color.DarkGreen);
}
// hand rotations
var time = DateTime.Now.TimeOfDay;
float seconds = time.Seconds;
float secRot = seconds / 60f * (float)Math.PI * 2f;
float minutes = time.Minutes + seconds / 60f;
float minRot = minutes / 60f * (float)Math.PI * 2f;
float hours = time.Hours + minutes / 60f;
float hrRot = hours / 12f * (float)Math.PI * 2f;
// hour hand
float hrX = (float)Math.Sin(hrRot) * hourHandLength;
float hrY = (float)-Math.Cos(hrRot) * hourHandLength;
canvas.DrawLine(
  centerX, centerY,
  centerX + hrX, centerY + hrY,
```

```
  hourPaint);
// minute hand
float minX = (float)Math.Sin(minRot) * minuteHandLength;
float minY = (float)-Math.Cos(minRot) * minuteHandLength;
canvas.DrawLine(
  centerX, centerY,
  centerX + minX, centerY + minY,
  minutePaint);
// second hand only in interactive mode.
if (!IsInAmbientMode) {
  float secX = (float)Math.Sin(secRot) * secondHandLength;
  float secY = (float)-Math.Cos(secRot) * secondHandLength;
  canvas.DrawLine(
    centerX, centerY,
    centerX + secX, centerY + secY,
    secondPaint);
}
```

Our watch face engine is complete. So now, we set up the wearable app to have a watch face service. We don't need any activities in either project, but just a service in the wearable project:

1. Our watch face service will inherit from a `WatchFaceService` type, such as `CanvasWatchFaceService`. We override the `OnCreateEngine()` method to return a new instance of our watch face engine:

```
public class WatchFaceService : CanvasWatchFaceService {
  public override WallpaperService.EngineOnCreateEngine() {
    return new WatchFaceEngine(this);
  }
}
```

2. The watch face service has a set of attributes that will be used to describe the service to the Android device. The first is declaring our type as a service by adding a `[Service]` attribute:

```
[Service(
  Label = "XamarinCookbook",
  Permission = Android.Manifest.Permission.BindWallpaper)]
```

3. Next, we specify that this service is started as a watch face using an `[IntentFilter]` attribute:

```
[IntentFilter(new [] {
  Android.Service.Wallpaper.WallpaperService.
  ServiceInterface
```

```
}, Categories = new [] {
  "com.google.android.wearable.watchface.
  category.WATCH_FACE"
})]
```

4. Then, in the wearable's resources, we add an XML resource named `watch_face.xml`:

```
<?xml version="1.0" encoding="UTF-8"?>
<wallpaper
xmlns:android="http://schemas.android.com/apk/res/android"
/>
```

5. Then, we add this resource to the service using a `[MetaData]` attribute:

```
[MetaData(
  Android.Service.Wallpaper.WallpaperService.
  ServiceMetaData,
  Resource = "@xml/watch_face")]
```

6. Similarly, we provide a preview image for the Android Wear companion app using two images. One should be a round preview and the other should be a square preview of the watch face. In our case, we save the images as `preview.png` and `preview_round.png` in the `drawable` resource folder.

7. Finally, we add these preview images to the watch face by also using the `[MetaData]` attributes:

```
[MetaData(
  "com.google.android.wearable.watchface.preview",
  Resource = "@drawable/preview")]
[MetaData(
  "com.google.android.wearable.watchface.preview_circular",
  Resource = "@drawable/preview_round")]
```

How it works...

Although we call them wearables, they were originally called smartwatches. The name changed to wearables after they grew to surpass the watch features. Wearables are much more than a smartwatch, but they still keep the basic idea of a watch, and one of the most important features of a watch, or rather, the only important feature of a watch, is to display the current time to the wearer.

Android wear is more than a watch operating system, but it is still a watch. And as a watch, it needs to display the current time. It does this by utilizing a special wallpaper that can handle displaying the current time when the device is awake, and when the device goes to sleep or enters the ambient mode.

Watch faces exist as a special type of service that are managed by the Android Wear companion app installed on the handheld.

An app that provides a watch face does not need to have any activities, but one might exist for configuration purposes.

When creating a watch face, we need to ensure that we design for both, square and round devices, as well as support the ambient mode properly. For the battery to last long, we need to ensure that when drawing in the ambient mode, we draw as little as possible.

Unlike traditional apps that support the ambient mode, watch faces cannot be closed by the user and are always displayed. As watch faces run continuously, we need to ensure that all the work is kept to a minimum, and network operations are done as little as possible.

Because a watch face supports the ambient mode and is also a wallpaper, we need to specify the wake lock and the `com.google.android.permission.PROVIDE_BACKGROUND` permissions.

 Creating a watch face consists of two parts: the engine that processes events and draws the face, and the service that instantiates and manages the watch face.

The watch face engine inherits from the `WatchFaceService.Engine` type. There are two types to inherit from: the 2D, canvas-based `CanvasWatchFaceService.Engine` and the 3D, OpenGL-based `Gles2WatchFaceService.Engine`.

Most watch faces can be created using the canvas-based drawing mechanism. In this case, we only need to override several watch face lifecycle methods to do so. Although, the watch face engine methods cover most of the events, we do need to create the mechanism that redraws the screen every second.

The simplest way to redraw the screen every second is to create a `Handler` instance and post delayed messages. As we want the screen to be redrawn every second, we use a delay of 1 second. We must make sure that we only use the handler when the device is not in the ambient mode and is actually visible on the screen. The base type provides two properties to test these cases: the `IsInAmbientMode` and `IsVisible` properties.

 The watch face engine does not provide a mechanism for updating these on hand position, this must be created soon.

To reduce any kind of overhead when drawing on the screen, we should initialize as much as we can in the `OnCreate()` method. This includes any drawing mechanisms, such as `Paint` instances and bitmaps.

Because the operating system needs to draw all the UI elements, such as battery indicators at the top of the watch face, we need to specify where and how to draw them. We do this in the `OnCreate()` method using the `SetWatchFaceStyle()` method. We pass in an instance of a `WatchFaceStyle` instance created using the `WatchFaceStyle.Builder` type.

Once we have set up all the pieces required to draw our watch face, we can start overriding the lifecycle events. Watch faces have a default update interval of one minute and at that time, the `OnTimeTick()` method is invoked. As we don't need to do anything special, we can simply request that the screen be redrawn by invoking the `Invalidate()` method. We use the `OnTimeTick()` method instead of using the handler to redraw the screen when in the ambient mode.

In the `OnVisibilityChanged()` and `OnAmbientModeChanged()` methods, we can also just request a redraw. We can even invoke the `Invalidate()` method here. However, as the device may be going to sleep or an app launching over the watch, we need to stop the `Handler` instance from requesting redraws. The device may also be waking up, so we may also need to start the `Handler` instance again.

 The second hand should not be drawn when in the ambient mode, and thus, the mechanism to update them can be disabled.

In addition to responding to ambient changes, we might need to handle cases where the screen has a reduced color mode. We can override the `OnPropertiesChanged()` method and read the `Bundle` argument. The `Boolean` bundle value for the `PropertyLowBitAmbient` key indicates whether the screen supports fewer bits for each color. So, we should disable the anti-aliasing and bitmap filtering. Also, the `Boolean` value for the `PropertyBurnInProtection` key indicates whether we need to avoid large areas of white pixels or drawing near the edges of the screen when in the ambient mode.

 Some devices have extra requirements when drawing in the ambient mode.

During initialization, and if the drawing surface changes for some reason, the `OnSurfaceChanged()` method is invoked. We can use this method to update any screen-related drawing parameters, such as the surface size. This method is useful for performing any kind of image scaling or size calculations. It is better to only perform these tasks once rather than to do them each time the face is drawn.

The last thing to do with the watch face is to draw it. We draw our watch face in the `OnDraw()` method using all the normal drawing tools. However, we do need to ensure that we check to see if the device is in the ambient mode using the `IsInAmbientMode` property. If so, then we should draw as little as possible and on a black background. We also need to keep in mind that in the ambient mode, drawing only occurs once every minute.

In the ambient mode, the background should be black, but this is more of a recommendation rather than a requirement.

Once the watch face engine is complete, we can create the watch face service and its metadata. The service is run on the wearable device, and the metadata is used when listing the watch face in the Android Wear companion app.

The watch face service is very simple; all we do is override the `OnCreateEngine()` method. Here, we return a new instance of our watch face engine. The service should inherit from the appropriate watch face type, such as the `CanvasWatchFaceService` type or the `Gles2WatchFaceService` type, depending on what our drawing engine is used for.

As the watch face service is just a specialized service, we need to add the `[Service]` attribute to it. We also need to add set the `Permission` property of the attribute to `android.permission.BIND_WALLPAPER`. Then, we need to add an `[IntentFilter]` attribute, and set the `Action` property to `android.service.wallpaper.WallpaperService` and the `Categories` property to `com.google.android.wearable.watchface.category.WATCH_FACE`.

We also need to add a `[MetaData]` attribute pointing to an XML resource. The XML resource should contain a `<Wallpaper>` element and be stored in the `xml` resource folder. The attribute `Name` should be `android.service.wallpaper` and `Resource` should point to the XML resource. If our XML is in a file named `watch_face.xml`, then the `Resource` property would be `@xml/watch_face`.

The code for the watch face service consists of one method with most of the work done through attributes on the service.

The last thing needed to list the watch face in the companion app is a preview. A preview for both, the round and square faces, should be provided in the `drawable` resource folder. We specify the previews for the service using a `[MetaData]` attribute. The metadata `Name` for a square preview is `com.google.android.wearable.watchface.preview`, and for a round preview is `com.google.android.wearable.watchface.preview_circular`. The resource for each of these would be set using the metadata `Resource` property. In the case of a square face, we might have a value of `@drawable/preview_square` and for a round face, `@drawable/preview_round`.

If no preview is specified, then the watch face will not appear in the picker.

When the app is installed on the wearable, both the companion app and the wearable will receive a new entry in the watch face picker. The user will then be able to select it as they would any other watch face. The preview images specified by the `[MetaData]` data attributes will be used as the picker item.

There's more...

In addition to displaying the current time, the watch face can also present information to the user. Such information could be of any upcoming events on the calendar, any unread emails, or fitness information. Similar to creating a `Handler` instance to redraw the screen every second, we can create a `Handler` instance to retrieve data from a calendar or inbox very so often.

Watch faces can also respond to tap events. To receive tap events, we need to specify that we handle these events when creating the `WatchFaceStyle` instance. The `WatchFaceStyle.Builder` type has a method, `SetAcceptsTapEvents()`, which is used to perform this. If we pass `true` into this method, when the user taps the watch face, the `OnTapCommand()` method of the watch face engine will be invoked. We can override this method to process the tap event.

Configuring watch faces

Awesome watch faces can be created to delight the wearer; however, users enjoy the ability to customize the final appearance of any personal technology.

How to do it...

Similar to communicating with wearables, our watch face configuration activity manages settings by synchronizing setting selections from the activities to the watch face service:

1. We need to create the configuration activity, and apply an `[IntentFilter]` attribute with a specification value that will be used to associate the watch face with this activity:

```
[Activity]
[IntentFilter(
  new[] { "com.xamarincookbook.wearables.CONFIG" },
  Categories = new[] {
    "com.google.android.wearable.watchface.category.
    WEARABLE_CONFIGURATION",
    Android.Content.Intent.CategoryDefault })]
public class WearableConfigurationActivity : Activity {
}
```

2. Then, to associate the activity with the watch face service, we apply a `[MetaData]` attribute using the activities action value as the metadata value:

```
[MetaData(
    "com.google.android.wearable.watchface.
    wearableConfigurationAction",
    Value = "com.xamarincookbook.wearables.CONFIG")]
```

Typically, we would use one of the Google Play services to synchronize the configuration between the activity and the watch face:

1. To receive Data API events, we implement the `IDataApiDataListener` interface on the watch face engine:

```
class WatchFaceEngine : IDataApiDataListener{
    public void OnDataChanged(DataEventBufferdataEvents) {
        // update variables
    }
}
```

2. We connect to, and disconnect from, the client in the `OnVisibilityChanged()` method of the watch face engine, making sure to remove the data listener before disconnecting:

```
if (visible) {
    client.Connect();
}
else if (client != null &&client.IsConnected) {
    WearableClass.DataApi.RemoveListener(client, this);
    client.Disconnect();
}
```

How it works...

Watch faces are great additions to any wearable, but sometimes, we want to provide fewer options so that the user can customize the final appearance. This is very easy to do and requires for us to create an activity that will be launched when the user wants to configure the watch face.

If we create a configuration activity for the wearable device, then a configure button will appear next to the watch face when picking a watch face. Similarly, there is an option to configure the watch face when picking one using the companion app.

Typically, the configuration activity is not launched directly by the user, but rather through the watch face picker. Thus, when adding the `[Activity]` attribute to our configuration activity, we can set the `MainLauncher` property to `false` (or leave it out altogether as `false` is the default value).

A watch face configuration activity does not need to appear in the app drawer of the device, because it is launched from the watch face picker.

To link a configuration activity with a watch face, we add attributes to both the configuration activity and the watch face service. Slightly different values will be used if the configuration activity is available on the handheld or wearable.

The configuration activity on the wearable requires us to add an [IntentFilter] attribute. The Actions value should be a name prefixed with the package name. For example, if our package name is com.xamarincookbook.wearables, then the action could be com.xamarincookbook.wearables.CONFIG. The Categories property requires two values to be provided; the first being com.google.android.wearable.watchface.category.WEARABLE_CONFIGURATION; and the second being android.intent.category.DEFAULT.

If the configuration activity is on the handheld, then the first category will instead be com.google.android.wearable.watchface.category.COMPANION_CONFIGURATION. The difference is in the last part, with the wearable value ending in WEARABLE_CONFIGURATION and the handheld value ending in COMPANION_CONFIGURATION.

For the watch face service, we specify the wearable configuration activity using a [MetaData] attribute. The Name parameter should be com.google.android.wearable.watchface.wearableConfigurationAction; Value being the value used for the configuration activity's Action value. In our case, the Value will be com.xamarincookbook.wearables.CONFIG.

 The value provided as the action for the configuration activity must match the value given to the metadata value for the watch face service.

Similar to the [IntentFilter] attribute, we need a slightly different Name value if the configuration activity is on the handheld. The Name parameter in this case will be com.google.android.wearable.watchface.companionConfigurationAction. Again, the difference is in the last part with the wearable value ending in wearableConfigurationAction, and the handheld value ending in companionConfigurationAction.

Once the service and configuration have their attributes, we can create the configuration activity as we would for any other activity. To send the configuration to the watch face, we usually make use of the Google Play services' Data API. The configuration activity will read the configuration when it is created, and then synchronize any option that a user selects.

Watch face configuration activities are just normal activities launched by the watch face picker.

One difference between the wearable and handheld configuration activities is what is displayed. As the wearable has a much smaller screen size, we only display the minimum required options. If there are many options, we should rather use the handheld configuration activity.

Configuration activities can be provided on both wearable and handheld.

A wearable configuration activity is usually very simple with only a few options, such as to select a new background. As a result, we can further enhance the user experience by automatically closing the activity once an option is selected. Then, the user will return to the watch face to see the change without having to manually close the activity.

If the Google Play service is used to manage the watch face settings, then the watch face service can be set up to receive these changes. Just like when we implement the `IDataApiDataListener` interface for communicating between the wearable and the handheld, we implement the interface on the service. Then, regardless of whether the configuration activity is on the handheld or on the wearable, the watch face service will receive the new data once the user makes changes.

When using the Google Play service with watch faces, we should connect and disconnect the client in the `OnVisibilityChanged()` method of the service. If the configuration changes when the watch face is invisible, we can always load the changes when the watch face becomes visible again.

There's more...

It is also possible to provide a configuration activity for a watch face on the handheld. This activity is shown when the user configures the watch face from the Android Wear companion app:

1. Our activity implementation is exactly the same, except we use a different `Category` value with the `[IntentFilter]` attribute:

```
[IntentFilter(
  new[] { "com.xamarincookbook.wearables.CONFIG" },
  Categories = new[] {
    "com.google.android.wearable.watchface.category.
    COMPANION_CONFIGURATION",
    Android.Content.Intent.CategoryDefault })]
```

2. Similarly, we register a different `Value` for the `[MetaData]` attribute on the watch face service:

```
[MetaData(
    "com.google.android.wearable.watchface.
    companionConfigurationAction",
    Value = "com.xamarincookbook.wearables.CONFIG")]
```

12

Adding In-App Billing

In this chapter, we will cover the following recipes:

- ▶ Preparing for in-app billing
- ▶ Integrating in-app billing
- ▶ Listing available products
- ▶ Purchasing products
- ▶ Listing purchased products
- ▶ Consuming purchases

Introduction

Everybody likes to go shopping—getting something new and shiny to play with is a great feeling. Unfortunately, shopping requires money, and nobody likes to give that up. However, in the end, people will go to work, earn money, and then go shopping anyway—whether it be to provide food to survive or things for entertainment, everybody goes shopping.

App developers can capitalize on this fact not only to provide users with cool features and apps for their devices but also to make money. One approach to making money is by asking the users to pay for the app before they can use it. Although this is very common, many users do not like the fact that they are required to spend money before getting to use the product.

Another approach is to give the app to the users for free, and then either restrict functionality until the user pays or give the user extra functionality when they pay. Either approach results in the user getting more when they pay. The app can keep giving them more as they pay more.

When selling an app, the price is fixed, and thus, it is usually fairly high for a virtual product. However, if the app is available for free with in-app purchases, the user often doesn't realize that they are in fact paying more than what they would if they had paid a once-off amount.

In-app purchases are advantageous for both parties. The user may not actually require all the features, and thus can use the app for free, or the user may only want some of the features and is willing to then pay a little bit only for the required features. The developer gains from having a larger install base due to the app being free of cost and thus having a larger market of people that may potentially spend money once they start using the app.

Another great approach to making money, is to publish the app with ads and then provide a method for the user to remove the ads for a small cost. This way, the developer gets money from the advertising and from the purchase.

Preparing for in-app billing

When implementing in-app billing, there needs to be a selection of products or subscriptions available for the user to purchase.

Getting ready

Before we can develop and implement in-app billing, we will require two Google accounts. One will be the merchant account, which will publish the app to the Play Store and provide the products. The other will be used for development and testing of purchases.

 Two accounts are required for testing because Google does not allow purchases to be made from the merchant account.

The merchant account should be registered as a Google developer (`http://play.google. com/apps/publish`) and linked to Google Wallet (`http://www.google.com/wallet/ merchants.html`). The other account only needs to be a Google account.

How to do it...

Before we prepare the Play Store app listing, we need to prepare the app package for upload:

1. We can either create a new, empty Xamarin.Android app project or use an existing project.

2. We then need to add the billing permission to the app:

   ```
   [assembly: UsesPermission("com.android.vending.BILLING")]
   ```

3. Finally, we need to build and sign the app package, ensuring that the package name and keystore is that of the final app. (Refer to *Chapter 13, Publishing Apps*)

Once we have our app package, we need to upload it to Google Play using the merchant account:

1. We need to upload the package we just created to the Alpha channel. (Refer to *Chapter 13, Publishing Apps*).

2. Then, we must ensure that we have added the developer/tester account to the uploaded package. (Refer to *Chapter 13, Publishing Apps*).

3. Lastly, we must publish the app.

Once the app is uploaded, we start creating the products that we will be providing to the user:

1. Select the **In-app Products** section in the console and click on the **Add new product** button at the top of the page.

2. Next, select the **Managed product** button, enter a product ID, and click on **Continue**:

Adding a new product

3. On the next page, we now enter the rest of the product details, such as the title, description, and price.

4. Finally, at the top of the page, we click on the **Save** button, and then activate the product using the adjacent dropdown:

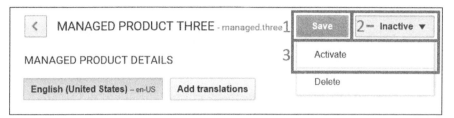

Save and activate the product

5. Similar to the process of adding products to purchase, we can also add recurring subscriptions by selecting the **Subscription** option in the dialog:

Adding a new subscription

6. On the next page, we complete the fields, just like we do with normal products, and with the additional billing and trial periods.

How it works...

Google has a few requirements before in-app billing can be implemented. The first is that the app be published to one of the channels on the merchant account. Then, the developer and the testers can use their own accounts to test the app.

 Two accounts are required for testing as Google does not allow purchases to be made from the merchant account.

The app must be signed and must include the `com.android.vending.BILLING` permission. This permission is required so that the app can communicate with Google Play Services.

 If the app is not available to be published, an empty app can be used as a placeholder.

If the `com.android.vending.BILLING` permission is not specified in the app, then products cannot be added to the app listing.

Once the app is uploaded and published, we can start adding the various products that are going to be available to the app. Adding products is easy and is done from the **In-app Products** section on the console. When adding new products, we can choose from either a managed product or a subscription.

Managed products are items that can be bought once and optionally consumed, so they can be repurchased. Subscriptions are recurring products that are periodically repurchased. In terms of a racing game, a nonconsumable product could be a new car, a consumable product could be fuel, and a subscription could be a club membership.

 Providing products that can be purchased repeatedly is achieved by consuming the product immediately after the purchase completes.

Both products and subscriptions require a product ID, which cannot be changed or reused. This ID is used when purchasing the item as well as when searching for items to buy. Although similar, both have various details that are used differently.

A product has a title, description, and a price, all of which can be localized to the user's region. Not all regions support in-app billing, so this must be considered if one of those regions is the target market.

 Not all regions support in-app billing because some regions do not support Google Wallet.

Subscriptions also have a title and description but they differ in how the pricing works. In addition to a price, they have a billing, trial, and grace period. The billing period is how often the user will be charged for the product. This can range from a week to a year, as well as a custom seasonal date range.

 Because pricing cannot be changed for a subscription, a new subscription can be created and used in the app instead. Existing users will be charged according to the old price, and new users will be charged the new price.

The trial period is useful for providing the user with the subscription for a short period before charging the user. The user can then use the subscription for free and can cancel at any time within that period to avoid any charges. The user is charged only after the trial period is over. If the user cancels the subscription, then it expires immediately even though there may be days remaining in the trial period.

Grace periods are slightly different; they come into effect if there are problems with the user's payment method. This allows us to provide a short period before Google automatically cancels the subscription due to nonpayment.

Integrating in-app billing

When Google Play is set up to handle in-app billing, the app must first connect to the Google Play service before it can request product details and make purchases.

Getting ready

Before the app can connect to Google Play, we need to create an app listing on the Google Play Developer Console (`http://play.google.com/apps/publish`).

How to do it...

Our first requirement before adding in-app billing to our app is the app's public key from Google Play:

1. We need to copy the Base64-encoded public key from the console under the app's **Services & APIs** section:

LICENSING & IN-APP BILLING

Licensing allows you to prevent unauthorized distribution of your app. It can also be used to verify in-app billing purchases. Learn more about licensing.

YOUR LICENSE KEY FOR THIS APPLICATION

Base64-encoded RSA public key to include in your binary. Please remove any spaces.

MIIBIjANBgkqhkiG9w0BAQEFAAOCAQ8AMIIBCgKCAQEA6/qyJCpfHmQfUHsk1eQ3iK1JAurZCD7+ri1erpZc
s/CRq5j+4gkTxhKcaxnQJ5Pdd8Axq1GUnFpcrqpjCBwhYC4btFZqJvgk6nfr8zYC1FbRYFypaIXAh6UfuUrk
cjGWa/EeT6LqMdOMYgjoh9bM4j7vRFLLS7XA5/OsnDeA0BMnQFmNZUW8Zr5117r1RTn/H5qPNWhOxxYO/Ys0
Lczu4uQnd0n8d75v0BBhAS5AIIrUjdCC74vLQJzDjRiAEMJvKuG2TpBXWbcI2tD5j5QbdKeC1aumf3AX5crC
wFyPTveHJZ1qiEfG60JaCvVWiQItLPFyiFA2a0txBgy+6YA8rwIDAQAB

The public app license key

2. Then, we paste that key into our app. For testing purposes, we can just store it in a field, but we should always obfuscate this key:

```
private const string PublicKey = "<app-license-key>";
```

Next, we will integrate the in-app billing library into our app:

1. To integrate the in-app billing library into our app, we first install the **Xamarin.InAppBilling** Component from the Xamarin Component Store.

2. Then, we create an instance of the `InAppBillingServiceConnection` instance, passing in the public key from Google Play and the current `Activity` instance:

```
connection = new InAppBillingServiceConnection(
   this, PublicKey);
```

3. If there are any errors during the connection attempt, we would want to be notified. Use the following code to enable error messages:

```
connection.OnInAppBillingError += (error, message) => {
   // there was an error with the service
};
```

4. We would also want to be notified when the connection succeeds:

```
connection.OnConnected += () => {
   // app is connected
};
```

5. Finally, we will initiate the connection using the `Connect()` method:

```
connection.Connect();
```

6. Once connected, all operations are performed through the `BillingHandler` property; thus, we need to get the following instance:

```
connection.OnConnected += () => {
  billing = connection.BillingHandler;
};
```

7. If an unknown error occurs while using the `InAppBillingHandler` instance, the `InAppBillingProcesingError` event is raised using the following code:

```
billing.InAppBillingProcessingError += (message) => {
  // unknown error processing a request
};
```

8. As soon as we are finished with our products and purchases, we will ensure that we release resources using the `Disconnect()` method:

```
connection.Disconnect();
```

How it works...

To support in-app billing, we need to have created the products and/or subscriptions on the Google Play Developer Console. This will require that the `com.android.vending.BILLING` permission be specified and the app be published to one of the channels.

Once this is done, we can start integrating the connection to the Google Play service. To do this, we will need the license key from the console. This allows the service connection to verify that the communication is really from the store and has not been tampered with. This key is found on the console under the app's **Services & APIs** section. The key should be obfuscated to prevent a malicious user from replacing the public key with another key and thereby removing one form of security.

 Google Play signs the responses with a private key, and the public key is used to verify the signature.

All logic needed to interact with Google Play is in the `Xamarin.InAppBilling` Component from the Xamarin Component Store. This library handles product listing, purchases, and purchase management. The library does not actually perform the tasks itself, but rather delegates the requests to the running Google Play service.

Once we have the key and library installed, we can now connect to the Google Play service. To do this, we create an instance of the `InAppBillingServiceConnection` type, passing in the `Activity` instance and the public key. Since the connection is asynchronously established, we must attach an event handler to the `OnConnected` event. This event is raised when a connection is successful. If there are any errors, the `OnInAppBillingError` event is raised instead. To actually initiate the connection, we invoke the `Connect()` method.

Connecting to Google Play requires a visible `Activity` instance because this is where the purchase events are sent to.

As soon as the connection is successfully completed, the `OnConnected` event is raised and we can get hold of the `InAppBillingHandler` instance through the `BillingHandler` property on the connection. This handler is then used to perform all further purchases and requests.

If there are any errors while making requests or processing responses, the `InAppBillingProcesingError` event on `InAppBillingHandler` will be raised. We can then handle these cases.

 Even though the `InAppBillingProcesingError` event exists, specific events for specific processing errors will be raised, such as the `BuyProductError` event.

As soon as the interaction with the store is complete, the purchases are made and the products are consumed, we must disconnect from the service. This requests that any resources that are being held be released and is done through the `Disconnect()` method on the connection. Disconnecting also destroys the billing handler; thus, we have to reconnect before interacting with it again.

Listing available products

We need to present the details about what products or subscriptions are available for purchase so that the users can verify what they want before making any purchases.

How to do it...

We can request a list of `Product` instances using the `QueryInventoryAsync()` method:

1. The `QueryInventoryAsync()` method returns the product details when invoked with the desired product IDs and the `Product ItemType` instance:

```
var productIds = new string[] {
   "managed.one",
   "managed.two"
};
var products = await billing.QueryInventoryAsync(
   productIds, ItemType.Product);
```

2. If we have any subscriptions, we can repeat the same process but we will use the `Subscription ItemType` type this time:

```
var productIds = new string[] {
  "subscription.one"
};
var subscriptions = await billing.QueryInventoryAsync(
  productIds, ItemType.Subscription);
```

3. Similar to do the process for all the requests, errors may occur, such as when there is no connectivity. We can respond to these errors using the `QueryInventoryError` event:

```
billing.QueryInventoryError += (code, details) => {
  // there was an error querying the inventory
};
```

4. Irrespective of whether it is a managed product or a subscription, each returned product has a set of properties that can be used to present the product to the user:

```
string id = product.ProductId; // managed.one
string title = product.Title;   // Managed Product One
string description = product.Description; // ...
string price = product.Price;   // R 10.00
```

How it works...

Once we are connected to the Google Play service, we can begin our product interaction. The first thing we will probably want to do is to present the user with a list of available items to purchase.

Obtaining a list of products is done through the `QueryInventoryAsync()` method, which is asynchronous and must be awaited. We provide a list of product IDs for which we want to get the product information. If we are requesting information about managed products, we use the `Product` item type. For subscriptions, we use the `Subscription` item type.

> The `QueryInventoryAsync()` method returns the product information for a set of product IDs rather than returning a list of available products.

We need this product list because it will now contain the names, description, and localized prices for the product or subscription. This information can then be presented to the user before making a purchase.

The price received from the server contains both the currency code as well as the number value, and can thus be presented directly to the user.

Google Play caches the result from the server, so we don't have to implement our own caching mechanism. Each time we need the product details, we can simply get it from the billing handler. We can locally cache when the app launches so that we don't have to keep the connection open, but it is not necessary to persist the cache between app launches.

 Because Google Play caches responses, subsequent requests do not involve network requests.

There's more...

There are also special products that are always available for testing purposes. No actual transaction takes place, but all the appropriate purchase events occur:

```
var productIds = new string[] {
  ReservedTestProductIDs.Canceled,
  ReservedTestProductIDs.Purchased,
  ReservedTestProductIDs.Unavailable
};
var products = await billing.QueryInventoryAsync(
  productIds, ItemType.Product);
```

In the case of `Canceled`, Google Play responds as though the purchase was canceled. This can occur when an error is encountered in the order process, such as an invalid credit card. For `Purchased`, the transaction always succeeds, representing a successful purchase. Finally, `Unavailable` acts as if the user has purchased an invalid item.

Purchasing products

Once the user has selected a product for purchase, we can start the checkout process.

How to do it...

When we have obtained a list of products, we can present the user with the opportunity to make a purchase. There are two ways to make a purchase, either using a `Product` instance or just the product ID:

1. The `QueryInventoryAsync()` method returns a list of:

    ```
    var products = await billing.QueryInventoryAsync(
        new [] { "managed.one" }, ItemType.Product);
    var product = products[0];
    billing.BuyProduct(product);
    ```

2. This method also has an overload that accepts a `string` payload that will be included with any server responses:

    ```
    billing.BuyProduct(product, "DeveloperPayload");
    ```

3. Another way to purchase a product is to simply pass the product ID to the `BuyProduct()` method along with the product type and an optional payload:

    ```
    billing.BuyProduct(
        "managed.one", ItemType.Product, "DeveloperPayload");
    ```

After the purchase has been made, we will be notified about the success, or failure, of the purchase. This is done through the use of several events:

1. Before any events are raised, we need to override the `OnActivityResult()` method on the `Activity` instance to pass the response to the billing handler:

    ```
    protected override void OnActivityResult(
    int requestCode, Result result, Intent data) {
      billing.HandleActivityResult(requestCode, result, data);
    }
    ```

2. Then, we can use the `OnProductPurchased` event to read any payload data that was passed to the `BuyProduct()` method:

    ```
    billing.OnProductPurchased += (resp, purch, data, sig) => {
      // product was purchased successfully
      var payload = purch.DeveloperPayload;
    };
    ```

3. As with all transactions, there may be a time when something fails for a valid reason. We can respond to these failures using the various error events:

    ```
    billing.BuyProductError += (code, sku) => {
      // error attempting to purchase
    };
    ```

```
billing.OnPurchaseFailedValidation += (purch, data, sig) =>
{
  // error validating the purchase
};
billing.OnUserCanceled += () => {
  // user canceled the purchase
};
```

Purchases made using the `ReservedTestProductIDs.Purchased` product will always succeed and can be used for testing the purchase workflow. However, when we want to test the app making actual product purchases, we have to ensure that the app is signed using the same keystore as the app that was uploaded to Google Play:

1. We can archive the app for publishing, sign the package and then manually install it on the device using the following command:

   adb install path/to/signed.apk

2. However, if we have access to the keystore, we can add the credentials to the project file:

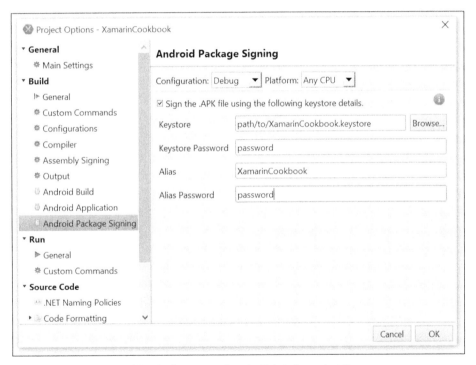

Adding the keystore and credentials to the project file

3. As with any password, we should never store this into any public location or check it in to a source control.

How it works...

Once the user has selected the desired product, we need to initiate the purchase request. There are two methods to do this. We can specify the `Product` instance that we obtained from the result of the `QueryInventoryAsync()` method, or we can just use the product ID and product type.

 The `BuyProduct` instance accepts either a `Product` instance or a product ID and product type.

When we specify the product by the product ID, we additionally provide a payload. When we use the `Product` instance, there is an overload method that accepts a payload. This payload can be any string and is always distributed with the `Purchase` instance when it is returned from the server. This occurs as part of the response to the purchase request as well as when requesting the list of purchased products. The payload is passed as an argument to `BuyProduct` and returned in the `DeveloperPayload` property on the `Purchase` instance.

 The purchase payload can be used to verify that the current user did indeed make the purchase.

To receive the purchase events, whether a success or an error, we need to catch the result from the purchase activity. As soon as the purchase completes, the response will be received and deserialized from the intent data and into a `Purchase` instance.

To do this, we override the `OnActivityResult()` method on the requesting activity. Then, we pass the `OnActivityResult()` method parameter values to the `HandleActivityResult()` method of the `InAppBillingHandler` instance. We must override the `OnActivityResult()` method because the purchase process is performed outside the activity, and the result is then passed to the activity via this method.

As the response is processed, various events are raised depending on the result. If the purchase is successful, the deserialized `Purchase` instance is provided in the `OnProductPurchased` event. In the case of an error, one of the several events is raised. If there is an error making the purchase, then the `BuyProductError` event is raised. If there is an error validating the signature on the purchase product, then the `OnPurchaseFailedValidation` event is raised. If the user cancels the purchase, then the `OnUserCanceled` event is raised.

 Purchasing the `ReservedTestProductIDs.Purchased` product can be used to test a complete successful purchase operation.

Testing purchases can be performed in two ways—either using a test product ID or by making a purchase from a test account. The `ReservedTestProductIDs.Purchased` reserved ID can be used to test a successful purchase without having to run the app as a signed package from the App Store. This is useful when testing the workflow of a purchase, with the other reserved product IDs being used to test error cases.

Once the purchase workflow is complete and a specific purchase is to be tested, we can purchase the product using a signed app package. We don't have to upload each build, but we do have to ensure that we sign the package with the same keystore as the one already uploaded. Another requirement is that the package name, version name, and version code match exactly.

In addition to the package matching the uploaded package, the user must be a tester that is not the merchant. Also, the user must have been added to the **Gmail accounts with testing access** section in the console settings. If the user is the owner of the console, then this happens automatically and does not need to be added.

When installing the app on the device, we can download the app from the store, or we can build a custom version during development. We should ensure that the package is still signed with the same keystore, but it can be a Debug build. One way to install the app is to build, archive, and sign the app. The final package can then be installed via ADB.

Another way is to add the credentials into the project file. This is done under the **Android Package Signing** section of the project options. However, all the values, including the passwords, are stored in plain text in the project file and should not be checked into source control.

There's more...

As the `Product` instance is nothing special, we can also just construct our own instance without having to first query the server:

```
var product = new Product {
  ProductId = "managed.one",
  Type = ItemType.Product
};
billing.BuyProduct(product);
```

This will work; however, we will be bypassing the initial confirmation that the product exists that we get from `QueryInventoryAsync`. Further, this might not be a problem if we are sure that the product exists. The advantage is that we do not have to first query the service before making a purchase.

Listing purchased products

After the user has purchased products or subscriptions, we need to be able to adjust the app accordingly when the app is launched the next time.

How to do it...

We can access the list of purchased products through the `GetPurchases()` method:

1. We list purchased products by passing the `Product` item type to the `GetPurchases()` method:

   ```
   var prods = billing.GetPurchases(ItemType.Product);
   ```

2. To list purchased subscriptions, we pass the `Subscription` item type instead:

   ```
   var subs = billing.GetPurchases(ItemType.Subscription);
   ```

3. The `GetPurchases()` method returns a collection of `Purchase` instances, each of which contain data that describe the purchase:

   ```
   Purchase purchase = prods[0];
   string id = purchase.ProductId;
   string token = purchase.PurchaseToken;
   string payload = purchase.DeveloperPayload;
   ```

4. If there are any errors processing the request, we can handle them in the error events:

   ```
   billing.OnGetProductsError += (code, bundle) => {
     // error loading the purchased items
   };
   billing.OnInvalidOwnedItemsBundleReturned += (bundle) => {
     // error validating the purchased items
   };
   ```

How it works...

Once the user has purchased products or subscriptions, they will want to be able to view those purchases. When the app begins, we might want to display the additional features on the basis of the purchase. We can do this by requesting the list of purchased products using the `GetPurchases()` method.

 As Google Play caches the list of purchases on the device, multiple queries should be made to the handler instead of implementing a custom cache.

The `GetPurchases()` method returns a list of `Purchase` instances, which we can use in our app. When we want to access the list of products, we pass the `Product` item type as a parameter, and for subscriptions, we use the `Subscription` item type.

The `Purchase` instances will contain details such as the product ID and purchase token. These values are stored in the `ProductId` and `PurchaseToken` properties, respectively. If we want to access other details, such as the title and price, we can invoke the `QueryInventoryAsync()` method by passing the product ID.

> The `Purchase` instance only contains the product ID, so the `QueryInventoryAsync()` method can be used to fetch the `Product` instance.

In addition to the product ID and purchase token, there is the `DeveloperPayload` property. This payload is the same data that was provided when the purchase was originally made. This data can be used to verify a purchase or perform some other form of validation.

In the event of any error, there are various events that can be raised. The `OnGetProductsError` event is raised if a valid error code from the Google Play service is received. If there is a problem validating the result data in the case of a successful response, the `OnInvalidOwnedItemsBundleReturned` event is raised. If there are any errors deserializing the result, outside the instance of an invalid service response, the `InAppBillingProcessingError` event will be raised.

> The `OnGetProductsError` and `OnInvalidOwnedItemsBundleReturned` events correspond to Google Play service errors, while `InAppBillingProcessingError` corresponds to library errors.

Consuming purchases

Some purchases are used to indicate additional features that are not initially available to the user. Other products are consumable products and only provide a once-off feature, which will have to be re-purchased to be re-used. These products are consumable products and only provide a once-off feature.

How to do it...

Some products are meant to be consumed, or exhausted, when used; the user is required to purchase them again before they can be reused:

1. To consume a product, we pass the purchase to the `ConsumePurchase()` method:

```
var success = billing.ConsumePurchase(purchase);
```

2. We don't really require the `Purchase` instance but rather just the purchase token. When a product is purchased, we can just store the purchase token and use that:

```
var token = purchase.PurchaseToken;
var success = billing.ConsumePurchase(token);
```

3. If the consumption is successful, we can use the return value, or make use of the `OnPurchaseConsumed` event:

```
billing.OnPurchaseConsumed += (token) => {
  // consumed product
};
```

4. Similarly, if there are any errors, we can use the return value, or the `OnPurchaseConsumedError` event:

```
billing.OnPurchaseConsumedError += (code, token) => {
  // error consuming the purchase
};
```

How it works...

Besides subscriptions, there are two main types of products: consumables and nonconsumables. Consumable products are meant to be purchased and then used once. To make use of the product again, they have to be repurchased. Nonconsumable products are only bought once and can be reused without having to be repurchased. If we want the user to repurchase the product, we have to first consume it.

 Products can be consumed, subscriptions cannot be consumed.

A nonconsumable product is a product that is bought once and never expires. An example of this type of product would be a feature, such as the removal of ads. Although it is possible to consume this product, we wouldn't.

Product consumption can be done after a period from the time of being bought or directly after the purchase. An example of a consumable purchase would be in-game money, where we would want the user to be able to buy the same amount multiple times.

 Consumable products should be consumed when the app is launched so that they can be purchased again.

In the case of money, we would actually consume the purchase immediately but track the total amount separately. Then, as the player uses the money, we would subtract from the local wallet. To protect against data loss, we would also backup or sync the wallet to an online storage. This will also allow the user to resume the game from a new device.

To consume a purchase, we can either pass the `Purchase` instance or the purchase token to the `ConsumePurchase()` method. This method will return `true` if the purchase is successful, or `false` if there is an error.

 It is a good practice to only perform the specified operation when a successful result is obtained from a consumption request.

In addition to the return value, the `OnPurchaseConsumed` event will be raised when the consumption is successful. If there is an error, the `OnPurchaseConsumedError` will be raised.

13
Publishing Apps

In this chapter, we will cover the following recipes:

- ▸ Protecting the content
- ▸ Protecting the code
- ▸ Preparing the app package
- ▸ Shrinking the app package
- ▸ Creating the app package
- ▸ Uploading the app package
- ▸ Adding preview testers
- ▸ Releasing for production
- ▸ Updating the app

Introduction

Even the greatest of apps will have no value if nobody can use them. All apps get their true value through the fact that they help users to perform a task. Great apps are a delight to use and provide the functionality to perform a task well. However, if no user has access to the app, the app is pointless.

The process of publishing an app on an app store is not just a matter of uploading the package for the users to download. Publishing involves adding polish to the finer, and not necessarily functional or even directly related, areas of the app.

An app can provide all the functionality to perform a task well. It can run well on the user's device. But, if the app only supports a single language or a single type of device, the app is actually very limited. Not all users speak the same language, and not all users use the same device. Android is one of the most popular operating systems because it runs on millions of different devices, and users expect the app to both look great and run well on all of them.

Publishing an app takes great code, releasing it onto users' devices, while continuing to maintain and grow the experience as time passes. If apps were just launched and then forgotten, the users would soon start looking for different apps as their requirements change.

In order for many apps to be economical for developers, they have to protect their app and its content. If an app provides content that requires the users to have bought the app, then the developer must ensure that the content is only accessible to those customers. Users will be unhappy if they have had to pay for the content, and then found out that they can access it for free somewhere else.

Just like protecting the content, the code must also be protected. There are many tools out there that can take an Android app and decompile it down to the source code. Because of this, nefarious developers might not only steal the content but also the code. This poses a risk, as there will now be a clone on the app store that will cause confusion for the users. And not only this, the clone may pretend to be the original and steal private data from unsuspecting users.

Once the content has been secured, the code protected, and the app packaged, the developer now needs to upload the app to an app store. This is not just a simple upload, but it involves creating marketing media. Users will not download an app without an icon, without screenshots, or without a decent description. This is why it is essential to spend time making the app desirable even before installation.

The final, and most important, part of publishing an app is the testing phase. No matter how great the app is, if it fails to meet the user's requirements or crashes, it will be uninstalled. Testing an app with real users, or a testing team, ensures that all the features that the app provides work, and work well.

Only once the app has been produced, protected, packaged, proved, and promoted, can it be said that the app has been published.

Protecting the content

When an app is published on Google Play, anyone can download and install it. This is great when the user has purchased the app. However, we need a way to prevent users from accessing the app if they have managed to get hold of the app without purchasing it.

Getting ready

Before we can add licensing to our app, we will need the app's public key from the Play Store app listing, which is created on the Google Play Developer Console (`https://play.google.com/apps/publish`).

How to do it...

One of the ways to prevent unauthorized access to our app's content is by adding Google Play licensing to our app. Then, when the app is launched, we can verify the user with Google Play.

The first thing that we will need to do before adding licensing to our app is to get the app's public key from Google Play:

1. We need to copy the Base64-encoded public key from the console under the app's **Services & APIs** section:

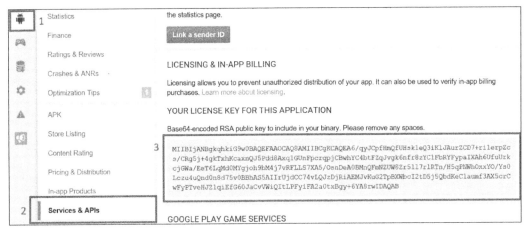

The public app license key

2. Then, we will paste that key into our app. For testing purposes, we can just store it in a field, but we should always obfuscate this key:

```
private const string PublicKey = "<app-license-key>";
```

Now that we have the public key, we set up our app so that we can perform the license check once the app has been launched:

1. First, we will need to install the **Android License Verification Library** NuGet.

2. Next, we need to add the licensing check permission to the app:

```
[assembly: UsesPermission(
  "com.android.vending.CHECK_LICENSE")]
```

3. Then, we implement the `ILicenseCheckerCallback` interface:

```
public class MainActivity : Activity,
  ILicenseCheckerCallback {
  public void Allow(PolicyServerResponse response) {
  }
  public void DontAllow(PolicyServerResponse response) {
  }
  public void ApplicationError(CallbackErrorCode errorCode)
  {
  }
}
```

The next thing that we need to do is to set up the license checker requirements:

1. First, we collect the unique information about the device, which we require when we will encrypt the server responses:

```
string deviceId = Settings.Secure.GetString(
  ContentResolver, Settings.Secure.AndroidId);
string appId = this.PackageName;
byte[] salt = new byte[] { 1, 2, 3, 4, 5, 6, 7, 8, 9, 0 };
```

2. Next, we create an instance of `AesObfuscator`, which will be used to encrypt the response:

```
var obfuscator = new AesObfuscator(salt, appId, deviceId);
```

3. Then, we create an instance of `ServerManagedPolicy`, which will process the server response to determine whether the user is authorized to use our app:

```
var policy = new ServerManagedPolicy(this, obfuscator);
```

4. Finally, we create an instance of `LicenseChecker`, making use of the public key:

```
checker = new LicenseChecker(this, policy, PublicKey);
```

Now, after the app is launched and we want to ensure that the user is authorized to access the app, we initiate the license check:

1. To start a check, or to retry a failed check, we invoke the `CheckAccess()` method of the license checker:

    ```
    checker.CheckAccess(this);
    ```

2. When a result comes back from Google Play, we are notified through the various methods of the `ILicenseCheckerCallback` interface. The `Allow()` method will be called if the user is licensed:

    ```
    public void Allow(PolicyServerResponse response) {
      // we are licensed
    }
    ```

3. If the user is not licensed, or there is a recoverable error, the `DontAllow()` method is invoked:

    ```
    public void DontAllow(PolicyServerResponse response) {
        if (response == PolicyServerResponse.Retry) {
          // we can retry the license check
        }
        else {
          // confirmed unlicensed user
        }
    }
    ```

4. If there is an app error, the `ApplicationError()` method is invoked:

    ```
    public void ApplicationError(CallbackErrorCode errorCode) {
      // handle the specific error code
    }
    ```

5. When we are finished with the checks, we clean up the resources using the `OnDestroy()` method:

    ```
    checker.OnDestroy();
    ```

As the publishing process usually takes a few days, we can test our implementation by specifying the server response manually:

1. First, we navigate to the **Account details** section of the developer console settings page.

2. Then, at the bottom of the page, we select **LICENSED** from the **Test License Response** dropdown, and click on the **Save** button:

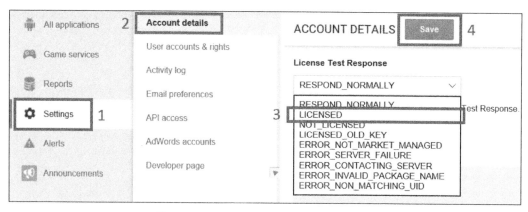

The steps to set the server response to Licensed

3. We will now receive the `Licensed` response in our app, and the `Allow()` method will be invoked.

How it works...

Some apps contain contents that we would like only legitimate users to be able to access. Although this is usually not the case with free apps, we almost always want to prevent access if the user has not purchase the app.

 Usually, only paid apps require licensing to be implemented.

Google Play provides a licensing service, which we can use to verify that the user did actually download the app from Google Play, either after purchasing the app or because the app was free. We use this service by querying Google Play at runtime to obtain a licensing status. Then we can determine, based on the response, whether the user is allowed to continue using the app, or should download the app.

 Google Play provides a licensing service only to apps distributed via Google Play. Other stores use other licensing mechanisms.

The only thing we need in order to get started is the public key from the Google Play Developer Console. We can either create a new app listing or use the existing app listing from a previous release. This key is also used when handling in-app billing, so we should always keep this key secure. One way to secure the key would be to obfuscate or encrypt the key.

Once we have the key, we start with the licensing implementation. We first need to install the **Android License Verification Library** NuGet, which contains the required assemblies. Once installed, we will need to add the `com.android.vending.CHECK_LICENSE` permission to our app.

 Even though the license check requires Internet access, the only permission that is required is `com.android. vending.CHECK_LICENSE`.

In order to handle the responses from the licensing sever, we need to implement the `ILicenseCheckerCallback` interface. This interface has three methods, one of which is invoked depending on what the response from the server is. The `Allow()` method corresponds to a confirmed licensed user. The `DontAllow()` method corresponds to a confirmed unlicensed user, or if there is a problem and we should retry. In the case of a retry, the `PolicyServerResponse` parameter value will be `Retry`. Also, the `ApplicationError()` method provides us with the `CallbackErrorCode` parameter in the case of an error when retrieving the license status.

Before we can initiate the license check, we will need an implementation of `IPolicy`, such as `ServerManagedPolicy`. Policies are used to determine whether the user with a given license is allowed to use the app. They contain the logic for allowing or disallowing user access based on the result of the license check. The `ServerManagedPolicy` instance uses server-provided settings and cached server responses to manage access to the app. Because this policy caches responses, the user can use the app even if the network goes down.

As the `ServerManagedPolicy` instance caches the server responses on the device, we need to encrypt the response to prevent unauthorized access to this response. To do this, we need to provide the policy an implementation of `IObfuscator`, such as `AesObfuscator`. This obfuscator uses the device ID, the app ID, and a random salt to encrypt the responses.

 Not all policies cache the response, such as `StrictPolicy`, thus, they do not require encryption or an obfuscator.

To actually perform the check, we create an instance of `LicenseChecker`, providing the policy and the public key from Google Play. Then, we invoke the `CheckAccess()` method, passing in the `ILicenseCheckerCallback` instance. As soon as the server responds, the provided policy will determine whether the user should be able to access the app, and invoke one of the methods of the `ILicenseCheckerCallback` instance.

Once we have determined whether or not the user can access the app, we must clean up any resources used by the license checker. This we do through the `OnDestroy()` method of the license checker.

 Once the license checker has been cleaned up, a new instance needs to be created to perform the check again.

To test our implementation against the various responses from the server, we will need to ensure that the app has been published, and is not just in the saved draft state. We need to publish our app even though it is not yet complete; this is because when we do the license check, we will need Google Play to know about our package name. The app only needs to be published to the Alpha channel, and does not even have to be a complete app. We should add a (see *Uploading the app package* recipe) bit here so that we don't have to go into detail until much later. We can just create an empty app, with our package name, and signed with the keystore that we will use for the final app.

 In order to test licensing, an app with the same package name, which is signed with the same keystore, must be published to Google Play.

After we have published our app to one of the channels, we do have to wait for a few days before the app can be tested with actual responses. But, we can also ask Google Play to respond with simulated responses. To simulate the various responses that we might receive, we select each response from the console settings. On the **Settings** page, under the **Account details** section and at the bottom of the page, we select the response from the **License Test Response** dropdown.

There's more...

There is also the `StrictPolicy` instance that we can use instead of `ServerManagedPolicy`. This policy does not persist the result from the server but instead just keeps it in memory. This results in the app checking with the server each time the app is launched. We might want to do this if we want to ensure that the user is licensed at the time of use. However, this comes at a cost in which the user has to be connected to the Internet each time the app is launched.

In the case where we need greater flexibility or control over the license checking, we can also create our own policy entirely. As the license checker only requires that the `IPolicy` interface be implemented, we can implement our own instance of that interface:

```
public class MyPolicy : IPolicy {
  public bool AllowAccess() {
  }
  public void ProcessServerResponse(
```

```
    PolicyServerResponse response, ResponseData rawData) {
    }
  }
```

We can also create our own obfuscator for an existing policy, such as the `ServerManagedPolicy` instance, by implementing the `IObfuscator` interface:

```
public interface IObfuscator {
  string Obfuscate (string original, string key) {
  }
  string Unobfuscate (string obfuscated, string key) {
  }
}
```

Protecting the code

As Android app packages are just ZIP files that contain the assemblies and metadata, the assemblies can easily be decompiled. As a result, we need a way to make it very difficult to understand the decompiled code, or even prevent it from happening altogether.

Getting ready

In this recipe, we will make use of the Babel for .NET obfuscator (`https://babelfor.net/products/obfuscator`). This is a commercial product, but they do have a demo version that can be used for free. The demo version does have a few limitations, and the obfuscated apps only run for a period of time, however this does not prevent us from using it.

There aren't many Mac/Linux obfuscators for .NET, and Babel for .NET is no different. We will also need a Windows machine to use the obfuscator, but we can use the MSBuild task to integrate with the build process for Xamarin.Android. As the MSBuild task does not have any specific IDE requirements, it will work with Xamarin Studio or Visual Studio.

How to do it...

Once we have installed Babel for .NET, we add the MSBuild task to our project file:

1. Open your solution in Xamarin Studio, and from the **Solution** panel, right-click on the project node and select **Unload**:

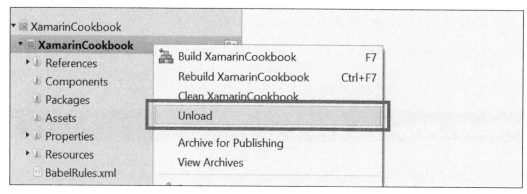

Unloading the project file

2. Then, right-click on the unloaded project and navigate to **Tools | Edit File**:

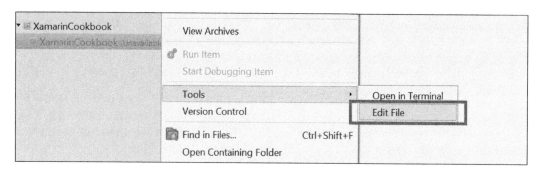

Editing the project file by hand

3. We now need to add the required `<UsingTask>` element into the project file as a child of the `<Project>` element:

```
<Project>
  <UsingTask
    TaskName="Babel"
    AssemblyName="Babel.Build, Version=8.0.0.0,
    Culture=neutral, PublicKeyToken=138d17b5bd621ab7" />
</Project>
```

4. Then, we add the `<Babel>` task element as a child of the `<Target Name="AfterBuild">` element:

```
<Target Name="AfterBuild">
  <Babel
     InputFile="$(TargetPath)"
     OutputFile="$(TargetPath)"
     VerboseLevel="5"
     ObfuscateTypes="true"
     ObfuscateEvents="true"
     ObfuscateMethods="true"
     ObfuscateProperties="true"
     ObfuscateFields="true"
     VirtualFunctions="true"
     FlattenNamespaces="false"
     UnicodeNormalization="false"
     SuppressIldasm="true"
     ControlFlowObfuscation=
        "goto=on;if=on;switch=on;case=on;call=on"
     ILIterations="5"/>
</Target>
```

5. To ensure that obfuscation only happens in the `Release` configuration, we can use the `Condition` attribute:

```
<Babel Condition="'$(Configuration)'=='Release'" ... />
```

6. Save the changes made to the project file and reload:

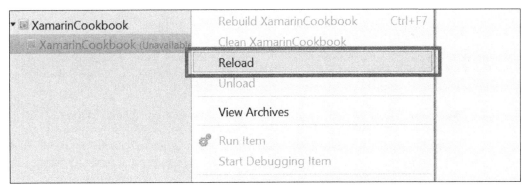

Reloading the project file

7. Now, we can switch to the release build and rebuild the solution. Xamarin Studio will create the app using the obfuscated assembly during the build process.

Some types and members shouldn't be obfuscated. This can be because we are using reflection or serialization to access them. As obfuscation might rename a type to something that we cannot use, we need tell the obfuscator to ignore or skip certain types and members. We do this by performing the following steps:

1. We first create an XML rules file that describes how and what to do. In our case, we name the file `BabelRules.xml`:

```xml
<?xml version="1.0" encoding="UTF-8"?>
<Rules
  xmlns:xsi=http://www.w3.org/2001/XMLSchema-instance
  version="2.0">
  <Rule name="Serializable types" exclude="true">
    <Target>Fields, StaticFields</Target>
    <Pattern><![CDATA[*]]></Pattern>
    <HasAttribute onEnclosingType="true">
      System.SerializableAttribute
    </HasAttribute>
    <Description>
      Skip fields of serializable types.
    </Description>
  </Rule>
</Rules>
```

2. Then, we add the `RulesFiles` attribute to the babel build task, setting it to be the name of the rules file:

```xml
<Babel RulesFiles="BabelRules.xml" ... />
```

How it works...

Even though we add licensing checks to ensure that unauthorized users cannot access our app, they might be able to tamper with the package to bypass the license checks. It is not possible to avoid this completely, but we can make it much more difficult to do so.

There are several ways in which we can prevent or detect tampering, and one of them is to obfuscate the assemblies. Obfuscation removes unused code and renames types and members with semantically obscure names. It can also perform control flow obfuscation, which produces spaghetti logic that can be very difficult for a cracker to analyze. The result is a smaller sized app package file that is more difficult to reverse engineer. As almost all the app logic resides in the managed .NET assemblies, this is what we must obfuscate.

 As Xamarin.Android assemblies are just normal .NET assemblies, most commercial .NET obfuscators can be used.

One such obfuscator that we can use, is babel for .NET. This obfuscator is great for Xamarin. Android projects because it provides a MSBuild task, which we use to easily integrate with the build process. There aren't many good obfuscators for non-Windows machines, and babel for .NET is one of the many that only run on Windows. But, it does work with both Xamarin Studio and Visual Studio as a result of its integration with MSBuild.

In order to integrate babel for .NET into our app's build, we do have to modify our project file manually in two places. The first is to add a reference to the build task that we want to include. This requires us to add the `<UsingTask TaskName="Babel">` element as a child of the `<Project>` element. This new element requires us to provide either the GAC-registered assembly name or the file path to the Babel.Build assembly. We provide the GAC-registered assembly name using the `AssemblyName` attribute, or the file path to the assembly using the `AssemblyFile` attribute.

The next place we modify the project file is in the `<Target Name="AfterBuild">` element. This target executes directly after the assembly is compiled, but before the app is packaged. In this element, we add a `<Babel>` child element and set the various obfuscator properties using attributes.

The two most important properties are set using the `InputFile` and `OutputFile` attributes. For both attributes, we must use the `$(TargetPath)` variable. This variable points to the final output file of the compiled project. The obfuscator will load the input file and then save the obfuscated file back in the same place. We need to do this in order to preserve the existing build process.

 Both the `InputFile` and `OutputFile` attribute values must be the `$(TargetPath)` variable.

We can also specify that the obfuscation only occurs when building with the release configuration. To do this, we set the `Condition` attribute to be the value `"'$(Configuration)'=='Release'"`. This makes use of the project variables and will only include the babel task when the `Configuration` variable's value is `Release`.

The remainder of the attributes are used to set which assemblies are obfuscated and how it is done. Some attributes, such as `UnicodeNormalization` and `FlattenNamespaces`, do not work well with Xamarin.Android and must be set to `false`. For example, if we enable `UnicodeNormalization`, then the types will be renamed with Unicode characters, which is not valid for the generated Java types or file names.

 As Unicode characters are not valid for the Java packager, the value of the `UnicodeNormalization` attribute must be `false`.

There might be instances where the obfuscation process renames a type or member that is used in reflection or serialization. At run time, the app will crash as it will not be able to find that type or member. In this case, we tell the obfuscator to ignore these types or members using the rules file.

Once we have the rules file created, we specify that we want to use it by specifying the path to the file using the `RulesFiles` attribute. Rule files are just XML files that follow a specific structure.

Preparing the app package

Once we have created an Android app, we may want to be able to upload it to Google Play for the users to download. This is no small task as there are many things that we can do to improve user reach and acceptance.

How to do it...

One of the first things we can do to get our app ready for the store is to ensure that we have all the textual translations ready for all the regions that we are going to release to:

1. We can specify our default resources in the `values/strings.xml` resource file. For example, if the English language is the default language, our resource file would contain:

```
<resources>
  <string name="message">English Text</string>
  <string name="popup">English Popup</string>
</resources>
```

2. We can provide a French translation in the `values-fr/strings.xml` resource directory:

```
<resources>
  <string name="message">Texte Français</string>
  <string name="popup">Popup Français</string>
</resources>
```

3. This can then be used in the layout files:

```
<Button android:text="@string/message" />
```

4. Alternatively, we can access the string from the code:

```
var text = Resources.GetString(Resource.String.popup);
```

Another way to enhance the experience on the wide variety of devices is to provide different image resources for the different screen resolutions and sizes:

▶ If our app icon is 72 x 72 pixels for high-density screens, we would store this in the `drawable-hdpi` resource folder.

▶ Then, to provide a scaled image for very high resolution devices, we would store the scaled up icon of 180 x 180 pixels in the `drawable-xxhdpi` resource folder.

▶ In a similar fashion, we can provide alternate layouts depending on the screen size. For a phone, we could store the layout in the `layout` or the `layout-sw320dp` resource folders.

▶ And for the tablets, we might store the alternate layout in the `layout-600dp` resource folder.

Although there are many other ways to improve the experience for different devices and users, we will only look at one more. We will make use of the Android Support Libraries to bring the modern styles, such as the material design, and functionality, such as toolbars, from the latest version of Android down to the older versions:

1. The first thing that we must do is install the **Xamarin Support Library v7 AppCompat** NuGet or Component into our app.

2. Then, we set the Minimum Android version to the older 2.3 and the Target Android version to the latest available, which is currently 5.0:

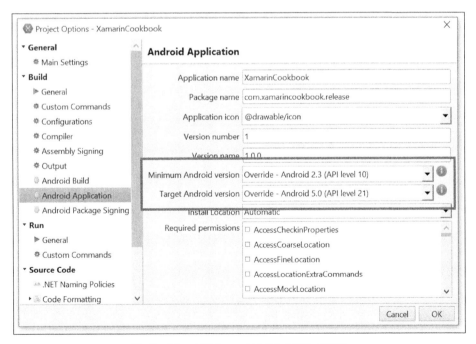

The Target and Minimum Android version options

3. Once the library is installed, we can make use of the various support types, such as `AppCompatActivity`, and apply the `Theme.AppCompat` themes:

```
[Activity(Theme = "@style/Theme.AppCompat.Light")]
public class MainActivity : AppCompatActivity {
}
```

Besides the Android versions, the language differences and the varying screen resolutions, we also need to consider the different hardware architectures of the various devices. There are a few different CPU architectures available, ranging from the older ARMv6 to the new ARMv8 to the Intel x86. As we do not know which users have which devices, we need to support as many as possible:

1. To ensure that our app runs on all of these different architectures, we specify that the compiler produce binaries for all the available ABIs:

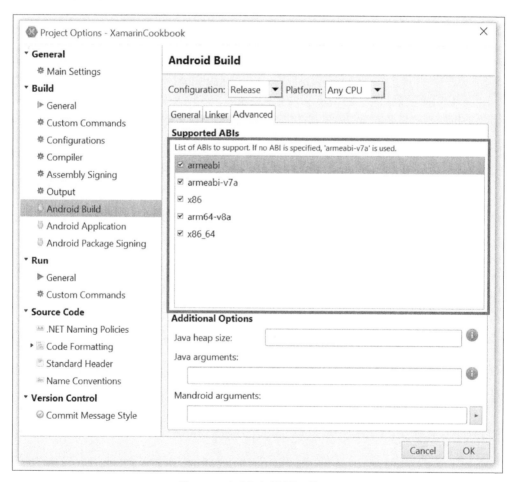

The supported Android ABI options

The next area to look at is the app packaging and the code itself. What we want to do here is to remove all the unnecessary, or debug-only, code as well as get the package ready for building in the `Release` configuration:

1. If we are making use of the `[UsesFeature]` attributes, we should remove any unnecessary `[UsesFeature]` attributes from our code.

2. Similarly, we remove all the unnecessary permissions. If we are using these attributes in code, we ensure that there are no unnecessary `[UsesPermission]` attributes.

3. If we are using the project options to edit the `AndroidManifest.xml` file, we ensure that we uncheck the unnecessary permission items:

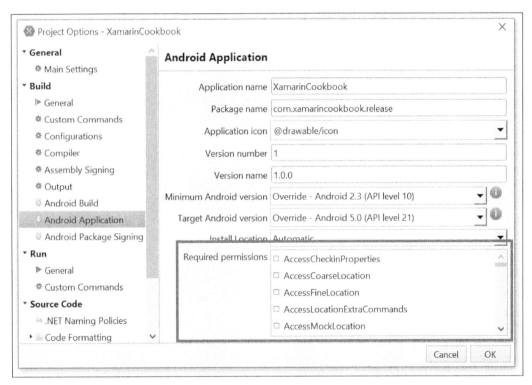

Specify the required permissions

As this app will be running on many devices that run many other apps, we don't want to waste CPU resources filling up the log file with all our debug information. We can now start removing the various debug logging:

1. We can start off by removing any unnecessary logging methods, such as `Log.Debug` or `Console.WriteLine`:

    ```
    Log.Debug("TAG", "message");
    Console.WriteLine("message");
    ```

2. Alternatively, we can use the `Debug.WriteLine()` methods, which are only included at compile time when building in the debug configuration:

    ```
    Debug.WriteLine("message");
    ```

3. Another way to do this is by simply wrapping chunks of code in preprocessor directives with the `DEBUG` conditional. This prevents the compiler from including this code when building in the release configuration:

    ```
    #if DEBUG
    WriteOutLogging();
    #endif
    ```

As the code is now mostly clean and ready for release, we can turn off the debugging permissions on the final app. We do this as it is possible to gain full access to the Java process and execute arbitrary code in the context of the application, if this debug state is not disabled:

1. One way to do this from the code using the `[Application]` assembly attribute:

    ```
    #if DEBUG
    [assembly: Application(Debuggable = true)]
    #else
    [assembly: Application(Debuggable = false)]
    #endif
    ```

2. Alternatively, we can add the `android:debuggable` attribute to the `<application>` element in the `AndroidManifest.xml` file:

    ```
    <application android:debuggable="false">
    ```

3. Finally, we need to specify that the app do not use the shared Mono runtime with the app, as it will not exist on the user's device:

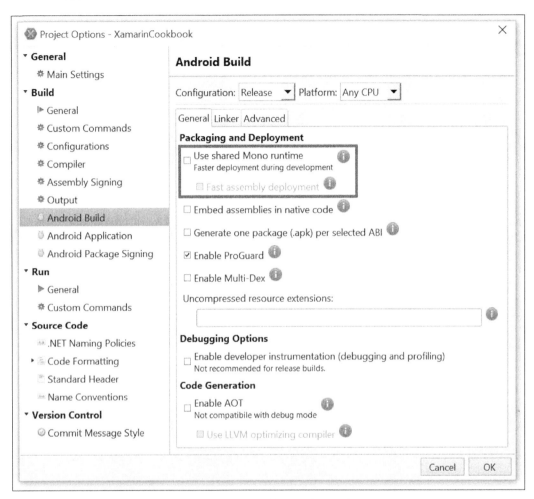

Don't use the shared Mono runtime package

How it works...

When releasing an app to the store, we want to be able to reach the widest possible audience. One of the things we can do is to make sure that we have created localized translations of the interface resources in the app. Often, this does not require any code changes, but makes the experience more delightful for users in other countries.

In order to do this, we need to ensure that we have extracted all the strings from the layout and code into a resource file for each culture. Android automatically selects the correct resource file depending on the device language that the user has set. We must ensure that there is a default resource for all resources so that Android can fall back to the default value if we miss a resource translation.

 When localizing resources, there should always be a default resource for every resource value. If there is none, the app may crash.

To make use of a string resource in the layout files, we replace the actual string value with a reference to the string resource. To access the resources from the code, we use the `GetString()` method on the `Resources` property of the `Context` instance.

In a very similar manner to strings, we can localize images and most other resource types. To create the localized resources, we add a suffix to the resource folders; for example, to localize strings to French, we use the `values-fr` resource folder. To localize images to Japanese, we use the `drawable-ja` resource folder.

Just like we can localize resources for different languages, we can customize resources based on the screen resolution or size. We do this so that we can provide higher resolution images for devices with higher resolution displays, or so that we can provide larger images for devices with more screen estate.

 Resources can be customized for any resource type, such as images and layouts, and in many different ways, such as languages and screen sizes.

Instead of adding the language code as a suffix to the resource folders, we add the display resource qualifiers. There are a few ways we can do this; one way is based on the screen density. Some values are low, high, or extra-extra-high. The resource folders for images at these densities would be `drawable-ldpi`, `drawable-hdpi`, and `drawable-xxhdpi`, respectively. Another way we can do this is by screen size, using the width of the smallest screen dimension. For small devices, such as phones, we would place the layout resources in the `layout-sw320dp` attribute, and for a 7-inch tablet, we would use the `layout-sw600dp` resource folder.

One of the first resources that we must always create multiple resolutions of is the launcher icon. This is the first thing that the user sees, and it represents the entire app. A good launcher icon provides a good first impression. In the following table are the common icon dimensions and relative resolutions:

Density Name	Resource Qualifier	Approximate DPI	Size Multiplier	Pixel Size
Low	ldpi	~120dpi	0.75x	36x36
Medium	mdpi	~160dpi	1.0x	48x48
High	hdpi	~240dpi	1.5x	72x72
Extra High	xhdpi	~320dpi	2.0x	96x96
Extra Extra High	xxhdpi	~480dpi	3.0x	180x180
Extra Extra Extra High	xxxhdpi	~640dpi	4.0x	192x192

The `xxxhdpi` qualifier only applies to launcher icons, and is not necessary for other images such as toolbar icons or app graphics.

Another area in which we can make the app more enjoyable to use is the overall theme or style. Each version of Android received a theme update, and they usually look nicer each time. Not all users will be running the latest Android version on their device, and not all devices will receive the latest updates. In order to ensure that our app always looks the best on all devices, we can make use of the Android Support Libraries.

After installing the **Xamarin Support Library v7 AppCompat** Component or NuGet into our app, we will get the libraries required to be able to use the latest styles on both the latest Android version as well as the older versions.

We let Android know what version to use as the base for the styles by setting the target Android version to be the latest available, and the minimum Android version to be the lowest we want to support. Android will then bring the functionality and features from the target version of Android to the minimum Android version.

Then, to use the features in the older Android versions, we need to ensure that we are using the types from the support libraries instead of the default types. For example, instead of inheriting from the `Activity` type, we inherit from the `AppCompatActivity` type. And, for themes, we apply or inherit from the `Theme.AppCompat` variants instead of the default `Theme` variants.

 The Android Support Libraries can be used to bring back both styles and functionality from the latest Android versions to the older versions.

Not only do we want to support older versions of Android, but we also want to support the various hardware configurations. The two main variations are the x86 and the ARM CPU architectures. The ARM architectures also have several variations from the older ARMv6 to the new 64-bit ARMv8.

To support the widest variety of device hardware, we ensure that we select all the desired ABI options for the app. This does increase the total size of the package by about 1.5 MB per ABI option, but this means that the app will run on almost all hardware configurations. The size increase is a result of the native Mono runtime being included for each ABI option. However, the actual managed assemblies are only included once.

Now that we have support for many devices and many device configurations, we must clean up any unnecessary requirements. The first thing to do is to remove all the unnecessary permissions and feature requirements. This is done by removing the `[UsesPermission]` and `[UsesFeature]` attributes that we do not require. We should also ensure that we have not included any unnecessary `<uses-permission>` or `<uses-feature>` elements in the `AndroidManifest.xml` file.

 Unnecessary permissions will not cause any problems with an Android app, but users may not install it if they see that the app requires too many permissions.

We should also remove all the debug logging from our app. Logging consumes CPU resources and can be detrimental to our app's performance. However, we should not remove any logging that we will need to debug errors or exceptions that may occur once we have released our app. Although we want to remove as much debug logging as possible, we still need to be able to solve problems when our users experience them.

There are a few ways to remove the unnecessary debug logging, the simplest being the removal of any `Log.Debug` or `Console.WriteLine` statements. If we want to keep these logging in our code for when we are developing further, we can use the `Debug.WriteLine()` method instead. When the compiler encounters these methods, it will automatically remove them when building in the release configuration. As these statements are removed entirely, any evaluations that happen as part of the statement will also be removed. Another way to remove statements when building for release is to wrap them with the `#if DEBUG` preprocessor directives. This allows us to remove entire blocks of code at compile time.

The debugging of an app is performed with the use of the **Java Debug Wire Protocol** (**JDWP**), which communicates with a JVM. While JDWP is important during development, it can pose a security risk for the released app. Thus, we must always disable debugging for released apps. We do this by setting the `Debuggable` property to `false` on the `[Application]` attribute in our code, or we can set the `android:debuggable` attribute to `false` on the `<application>` element in the `AndroidManifest.xml` file.

When developing apps with `Xamarin.Android`, we want the process of building and deploying to the device to be as quick as possible. As copying and installing a package on a device is a relatively slow operation, we want the package size to be as small as possible. One way to do this is to use the linker, but this is also very slow.

Instead, the app is broken into the `Shared Runtime` package, the shared platform and our app package. The `Shared Runtime` package contains the Mono runtime and BCL, the shared platform contains the Android APIs, and our app package just contains the libraries referenced by our project. The `Shared Runtime` and `Shared Platform` packages are only copied once to the device, but our app assemblies are updated each time we build and deploy.

As a result, the app package will not include the runtime and Android APIs, but are installed separately. However, as we will not have these packages installed on the users' devices, we need to specify that it should be included with our app by unchecking the **Use shared Mono runtime** checkbox in the project options.

 When releasing apps, debugging support must always be disabled and the shared Mono runtime cannot be used.

Shrinking the app package

No app uses all the features of all the included libraries. The .NET libraries are quite big, and we often only use a tiny subset. To reduce the size of an app, we need to remove any unnecessary code or libraries that exist in it.

How to do it...

To reduce the overall size of the app, we enable the linker. This is used to remove any unused code from our app, or from any assemblies that are used:

1. We select either the **Link SDK assemblies only** option or the **Link all assemblies** option from the **Linker behavior** dropdown:

The linker options

2. When we link assemblies, types and members are removed. To prevent members from being removed, we can add the [Preserve] attribute to those members:

```
public class MyClass {
  [Preserve]
  public string MyMember() {
  }
}
```

3. We can also request that the linker skip all the members on an entire type:

```
[Preserve(AllMembers = true)]
public class MyClass {
}
```

4. If we can't, or don't, want to use the `[Preserve]` attribute, we can provide a block of code that prevents the linker from removing the referenced members:

```
public class MyActivity : Activity {
  static bool falseflag = false;
  static MyActivity() {
    if (falseflag) {
      var ignore = new MyClass();
    }
  }
}
```

5. The last thing we can do to stop the linker, is to specify which assemblies it must not process:

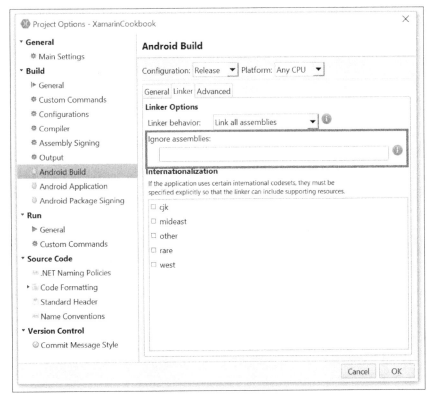

Specify which assemblies to skip

6. Once the linker is enabled for the .NET assemblies, we enable ProGuard to remove the unnecessary Java bytecode:

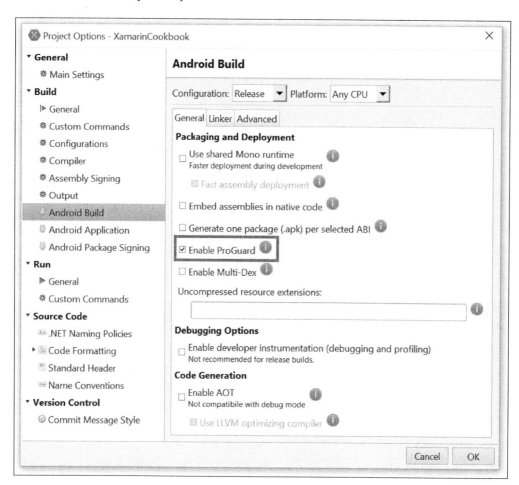

The option to enable ProGuard

How it works...

Most apps contain libraries, or parts of libraries, that aren't being used by the app at all. If the app never connects to the Internet, the entire networking stack is unused and can be removed. As a result of removing the unnecessary code, the final size of the assemblies is much smaller than the initial size. To remove unnecessary code from our app, we use the linker.

Using a linker with Xamarin.Android is essential, as we are including the entire Mono framework and runtime, which is over 40 MB. As Google Play only allows up to a maximum of 50 MB for the app package, we will be severely limited in the amount of extra resources we can add. And, users will not want to download a very simple app if the app has a very large download size.

When we enable the linker, we can reduce the total size of the app package to around 5 MB for simple apps. This is far more desirable, and usually, only extra resources increase the app size.

> Enabling the linker is essential for almost all apps, as this significantly reduces the final app size.

There are two ways in which we can enable the linker. We can select the **Link SDK assemblies only** option, which specifies that the linker should only processes the Xamarin.Android platform and the runtime assemblies. This will reduce the size of only the framework, but will leave any additional assemblies as is.

However, we can rather select the **Link all assemblies** option, which will try and remove any unused code from all assemblies, including from any referenced libraries. Removing code from referenced assemblies is very useful if we are making use of many, or large, libraries.

When we link assemblies, some types and members will be removed. This sometimes causes problems if we are accessing these types through reflection or serialization. These members are removed as a result of the linker not being able to see where they are being referenced in the code.

> The linker may sometimes remove the code that is actually being used. When this happens, steps can be taken to prevent it for occurring.

There are several ways to prevent the linker from removing types and members. One way to do this is by adding the `[Preserve]` attribute to those members. In the cases where we can't, or don't, want to use the `[Preserve]` attribute, we can provide a block of code that causes the linker to think that the members are used, but in fact, they aren't used at runtime.

Another way we can prevent the linker from processing certain assemblies, is to specify in the project options the list of assemblies to ignore. This method is very useful if there is an assembly that is being used specifically for serialization, or if there are many types that need to be preserved. However, this results in the entire assembly being skipped, which is mostly unnecessary.

With Xamarin.Android, there are two sets of libraries, the .NET assemblies and the Java libraries. For example, if we create an app that uses the Android Support Libraries, the actual .NET assembly that gets referenced is actually just a wrapper for the underlying Java library. Thus, when we link the .NET assembly, we are only linking a tiny wrapper instead of the large Java library.

As many Xamarin.Android apps make use of many Java libraries, we need a way to link the underlying Java libraries as well. When compiling our app, there is the option to use ProGuard, which is the Java linker and obfuscator.

 ProGuard will link only the Java libraries, and is used together with the managed linker, which links only the managed code.

ProGuard is similar to the managed linker, and it will remove the unused Java code. However, it is also an obfuscator. This means that it will also obfuscate and optimize the generated and included Java code.

There's more...

The maximum size for a package published on Google Play is 50 MB. If an app exceeds that size, Google Play will allow extra assets to be delivered through APK Expansion files. Android Expansion Files permit the app to have two additional files, with each being up to 2 GB in size. Google Play will host and distribute these files at no cost.

To use these expansion files, we must install the **Android APK Expansion Downloader** NuGet. We create a service that inherits from `DownloaderService` and also implements the `IDownloaderClient` interface. Although not as simple as this, we connect to the service and start the download.

Creating the app package

Now that our app is finally finished, we can get started creating the final app package. We need to ensure that the actual package meets Google Play's requirements and is signed with a key from a keystore.

How to do it...

Before we can create the app package, we need to ensure that the package will be accepted by Google Play and the metadata describes the app correctly. To do this, we use the app's project settings to provide the correct values for the packaging process:

1. We first need to provide a name that will be used when listing the app on the device. This should be a string resource, but can be a normal string:

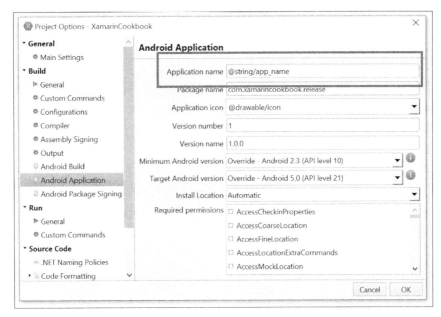

The application name field

2. Next, we will provide a unique package name, which is the ID that is used to identify our app on Google Play:

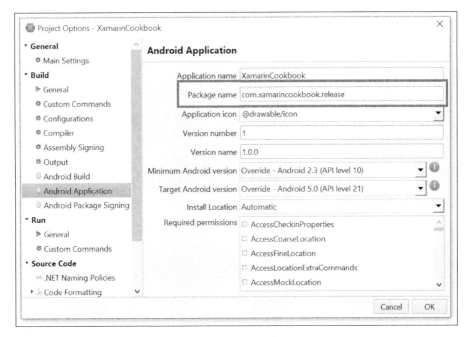

The package name field

3. We now specify the **Application icon**, which represents the default image used for the app. We can do this using the `[Application]` attribute:

```
[assembly: Application(Icon = "@drawable/iconit is just an
alternati")]
```

4. Also, we can set the Application icon in the `AndroidManifest.xml` file, using the project options:

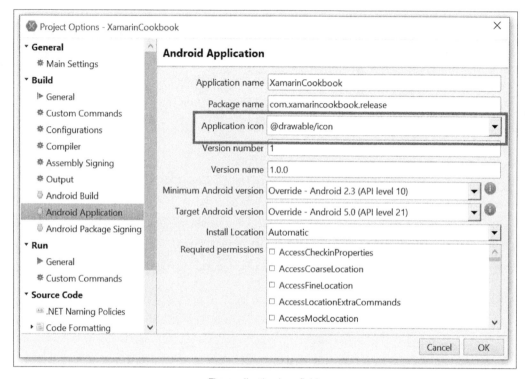

The application icon field

5. Then, we provide versioning information. The **Version number** text box is an integer used internally by Android, and the **Version name** text box is a user-facing string:

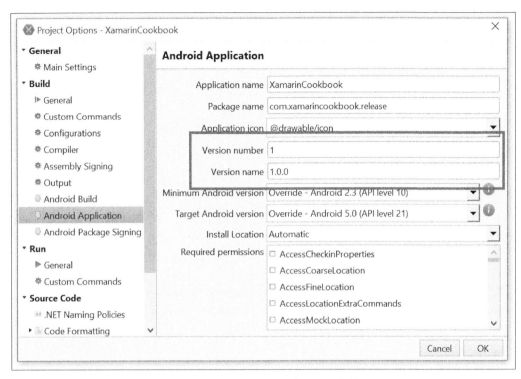

The version number and version name fields

6. Finally, we specify the preferred install location of the app on the device:

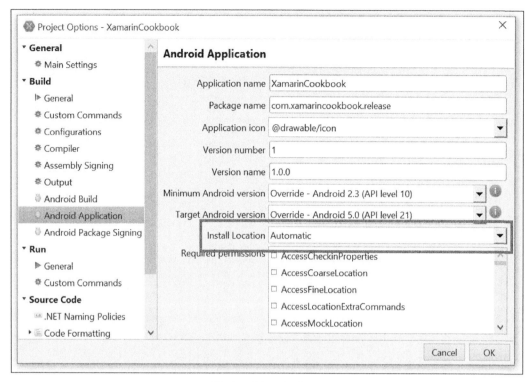

The install location field

Now that the package is ready to be created, we can switch to the release configuration and start the build process:

1. First, ensure that we are on the **Release** configuration.

2. Next, we must package the app. In Xamarin Studio, we select the **Build | Archive for Publishing** menu item. In Visual Studio, this step is not required:

Archive for publishing

3. After the project has been archived in Xamarin Studio, we select the archive that was just created and click on the **Sign and Distribute** button:

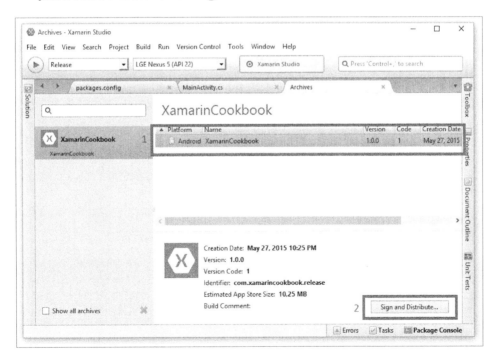

4. In the case of Visual Studio, we navigate to **Tools | Android | Publish Android App...** menu item. This performs both the archive and sign steps in a single wizard:

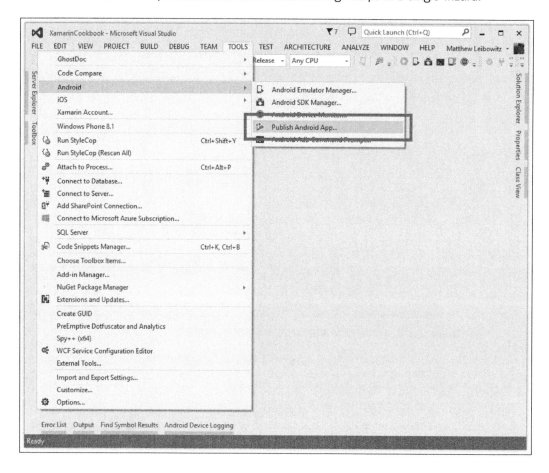

5. In either case, the packaging and signing wizard will appear and we just have to follow the onscreen instructions. The wizard will ask us to select a key from a keystore, and a location to save the final app package. If we don't have a keystore yet, we will create one in the wizard.

How it works...

Once an app's code is complete and the various compiler options have been set, we will create the final package that will be uploaded to Google Play. Just before we build the package, we need to first check that the packaging options are correct for this release of the app. These options are used to display and categorize the app of both the device as well as Google Play.

The first option is the **Application name**, which is used as the title for the app on Google Play. Once the app is installed, the name that appears on the launcher will actually be the name of the activity. In the same way, the Application icon option is also only used on Google Play, and the activity icon used on the device launcher. As these two fields are user-visible resources, they should be localized. The **Application name** field can be a plain string, but this is not recommended.

The app icon can also be provided using the `Icon` property of the `[Application]` attribute.

The **Package name** field is really the ID that is used to identify our app on Google Play. This has to be unique across the entire store and cannot be changed once the app has been published. As a result, it is important that we select a name that will remain relevant throughout our app's lifetime.

The package name must be unique across the store and cannot be changed.

The next important part of the package is the version. Versioning consists of the internal, integer number representing our app's version. Every release must receive a higher number, and this is used by Google Play to determine whether the app needs to be updated on the user's device.

The other component to the version, is the user-friendly **Version name**. This can be any string that we want to present to the user, and it is not used by Google Play. Usually, this is in the form `<major>.<minor>.<point>`, or in the case of .NET versioning, `<major>.<minor>.<build>.<revision>`.

The version number is an internally-used integer, and the version name is a publicly-visible string.

The last packaging option to set, is the install location. Here, we specify where to try and install to. We can request that we install to the external storage, or specify that we must always, and only, install to the internal storage. If the app is quite large, we should prefer the external storage.

When we want to actually create the app package, that is, the `.APK` file that we upload to Google Play, we must build the release configuration. When using Xamarin Studio, we must archive the app before signing the package for distribution. In Visual Studio, we do both steps when we publish the app.

An APK file is the name given to the final Android application package, which is uploaded to an Android app store, such as Google Play.

When signing, we use a key, or certificate, from a keystore. This key is used by Android to verify the author of the app. We can reuse an existing keystore, or we can create a new one in the wizard. However, we must use a keystore that only expires after October 22, 2033.

All versions of the same app must be signed with the same key, otherwise Google Play can't verify that the app update was created by the same author. A new key will make it necessary for us to create a totally new app with a new package name. Although not required for many apps, only those signed with the same key can run in the same process and share code.

 The same key must be used to sign each version of the app, otherwise the app cannot be updated seamlessly.

There's more...

Maintaining the security of our keystore is of critical importance, both for us as developers and for the user. The keys can be used to impersonate the publisher and access users' private data.

The keystore is required for signing all future versions of our app. If we lose or misplace our keystore, we will not be able to publish updates to our existing app. This is because we cannot regenerate a previously generated key.

Uploading the app package

After the app has been developed and packaged, we want to be able to release it into the wild. There are many different Android app stores available, such as Google Play or Amazon Appstore.

Getting ready

To distribute our app through Google Play, we need to have created a developer account on the Google Play Developer Console (`https://play.google.com/apps/publish`). This only needs to be performed once, and involves a one-time fee of $25 USD.

If we are going to distribute paid apps or apps that have in-app billing, we need to link the developer account to a Google Wallet account (`http://www.google.com/wallet/merchants.html`). Google Wallet is only available in certain countries, so we need to ensure that we have created the merchant account in one of them (`https://support.google.com/googleplay/android-developer/table/3539140`).

How to do it...

Once we have signed the app package, we can prepare the Google Play app listing for the upload process as follows:

1. When logged into the console, click on the **Add new application** button, enter the new app's title, and click on **Prepare Store Listing**:

The Add New Application dialog

2. When the listing has been created, we upload the package to the Alpha channel. We first select the **APK** section on the left-hand side. Then, under the **Alpha Testing** tab, click on the **Upload your first APK to Alpha** button, which can be seen in the following screenshot:

Uploading the first APK to Google Play

3. In the dialog that appears, browse to and select the package that we just packaged using our IDE.

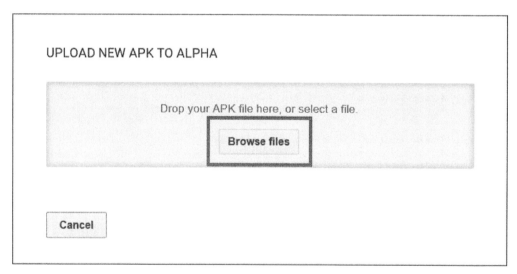

The upload APK dialog

4. When the upload completes, we can select the package item in the list and review the details and add release notes.

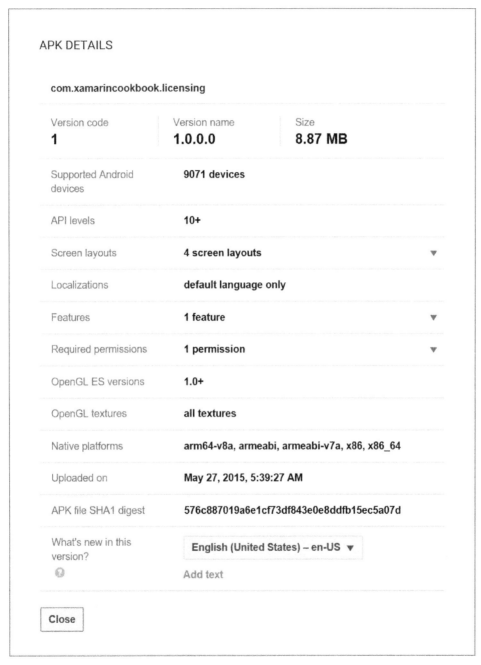

APK DETAILS

com.xamarincookbook.licensing

Version code	Version name	Size
1	**1.0.0.0**	**8.87 MB**

Supported Android devices	**9071 devices**
API levels	**10+**
Screen layouts	**4 screen layouts** ▼
Localizations	**default language only**
Features	**1 feature** ▼
Required permissions	**1 permission** ▼
OpenGL ES versions	**1.0+**
OpenGL textures	**all textures**
Native platforms	**arm64-v8a, armeabi, armeabi-v7a, x86, x86_64**
Uploaded on	**May 27, 2015, 5:39:27 AM**
APK file SHA1 digest	**576c887019a6e1cf73df843e0e8ddfb15ec5a07d**
What's new in this version?	**English (United States) – en-US** ▼
	Add text

Close

The APK details dialog

5. After the APK has been uploaded, we now complete the fields required in the various sections. As we complete each section, we click on the **Save draft** button at the top of the page. Once all the required fields are completed in each section, the check mark next to the section turns green:

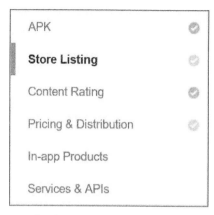

The Google Play package sections

6. The first section after the **APK** section is **Store Listing**. All of these fields can be localized, and are used to describe the package as it appears in Google Play.

7. One of the fields in the **Store Listing** section is **New content rating**. We specify a rating here by completing the questionnaire in the **Content Rating** section.

8. The last section we need to complete is the **Pricing & Distribution** section. Here, we specify whether the app is paid or free, and which countries the app will be available in.

9. Once all the fields are filled in, we can click on the **Publish app** button at the top of the page. It usually takes a few days before the app will appear on the store.

10. If the button is not enabled, we can click on the **Why can't I publish?** link above the publish button:

The link to view outstanding fields

11. This will show a dialog that lists all the fields that still need completion:

WHY CAN'T I PUBLISH?

You need to complete the points below before you can publish your application.

You need to add a high-res icon. [English (United States) – en-US]
You need to add a feature graphic. [English (United States) – en-US]
You need to add at least 2 non-Android TV screenshots. [English (United States) – en-US]
You need to select a category.

Close

The fields that still need to be completed

How it works...

Google Play requires that there be metadata describing the app and its content. This is the app listing, which is used for categorization and filtering. This information ranges from the description and icon to the content rating and supported platforms.

When creating a store listing, we start off by specifying just the app title. The package name and version numbers are obtained from the upload package. Uploading of a package is performed on the **APK** section of the listing. Here, we specify the channel to which the app is to be released on, which should initially be one of the testing channels.

Testing channels are used to provide phased rollouts of new app versions to only a subset of the users. Then, based on those users' feedback, we can improve the package before we release it to everyone. This is important, as even though the app may run smoothly, the users may not enjoy some of the functionality.

 The testing channels can be used to test the app before it is released to production, potentially avoiding bad reviews.

After we have uploaded a package, we get the opportunity to review the package details. We do this to ensure that we have not accidentally included unnecessary permissions or features. Also, we can confirm that we are supporting the desired platforms and languages.

Another important thing that we can do is to add release notes. Release notes is a way in which we are able to advertise new features in our app, as well as point out any bug fixes.

Once the package has been uploaded, we complete the required fields in the various sections. As we complete each section, we save the changes using the **Save draft** button at the top of the page. As required fields are completed in each section, the check mark next to that section goes green. Once all the sections are green, we will be able to publish the app.

The first section after the **APK** section is **Store Listing**. All of these fields can be localized, and are used to describe the package as it will appear in Google Play. The first three fields are the textual descriptions of the app, the app title, a short description and a longer, full description.

 All the values under the **Store Listing** section should be localized for the regions in which the app is released.

The next set of fields are the graphic assets and video fields. These include the various screenshots, icons, and other promotional graphics. Screenshots can be provided for phones, tablets, and TVs. At least two screenshots are required, but we don't have to provide screenshots for all displays. Other graphics include a high resolution icon used on the website, along with some promotional graphics.

After the graphics, we fill in categorization fields. These are used when organizing the apps in Google Play. One of the fields here is **New content rating**, which we specify by completing the questionnaire in the **Content Rating** section.

The final fields in the **Store Listing** section are the contact details and any privacy policy information. Although optional, we should provide a privacy policy that discloses the ways in which our app gathers and manages user data.

The next section, **Content Rating**, is a questionnaire that Google uses to provide a rating of the app content. Then, consumers, such as parents, can decide whether an app is suitable for the intended audience.

 The content rating field in the **Store Listing** section is populated by applying a questionnaire in the **Content Rating** section.

Next, we will complete the **Pricing & Distribution** section. This section controls where and how the package is distributed to the many countries. Here is where we specify whether the app is a paid app or a free app. This is an important step as once the app is free, we cannot change it back to a paid app. If we select **paid**, we must enter a default price, and any specific regional prices.

After the pricing fields, we are provided a checklist with all the countries that we can distribute to. Here, we check all the countries in which we want our app to be available. If this is a paid app, we can adjust any local pricing here. Usually, we would want to distribute the app to as many regions as possible, but we may want to restrict the initial release to fewer regions.

 The various prices can be changed once the app has been published, but a free app cannot become a paid app.

The next group of fields is where we select the distribution areas, such as for Android Wear, TV, Auto, or work. And, we have to indicate that our app complies with the content guidelines and US export laws.

The last two sections, **In-app Products** and **Services & APIs**, are used when we are going to be adding in-app billing or licensing into the app. These are not required for many of the apps we will create, so we can skip them.

Once all the fields are filled in, our app is ready to be published. We can check whether the check marks next to each section are all green. If they aren't, or the **Publish app** button at the top of the page is disabled, we can click on the **Why can't I publish?** link above the publish button. This will show a dialog that lists all the fields that still need completion.

Finally, once all the requirements are met, we click on the **Publish app** button at the top of the page. Once we have published the app, it usually takes a few days before it will appear on the store. This is because Google will process the package to ensure that it conforms to their guidelines and does not infringe on any copyrights.

 The publishing process usually takes a few days.

Adding preview testers

It's always valuable to get real-world feedback from users, especially before we release the app. Google Play allows us to distribute preview versions of our app test groups.

How to do it...

To add testers to the Alpha or Beta channels, we have to create a Google group, to which we are going to add all the developers and testers:

1. First, we log into Google Groups (`https://groups.google.com`) with the publisher account credentials, and create a new group using the **Create Group** button.

2. Then, in the create group page, we fill in the fields, ensuring that we make note of the group e-mail address (`alpha-testers-channel@googlegroups.com`):

The Create Group page

3. A captcha dialog will appear, where we just enter the characters and click on **Continue** to create the group.

4. Now that we have the group created, we can start adding the testers to it. To do this, we click on the **Manage** link next to the group name.

5. When the page opens, we select the **Invite members** section, enter the testers' and developers' e-mail addresses, and then click on the **Send invites** button:

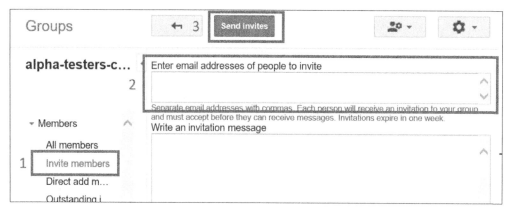

The Invite Members page

Now that we have our group of testers, we must assign this group to either the Alpha or the Beta channels by following these steps:

1. On either the **Alpha Testing** or **Beta Testing** tabs of the **APK** section, depending on where the app was released to, select the **Manage list of testers** link:

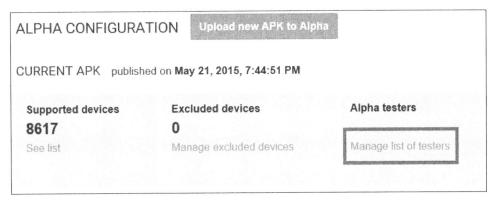

ALPHA CONFIGURATION   Upload new APK to Alpha

CURRENT APK   published on **May 21, 2015, 7:44:51 PM**

Supported devices	Excluded devices	Alpha testers
8617	**0**	
See list	Manage excluded devices	Manage list of testers

The link to add the testers group

2. In the dialog that appears, enter the e-mail address of the group, click on **Add**, and then click on **Close**. We can copy the link at the bottom of the dialog and send it to the testers:

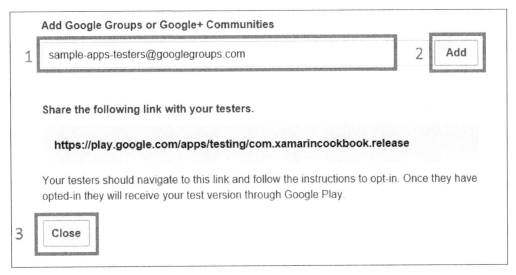

Add Google Groups or Google+ Communities

1   sample-apps-testers@googlegroups.com   2   Add

Share the following link with your testers.

https://play.google.com/apps/testing/com.xamarincookbook.release

Your testers should navigate to this link and follow the instructions to opt-in. Once they have opted-in they will receive your test version through Google Play.

3   Close

The dialog for adding testers

3. All users in the testers group will be able to navigate to the testing URL and download our app.

How it works...

Being able to release apps to the Alpha and Beta channels is a great way to test our app before we release it to production. However, these channels are not publicly accessible, and if we are working in a team, the testers will not be able to access the app. By default, only the publisher can view the app when it is in Alpha or Beta stage. This is especially limiting if we were adding in-app billing to our app, as the publisher cannot buy any products.

> Testing groups are required when testing in-app billing, as the publisher cannot make purchases.

Google Play provides a way to add groups of testers to a specific channel, so that all members of those groups can access the app. There are two types of groups, Google Groups and Google+ Communities.

If we are using Google Groups to organize the testers, we have to create a new Google Group and invite the testers. We can manage Google Groups on the website (`https://groups.google.com`) using the publisher account credentials.

We assign the new group to either the Alpha or the Beta channel, using the Google Group e-mail address that was created when we created the group. Both the Alpha and Beta channels have a **Manage list of testers** link that allows us to add the various groups of testers to a specific channel.

In the dialog that we are using to add the groups to the channel, there is a URL that we can send to the testers. This URL will take the tester to a page where they are provided with a download URL, which will install the app on their device.

There's more...

We can also make use of Google+ Communities (`https://plus.google.com/communities`) to organize the groups of testers. In a similar manner to creating Google Groups, we can create a community and add the URL to the testers list.

Releasing for production

After a period of our app being in the preview stages, we would want to release it to everyone. Or, we might just be going straight to a full public release. Either way, we want to move the app from the Alpha cannel and into the Production channel.

Getting ready

Before we can release an app to the Production channel, we will need to have uploaded an app the either the Alpha or Beta channels. We can upload directly to Production, but this is not recommended.

How to do it...

Moving an app from Alpha or Beta into Production, is just a matter of a few clicks:

1. First, we navigate to the **APK** section on the Developer Console.

2. Next, we navigate to either the **Alpha** or **Beta** tab, depending on where our current release package is.

3. Then, we click on the **Promote...** dropdown on the APK that we want to push to the production channel, and select the **Promote to Prod** item:

Pushing an APK to a new release channel

4. In the dialog that appears, ensure that we have completed any release notes, and then click on the **Move and publish** button, which can be seen here:

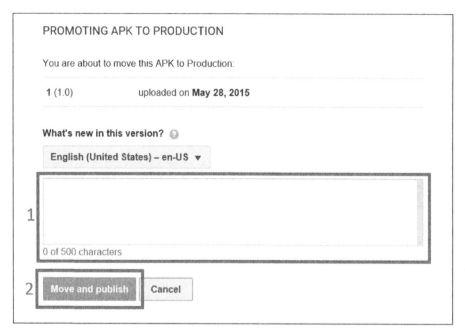

The promote APK dialog

5. This publishes our APK to production, where all Google Play users can view it. The publication process may take a few hours to propagate through Google Play, so the app may not appear immediately.

How it works...

When we release a new version of our app to Google Play, we want to first do some user acceptance testing. After internal testing, which ensures that the app runs smoothly, we can start the rollout to a smaller subset of the users through the use of the testing channels. As new features are added and existing features changed, it is important that the users like the changes. The subset of the users that will be testing the app in the real world can use the testing channel to provide valuable feedback, before the app is published to the general public.

Once the testing phase is complete, we want to take that app and move it from a testing channel into the production channel. With Google Play, this is easy to do, and only requires a few console actions.

We can select any package, from either the Alpha or Beta channels, and move it to the production channel. We can also move the package from the Alpha channel into the Beta channel and perform more testing for a different set of users. This way, we can provide a phased rollout through first the Alpha, then the Beta, and then the Production channels.

Updating the app

Once an app has been released, we will want to provide additional features or fix any bugs. We can easily do this by uploading a later version of our app to Google Play.

Getting ready

When we want to update an app, we will need to ensure that our new app will have the same package name and can be signed by the same keystore.

How to do it...

Releasing updates to an existing app on Google Play is straightforward, only requiring that the version numbers be increased besides any code changes:

1. The **Version number** field needs to be a greater integer value than the current release, and the **Version name** field should be a higher semantic version:

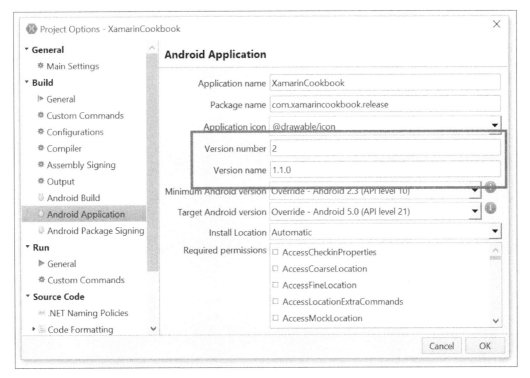

Increasing the app version numbers

2. Next, we must archive and sign the app package in the same manner as with the previous release.

3. Then, we go to the **APK** section in the dashboard of the app we want to update. On the **Alpha** tab, click on the **Upload new APK to Alpha** button.

4. In the dialog that appears, browse to and select the APK that we just packaged using our IDE.

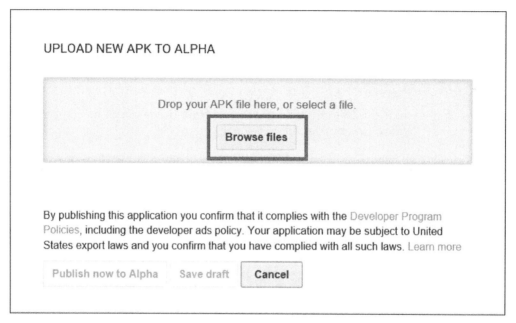

UPLOAD NEW APK TO ALPHA

Drop your APK file here, or select a file.

Browse files

By publishing this application you confirm that it complies with the Developer Program Policies, including the developer ads policy. Your application may be subject to United States export laws and you confirm that you have complied with all such laws. Learn more

Publish now to Alpha   Save draft   Cancel

The upload new APK dialog

5. Once the upload is complete, enter any release notes before clicking on the **Publish now to Alpha** button:

UPLOAD NEW APK TO ALPHA

com.xamarincookbook.release

Version code	Version name	Size
2	**1.1.0**	**8.87 MB**

APK details Show

Use expansion file

No expansion file ▼

What's new in this version?

English (United States) – en-US ▼

1

0 of 500 characters

By publishing this application you confirm that it complies with the Developer Program Policies, including the developer ads policy. Your application may be subject to United States export laws and you confirm that you have complied with all such laws. Learn more

2 Publish now to Alpha   Save draft   Cancel

The upload new APK dialog

How it works...

App updates are very important, as they let the user know that we are still supporting them, especially if this was a paid app. The actual release process is just the package and upload steps. We do not have to create a new store listing or new keystores.

Once the app update has been developed, we just package and sign the app. We must ensure that the package name is the same as the previous version, the version numbers have been increased, and the final package is signed with the same key.

When the package is created, we then go ahead and upload the new package to any one of the channels. Usually, we would want to upload to a testing channel so that the new package can be tested before the final release.

> Release notes let the users know about new features that they may have otherwise missed.

Testing updates is important as we may have an app with a high rating, but a poor update can result in a drop in the ratings. Also, testing an app with a few users allows us to make changes before the app goes to production and to the rest of the users.

Index

Thank you for buying
Xamarin Mobile Development
for Android Cookbook

About Packt Publishing

Packt, pronounced 'packed', published its first book, *Mastering phpMyAdmin for Effective MySQL Management*, in April 2004, and subsequently continued to specialize in publishing highly focused books on specific technologies and solutions.

Our books and publications share the experiences of your fellow IT professionals in adapting and customizing today's systems, applications, and frameworks. Our solution-based books give you the knowledge and power to customize the software and technologies you're using to get the job done. Packt books are more specific and less general than the IT books you have seen in the past. Our unique business model allows us to bring you more focused information, giving you more of what you need to know, and less of what you don't.

Packt is a modern yet unique publishing company that focuses on producing quality, cutting-edge books for communities of developers, administrators, and newbies alike. For more information, please visit our website at www.packtpub.com.

Writing for Packt

We welcome all inquiries from people who are interested in authoring. Book proposals should be sent to author@packtpub.com. If your book idea is still at an early stage and you would like to discuss it first before writing a formal book proposal, then please contact us; one of our commissioning editors will get in touch with you.

We're not just looking for published authors; if you have strong technical skills but no writing experience, our experienced editors can help you develop a writing career, or simply get some additional reward for your expertise.

Xamarin Essentials

ISBN: 978-1-78355-083-8   Paperback: 234 pages

Learn how to efficiently develop Android and iOS apps for deployment using the Xamarin platform

1. Explore the Xamarin platform and understand the architecture behind Xamarin.iOS and Xamarin.Android.

2. Learn how to build and run iOS and Android apps using Xamarin Studio and Visual Studio.

3. This is a practical tutorial with a clear and concise approach that teaches you how to create, share, and reuse code across your iOS and Android apps.

Xamarin Mobile Application Development for iOS

ISBN: 978-1-78355-918-3   Paperback: 222 pages

If you know C# and have an iOS device, learn to use one language for multiple devices with Xamarin

1. A clear and concise look at how to create your own apps building on what you already know of C#.

2. Create advanced and elegant apps by yourself.

3. Ensure that the majority of your code can also be used with Android and Windows Mobile 8 devices.

Please check **www.PacktPub.com** for information on our titles

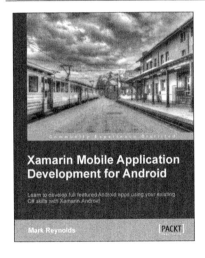

Printed in Great Britain
by Amazon